Creating Christian Granada

From the baptismal registers of the parish church of Santa María in the Alhambra (Granada). Source: Archivo de la Parroquia de San Cecilio (Granada), Libro I de bautismos de Santa María de la Alhambra, f. 81. Photo by author.

Creating Christian Granada

Society & Religious Culture in an Old-World Frontier City, 1492–1600

David Coleman

CORNELL
UNIVERSITY
PRESS

*Ithaca &
London*

This book is published with the aid of a grant from the Program for Cultural Cooperation between Spain's Ministry of Education, Culture, and Sports and United States Universities.

First published 2003 by Cornell University Press

Printed in the United States of America

Library of Congress Cataloging-in-Publication Data

Coleman, David.
   Creating Christian Granada : society and religious culture in an Old-World frontier city, 1492-1600 / David Coleman.
      p. cm.
Includes bibliographical references and index.
ISBN: 978-0-8014-7883-3
   1. Granada (Spain : Reino)—Ethnic relations—History. 2. Granada (Spain : Reino)—History. 3. Granada (Kingdom)—History—Spanish Conquest, 1476-1492. 4. Christians—Granada (Spain : Reino)—History. 5. Muslims—Granada (Spain : Reino)—History. 6. Jews—Granada (Spain : Reino)—History. 7. Granada (Spain: Reino)—Church history. I. Title.
   DP302.G66C65 2003
   946'.8203—dc21

                                          2003009188

Cloth printing   10 9 8 7 6 5 4 3 2 1

Contents

Acknowledgments

The writing of this book and the research on which it is based have been made possible by fellowships and grants from a variety of organizations and individuals, and to all of them I offer my thanks: the Fulbright Foundation; the Tinker Foundation; Miriam Usher Chrisman; the Society for Reformation Research; the Charlotte W. Newcombe Foundation; the Graduate College and History Department of the University of Illinois; the History Department of Yale University; the Office of the Vice President for Research of the University of Minnesota; and the History Department, College of Arts and Sciences, and Office of the Vice President of Academic Affairs of Eastern Kentucky University. I would also like to acknowledge and thank the dozens of archivists and librarians in Granada, Madrid, and Simancas, Spain, who likewise played crucial roles in the completion of this project.

The list of scholars, editors, graduate assistants, and friends who have contributed research advice, commentary on my writing, and other important assistance is lengthy, and I express my gratitude to all of them: Jodi Bilinkoff, Enrique Soria Mesa, Gretchen Starr-Lebeau, Amalia García Pedraza, Sara Nalle, Richard Kagan, Katie Harris, Helen Nader, John Ackerman, Henry Tom, Bob Tombs, Dick Gilbreath, Tom Appleton, Jennifer Spock, Brad Wood, Ron Huch, David Sefton, Mick Lewis, Chris Taylor, Richard Burkhardt, Harry Liebersohn, Aurelia Martín Casares, Pamela McVay, Nancy van Deusen, Nils Jacobsen, Miguel Luis López Muñoz, Alberto Martín Quirantes, Javier Castillo Fernández, Curt Gardner, Dian Tyer, Rita Brown, Dick Underwood, Chris Snow, Joe Smyth, Rebecca Williams, Erica Jones, Michelle Chapman, the late Don Queller, and above all, my mentor and friend Geoffrey Parker. I am also indebted to the anonymous reviewers who read the manuscript for Cornell University Press and who provided many outstanding suggestions for improvement. All of these individuals have in some way helped to make this a better book than it would have been otherwise. Of course, any remaining errors, whether of fact or judgment, are entirely my own responsibility.

I also return love and thanks to my entire family for their support and understanding through this process. My mother, my father, my brother, and my grandmother have all listened patiently for nearly a decade as I have shared with them the joys and the frustrations of my research and writing. With regard to my children Ian, Alison, and Lydia, one perhaps unrealistic goal of mine in publishing this book is that they might one day read it, enjoy it, and in the process, I hope, feel for me even a tiny fraction of the pride that I take in them every day. Finally, in love and in admiration for all that she is, it is to Beth Underwood, my wife and my partner in all matters intellectual and otherwise, that I dedicate this work.

DAVID COLEMAN

Richmond, Kentucky

Abbreviations

ACG   Archivo de la Catedral de Granada
AChG   Archivo de la Real Chancillería de Granada
AMG   Archivo Municipal de Granada
APG   Archivo de Protócolos de Granada
AGS   Archivo General de Simancas
AHN   Archivo Histórico Nacional, Madrid
BNM   Biblioteca Nacional, Madrid
CODOIN *Colección de documentos inéditos para la historia de España.*
MHSI   *Monumenta Historica Societatis Iesu*

Creating Christian Granada

KINGDOM OF NAVARRE

KINGDOM
OF
ARAGON

Barcelona

KINGDOM
OF
•Valladolid

KINGDOM
OF

•Madrid
Toledo

Valencia

PORTUGAL

CASTILE

•Seville

KINGDOM OF GRANADA

•GRANADA

Málaga

Almería

Mediterranean Sea

0   50   100
miles

Map prepared by Dick Gilbreath at the University of Kentucky Cartography Lab

The Iberian Peninsula circa 1500

A Conquered City

When did Granada become a "Christian" city? The most obvious answer to this question is misleading: January 2, 1492—the date on which the "Catholic Monarchs" Isabella and Ferdinand of Castile and Aragon triumphantly entered this city in the southeastern corner of the Iberian Peninsula, thus subduing Islam's last bastion in Western Europe and completing the centuries-long Christian "reconquest" of Spain. Although under Christian political control after 1492, Granada long remained in many ways an Islamic city. For eight years after the conquest, for example, Islam remained the religion practiced by the overwhelming majority of the city's residents. The resounding voices of the muezzins from the city's minarets continued to call the Muslim faithful to prayer five times each day in the more than two hundred mosques that still filled the urban landscape.[1] In 1500, after a local Muslim uprising, and with rebellion yet raging in the nearby Alpujarras Mountains, a royal order mandated that all of the city's Muslims convert to Christianity or leave the kingdom. After the ensuing mass baptisms, all of Granada's remaining residents were technically "Christian." Nonetheless, the traditional language, dress, and customs of Muslim Granada endured among many of the city's *moriscos* (formerly Muslim converts to Christianity) well into the sixteenth century. Even after the expulsion of the vast majority of the city's moriscos in 1569–1570 at the height of a second major rebellion in the Alpujarras (1568–1571), Granada retained much of its preconquest physiognomy and character. The towering minaret of Granada's great mosque, for example, continued to be a dominant feature of the city's skyline until it was finally destroyed in 1588—nearly twenty years after the expulsion of the moriscos. Even today, Granada remains the most apparently Islamic of Spain's major cities. Tourists by the thousands flock each day to the city primarily to see the Alhambra—the magnificent palace and fortress complex built by the sultans—and other surviving reminders of the city's Muslim heritage. In short, the creation of Christian Granada—the subject of this book—was not an event but rather an historical process, and a gradual and incomplete one at that.

The resonance of the date of the city's conquest among scholars and non-

scholars alike—Spain's *anno mirabilis* of 1492—underscores dramatically
the fact that the Granada story was no isolated or peripheral development.
Inherently, an examination of Granada's transformation from a Muslim
city into a Christian one brings us directly to the heart of three vital and in-
terrelated themes in the history of medieval and early modern Spain: first,
the nature of Spanish imperial expansion; second, the fate of Christian
Spain's religious minorities; and third, the growth in the power and institutional strength of the Spanish church in the era of the Catholic Reformation. On each of these three critical matters, careful study of the Granada
case suggests new perspectives on which the central arguments of this book
are based.

First, the conquest and settlement of new territories is a recurring and in
some ways defining feature of medieval and early modern Spanish history.
The creation of Christian Granada was an important and transitional episode
in a much larger story of Spanish expansion both within the Iberian Peninsula
and overseas. On the one hand, the conquest of the Nasrid sultanate of
Granada represented a long-delayed last step in the Christian "reconquest" of
Spain from Muslim rule—a process that had remained stalled since the
thirteenth-century capture of Córdoba, Seville, and the rest of northern and
western Andalusia. On the other hand, the conquest of Granada preceded by
only eight months the August 1492 departure of Columbus's first voyage. In
Columbus's wake, of course, Spanish conquerors and settlers embarked on an
unprecedented wave of overseas imperial expansion that would carry them as
far away as the vast reaches of North and South America and the remote is-
lands of the Philippines, thus creating the world's first territorial empire of
truly global scale. The coincidence of Granada's conquest and Columbus's
first voyage, moreover, was not merely chronological. The Genoese adven-
turer in fact received his April 1492 commission from Queen Isabella in the
newly founded village of Santa Fe—on the site of the Catholic Monarchs' former siege camp just outside of Granada—only after the successful conclusion
of the costly ten-year military campaign against the Nasrid sultanate finally
freed up a small amount of funds for the queen to risk on Columbus's specu-
lative venture.

The capture and incorporation of Granada into Christian Spain constituted a distinct case of Spanish colonial expansion that provides a useful
point of comparison with and contrast to the cities of the medieval *reconquista* frontiers on the one hand and conquered locales throughout
sixteenth-century Spain's overseas empire on the other. Crown policy regarding Christian immigrant settlement and, at least initially, the legal status of Granada's conquered Muslim and Jewish populations clearly drew on
medieval precedents.[2] Yet the circumstances and outcome of the Granada
case also differed in fundamental ways from the reconquest frontiers of
Castile and Aragon, and where appropriate, I have tried to make clear some
of the critical similarities as well as differences. The Granada precedent also

played a role in influencing sixteenth-century Spanish overseas imperial projects in the New World.[3] Yet the differences between Granada and the more remote venues of Spanish colonial expansion included more than just the obvious issues of distance and the relative long-term historical and cultural familiarity between conquerors and conquered in the Granada case compared with the complete absence of knowledge of each other's culture and traditions that characterized initial encounters overseas. Again, where appropriate, I have tried to clarify some of the key similarities, differences, and possible points of influence.

Central to an understanding of Granada's history in the late fifteenth and sixteenth centuries is the fact that, for moriscos and Christian immigrants alike, daily life in the city's streets and plazas reflected the demands of a frontier society. The applicability of the term *frontier* to the case of the postconquest city of Granada may no doubt be disputed by some—particularly those whose definition of "frontier" excludes any place over which one of two or more previously contending groups has already established firm and lasting political control, as was the case in Granada after 1492.[4] To clarify, I employ the term *frontier* in this book in much the same way as did Father Robert Burns in his classic studies of the thirteenth-century Kingdom of Valencia in the crown of Aragon (although, again, I acknowledge significant differences between the two cases).[5]

Specifically, I contend that Granada during the nearly eight decades that separated the 1492 conquest from the 1569–1570 local expulsions constituted a "frontier" community in at least three distinct senses of the term. First, the city remained even after 1492 a political and military frontier. Despite the fact of the conquest, Christian immigrants and state authorities continued for decades to fear not only possible rebellions among the moriscos but also a potential Ottoman seaborne invasion of the peninsula via the old Nasrid sultanate that would employ the moriscos as an internal "fifth column."[6] Even as late as 1572, in the aftermath of the second rebellion of the Alpujarras, Granada's municipal councillors continued explicitly to refer to their city as a "frontier" city (*ciudad frontera*) in this sense in a lengthy report to the crown on the state of local military preparedness.[7] Second, postconquest Granada obviously long remained a cultural and religious frontier zone in which elements of traditional Iberian Islamic and Christian faith and practices met, coexisted, blended, and frequently clashed. Third and finally, postconquest Granada long housed a particularly fluid and dynamic frontier society distinct from the more established social orders of many of Spain's other major cities, particularly those to the north. Like many frontier communities, Granada not only suffered from political instability, but it also offered many of its residents a variety of possibilities for social and economic advancement.

With regard to the second theme, Granada clearly constituted a central chapter in the history of religious and ethnic minorities in Spain's Christian kingdoms. The coincidence of the city's conquest with the 1492 expulsion of the Jews from Castile and Aragon provided a chilling portent of the fate that would eventually befall conquered Granada's "native" population: exile or mandatory conversion to Christianity in 1500, expulsion from the city 1569–1570 for resettlement in dispersed areas of the crown of Castile, and the final exile of the moriscos from the Spanish kingdoms in 1609–1614. Medieval and early modern Spain's intrinsic appeal as a subject of study among today's scholars lies to a large degree in the lessons that it may hold concerning questions of multiethnic and religiously plural societies of the sort that have become so common in our own world. Yet those who approach Spanish history expecting such lessons to be simplistic ones are often disappointed. According to the most romantic interpretations, medieval Spain, the "land of the three religions" (Islam, Judaism, and Christianity), experienced an idyllic golden age of dynamic intercultural exchange and cross-fertilization. Beneath the intermittent clamor of Christian crusade and Islamic jihad that characterized the *reconquista* centuries, there remained according to such interpretations a startling degree of what Américo Castro called *convivencia*—a term he coined to describe the more or less peaceful coexistence and interaction of Muslims, Jews, and Christians.[8] The merits of the term *convivencia* as an organizational concept for understanding medieval Spanish history have been questioned and debated for decades, and recent studies of religious violence in medieval Spain have effectively exploded the romantic mythology. Although adherents to the three faiths may indeed have "coexisted" in communities throughout medieval Iberia, they by no means did so in ways that can be uniformly characterized as "peaceful."[9]

It is nonetheless clear that by the time of Philip III's 1609 royal decree expelling the moriscos from all of his kingdoms, Spain had become a very different place. In the high Middle Ages, Muslims and Jews practiced their faiths openly in Iberia's Christian kingdoms, and Jews and Christians similarly did so in Muslim-ruled areas of the peninsula. By the seventeenth century, Spain had become a land of rigorously enforced Catholic identity that had formally excluded not only open practitioners of Islam and Judaism on strictly religious grounds but also even baptized Christians of ethnically morisco descent. Importantly, Christian descendants of converted Jews (called *judeoconversos,* or simply *conversos*), by contrast, were never subject to such expulsion, but conversos continued throughout the early modern period to endure various forms of official and unofficial exclusion and social stigmatization. In short, the decline of *convivencia*—so long as the term is defined simply as "coexistence" and shorn of all connotations of a medieval utopia of multicultural understanding—is still a useful concept in understanding Spain's transformation from the medieval to the early modern period.[10]

The policies of religious and ethnic exclusion enacted by the Catholic

Monarchs and their Habsburg successors broke down the conditions that had sustained medieval *convivencia,* and at the heart of the deliberations of these rulers always stood the vexing problems of Jewish and Muslim conversion to Christianity. With regard to Granada and the Spanish kingdoms as a whole, many historians have expertly covered the often-bewildering complexity that characterized the evolution of crown policy toward religious and ethnic minorities, and it is not the primary intent of this book simply to repeat their findings and revisit their debates.[11] This book focuses on the gradual creation of a new local society and culture by and among the Christian immigrant and morisco residents of postconquest Granada—a topic about which we still know surprisingly little—rather than on the development of official policies of persecution. In Granada as elsewhere, however, creation and destruction were processes that were intimately linked. Understanding the nature of the local society and culture that developed in Granada is impossible without a basic grasp of the deteriorating legal and social conditions under which the city's "native" population lived.

Official concern with the issue of religious conversion long predated 1492, and the context within which Christian Granada was created is thus also incomprehensible without a brief retreat into the religious politics of the late medieval period. In the wake of a peninsulawide wave of pogroms of 1391, as much as one-third of Spain's Jewish population converted to Christianity under conditions that can be described at best as highly pressured. Theologians hotly debated the validity of such conversions, but the most common conclusion, and the one that ultimately shaped royal policy toward judeoconversos and moriscos alike in the era of the Catholic Monarchs, was that baptism, once received, was ineffaceable regardless of the circumstances under which it occurred. Church and state authorities nonetheless constantly suspected formerly Jewish converts and their descendants of secretly adhering to their ancestral faith and law. It was explicitly in response to this persistent "converso problem" that Isabella and Ferdinand enacted two policies of monumental significance for the future history of Granada and all of the Spanish kingdoms. First, they established the Spanish Inquisition in 1478 to root out crypto-Judaism among converts. Second, with the expressed intent of safeguarding the Catholic faith of the conversos from the potentially damaging influence of their former coreligionists,[12] they issued the March 1492 decree expelling from the kingdoms of Aragon and Castile all Jews who refused to accept baptism.

In terms of the evolution of official crown policy toward religious and ethnic minorities, the history of the city of Granada in the period 1492–1570 included two critical and broadly influential innovations. The first came in January 1500, when for the first time the Catholic Monarchs presented to a group of their *mudéjar* (or Muslim) subjects—those of the city of Granada—the same choice that they had given to all of their Jewish subjects eight years earlier: convert to Christianity or leave the kingdom.

Historians have long debated whether or not a policy of forced conversion or expulsion toward Granada's conquered Muslims was an inevitable corollary of a broader, preconceived program on the part of Isabella and Ferdinand to forge religious unity as a means of furthering the political centralization of their kingdoms.[13] As Mark Meyerson has argued, however, the persistence of a crown-protected and numerically significant Muslim minority in Ferdinand's Aragonese kingdom of Valencia throughout the Catholic Monarchs' reign and well into the 1520s weighs strongly against the existence of such a master plan.[14] Although Isabella is widely known to have pursued a much sterner line than her husband with regard to the religious minorities of her Castilian kingdom into which conquered Granada was being incorporated, the evidence suggests that the mass baptisms of Granada's remaining Muslims in January and February of 1500 resulted from royal policy characterized more by inconsistency and blunder than by coordinated, purposeful intent.

The terms of Granada's surrender treaty negotiated in the final months of 1491 and enacted on January 2, 1492, explicitly guaranteed all Muslims who chose to stay in the city the freedom to practice their ancestral faith. In the early postconquest years, these terms were generally observed by Granada's first archbishop—the queen's former confessor and trusted advisor Hernando de Talavera. Talavera's respect for the cultural traditions of the city's native population, combined with his emphasis on evangelization by gentle persuasion rather than by force, made him a popular figure among the conquered city's Muslim majority. Frustrated by the slow progress of Talavera's peaceful missionary efforts, however, Isabella conceded in the fall of 1499 to the more aggressive plans of the archbishop of Toledo, Francisco Jiménez de Cisneros. In clear violation of the surrender treaty terms, Cisneros came to Granada and embarked on a forceful conversion campaign. Outraged by Cisneros's efforts and by his reported use of torture, Granada's Muslims in December 1499 rose up in an open rebellion that quickly spread to the nearby Alpujarras Mountains. As the violence of the first rebellion was quelled, Isabella—on Cisneros's advice and against the misgivings of Ferdinand—made the acceptance of baptism a necessary condition of royal pardon for the act of rebellion. First in the city and later throughout the former sultanate, the impact was twofold: widespread emigration of those Muslims who had the means and inclination to do so, and baptism en masse of the rest.

For the first time, the Catholic Monarchs now faced a large-scale "morisco problem," and its effects reached far beyond the borders of the old Nasrid sultanate. Following the precedent that had been set for the solution of the "converso problem," Isabella decreed on February 12, 1502, that all Muslim subjects in the kingdom of Castile who had not converted to Christianity would be expelled. Ferdinand, by contrast, continued until his death in 1516 to allow the practice of Islam among the mudéjares of his

Aragonese kingdoms. Ultimately, however, the creation of a new "morisco problem" in Valencia as a result of popular anti-Muslim violence and pressured conversions during the *Gemanías* rebellion of 1520–1522 led Ferdinand's grandson Charles V to order on November 25, 1525, the expulsion or conversion of Spain's final remaining mudéjar population.[15]

The second broadly influential innovation in royal policy toward minorities to arise from Granada came in July 1569, when King Philip II for the first time in Spain's history enacted a policy of expulsion based not on strictly religious grounds, but rather against a baptized Christian ethnic minority—the moriscos of the city of Granada. Although the city's morisco masses played little direct role in the "second rebellion" raging at the time in the nearby Alpujarras, state and church authorities saw them as a potential security threat. Ever since the mass baptisms of 1500, the sincerity of their Christian faith and loyalty to the Castilian crown had remained a matter of serious doubt. Crown and church officials had made many attempts to accelerate the cultural assimilation of Granada's moriscos—attempts that often backfired by sharpening rather than ameliorating local ethnic hostilities. A series of edicts beginning in 1508, for example, banned various customs and traditions that the authorities believed contributed to the persistence of crypto-Muslim practices and distinct community identity among the moriscos, including the use of the Arabic language and the wearing of their traditional clothing. These efforts culminated in 1526 in the Royal Chapel Congregation called and personally attended by Emperor Charles V with the explicit intent of resolving Granada's "morisco problem" once and for all. In addition to condemning a variety of abuses committed against the moriscos by local church and state officials, the mandates of the conference repeated most of the earlier bans on traditional morisco customs and ordered for the first time the introduction into Granada of a tribunal of the Spanish Inquisition. Local morisco leaders lobbied their monarch vigorously to annul the congregation's prohibitions, arguing that the customs in question were merely regional traditions that bore no religious significance whatsoever and in no way inhibited their ability to be good, practicing Christians. Whatever level of credence he gave to their arguments, the cash-strapped emperor, beset as he was by ongoing conflicts throughout his scattered realms, proved unable to ignore the moriscos' money. In exchange for an extraordinary grant of ninety thousand ducats and the offer of a new annual levy of twenty-one thousand ducats from the moriscos of the city and kingdom of Granada, Charles agreed to suspend for forty years the mandates of the Royal Chapel Congregation, with the sole exception of the establishment of Granada's Inquisition tribunal, which opened the following year.

When the forty-year grace period expired in 1566, still-suspicious church and state authorities revived all of the suspended cultural prohibitions and added some new ones concerning morisco music and dance, and King Philip

II ordered their stern enforcement. Renewed persecution, combined with deterioration through administrative corruption and increased royal taxation of Granada's vital silk industry on which many of the moriscos depended, sparked the second rebellion of the Alpujarras, which broke out in December 1568.[16] It was at the height of the rebellion that King Philip ordered the city's morisco population expelled from their homes and redistributed in smaller groups in various towns and cities throughout the crown of Castile, where it was believed they might be more effectively assimilated into the Castilian Christian social mainstream. A series of three separate expulsions—conducted in June and December 1569 and July 1570—carried away the vast majority of the city's morisco population, with exceptions being granted only to those artisans and professionals whose skills were deemed essential to the local economy and to a number of upper- and middle-class morisco families who had managed to integrate themselves into positions of authority within the society of the conquerors.

Again, the fate of the city's moriscos proved a preview of developments elsewhere. As royal forces gradually overcame rebel resistance in the Alpujarras by 1571, one after another of the morisco communities of the former sultanate were expelled and resettled in dispersed areas of Castile. In 1609, the government of Philip III carried the process one step further. Convinced that they would never become faithful Christians or loyal subjects, Philip ordered the expulsion of all moriscos from his realms—a process that was completed by 1614.

Within this broader pattern of persecution, one might reasonably expect to find that the role of the local mudéjar/morisco community in postconquest Granada amounted to little more than that of a uniformly hostile and marginalized subculture bound firmly together by shared persecution. Traditional historical accounts have until recently accepted at face value the generalized descriptions to this effect offered by contemporary observers such as the Jesuit Father Ruiz, who as late as 1556 wrote of Granada's moriscos: "They are commonly as Muslim now as before they were baptized."[17] Its "native" population thus characterized as the extreme case of an embittered minority unswervingly hostile toward authorities and immigrant settlers alike, postconquest Granada often serves as the paradigmatic counterpoint in studies that stress the partial survival of essentially medieval patterns of *convivencia* in other peninsular locales well into the sixteenth century. Contrasting mudéjar-Christian relations in Valencia from 1479 to 1525 to the state of affairs in Granada, for example, Meyerson writes:

There is almost no comparison between the situations in Valencia and Granada. In Valencia Muslims and Christians had been coexisting for well over two centuries, and, although there were problems, society remained cohesive. Valencia's Christians and Muslims had long ago experienced the shock of having to inhabit the same kingdom. As for Granada, one is hard pressed to speak of a single society; rather, it was more a case of two societies that had glowered at each other across the Granadan frontier being forced together by virtue of Granada's conquest.[18]

On the whole, the evidence presented in this book confirms that this generalized image of mudéjar/morisco resistance is, at least to a point, valid. Most of Granada's mudéjar/morisco community did, in fact, maintain a great degree of solidarity in the face of the hostility not only of church and state authorities, but also of much of the ever-growing local Christian immigrant community at large. Over the past decade, however, a fresh wave of research into previously untapped archival resources in Granada has begun to uncover a startling degree of economic, political and religious variation within the postconquest city's mudéjar/morisco community, as well as much more complicated patterns of mudéjar/morisco-Christian immigrant interaction than previously realized.[19] Without ignoring the simultaneous patterns of persecution and confrontation that led ultimately to the 1569–1570 local expulsions, this book makes an original contribution to this line of research. I argue that much can be learned not only by contrasting differences but also by comparing similarities in the social realities faced by the postconquest city's immigrants and moriscos. Both groups, for example, remained throughout the period 1492–1569 dynamic communities in a state of continuous transformation. Postconquest Granada long remained a "frontier society" constantly reshuffled on each side of the ethnic divide by ongoing emigration and immigration among both the settler and morisco communities alike. I also contend that Granada in some ways resembled rather than differed from cases such as Meyerson's Valencia. It remained throughout this period not only a city of endemic religious and ethnic confrontation but also a place where thousands of moriscos and Christian immigrant settlers interacted closely with one another on a daily basis in a mostly peaceable manner.

The third and final central theme of this book is the creation of a new local Christian religious culture in postconquest Granada—a process that not only coincided chronologically with the early stages of the Catholic Reformation but also produced a remarkable list of broadly influential religious reformers perhaps unparalleled by any other city in Catholic Europe, and certainly any other city of comparable size.[20] The impressive list includes among others archbishops Hernando de Talavera and Pedro Guerrero, the future saints Juan de Dios and Juan de Avila, and the spiritual writer and Spain's "best-selling" author of the sixteenth century, Luis de Granada. Ironically, even though it was located in a peripheral "frontier" zone on the very edge of Catholic Europe, Granada produced many key contributors to devotional and institutional reform movements that would transform Roman Catholicism worldwide in the sixteenth and seventeenth centuries. Could this have been mere coincidence, or did the distinct social and cultural circumstances of frontier Granada make it particularly productive of innovative reformers and reform movements?

My answer to the latter question is a qualified yes. In many ways, Granada did play a privileged role in the production of broadly influential sixteenth-century reform ideas and programs. From the enduring image within Spain and abroad of Talavera as an exemplary prelate, to the rapid spread of Juan de Dios's Order of Brothers Hospitallers, and to the Council of Trent itself—where Granada's archbishop Guerrero championed the reform cause as president of the Spanish delegation, and where the reform agenda was deeply influenced by Juan de Avila's proposals—Granada's influence on sixteenth-century Catholic reform was far-reaching.[21] In analyzing the work of these broadly influential reformers, moreover, I argue that many of their specific ideas and programs should be understood largely, although not necessarily exclusively, as responses to the specific social and religious circumstances of the frontier city in which they worked.

In introducing this argument, three clarifications must be stated. First, I am by no means interested simply in identifying local "precedents" for Trent of the sort that have been repeatedly discovered and discussed for decades by historians of various dioceses throughout Catholic Europe.[22] What makes Granada of particular significance to our understanding of early modern Catholicism is the *direct* role played by local developments, through clergymen such as Avila and Guerrero and lay leaders such as Juan de Dios as conduits and as agents, in the production of various reform programs of churchwide significance—including, for example, the actual text of the Tridentine decrees themselves. I fully recognize that prelates and reformers in other dioceses shared many of the concerns voiced by Avila and Guerrero in their dealings with the council, and Avila and Guerrero both had worked with reform-minded clergymen in other communities before coming to Granada in the 1530s and 1540s, respectively. Both men, moreover, were also deeply influenced by intellectual fashions of the era such as Erasmian humanism, as well as by the general European spiritual and devotional ferment that was transforming the nature and practice of Christianity across the continent, in Catholic and Protestant lands alike, through the middle decades of the sixteenth century. Still, I argue that, as a newly conquered frontier city whose local religious culture remained a work in progress throughout the sixteenth century, Granada exerted direct, specific, and tangible influence on the reform ideas of both men—a relationship that sheds critical light on their activities relating to the ecumenical council.

By making such an assertion, however, I must also clarify that I by no means intend to suggest that postconquest Granada somehow became an "exemplary" or "laboratory" archdiocese that Guerrero, Avila, and other shapers of the Tridentine decrees put forward as a model to be imitated by the rest of Catholic Christendom. On the contrary, I demonstrate that during most of this period Granada ironically remained a particularly troubled archdiocese. Even aside from the enduring and often crippling "morisco problem," for example, Granada's ecclesiastical establishment in the formative four decades between the death of Archbishop Talavera in 1507 and the arrival of Archbishop Guerrero in 1546 suffered from a glaring absence of effective leadership, owing to a string of archbishops who were either nonresident or rendered ineffective by staunch local opposition. Granada was, of course, hardly unique in this regard; many early-sixteenth-century dioceses throughout Catholic Europe lacked strong episcopal leadership. Granada was distinct, however, in that it was the only archdiocesan seat in sixteenth-century Europe in which such absenteeism and/or archiepiscopal impotence occurred within the context of a newly conquered city that had no longstanding local Christian tradition and a city in which the ongoing development of a new local religious culture was therefore quite literally a continuous process of innovation and invention. Lacking firm guidance or control from the archbishops and other local high clergy in the critical early decades, many of the most important local religious traditions and institutions that characterized the public religious life of the newly conquered city thus originated and developed under the direction of lay individuals and groups—mostly from the city's Christian immigrant community. Among the central questions that I address are exactly who created Granada's new local Christian culture? How was this culture created, and to what ends? One of the most consistent tendencies that I have discovered in examining this process is that, far from resisting the incursions of the church, Granada's immigrant laity demanded from their clergy extensive participation in a broad variety of civic and charitable functions, and responded best to those local ecclesiastical institutions that met these expectations. These included, for example, various local Franciscan establishments, which, as had often been the case on the *reconquista* frontiers of the thirteenth century,[23] and as would again be the case among early settler communities in the Americas,[24] played many critical roles in the public religious culture of early postconquest Granada. Under these circumstances, it is not surprising that frontier Granada in the middle decades of the sixteenth century proved especially productive of influential reform ideas and groups such as the Brothers Hospitallers of Juan de Dios and his spiritual mentor Juan de Avila's "sacerdotal school." Their promotion of active and apostolic notions of the role of the clergy and church institutions in the life of the community, I argue, must be understood not only in the context of the intellectual critique of the church provided by contemporary humanist scholars, but also more specifically as a response to the distinct historical and social circumstances of the community in which they worked.

A full appreciation of the continentwide multiplicity and complexity of forces that contributed to the production of sixteenth-century Catholic reform, however, leads to a third critical clarification. It is not my intent to resurrect in a new "Granadan" form the oversimplified "Spanish thesis" of the influential late-nineteenth-century German Hispanist Wilhelm Maurenbrecher, who argued that most of the principal devotional and institutional reform movements that powerfully transformed Roman Catholicism in the sixteenth and seventeenth centuries traced their historical roots to the Spanish church in the time of the Catholic Monarchs.[25] With regard to Trent, for example, Guerrero and Avila were by no means the only shapers of the council's reform decrees, nor were they even necessarily the most influential. According to all accounts of the council, however, they were very important. Even more significant to me is the fact that their impact on Trent is emblematic of what I contend is a still poorly understood general process of negotiation, dialogue, and exchange between local concerns and church-wide policy that underlay early modern Catholic reform—a process that affected not only Guerrero and Avila, but also other reformers who made critical contributions to what would eventually become the Tridentine reform program. These would include, most obviously, men such as the Venetian diplomat and later cardinal, Gasparo Contarini, upon whose reform ideas the influence of specifically Venetian religious and political factors have been insightfully illuminated by Elizabeth Gleason.[26]

What I am suggesting, in short, is that the story of the production of Catholic reform is, no less than the story of the post-1563 "reception" or "application" of the Tridentine reforms examined in many recent studies,[27] one that must be written locally, or at least one that must take into account the effect of formative local experiences on many of the key contributors to reform.[28] Such perspective, provided in an especially clear fashion by the case of frontier Granada, calls into question all characterizations of sixteenth-century Catholic reform programs as movements that were imposed from above or even externally induced.

The recent historiographical focus on "local religion,"[29] despite providing innumerable critical insights concerning the differences between Catholicism "as prescribed" and Catholicism "as practiced" in early modern European communities, has perhaps, as Craig Harline and others have argued, left us with an image of the upper clergy and their supposedly uniform notions of "official religion" as somewhat monolithic and univocal.[30] Harline in particular has suggested that it may be time for ecclesiastical historians to take the lessons learned from a generation of local studies of lay religious practice and apply them to a renewed, more nuanced, and better-informed study of the institutional church, especially the episcopacy.[31] By shedding light on the relationships between Granada's influential religious reformers and the frontier community in which they worked in the decades leading up to the Council of Trent, this book aims at providing an original and useful contribution to the rethinking of the institutional nature of the church in the early modern period.

CHAPTER ONE

A Frontier Society

The Christian Immigrant Community,
1492–1570

Juan de la Torre was one of the thousands of Christian immigrants who came to Granada seeking opportunity and fortune in the decades after the city's 1492 conquest. He had grown up in Toledo as a member of a wealthy judeoconverso merchant family that played a leading role in that city's endemic violence between Jewish converts and "Old Christians." Two of his kinsmen had been hanged in 1467 for entering Toledo's cathedral armed to do battle with Old Christians; another had been hanged for allegedly leading a 1485 plot to murder local inquisitors during the city's Corpus Christi procession.[1] Though Juan did not participate in the violence, he actively shared in the family tradition of shrewd business. Viewed from Toledo, newly conquered Granada appeared to him a golden opportunity for investment. His name first appears in Granada's records shortly after the city's conquest, when in 1493 and 1494 he issued loans to Archbishop Talavera and royal secretary Hernando de Zafra.[2] He may have purchased from the crown part of the Granada silk-tax contract as early as 1504, and by 1517 his name appears in royal documentation as the primary *arrendador* (tax collector) of the local silk trade. Along with his in-laws, also from Toledan converso families, Juan de la Torre dominated the Granada silk-tax contract for the better part of the first half of the sixteenth century. Granada was among the principal centers of European silk production, and Juan quickly amassed an enormous fortune.

Meanwhile, he maintained close ties with relatives back in Toledo and even kept a house in his native city. His fortune had, in fact, allowed him to become one of the most powerful men in both cities, and for more than three decades he shuttled back and forth between the two. He purchased an office as municipal council member (*regidor*) in Toledo in 1529, and served as Toledo's representative (*procurador*) in the Castilian Cortes of 1539. In the same year, Granada's city council borrowed from Juan de la Torre a sum of four thousand ducats. The city of Granada remained indebted to him for years.[3] In 1544, he renounced his position on Toledo's municipal council, and from that point on lived in Granada full time. After losing the silk-tax contract to a higher bidder in 1546, Juan continued to be a major player in Granada's local power structure. In 1553, he became lord of a village some forty kilometers south of the city, and his fortune allowed his son to purchase a seat as a voting *regidor* on Granada's municipal council.[4]

Unlike Juan de la Torre, Domingo Pérez de Herrasti was not socially scarred by any known Jewish lineage, nor was he blessed by family wealth. Instead, he was a soldier who came, his family later claimed, from a proud but relatively poor noble family from the Basque village of Azcoita. Domingo, like Juan de la Torre, took advantage of the opportunities presented by the Granadan frontier. He served in the Catholic Monarchs' army during the conquest of the city, and Queen Isabella rewarded him in 1492 with two offices: public scribe of the city of Granada and *jurado* (nonvoting official at municipal council meetings) of the city, representing the parish of San Pedro y San Pablo. He held a variety of offices, and the powerful captain general of Granada, Iñigo López de Mendoza, repeatedly accused him of corrupt abuse of his position for personal gain. Despite Mendoza's disfavor, Pérez de Herrasti continued to milk royal patronage, especially through friends such as Isabella's royal secretary Hernando de Zafra and, later, Charles V's advisor Francisco de los Cobos. He also forged alliances with powerful local families by arranging the marriages of his sons to daughters of municipal councilmen. Domingo's ascent culminated in royal grants of seigneurial control of lands near Granada and the purchase by his son Francisco in 1541 of his own seat as a member of Granada's municipal council.[5]

If Granada promised opportunity to men such as Domingo Pérez de Herrasti and Juan de la Torre, it did not always deliver. The cases of these two highly successful men must be balanced against the experiences of most immigrants to the frontier city. The husband-and-wife merchant team of Pedro Sánchez and Juana González, for example, came to Granada from the Plasencia region of Extremadura (in southwestern Spain) with similarly high aspirations. Bad business fortune, however, gradually drove the couple into poverty. After the death of her husband, Juana González attempted to continue the business, running up a string of debts that stretched from Granada itself to the nearby towns of Pinos Puente and Ronda to her Extremaduran hometown of Plasencia. In her 1577 last will and testament, she reported that she had been reduced to begging for food in the streets of Granada. Having no money to order funeral masses for herself, Juana entrusted her executors to contact her family back in Plasencia to arrange for masses to be said there for her departed soul.[6]

Alongside such stereotypical frontier stories of boom and bust, many Christian immigrants found in frontier Granada economic conditions that allowed them simply to make do. During his 1526 visit, Venetian traveler Andrea Navagero reported that, compared with other cities, Granada appeared to him to have relatively few wealthy individuals and families. Most of the immigrants, he claimed, made modest livings working in various professions—above all in the production and trade of silk.[7] Still, even if Granada's promise often proved illusory, the perception of nearly limitless opportunity was powerful enough to attract Christian immigrants by the tens of thousands.

A brief overview of the city's demographic history from the conquest in 1492 to the end of the sixteenth century makes clear the quantitative significance of Christian immigration to Granada. On the eve of the conquest, Granada housed a population of approximately fifty thousand. This figure, although admittedly swollen significantly by wartime refugees from other, already-conquered areas of the Nasrid kingdom, made Muslim Granada one of the Iberian Peninsula's largest cities at the time of its surrender.[8] This preconquest population, however, included only a handful of Castilian Christians—mostly wartime captives and a small number of fugitives who had fled to the Muslim kingdom to hide from Spanish state or church authorities.[9] After 1492, however, Christian immigrants began to stream into the conquered city in numbers that would eventually surpass those of Granada's remaining indigenous, formerly Muslim population, which declined significantly as a result of emigration to Muslim North Africa. By 1561, the date of the first royal census of the city, Granada housed a Christian immigrant community of slightly more than thirty thousand people—a figure twice as large as the approximately fifteen thousand moriscos who still shared the city with them at that date.[10] Most of the moriscos who remained in the city in 1561, however, were driven from Granada during the second rebellion via the crown-mandated expulsions of 1569–1570. By the end of the sixteenth century, the city housed between thirty-five and forty thousand people—the overwhelming majority of them Castilian immigrants or the immediate descendants of such immigrants.[11] Overall, Granada's transformation from a Muslim city to one inhabited almost entirely by Christians of Castilian descent had thus resulted in a net population decline when compared with the preconquest figures. Despite the loss of almost all of the indigenous population, Christian immigration to Granada had nonetheless managed remarkably to produce by 1600 a city that ranked as the fourth largest in the crown of Castile. Only Seville, Toledo, and Madrid had more people.[12]

The influx of immigrants into the frontier city, however, began slowly. Christian immigrant settlement in Granada in the period under study is, in fact, best understood as a two-stage process. The first wave of Christian immigration in the years immediately after the conquest in 1492 was strictly limited by the legal conditions and protections of Muslim property guaranteed by the treaty of surrender. The lifting of these restrictions as a result of the events of 1498–1499 initiated a second, longer, and much larger wave of immigration that would endure into the middle decades of the sixteenth century.

The conditions surrounding postconquest Granada's first wave of immigration (1492–1499) restricted Christian settlement in the city itself largely, though not exclusively, to soldiers and royal bureaucrats. During this initial stage, the crown remained bound by the terms of the 1492 surrender agreement to protect the property of the resident Muslim population and thus bar any seizure or direct purchase of that property by Christians. Under these conditions, Christian immigrants could gain access to residence in the city only by two means. First, an immigrant could purchase the house or place of business of a Muslim who had chosen to flee to North Africa rather than live under Christian political control. Second, an immigrant could purchase from the crown the properties that had before the conquest pertained to the Nasrid royal patrimony, which were now in the hands of Isabella and Ferdinand as successors to the sultans. Especially in the first three or four years after the conquest, these constraints greatly impeded Christian immigration to the city. As a result, Granada's Christian community in these early years consisted mostly of royal administrative appointees, such as the count of Tendilla and crown secretary Hernando de Zafra, and soldiers who, like Domingo Pérez de Herrasti, had participated in the conquest and received rewards and offices in the new city in return for their services.[13]

Moreover, the vast majority of this nascent Christian community remained concentrated within the Alhambra castle-palace complex on a hill overlooking Granada—largely isolated from the daily life of the Muslim city below. In an account of his visit to the conquered city in October 1494, Tyrolean traveler Hieronymus Münzer made scant mention of Castilians in the city outside the Alhambra. After entering through the Guadix gate on the city's eastern edge, he rode straight into the heart of the city to the old main mosque without noticing anyone besides those whom he called the "infinite saracens."[14] The Christian immigrant community in the Alhambra complex in the 1490s, Miguel Ángel Ladero Quesada has estimated, probably numbered no more than one thousand permanent residents.[15]

Though not a large group in numerical terms, this seed of Granada's Christian immigrant community proved extremely important in the subsequent political development of the city. For the Pérez de Herrasti and many other families, participation in the conquest and presence among Granada's early Christian community conferred considerable prestige and often provided a basis for later claims to power within the local political order. Juan Arias de Mansilla, for example, rose from an apparently humble childhood in the village of San Ceprián near the Old Castilian city of Zamora to become an infantry captain in the forces of Queen Isabella. After participating in the conquest of Granada in 1492, he took up residence in the Alhambra and there raised four sons. In 1540, Granada's royal appellate court rejected as ridiculous a claim by these four Arias de Mansilla brothers that their ancestors in San Ceprián had enjoyed the privileges of noble status.[16] Nonetheless, their father's presence in the conquering armies proved politically advantageous, as two of the brothers rose in the 1550s to powerful voting positions on Granada's municipal council.[17] Granada's governing institutions throughout the period under study were filled with families such as the Pérez de Herrasti and Arias de Mansilla, whose prestige stemmed largely from their recent ancestors' presence among the conquering armies and Granada's nascent Christian immigrant community in the 1490s.[18]

While legal restrictions impeded large-scale Christian entry into the city of Granada itself in these early years, immigrants by the thousands streamed into the nearby villages and other major cities of the formerly Muslim kingdom. In Málaga, for example, the 1487 Christian takeover had resulted from a lengthy and bloody siege rather than a negotiated surrender. Christians who wished to enter this, the kingdom's principal port city, did not face the sort of legal obstacles that the 1492 surrender agreement created for would-be Christian residents of the kingdom's capital. As a result, Málaga, unlike Granada, already had in the 1490s a large and vibrant Christian immigrant community.[19]

Ladero Quesada has estimated from his study of royal land distribution records (*repartimientos*) that a total of between thirty-five and forty thousand Castilian subjects moved to the towns and villages of the formerly Muslim kingdom of Granada in the 1490s.[20] Besides Málaga, other important destinations of these early Christian immigrants included the villages of the area immediately surrounding the city of Granada itself. Hieronymus Münzer, in fact, mentioned in his 1494 travelogue that the possibility of rebellion among the city's conquered Muslim population was decreasing each day as the surrounding countryside was rapidly filling with Christian immigrants, leaving the local Muslims surrounded.[21] Particularly important in this regard was the nearby village of Santa Fe—a new town founded by the Christians on the spot where the Catholic Monarchs had set up their base camp as they prepared for a final attack on the city of Granada in 1491.

The Christians who filled Santa Fe and other villages near Granada included large numbers of Castilian merchants in search of profit in the city's lucrative silk trade. They exerted considerable political pressure on the crown to disregard the stipulations of the surrender agreement and allow them freely to set up enterprises within the city of Granada itself. Moreover, when properties in the city opened up for sale as the result of Muslim emigration, it was often such traders who had the most money and motivation to make the purchase. Thus, in addition to the aforementioned soldiers and royal administrators, Granada's early Christian immigrant community in the 1490s included a small but growing number of merchants.[22]

Castilian women played only a small role in this brief, initial stage of Christian immigration to the city of Granada between 1492 and 1500. Filled as it was with soldiers, bureaucrats, and traders, postconquest Granada's earliest Christian immigrant community was dominated by men.

Some sixteenth-century local historians characterized Granada's highly militarized, mostly male immigrant community of the 1490s as rowdy and roguish. Luis de Mármol Carvajal, for example, claimed that an archbishop of the even temperament and unquestionable moral rectitude of Hernando de Talavera had been absolutely necessary in Granada in those early years, not only to deal with the local Muslim community, but also with the city's Christians: "Such a prelate was very necessary for the Christians of the city, because the majority of those who came to populate it were men of war or upstarts, and among them there were many who were so unruly in the evils that the military life brings with it, that Talavera's work, diligence and industry were essential in order to reform them."[23]

As the turn of the century approached, Muslim emigration and shifting royal policy gradually undermined the protections that Granada's remaining Muslim population had previously enjoyed under the terms of the surrender agreement. On one hand, abandoned Muslim properties increasingly provided Christian immigrants opportunities for legal entry. On the other hand, frustrated by the slow growth of the Christian immigrant community in the years immediately after the 1492 conquest, the Catholic Monarchs began to issue incentives and privileges (*franquezas*) to those Castilian subjects who would take up residence in the frontier city.

Such crown incentives had been common in the thirteenth century, when Aragonese and Castilian kings had found it exceptionally difficult to attract settlers to the then newly conquered regions of Valencia and northern and western Andalusia.[24] On the medieval Andalusian frontier, such incentives in some cases had even included royal pardons for murderers and other criminals who would settle in the conquered zones.[25] In postconquest Granada, by contrast, such incentives usually came only in the form of tax exemptions. The most important of these *franquezas* was issued for the first time in 1495, when the crown granted all Christian immigrant residents of Granada exemption from the royal sales-tax (*alcabala*) and all other forms of royal taxation for the next ten years. In 1500, the crown ordered that these incentives be proclaimed in every city and town of the kingdom of Castile.[26] Not content to rely exclusively on crown publicity, Granada's municipal council also sent out its own commissions to various Castilian cities to announce the incentives and recruit new immigrants.[27] As if the economic opportunities to be found in Granada were not already sufficient to lure northern money and immigrants, these royal *franquezas* vastly increased the possibilities for profit and the flow of newcomers. Granada's growing Christian immigrant community in subsequent years guarded these royal privileges jealously and lobbied the crown frequently both for their renewal and for new incentives. In the Castilian Cortes of 1510, for example, Granada's representatives greedily petitioned the crown for broader tax exemptions to attract even more immigrants. Like the mother of a spoiled child, the crown responded flatly that "the ones you have already are sufficient."[28]

In addition to the royal *franquezas,* two events of 1498–1499 signaled a definitive end to the early stage of slow growth for the Christian immigrant community. First, in 1498, Granada's Christian and Muslim communities negotiated an agreement by which the city was officially divided into two residential zones. According to the terms of the treaty, local Muslim leaders consented to a segregation plan by which the Muslim community would concentrate itself in the Albaicín—a hilly district on the city's northeastern edge. The treaty opened up most properties in the lower areas of the city for Christian purchase and settlement.[29] Second, in the wake of the 1499 local Muslim uprising against Christian rule, the crown officially annulled all protections guaranteed the local Muslim population by the 1492 surrender agreement—terms that by this time had become largely meaningless anyway.[30] In addition, the forced conversions and mass baptisms of January and February 1500 brought on a renewed wave of Muslim emigration. By 1500, in short, all barriers to Christian immigrant settlement in the frontier city had disappeared.

The year 1500 thus marked the beginning of a second stage of Christian immigration to Granada, which would continue at least until midcentury. During this period, men and women from various sectors of Spanish society streamed into the city in numbers that produced by 1561 a local Christian immigrant community of more than thirty thousand people. Despite the large number of settlers, surviving documentary sources that address directly and explicitly the issue of Christian immigration to the frontier city are relatively few. Comparison with studies of migration to other medieval and early modern Spanish "frontiers" clarifies the challenges of studying the Granada case. Because the Castilian crown directed the flow of emigrants to the New World through the port of Seville, for example, those who study the movement of Spaniards to the early colonial settlements in the Americas have the advantage of detailed passenger inventories stored in Seville's Archivo General de Indias and surveyed in general quantitative terms in the works of Peter Boyd Bowman.[31] For their part, medievalists concerned with Christian migration to rural regions of the reconquest frontiers of the crowns of Castile and Aragon have long benefited from the richly detailed land distribution inventories contained in the *Libros de Repartimiento.*[32] Similarly precise land registers record the transfer of properties in much of the old Nasrid sultanate to new immigrant proprietors in the years during and immediately after the 1482–1492 war of conquest,[33] but they tell us nothing about the changing society of the city of Granada itself. For the city's Christian immigrants, the earliest surviving comprehensive documentary profile of the community as a whole is the 1561 royal census—a survey carried out nearly seventy years after the conquest. In order to gauge the nature and pace of Christian immigration to the frontier city over the intervening seven decades, it has therefore been necessary to trawl through a variety of forms of surviving evidence, including not only the qualitative impressions of contemporary observers, but also the more quantifiable data provided by notarial documents, parish registers, and court records.[34]

Used carefully, the available sources strongly suggest that the growth of Granada's Christian immigrant community through the first half of the sixteenth century occurred at a fairly steady and continuous pace. Immigration appears not, in other words, to have been concentrated disproportionately within any specific time period. Table 1.1, for example, summarizes the responses of fifty-one members of Granada's Christian immigrant community who, as witnesses in civil court trials in the decade 1551–1561, provided specific and detailed information regarding their time of residence in the frontier city.[35] Reliable testimony of this sort is rare in the court records, and as a result, this database is admittedly too small to be absolutely conclusive.[36] In terms of socioeconomic class, however, the sample is reasonably representative of Granada's immigrant community as a whole.[37] Of thirty-six whose testimony provided explicit indication of profession, for example, eight were laborers, ten were artisans, ten were merchants, two were tavern owners, four were soldiers, one was a town crier, and one held a nonvoting seat as *jurado* on the city's municipal council. The only category in which this sample is grossly nonrepresentative of the immigrant community as a whole is sex of the witness. Although women, as we will see, constituted as much as half of Granada's post-1500 immigrant community, they were rarely called to testify in trials. As a result, this database unfortunately includes only one woman.

Of the total of fifty-one witnesses, nineteen indicated that they had been born and/or raised in the city—suggesting that they were the second or third generation children or grandchildren of immigrants who had come to Granada in the first few decades after the conquest. Significantly larger, however, was the number of respondents—thirty-two, or more than 60 percent of the total—who stated clearly that they had come to the frontier city as first-generation immigrants. Perhaps most surprising, especially since the reasonable expectation would be that a database of witnesses chosen by civil litigants to testify in their favor might be heavily weighted toward long-established (and thus presumably well-respected) city residents, is the fact that a full twelve of the respondents—nearly a quarter of the total—stated that they first arrived in Granada after 1540. Notably, moreover, of the thirty-two witnesses who came to Granada as immigrants, the vast majority claimed to have arrived in the city at a young age—most of them in their twenties. In short, the experiences of these fifty-one people underscore the frontier nature of immigrant society in Granada in the period under study. As late as the 1550s, the majority of the city's Castilian Christian residents

TABLE 1.1 Immigration Data of Fifty-One
Witnesses in Civil Court Trials, 1551–1561

Date of Immigration to Granada		Age at Time of Arrival	
Born/Raised in Granada	19	Born/Raised in Granada	19
Before 1500	1	<20	4
1500s	2	20s	17
1510s	4	30s	8
1520s	7	40s	2
1530s	6	50s	0
1540s	10	60s	1
1550s	2		
TOTAL	51	TOTAL	51

appear to have been first-generation immigrants. Moreover, the growth of
Granada's Christian immigrant community seems to have been fairly steady
and continuous through the first half of the sixteenth century. The result
was a particularly dynamic community in which the contours and ranks of
local society were constantly reshuffled and remade through the continuing
arrival of new faces.

The steady growth of Granada's immigrant community proves somewhat
surprising when viewed within the broader context of late medieval and
early modern Spanish expansion and colonization. As noted earlier, most of
the conquered cities of thirteenth-century Valencia and Andalusia had experienced only slow and uneven Christian settlement. Historians have attributed the slow growth of Christian communities in these cases to a variety of
factors, including not only the continuing threat of violence from local
Muslim rebellions and intermittent raids from the nearby Muslim kingdom
of Granada, but also a series of poor harvests that endured well into the
fourteenth century. Under these conditions, Christian settlers frequently
gave up and returned to their hometowns to the north.[38] Ironically,
Granada's sixteenth-century immigrant community grew steadily not because of the absence of such hardships, but despite them, as evidenced by
the rebellions of 1499–1501 and 1568–1571 as well as local epidemics and
famines in 1521–1522 and 1529.[39]

Moreover, the continuing stream of immigrants to Granada is also surprising given the fact that it coincided with substantial waves of Castilian
migration not only to the New World, but also to other locales in Europe.
Beginning in the opening decades of the sixteenth century, settlers by the
tens of thousands flowed first into the Caribbean colonies and, later, beginning in the 1520s and 1530s, into conquered regions of Mexico and Peru.
In addition, as Thomas Dandelet has shown, sixteenth-century Spaniards
moved to Rome in sufficient numbers to produce an expatriate community

that constituted as much as a quarter of the "Eternal City's" population of some 110,000.[40] It was, in short, was an era of extensive Spanish migration, and the "frontiers" to be settled were numerous. Yet Granada's Christian immigrant community continued to grow despite the dangers of frontier life and the attraction of other frontiers in the New World and the Old.

Understanding Granada's place within the broader context of late medieval and early modern Spanish expansion depends above all on an understanding of the particular advantages offered by the city to Christian immigrants who chose to live there. Immigrant society in Granada did not constitute, on the one hand, a simple projection and reproduction of traditional Castilian social structures. Nor, on the other hand, did the growth of Granada's Christian immigrant community mirror the contemporaneous development of local societies among Castilian settlers in the New World. Granada constituted, in sum, a unique case of early modern Spanish expansion and settlement. Detailed qualitative analysis of Granada's sixteenth-century immigrant community clarifies these distinctions.

As was the case in the New World colonies, all of the major geographic regions of the kingdom of Castile and nearly all sectors of Spanish society contributed in some way to the growth of Granada's Christian immigrant community. However, in Granada and the New World alike, frontier life proved more attractive to certain segments of Spanish society than to others. In terms of geographic origins, for example, the New World tended to attract settlers from southern Spain—particularly Extremadura and Andalusia—at higher rates than from other areas of the kingdom of Castile.[41] In Granada, too, southern Spain not surprisingly provided the majority of the settlers—particularly the nearby regions of Andalusia and La Mancha.[42] As we will see, moreover, immigrant society both in New World and in Granada was characterized by a somewhat greater degree of social mobility than was possible in many of the more established communities of central and northern Castile—especially in the early decades of Spanish settlement.

Despite the similarities, local Christian society in postconquest Granada also differed in many ways from settler communities in the conquered regions of the Americas. For Spanish women and judeoconversos, for example, access to Spain's early colonies in the New World proved difficult or impossible to attain. Both groups, however, constituted highly significant elements of Granada's Christian immigrant community, particularly after 1500.

Studies of immigrant society in the earliest colonial settlements in the Americas, for example, have estimated that Spanish men outnumbered Spanish women as much as seven or eight to one.[43] At least after 1500, by contrast, there was no such imbalance among Granada's Christian immigrant community. The steady stream of settlers who entered the city in the first half of the sixteenth century, in fact, appears to have included Castilian women in numbers roughly equal to those of Castilian men. Surviving Christian immigrant last wills and testaments in Granada's notarial archive, for example, are equally divided between men and women testators. Of 163 Christian immigrant wills collected for this study, covering the period from the 1520s through the 1570s, 83, or slightly more than half, are those of immigrant women. Even in the earliest period covered by this database, women's and men's testaments survive in equal numbers; of 56 wills written between 1520 and 1540, 28 are women's.[44]

Analysis of these testaments suggests that Granada's Christian immigrant women, like their male counterparts, represented a broad cross-section of sixteenth-century Spanish society. For example, of the forty-one female testators who gave specific indication of their socioeconomic status, roughly two-thirds were from families of artisans or laborers, while the remaining third indicated that they came from wealthier merchant, bureaucratic, or noble backgrounds. Nearly all of the eighty-three women testators represented in the database were either married (52 percent) or widowed (41 percent), while only six (or 7 percent) of these women indicated that they were single. The lack of single women in this database is in large part a function of the nature of the documentation itself. Besides elderly widows, those most likely to write wills were younger women—usually married—who faced the perils of childbirth. The percentage of single women among frontier Granada's immigrant community was almost certainly higher than the tiny fraction represented in this database.

Married or single, immigrant women in postconquest Granada were drawn to the city for a variety of reasons, and they occupied a wide array of positions within the local economy. Some, like the struggling Extremaduran merchant Juana González discussed above, worked alongside their husbands or even took over family businesses after their husbands' deaths. Others, such as the linen-weaver Catalina González, sold goods they produced within the home in order to increase family income.[45] Many single or widowed women—such as Francisca de Prados, the elderly widow of a former velvet-weaver—found employment as household servants in the homes of Granada's wealthiest families.[46] In short, Castilian immigrant women were a large, varied, and highly active segment of frontier Granada's broader Christian immigrant community. They were also, as we will see, among the principal shapers of the conquered city's developing local religious culture and traditions.

For their part, Castilian judeoconversos—male and female alike—were legally prohibited from Spain's New World colonies.[47] In frontier Granada, by contrast, conversos faced no such restrictions, and they quickly came to comprise a very large segment of the Christian immigrant community. Exactly how large their presence in Granada was is impossible to know from census data or court records, since, like the Toledan converso Juan de la

Torre, they carried names indistinguishable from those of their Old Christian neighbors. Qualitative evidence, however, leaves no doubt as to their presence and significance at all levels of Granadan immigrant society.

Like Old Christian immigrants, judeoconversos had a wide variety of motivations to settle in the frontier city. At times faced with violent resistance against their attempts to penetrate established local power-structures, particularly in the cities of northern and central Castile,[48] many wealthy conversos found social advancement somewhat more easily attained in Granada's dynamic frontier society. Granada's governing institutions, secular and ecclesiastical alike, were filled with judeoconverso immigrants.[49] Moreover, conversos at all levels of local society—not just the wealthy—enjoyed in the frontier city a level of freedom from Inquisitorial harassment that could be found in none of the other major cities of the kingdom of Castile. For more than three decades after the city's conquest, there was no permanent Inquisition tribunal in Granada. Until the final establishment of Granada's Inquisition in 1526, the city was subject only to sporadic attention from the Holy Office's Córdoba tribunal. In 1510, for example, a visit by inquisitors from Córdoba led to the arrest of dozens of suspected crypto-Jews. In the Castilian Cortes held later that year, Granada's representatives issued official complaints to the crown regarding the disruptions caused by the Córdoban inquisitors, providing in the process startling testimony to the significance of conversos within Granada's Christian immigrant community:

> [The Inquisitor] took into custody more than eighty people, all of whom were wealthy merchants or other principal members of the community. After he finished this wave of arrests, many similar men [conversos] fled the city, and those who remained were very disheartened, and this city was greatly harmed in the process. If no remedy is taken, the city will become very underpopulated, and much business will be lost, and business is the most important means by which this city sustains itself and attracts new residents. The bad reputation of our city and its residents is such that the inquisitor and his familiars and officials called it "Little Judea," and did so publicly.[50]

Shortly after the definitive foundation of a tribunal of Spain's "Holy Office" in Granada in 1526, Venetian traveler Andrea Navagero provided further commentary on the importance of these Jewish converts in the growth of the Christian immigrant community:

> Because this city has thus far enjoyed the privilege of not having an Inquisition tribunal for nearly four decades, many people of suspicious backgrounds from all over Spain have come here to live securely, and this [the establishment of an Inquisition tribunal in Granada] will greatly damage the beauty and growth of the city, because these people have

built many very nice houses, and many of them are highly wealthy merchants. If no more of these people come to the city, and if [the Inquisi-
tion] drives away those that are already here, the entire city will rapidly
decline.[51]

In the early years after its 1526 establishment, Granada's Inquisition tribunal did indeed target suspected crypto-Jews among the city's large converso populace. Of eighty-nine penitents in Granada's first *auto de fe* of
1529, only three were moriscos, while most of the remainder were accused
of crypto-Judaism.[52] Nonetheless, after an initial period of targeting judeoconversos, Granada's tribunal turned its attention in the years around mid-
century principally to the eradication of vestiges of Islam among Granada's
moriscos.[53] In any case, judeoconverso immigrants remained throughout
the period one of the most powerful and influential elements of Granada's
economy, society, and culture. A morisco resident of the Albaicín in the
1560s, in fact, complained that one of the greatest injustices of Christian
rule in the city was the fact that the conquerors "have placed us under the
control of Jews."[54]

Well-educated royal bureaucrats, many of them from judeoconverso
backgrounds, were another important source of Christian immigration to
frontier Granada.[55] Especially significant among this group were hundreds
of lawyers, judges, and scribes who were drawn to Granada in the decades
after the transfer of the royal appellate court (*Real Chancillería*, or
Chancery) from the La Manchan city of Ciudad Real to Granada in 1505.
Often ambitious and "upwardly mobile," the jurists and bureaucrats of the
Chancery proved through the course of the sixteenth century to be a dynamic force in local society, as well as a particularly confrontational group
greatly concerned with issues of prestige. As a result, they frequently found
themselves at odds with other local governing institutions, including the
municipal council and, especially, the powerful aristocratic Mendoza family
as captains general of Granada.

For merchants, jurists, and many other well-to-do members of the Christian immigrant community, frontier Granada was a bonanza of opportunity
for the sorts of economic, social, and political advancement that could not
as easily be found in many other Spanish cities in the early sixteenth century. Numerous recent studies of other locales have shown that, despite
general economic growth and increasing social mobility throughout the
peninsula in the decades after 1500, Spain's increasingly wealthy middle
classes still found it difficult in many cities to penetrate the rigid ranks of
long-established local ruling oligarchies. In Barcelona, for example, James
Amelang has argued that local political and economic structures remained,
in his words, largely "ossified" throughout the early modern period.[56] As
Jodi Bilinkoff has effectively demonstrated, the Old Castilian city of Avila's

ruling elite during this period effectively resisted the entry of newly wealthy merchant families, particularly those of judeoconverso descent.[57] Even in the some of the cities of southern Spain, sixteenth-century local elites proved largely impenetrable to new members, as John Edwards has illustrated in the case of Córdoba.[58]

By contrast, social ranks within frontier Granada's Christian immigrant community were significantly more fluid and dynamic. In Granada, there was no long-established oligarchy among the immigrants of the sort that could be found in many of Spain's other major cities. Access to positions of power and influence in frontier Granada remained open to many ascendant immigrant families such as the Arias de Mansilla brothers and the judeoconverso de la Torre. As was often the case in newly conquered regions of the New World, Granada's ruling elite throughout the period under study remained, in the words of Bernard Vincent, "a world in continuous renovation."[59]

Even in frontier regions such as sixteenth-century Granada, however, social mobility had limits. Along with the large numbers of upwardly mobile merchants and jurists, Granada also attracted thousands of working-class immigrants who lacked sufficient resources to advance to official positions of power in Granada's municipal council or ecclesiastical establishment. Nonetheless, Granada proved appealing to these more humble members of Spanish society for many of the same reasons that brought the socially ascendant to the frontier city. The freedom from royal taxation provided by the city's *franquezas,* for example, applied to wealthy and poor alike. Similarly, Granada's relative freedom from inquisitorial harassment in the century's early decades drew Castilian conversos from all social classes to the city, not just wealthy merchants and ambitious bureaucrats.

A glimpse into the broader economic life of the Christian immigrant community as a whole is provided by the results of the 1561 census, in which a handful of parish reports identified the professions of residents. Table 1.2 summarizes the census's findings concerning the number of practitioners of a variety of professions and trades among a total of 2,241 individuals in five Christian immigrant majority parishes.[60] Though incomplete with respect to the city as a whole, the five parishes included here do in fact provide a reasonable cross-section of immigrant society, including as they do one parish in the commercial heart of the city (Sagrario/Iglesia Mayor), two in fairly wealthy parishes in Granada's eastern sector (Santa Ana and San Pedro y San Pablo), and two in heavily populated, largely working-class peripheral neighborhoods on the city's western and northern edges (Magdalena and San Ildefonso).

From these data it is clear that Christian immigration had managed by 1561 to bring to frontier Granada representatives of all the economic structures typical of Spanish cities of the era.[61] Even before the conquest, however, Nasrid Granada had long been a center of silk production, regional

TABLE 1.2 Economic Activities/Professions of 2,241 Immigrants According to the 1561 Royal Census

Profession	Total #	%
Agriculture/husbandry	106	4.7
Construction	94	4.2
Hides and leather	155	6.9
Cloth (mostly silk and wool)	169	7.5
Metalwork	32	1.4
Fine arts/glass/ceramics	33	1.5
Other crafts	157	7.0
Victualing trades	133	5.9
Small shop owners	251	11.2
Merchants/commerce	86	3.8
Professionals (doctors, lawyers, etc.)	86	3.8
Public employees	152	6.8
Soldiers	8	<0.1
Domestic service	37	1.7
Clergy	38	1.7
Widows*	645	28.8
Day laborers	59	2.6
TOTAL	**2241**	

* Specific profession, if any, not indicated. Only the parishes of Iglesia Mayor/Sagrario, Santa Ana, and Magdalena specified which heads of household were widows.

commerce, and political administration, and in this regard the waves of Christian immigrants who came to the city in the decades after 1492 transformed surprisingly little of the overall economic character of the city.[62] The production and trade of silk, for example, remained one of the city's principal economic engines—a fact apparent even in these data despite the absence in this sample of the parishes that were the primary centers of the local silk industry (e.g. Santa Escolástica and San Cecilio). The former Nasrid capital also remained after the conquest a center of administration, attracting large numbers of well-educated scribes and royal bureaucrats.

One important way in which Granada's economy was transformed as a result of the conquest, however, was in the preponderance of the construction industry. Throughout the sixteenth century, the conquerors engaged in literally dozens of major, new building projects that gradually began to transform the physical face of the formerly Muslim city, including the cathedral, Charles V's imposing Renaissance-style palace in the heart of the Alhambra, the enormous Royal Hospital on the city's western edge, and more than forty new monasteries and parish church edifices. The city's long-lasting construction boom not only provided steady jobs for skilled crafts-men and architects, but also intermittent work for unskilled day laborers.[63]

Frontier Granada, like all European cities of the era, certainly produced its own poor urban underclass that does not show up clearly in the numbers presented here.[64] On balance, however, the available data suggest that the variety and quantity of economic opportunities offered by the frontier city for skilled and unskilled labor alike in industries such as construction and silk production made Granada's population much more economically "ac-tive" than those of other cities in the crown of Castile. Vincent, for ex-ample, has shown that the percentage of economically active "producers" in Granada's population as a whole was higher than that of any other major city in the sixteenth-century crown of Castile except Segovia.[65]

For many working-class immigrants, frontier Granada simply repre-sented an opportunity to make a fresh start. In his 1548 last will and testa-ment, for example, the agricultural laborer Alonso de Cuéllar reported that he had come to Granada many years before, leaving behind in his Catalan hometown of Aviá high in the Pyrenees a total of more than 17,000 mar-avedís of debts that he owed to some two hundred different people whose names he could no longer fully remember.[66] Diego Hurtado de Mendoza, the aristocratic son of the captain general and historian of the second rebel-lion, described the Christian immigrant community in which he had been raised as one that was filled with such fugitives, renegades, and oppor-tunists: "A new city, populated by immigrants from various parts of Spain who were poor or had lost their way in their own lands, who were moti-vated to come to this city by the opportunity for profit, and the dispossessed who could not stay in their own houses with their own families."[67]

Even among these humbler elements of the Christian immigrant commu-nity, however, Granada often appeared to be a city of extraordinary oppor-tunity. Tales of forgotten hordes of gold and jewels left by former Muslim rulers were common in many areas of late medieval Spain, and in postcon-quest Granada such legends abounded in particularly powerful and imme-diate ways. Stories of hidden gold left by Granada's Nasrid sultans, often protected by magical spells, survived in the local oral tradition well into the nineteenth century, when the North American traveler Washington Irving recorded them in his *Tales of the Alhambra*. Besides such lost treasures, ru-mors spread in postconquest Granada of gold to be found in the streams of the area. A group of Frenchmen who came to Granada in the first two years after the conquest, for example, reportedly discovered gold in the sands of the Darro River—a small creek that ran through the heart of the city.[68] De-spite the fact that King Ferdinand immediately prohibited private searches for gold in the Darro, Granada's municipal council apparently used such ru-mors to entice even more Christian immigrants to the city. In 1537, for ex-ample, the municipal council issued an ordinance that banned the removal of stones from the Darro. They carefully and explicitly exempted from this ordinance, however, anyone who was searching for gold.[69] Ultimately, little gold was found in the Darro, but such treasure-hunting might well stand as a compact metaphor for the broad variety of motives that brought immigrants of all sorts to the frontier city.

Whatever their origin, social class, or level of wealth, all of Granada's Christian immigrants shared the common experience of belonging to an empowered group of conquerors amidst a large, often exploited, and at times hostile native population. The constant threat of rebellion among the moriscos led local authorities to emphasize military preparedness among all of Granada's male immigrants, rich and poor alike. In 1572, for example, King Philip II wrote to Granada's municipal council recommending the establishment of a new brotherhood of fighting men who might practice military skills with one another. The municipal council's response to Philip makes clear their notion of the military nature of their community as a whole:

> Because this is a *frontier* city [*ciudad frontera*], the nobility as well as the
> community at large have served Your Majesty in the defense of the
> coasts of this kingdom, and there have always been both suspicion of
> and actual instances of attacks by armed enemies, most recently with the
> uprising and rebellion [of the Alpujarras 1568–1571], as Your Majesty
> has seen and been informed, and these instances have made both the no-
> bility and the rest of this community arm themselves well, and all are
> well-practiced either in the art of horseback warfare or in that of the in-
> fantry, and, in addition, this city has certain days set aside for military
> exercises and musters.[70]

The municipal council's pride in the military prowess of the local Christian immigrant community proved under fire, however, to be largely misplaced. In his history of the second rebellion of the Alpujarras, Diego Hurtado de Mendoza explained that Granada's militia regiments were poorly trained, undisciplined, and militarily ineffective when compared with the crown's regular forces.[71] Similar in this way to the settler community in early colonial Peru described by James Lockhart, many of Granada's male immigrants appear to have been brawlers rather than soldiers.[72]

Finally, the dynamism of postconquest Granadan society is further underscored by the remarkably transient nature of much of the local immigrant community. Not all who came to frontier Granada came to live on a permanent basis, and outsiders were a common sight in the streets of the city. The presence of the royal appellate court in Granada, for example, brought hundreds of litigants each year from all over southern Spain for short stays in the city. In addition, the city's silk markets attracted a constant flow of both Spanish and foreign merchants, many of whom took up temporary or even permanent residence. A small but wealthy Genoese commercial community, moreover, had existed in the city of Granada under the

Nasrid sultans, and they continued under Christian rule to constitute a highly active and visible element of local society.[73] French visitors and residents, too, were fairly common in frontier Granada, playing a variety of roles in the local economy. Aside from such wanderers as the French gold prospectors mentioned earlier, Granada's more permanent French expatriate community included the head of the local mercury trade in the 1530s, Ramon Nonbeal,[74] as well as two of the city's three book printers in the 1550s, 1560s, and 1570s: René Rabus and Hugo de Mena.[75]

Even much of Granada's ostensibly permanent Christian immigrant community proved to be quite transient. Ties to local society in the hometowns from which the immigrants had come, for example, often remained strong. Some, like the Toledan converso Juan de la Torre, maintained for many years both resident status in and social ties to their hometowns to the north. Even after taking up residence in Granada sometime before 1539, for example, Pedro de Góngora kept his position on the municipal council of his hometown of Córdoba.[76] As Ida Altman has shown, Spanish settlers in the New World similarly maintained close ties to their hometowns in Spain, and some, albeit a small minority, even returned to Spain for short visits or to live.[77] The Granada frontier was, of course, far more accessible than Mexico or Peru, and travel back and forth between Granada and the cities and towns of the north was much more common.

Such travel among Granada's Christian immigrants was not, moreover, limited to visits home. Early modern Spanish society at nearly all levels was highly mobile (a phenomenon ignored until recently by historians), and perhaps nowhere in the Iberian Peninsula is this propensity for travel more apparent than among the Christian immigrants of frontier Granada.[78] Particularly poignant testimony to this geographical mobility is found in a 1555 local civil court trial in which witnesses from across Granada's social spectrum (although, again, only men) were asked if they had visited Seville, Toledo, Valladolid, or other major cities in Spain. Of seventeen witnesses called, eight were merchants, and seven of the eight reported having been called away by commercial interests to spend months at a time in one or more of Spain's other principal cities. More surprising are the responses of the remaining nine witnesses—a group that included not only four artisans (a silversmith and three tailors), but also three laborers (one silkworker, one cloth weaver, and a clothes washer) and two who gave no indication of their professions. Of the artisans and laborers, only the silversmith reported that he had not spent time in Spain's other cities. Especially revealing is the testimony of the silkworker Juan Sánchez. Although only thirty years old and by no means a wealthy man, he testified that he had spent time in locales as widespread as Seville, Toledo, Valladolid, Barcelona, and Valencia.[79]

Of the cities mentioned in this trial, Seville—the gateway to the New World—was the most frequently visited, appearing in the lists of ten of the seventeen witnesses. (Toledo and Valladolid were second with eight mentions apiece.) Granada's connection with Seville was in part a function of geographic proximity and in part a reflection of sixteenth-century Seville's growing significance as a world center of commerce. However, Seville's precedence in this list is also emblematic of the degree to which many of Granada's Christian immigrants simultaneously felt the pull of Spain's other early modern frontiers. Antonio Garrido Aranda, for example, has traced the migration of several clergymen who began their careers on the Granadan frontier before moving on to missionary work in the New World.[80] Another clergyman, Cristóbal de Arévalo, served more than twenty years in Granada's San Cecilio parish before moving in 1542 to missionary work in the North African city of Tunis, which had been recently conquered by the forces of Charles V.[81] Besides such migrant clergymen, Spain's other frontiers also proved attractive to some lay members of the Christian immigrant community. For example, Hernando Arias de Mansilla, the younger brother of the future municipal councilmen Francisco and Juan Arias de Mansilla, set out from Granada in or before 1540 to seek opportunity of his own in the Indies.[82]

In short, immigrant society at all levels in frontier Granada remained through the middle decades of the sixteenth century in a state of flux and transition. The men and women who comprised Granada's Christian immigrant community—merchants, soldiers, bureaucrats, artisans, and laborers alike—all participated in a new society forged amidst the unique circumstances of the frontier city. Though the great majority of the immigrants had come from the kingdom of Castile, the community that they produced in Granada was no mere transplant of traditional Castilian local social orders. Granada was in many ways unique among Spanish cities, and not just in terms of the presence of an enormous morisco community within the city's walls. Granada's Christian immigrant social landscape was characterized by a level of fluidity and dynamism that exceeded that of most of Spain's other principal cities. Tradition among frontier Granada's Christian immigrant community was not something simply to be followed or observed; it was something to be created.

CHAPTER TWO

Mudéjares and Moriscos

Change and Continuity in Granada's "Indigenous" Community

Judging by the 1563 distribution of his six-million *maravedí* estate among his heirs, the morisco merchant Alonso Hermes had become by the middle decades of the sixteenth century one of Granada's wealthiest residents. Yet little is known of his family's past. His recent Muslim ancestors certainly had not been members of Nasrid Granada's ruling elite, and his parents and/or grandparents were probably converted to Christianity along with the city's mudéjar masses in January or February 1500 in the wake of the failed first rebellion. Alonso's wealth, however, had allowed him to arrange particularly advantageous marriages for his children, including that of his son Miguel Hernández Hermes to the granddaughter of the powerful local morisco leader Diego Luis Abencerraje, who held an influential position as a *jurado* on Granada's Christian immigrant-majority municipal council. From his connection with the Abencerraje family, Miguel himself eventually fell heir to the *jurado* office—a post he still held at the time of the outbreak of the second rebellion in December 1568. Although his brother Francisco Hermes was among the overwhelming majority of the city's morisco population who were expelled from the city 1569–1570, Miguel's position in local government enabled him and his wife and children to remain in Granada, where the family continued in the years after the expulsion to strengthen its position in the local oligarchy. Miguel's granddaughter Isabel, for example, married a prominent "Old Christian" jurist in Granada's royal appellate court, and his descendent Álvaro Hermes even gathered in 1610 enough perjured testimony from "Old Christian" friends to convince crown authorities that the family was in fact not morisco at all, but rather descendants of Milanese merchants, and thus not subject to the 1609 order expelling all moriscos from Spain. From fairly humble middle-class Muslim roots, some members of the Hermes family managed in frontier Granada to integrate themselves effectively into long-lasting positions in the ruling elite of the Christian city.[1]

The story of the Hermes family is emblematic of startling evidence that has emerged from a recent wave of research into largely untapped material in Granada's archives—evidence that has raised important questions concerning the traditional historiographical portrayal of the city's moriscos as a unified community whose cohesion was forged and constantly strengthened by the ongoing hostility and persecution of church and state authorities. Their status as a persecuted minority in Christian Spain and the protagonists of two major rebellions against the crown has long made the "native" community of the city of Granada, the nearby Alpujarras mountains, and other surrounding regions of the old Nasrid sultanate a popular subject of study. Contemporary travelers and observers such as Hieronymus Münzer and the Venetian diplomat Andrea Navagero, for example, typically coupled their lavish praises for the city's staggering physical beauty and exotic Muslim architecture with blanket generalizations in which they characterized Granada's "native" population as a uniformly disgruntled and rebellious lot. "They are Christians," Navagero wrote during his 1526 visit, "only by means of force, and are poorly instructed in matters of the faith. . . . On the inside, either they are more Muslim than before (the conversion), or they believe in nothing. They are enemies of the Spaniards, who, in truth, do not treat them very well."[2] Although similarly critical of royal and ecclesiastical authorities for mismanaging morisco affairs, the classic "eyewitness" histories of the second rebellion by the aristocratic scholar Diego Hurtado de Mendoza and the soldier Luis de Mármol Carvajal left this monolithic image of Granada's recently expelled morisco community largely intact. Mármol Carvajal characterized the morisco masses of his hometown as generally bitter and recalcitrant: "Although with feigned humility they engaged in some good moral customs in their business, communications, and dress, on the inside they despised the yoke of the Christian religion, and in secret they taught and indoctrinated one another in the rites and ceremonies of the Mohammedan sect. This stain was universal among the common folk."[3]

More recently, Granada's moriscos became the subject of studies by some of the twentieth century's most distinguished historians of Spain, from Henry Charles Lea to Julio Caro Baroja to Antonio Domínguez Ortiz and Bernard Vincent.[4] Continuing to view morisco history principally through the lens of the second rebellion and consequent expulsions, however, these "modern" accounts did not significantly revise the traditional image of morisco unity. All acknowledged the existence of a tiny group of powerful and well-assimilated morisco aristocrats typically termed the "collaborator" elite, but this group is customarily dismissed as being so small as to be numerically insignificant.[5] As late as 1990, in fact, prominent French Hispanist Bernard Vincent explicitly characterized Granada's morisco community as a "practically solid bloc" void of significant internal fissures.[6]

To be sure, the evidence presented in this book will do much to confirm the traditional stereotype. The bulk of the city's "native" community does in fact appear to have resented and rejected to varying degrees the culture and/or the religion of the immigrants. Most, in fact, resisted conversion and acculturation simply by emigrating, either before or after the mass baptisms of 1500, to Muslim-controlled areas outside the Iberian Peninsula. As we will see in chapter 3, even those who remained in the city up until the 1569–1570 expulsions tended as a community to isolate themselves ever more deeply in the winding and hilly streets of the Albaicín—as far removed as possible from the predominantly immigrant neighborhoods of the lower city below. Despite the mass baptisms of 1500, moreover, many also continued to adhere privately to Islam. Although conclusive evidence concerning personal beliefs is far too scarce to permit even a reasonably safe guess at the percentage of local moriscos who clung self-consciously to the faith of their ancestors, the number was no doubt high, and the community as a whole was certainly characterized by a high degree of "Islamic consciousness."

But what do we make of the Hermes—and many other recently "discovered" morisco families and individuals like them from various sectors of local society—who fared quite well in the economic, political, and social climate of sixteenth-century Granada? In a landmark 1992 article, Mercedes García Arenal complained that the historical study of morisco communities throughout early modern Spain had descended into what she called a state of "methodological sclerosis" and urged historians to look to anthropological literature in order to equip themselves with theoretical tools and concepts better suited to coming to terms with questions of ethnicity and religious identity.[7] Perhaps precisely because of the surprising nature of recent discoveries, moreover, the proliferation of local archival research on Granada's moriscos over the past decade has ironically done more to complicate than to cure this alleged interpretive paralysis.[8] It is clear, nonetheless, that our understanding of Granada's "native" community must somehow be nuanced in order to account for a range of morisco experiences in the frontier city that was far broader than previously realized. Successful adaptation to life under the city's new rulers was not, in other words, the exclusive domain of a handful of individual "collaborators" from the old Nasrid elite.

In no way do I claim in this book to offer the sort of grand social scientific synthesis envisioned by García Arenal—a synthesis that may still be premature. Yet I argue that viewing the frontier city's mudéjar/morisco community alongside chapter 1's examination of local Christian immigrant society offers some important comparative insights. Despite the obvious differences between the society of the conquerors and that of the conquered, an important key to making sense of Granada's highly complex "native" community is, specifically, to understand how much the moriscos' experience in the conquered city paralleled that of their Christian immigrant neighbors. While the traditional interpretation is no doubt correct in asserting that the legacy of their divergent cultural and religious heritages clearly set them apart from one another, frontier Granada's Christian immigrant and morisco communities also resembled each other in at least two significant and fundamental ways.

First, Granada's moriscos, like the Christian immigrants, comprised, especially in the first few decades after the conquest, a dynamic community in a state of near-constant flux. As emigration significantly trimmed its ranks, the city's remaining "native" population was supplemented by Muslims (and later moriscos) who were not native to the city at all, but rather immigrants themselves from other Spanish kingdoms and from nearby towns and villages in the recently conquered kingdom of Granada. Well into the early decades of the sixteenth century, patterns of emigration and immigration thus made the frontier city's morisco community subject to similar sorts of constant reshuffling as we have already witnessed among Granada's Christian immigrants.

Second, the internal power structures of postconquest Granada's Muslim and later morisco community long remained, like those among the Christian immigrants, unstable and open to penetration by newly ascendant families and individuals. This was made possible by the fact that the overwhelming majority of the Muslim political, military, and religious elites who had dominated the Nasrid capital under the sultans emigrated en masse in the first few years after the conquest. Some ambitious and opportunistic upper- and middle-class Granadan moriscos such as the Hermes even managed to secure for themselves positions of authority in the developing official church and state hierarchies of the newly Christian city. Thus, alongside the familiar story of official persecution and morisco resistance leading to the second rebellion and the local expulsions of 1569–1570, recent research has revealed a variety of ways in which frontier Granada offered significant possibilities for social advancement not only to the conquerors, but also to at least some of the conquered.

Emigration was by far the most important factor in the reshaping of Granada's Muslim/morisco community in the years between the conquest and the expulsion—a fact made abundantly clear by a brief look at the demographic evidence. The Muslim city's population at the time of the surrender was approximately fifty thousand. By the time of the royal census of 1561, however, Granada's morisco community numbered only about fifteen thousand persons. While a small part of this reduction may be attributable to a relatively low birthrate among the city's moriscos,[9] the bulk of the decline was clearly the result of Muslim and morisco emigration. As was the case with Christian immigration, however, the exodus of the majority of the city's native population was not a phenomenon that occurred all at once. Understanding who chose to leave the city and when they chose to do so provides critical clues to explaining the social and political contours of the morisco community that remained in Granada up until the outbreak of the rebellion in 1568 and the local expulsions of 1569–1570.

The emigration process, in fact, began slowly. The triumphant entry of the Catholic Monarchs, of course, brought all of Granada's Muslim residents face-to-face with the difficult question of whether to remain in their native city or leave and seek a more secure life elsewhere. In practice, however, emigration proved to be a realistic option only for the wealthiest and most powerful among the city's "native" population. The surrender treaty negotiated in the final months of 1491 and enacted on January 2, 1492, defined to a large degree the legal terms and political contexts within which such decisions were made. The treaty itself stipulated not only the terms under which Granada's Muslims would be allowed to emigrate, but also the legal conditions under which those Muslims who chose to remain in the city would live.

Dating back to the eleventh-century conquest of Toledo, the Castilian crown had traditionally granted extensive legal protections to Muslim communities who surrendered to Christian control without a fight. This tradition of "mudejarism"—the official sanctioning and protection of conquered Muslim communities under Christian rule—was clearly reflected in the generous official provisions of Granada's surrender treaty.[10] Most important, the treaty guaranteed that no Muslim who chose to stay in the city would ever be forced to convert to Christianity against his or her will.[11] This respect for the right of Granada's Muslims to maintain their faith was even extended explicitly by the terms of the treaty to the city's *elches*—those Muslims, mostly former wartime captives or recent descendants of such captives, who had themselves been converted to Islam from Christianity. Beyond the protection of formal Muslim religious practice, the treaty also stipulated among other things that Muslims who remained in the city would continue to live under their traditional laws and judicial system, that matters of local government would continue to rest in the hands of a mudéjar municipal council and bureaucracy, and that the Muslims would continue to have the right to carry all forms of weaponry except firearms.

Nasrid Granada at the time of the conquest also housed a small Jewish minority of approximately five hundred persons,[12] and the surrender treaty specified that the city's Jews were to enjoy the same religious and legal protections afforded the Muslims. In a provision that provides particularly poignant testimony to the status of Jews in Granada at the time of the surrender, however, the treaty also guaranteed the city's Muslims that no Jew, whether Castilian or Granada native, would be placed in a position of authority over them.

For those Muslims who chose to leave rather than remain in the city under Christian rule, the terms of the surrender agreement were also, at least on the surface, fairly generous. The treaty granted, for example, a three-year gratis period during which all Muslim residents of the city of Granada would be free to emigrate without having to pay any sort of tax or fee, and the crown even guaranteed that it would find and pay for ships for the passage. Even with such royal favor, however, the choice to emigrate would prove financially impractical or even impossible to most mudéjares of average or below average means. Beyond breaking emotional ties to their ancestral hometown and community, leaving also required liquidating family resources by selling homes and properties at the ridiculously low prices offered by the small wave of Christian immigrant speculators who hovered in and around the city in the wake of the surrender.[13] Moreover, after the three-year gratis period expired at the beginning of 1495, the surrender treaty stipulated that Muslim emigrants from the city would be required to pay the crown one gold *dobla* per head—a nearly prohibitive sum that represented as much as an entire month's wages for an average worker.[14] While some of the city's working-class Muslims managed to flee clandestinely in order to avoid these royal exactions,[15] surviving documentation makes it clear that emigration by legal means remained in these early years limited to the former religious and political elites of the Nasrid capital and their families.

The question of the sincerity and security of the guarantees provided by the surrender agreement certainly weighed heavily on the minds of many of Granada's Muslims, rich and poor alike, as they pondered their futures in the early months of 1492. Similar legal protections had been granted before by the crown, only to be rescinded later as political circumstances changed, both in recently conquered nearby areas of the former Nasrid sultanate and on the medieval Castilian frontier in the eleventh, twelfth, and thirteenth centuries.[16] Nonetheless, for an example of a thriving mudéjar community in the Spain of the Catholic Monarchs, Granada's Muslims had only to look to their northeast, to Ferdinand's Aragonese kingdom of Valencia, where a fairly prosperous and well-protected mudéjar minority constituted nearly one-third of the total population.[17] In Isabella's Castilian kingdom into which Granada was being incorporated, by contrast, the legal, economic, and social status of Muslims was generally worse than that of their coreligionists in Valencia. Still, even Castile's Muslims were at least allowed to practice their ancestral faith, and at the time of the fall of Granada, most of Castile's major cities continued to house an appreciable, albeit largely marginalized, mudéjar minority.[18] The long and complex history of mudejarism in Spain's Christian kingdoms had, in fact, left even contemporary Muslim intellectuals deeply divided over the question of whether or not Muslims were religiously obligated to flee from areas ruled by Christian princes. Some, such as the prominent mid-fifteenth-century scholar from Fez Abd Allāh al-'Abdusī, maintained that it was permissible for Muslims to remain in Christian lands so long as the practice of Islam remained legal and if emigration presented a danger to self or family. Others, such as the influential jurist al-Wanšarīšī, argued by contrast that the spiritual and physical perils of living under Christian rule obliged all good Muslims to emigrate regardless of all short-term dangers and financial hardships.[19]

Fears such as those expressed by al-Wanšarīsī proved in Granada's case to be more than justified. For the Muslims of the newly conquered city, all questions concerning the absolute inviolability of the treaty provisions were quickly answered in the negative. Barely one month after Ferdinand and Isabella's entry into the city, a royal proclamation issued on February 6, 1492, announced that Muslims in the city would no longer be allowed to carry weapons and that the treaty provisions guaranteeing the right to bear arms were thereby rescinded. The fact that Granada's Muslim leadership had agreed to this violation of the treaty agreement one week earlier as a concession in return for sufficient supplies of wheat to feed the hungry city probably provided little comfort to those Muslims who remained suspicious of the crown's intentions.[20] Less than two months later, Granada's Muslims may have drawn further confirmation of their fears from the fate that befell their Jewish neighbors. On March 31, Ferdinand and Isabella issued their landmark edict ordering all Jews in the crowns of Aragon and Castile to convert to Christianity or leave their kingdoms. Included among the expelled, despite the specific protections guaranteed by the surrender treaty only three months earlier, was the Jewish population of the city of Granada. Violations of both the spirit and the letter of the surrender agreement continued throughout the 1490s, culminating in the aggressive conversion campaign spearheaded by the archbishop of Toledo and royal confessor, Francisco Jiménez de Cisneros, against suspected *elches* in Granada in the final months of 1499. In the eyes of the city's Muslim community a clear violation of the 1492 treaty guarantees, Cisneros's reportedly harsh treatment of imprisoned *elches* provided the proximate cause of the outbreak of the local Muslim rebellion in 1499.

Faced with the troubling uncertainties of a future under Christian rule, most of Granada's Muslim population who were financially capable of doing so had already fled to North Africa in the first few years after the conquest. In strictly quantitative terms, the first wave of emigration during the three-year gratis period 1492–1494—limited as it was largely to the wealthy and powerful—reduced the city's preconquest Muslim population by only a few thousand. The letters of royal secretary Hernando de Zafra, who was charged by the Catholic Monarchs with overseeing the administrative details of the emigration process, make it clear that the scale of the exodus, while significant, by no means amounted to the wholesale emptying of the city's neighborhoods.[21] Moreover, after 1494, with the three-year gratis period for Muslim emigration coming to a close and the royal ships that had been used in the process diverted to the task of transporting troops to the wars in Italy, emigration slowed to a trickle of mostly clandestine refugees.[22]

More important than the relatively small number of emigrants, however, was the fact that the emigration process in this earliest stage robbed Granada's Muslim community of nearly the entirety of its traditional ruling classes. The degree to which emigration in the early 1490s gutted the city's

Muslim elites is made strikingly evident by the incomplete surviving records of the mass baptisms that followed the defeat of the local rebellion in January and February 1500. Of more than eight thousand men, women, and children whose baptisms are listed, only a handful came from families of the old Nasrid city's religious, military, and political governing class.[23] The implications of this for the future of Granada's "native" community were profound. For example, among those few elites who did remain, as well as for a number of ascendant newcomers to the upper echelons of mudéjar/morisco society such as the Hermes family, the rapid and nearly complete disappearance of the city's traditional powers presented a variety of opportunities for social, political, and economic advancement.

A second, larger, and much more socially broad-based wave of Muslim emigration began in 1499, months before the outbreak of the first rebellion that December. The causes of renewed emigration in 1499 were various. The continuing erosion of the surrender treaty's protections and the 1498 official segregation of the city into distinct Christian and Muslim residential zones, for example, contributed to an increasing sense of desperation among the city's mudéjar majority. Many Muslims of all social classes were by this point willing to leave regardless of the physical risks and financial losses involved. In the chaos that surrounded the Albaicín uprising and forced conversions from December 1499 through February 1500, the wave of emigrants became a flood, as thousands of faithful Muslims sought out whatever means possible to escape to North Africa.[24] After the mass baptisms of 1500, the now Christian morisco residents of the city were officially forbidden to flee to Muslim lands, but over the next six decades, clandestine emigration nonetheless continued to provide a constant drain on Granada's morisco population. Lists of penitents at the autos de fe of Granada's Inquisition tribunal in the 1560s, for example, were filled with individual examples of moriscos among whose announced offenses were attempts to flee to North Africa or to assist other moriscos in doing so.[25] Some moriscos were even penanced "in absentia" for this offense, suggesting that they either succeeded or were killed en route.[26]

Ironically, however, while tens of thousands chose to leave the city in the decades after the conquest, Granada in these years also became a pole of attraction for thousands of Muslim and later morisco immigrants from the crowns of Castile and Aragon as well as from the nearby towns and villages of the old Nasrid sultanate.[27] Although the quantity of mudéjar/morisco immigration was far from sufficient to compensate for the demographic decline caused by emigration, the continuing arrival of new immigrants provided Granada's "native" community a measure of the same sort of dynamism and flux that characterized the frontier city's Christian immigrant community. Officially, Muslim immigration from other areas of the peninsula remained legal only through 1501, when a royal decree aimed at protecting Granada's newly Christian moriscos from the influence of Castilian or Valencian Muslims ordered under penalty of death that the entire kingdom of Granada be cordoned off from the entry of any and all Muslims.[28] Despite this mandate, additional bans not only on morisco but also mudéjar immigration to Granada issued by the crown in 1514 and 1515 attest to the fact that clandestine Muslim migration to the frontier city remained a concern of royal officials well into the early decades of the sixteenth century.[29] Even after the last vestiges of the legal practice of Islam in the Spanish kingdoms were destroyed by the 1525 crown-mandated conversion of Valencia's Muslims, the entry of newly converted morisco immigrants into the city of Granada—mostly from the nearby towns and villages of the old Nasrid sultanate—continued to trouble both crown and local authorities. In 1567, in the midst of the escalating tensions that eventually culminated in the outbreak of the second rebellion, for example, all moriscos who were not native to the city were ordered to leave and return to their own hometowns.[30]

Despite the hardships of state and church persecution under which Granada's "native" population lived, these mudéjar and morisco immigrants, like the Christian immigrants, were in many cases attracted to the frontier city by a perceived opportunity for social and economic advancement. Some of the newcomers, in fact, even managed to secure positions of authority in the emerging political structures of the postconquest city. One Muslim merchant, Yaya el Fistelí, left his home in Málaga and took up residence in Granada shortly before the conquest in January 1492, and he may have been among the participants in the negotiation of the surrender treaty. In his new city, the opportunistic el Fistelí managed through collaboration with the city's Muslim and Christian elites to secure in 1494 a powerful administrative post as constable (*alguacil*) of the city's Muslim majority. The following year, he traveled to the royal court as a representative of Granada's mudéjar community in the negotiation of a sizeable extraordinary tax. In return for his services, he received from the crown a variety of new offices and lands near Granada. In 1498, el Fistelí converted to Christianity, taking the Christian name Fernando de Morales, and he appears for at least the next few years to have shuttled back and forth between his native Málaga, where he attained a voting position on the municipal council, and Granada, where he held a nonvoting seat as *jurado*.[31]

Although by no means the rule, the sort of opportunistic cooperation with state and church authorities represented by the cases of the Hermes family and Yaya el Fistelí was common enough in frontier Granada's mudéjar and morisco society to make untenable the old characterizations of the city's "native" population as monolithic or univocal. In the constantly shifting social landscape of postconquest Granada, a wide variety of mudéjar and morisco "collaborators" from diverse backgrounds played critical roles in the cultural and political development of the frontier city. Just how large this group was, and exactly how deeply such collaborationist efforts penetrated the middle and lower ranks of Granada's morisco society, are questions that remain to be answered. It is clear, however, that such activity was by no means confined solely to a handful of wealthy holdovers from the city's pre-1492 Muslim elite.

It is nonetheless true the most powerful and influential of the collaborators were the few prominent families from Nasrid Granada's old ruling class who chose to remain in the city after the conquest rather than emigrate, including most importantly the Granada-Venegas, the Zegrí, and the Córdoba lineages—all of whom maintained powerful voting seats on the city's municipal council. In addition to these surviving vestiges of the preconquest Muslim city's power structure, however, Granada's collaborator elite also included, as we have seen, socially ascendant merchants as well as, ironically, a number of middling religious leaders who, up until the time of their conversions to Christianity in the years around 1500, were called al-faquís, or Muslim holy men.

From this third group, in fact, emerged the man who would become the principal leader of Granada's mudéjar community in the years between the conquest and the outbreak of the first rebellion seven years later—the al-faquí Mohammed el Pequeñí. In the final months of Nasrid rule, el Pequeñí had been among the partisans of peaceful surrender, and he had also participated in the negotiation of the terms of the surrender treaty itself. From a family of fairly well known Granadan Muslim jurists and intellectuals, el Pequeñí was by no means a member of the old royal family or Nasrid elite. Nonetheless, in the years immediately after the conquest, he became the leading representative of mudéjar interests in ongoing negotiations with the crown and its officials, despite the fact that as late as 1498 he still did not speak Castilian. With royal favor, he occupied the powerful traditional post of qādī, the supreme judge of Islamic law among the Muslims of the city and kingdom of Granada, as well as a spot as a regidor (voting member) of the new mudéjar municipal council guaranteed by the surrender agreement. Although the most reticent members of the conquered Muslim community probably resented his open cooperation with the crown in matters such as the 1492 revocation of the treaty guarantees concerning the right of the mudéjares to bear arms and the 1498 residential segregation agreement, he seems to have remained through the course of the 1490s a fairly popular and well-respected figure among most of his fellow Muslims. His surprising popularity in this regard may have owed much to the fact that, as surviving records of his possessions indicate, he appears not to have abused his political power in order to become extremely wealthy. The common perception among local Muslims and Christians alike seems to have been that he was a sincere man and one of the few municipal officials, mudéjar or Christian immigrant, who did not use his offices for personal gain.[32]

Along with el Pequeñí, and often under his patronage or tutelage, an entirely new group of Muslim "collaborators" stepped into official positions of authority in the internal government of frontier Granada's mudéjar community as the city's traditional elites emigrated between 1492 and 1494. With almost all of the old judges and administrators and most of the religious leaders gone, Granada's Muslim community obviously required leadership in matters of local government, the administration of justice, and spiritual guidance. Moreover, the surrender treaty itself explicitly provided for governmental structures and administrative positions that had to be filled. Of the twenty-one men appointed by the crown as *regidores* on postconquest Granada's original mudéjar municipal council, nine, including Mohammed el Pequeñí, were *alfaquís*. Although the exact preconquest social origins of the remaining twelve Muslim *regidores* are unclear, many were probably merchants, and none came from the old Nasrid city's ruling elite. In addition to the influential voting positions on the municipal council, Granada's postconquest mudéjar bureaucracy also included dozens of appointed officials charged with overseeing matters ranging from water rights to preaching to the regulation of commerce in the city. Moreover, through the first four or five years after the conquest, most of these offices changed hands frequently, with new appointments going mostly to those who best proved their loyalty to their new monarchs. That is to say, the administrative structures installed among the postconquest city's mudéjar community provided ample opportunities for social advancement to dozens of local Muslim individuals and families willing to work within the city's new political order and under the rule of the Catholic Monarchs.[33]

As Christian immigrants streamed into the city in ever larger numbers in the years around 1500, however, Granada's "native" population came to occupy fewer and fewer positions of authority in the city's institutional structures. Nonetheless, the exclusion of the moriscos from the city's official power structures was gradual, and it was never complete. At least some of the ascendant officials who had risen to positions of power in Granada's mudéjar community in the 1490s managed to parlay their newfound prestige into lasting positions in the city's predominantly Christian immigrant emerging elite. A former *alfaquí* and voting member of the mudéjar municipal council, for example, the morisco Andrés de Granada el Basti continued to serve in the influential position of *regidor* on Granada's Christian immigrant majority municipal council after 1500.[34]

Of even greater long-term significance than such social climbers among the emerging collaborator elite of morisco Granada, however, were the handful of prominent members of the old Nasrid elite who chose not to emigrate, including most importantly the Granada Venegas family. Descendants of the former sultan of Granada, Yuçuf IV (1431–1432), and hence members of the Nasrid royal family, the collaborators Yaya al-Nayyar and his son remained in Granada after the conquest, where they received baptism in 1500 and 1492, respectively, taking the Christian names Don Pedro de Granada and Don Alonso de Granada Venegas. During the uprising of

1499, both father and son participated in the suppression of the Muslim rebels, and both became knights of the prestigious Castilian military order of Santiago. From 1499, Don Alonso also held a voting position on Granada's municipal council, and he solidified the family's position among the city's emerging sixteenth-century elite by arranging marriages for two of his children to the offspring of Christian immigrant fellow *regidores* Luis Maza and Francisco de Alarcón. Throughout the sixteenth century and into the seventeenth, well after the expulsion of the morisco masses from the city in 1569–1570, the Granada Venegas descendants of Yaya al-Nayyar would remain one of the city's most influential families.[35]

Understandably, this sort of overt opportunism made collaborators such as the Granada Venegas and Hermes families the objects of intense hatred and, when possible, violent retribution among the most rebellious members of Granada's conquered population. In the violence surrounding the second rebellion, for example, morisco raiders made it a point to target the rural properties of the collaborator elite. The lands of the Granada Venegas, for example, were especially hard hit; the family reported after the rebellion that, as a result of the sacking of their seigneurial holdings near Granada, they had lost more than three thousand ducats in annual rents.[36]

Regardless of how broadly such outright collaboration may have permeated various levels of local morisco society, it was nonetheless never characteristic of the majority of Granada's "native" population. Most of Granada's remaining morisco families simply endured the difficulties of the postconquest years, earning respectable livings in a variety of trades ranging from labor in the frontier city's numerous construction projects to cultivating gardens in the nearby countryside to, above all, the production and sale of the silk cloth for which the city and region were so well known.[37] Yet, as noted earlier, contemporary observers, as well as many subsequent historians, were convinced that these working-class morisco "masses" were potentially rebellious and uniformly hostile toward their Christian conquerors. If on the one hand the majority of the city's native population were not active collaborators, however, it would be similarly inaccurate on the other hand to characterize them in absolute terms as a unified and violent resistance.

The most obvious evidence in favor of such generalizations comes, of course, from the two major rebellions. Yet the role of the urban morisco population of the city of Granada itself in these uprisings is problematic. The most open and violent expression of hostility among the city's conquered population was the December 1499 revolt against Cisneros's aggressive conversion campaign in the Albaicín that signaled the beginning of the first rebellion. The violence in the city itself, however, was quickly quelled, and, after the mass baptisms of January and February 1500, the center of the rebellion shifted for the remainder of 1500 and 1501 to the Alpujarras and surrounding countryside. Moreover, the second rebellion of 1568–1571 was from the beginning predominantly a rural movement in which the city's morisco community as a whole played an even smaller role,[38] although the city did produce many of the rebellion's key leaders, including the particularly militant former silk-dyer turned rebel commander Fárax aben Fárax.[39]

When the rebellion began in December 1568, the great majority of the city's supposedly seething morisco masses proved in fact to be quite cautious and pacified. On Christmas Eve night, Fárax entered Granada with 150 armed rebels from the Alpujarras fully expecting his native city's morisco community of some fifteen thousand to rise as one and join him in violent retribution against the Christian immigrants and their authorities, restoring the city once and for all to the Muslim faith of their ancestors. His rousing cries in the streets of the Albaicín, however, were met only by silence and locked doors. Embittered by this betrayal, Fárax and his men managed to escape the city before morning, returning to the Alpujarras to join with the rebel forces there.[40]

Additional evidence of morisco resistance comes from the persistence of crypto-Muslim religious practices among the supposed new converts. Again, however, evidence revealed by recent research is increasingly pointing to complex variation rather than unanimity among the city's morisco "masses." That many of the city's moriscos continued clandestinely to practice the faith of their ancestors is clear enough even if we acknowledge the "hostile" nature of the documentary sources that provide the most concrete evidence, including above all Inquisition reports. Granada's tribunal of the "Holy Office" was established in 1526, but we unfortunately have very few documentary sources through which to study its activities. As is the case with most of Spain's Inquisition tribunals (the most important exceptions being the exceptionally rich archival resources of the Toledo and Cuenca tribunals), the actual trial records of Granada's Inquisition have been lost.[41] In addition, the local tribunal's *relaciones de causa*—reports drawn up by local inquisitors and sent to the Supreme Council of the Inquisition, listing each penitent who appeared at autos de fe alongside his or her offense and penalty assigned—survive in Granada's case only from 1550 on.[42] According to these reports, in each of the nine autos "celebrated" in Granada from 1550 to the aftermath of the second rebellion in 1571, the majority of the penitents were in fact moriscos charged with various Muslim practices, ranging from the possession of Arabic-language prayer books or copies of the Koran[43] to indiscreet statements of conscious affinity for Islam or against Christianity.[44] The elderly Granada morisca Isabel Zapatayra faced charges in 1569 simply for having requested that her bones be buried in North Africa.[45]

Overall, however, the total number of moriscos tried by the inquisitors was quite small, especially if we restrict our attention to those from the city of Granada rather than those of the more heavily morisco majority towns and villages of the Alpujarras and other parts of the former Nasrid sultanate over whom the Granada tribunal also held jurisdiction. Of a total of 442 moriscos who appeared in five autos de fe (1560, 1563, 1566, 1569, and 1571), only 43, or slightly less than 10 percent, were from the capital city.[46] That is to say, of a total urban morisco population of some 15,000 in the 1560s, only a tiny handful actually faced Inquisition charges for Islamic practices. By themselves, of course, these figures prove nothing; most crypto-Muslims probably simply escaped inquisitorial notice. The number of moriscos who secretly held to the beliefs and, when possible, the practices of their ancestral faith while feigning allegiance to Christianity according to the Koranic principle of *taqīya* (dissimulation) must have been much higher than the number who were actually tried by the inquisitors—especially if we lend even an ounce of credence to the perceptions of contemporary observers who described the bulk of them as closet Muslims.

Matters of personal faith, of course, are extremely difficult, if not impossible, to quantify. Evidence is mounting, nonetheless, that at least a significant portion of the city's morisco community—and not just a handful of members of a "collaborator elite"—were in fact increasingly embracing the Christian faith of the conquerors, especially as we proceed into the second and third generations *after* the mass baptisms of 1500. Early missionary and catechization efforts among the city's new converts in the opening decades of the sixteenth century were, even according to the accounts of contemporary clergymen, woefully inadequate to the scale of the task, but there were some important initiatives. The city's first archbishop, Hernando de Talavera, established soon after the conversions a small school for the religious instruction of the city's morisco boys, and as was often the case later in conquered regions of the Americas, the mendicant orders, especially the Dominicans and Franciscans, actively led the way in sending preachers and teachers into the morisco communities of the city and kingdom of Granada.[47] In 1513, Franciscan friar Juan de Oliva was commissioned by his order to preach and teach daily in the Albaicín. According to a letter written to the crown that year by a local magistrate, Oliva's sermons led to the outbreak of violent scuffles *among* the city's moriscos, suggesting that morisco reaction to Christian evangelization was varied rather than uniformly hostile.[48] Some prominent moriscos, too, became involved in early religious instruction efforts among their fellow former Muslims. In his 1542 last will and testament, for example, the morisco municipal councilman Gonzalo Fernández el Zegrí mentioned that he had regularly taught the catechism in the Albaicín as well as in the nearby town of Guadix.[49] That there was still a profound need for such basic instruction in the 1550s when the Jesuits arrived in the city and established the best-known and most successful of Granada's schools for the religious instruction of morisco youth—the Casa de la Doctrina, headed by the native Granada morisco Jesuit father Juan de Albotodo—is testimony to the insufficiency of earlier efforts. Nonetheless, later evidence suggests that catechism campaigns among the moriscos were not altogether fruitless. In 1581, moriscos who had been exiled from the kingdom of Granada and resettled in the diocese of Cuenca were subjected to an extensive inquiry concerning the status of their knowledge of the basic tenets of Catholic belief, and the survey revealed that more than half of them could at least recite the basic prayers, the Ten Commandments, and the Articles of Faith.[50]

Rote memory is, of course, one thing; genuine dedication to the Christian faith is something else. In an effort to provide some tangible gauge of morisco devotion, Amalia García Pedraza recently compiled a database of nearly three hundred surviving last wills and testaments written by morisco men and women in sixteenth-century Granada. In their mentions of religious matters, many morisco wills simply follow standard formulae dictated or suggested by the notaries who recorded the testators' wishes. Behind much of this mute adherence to standard form, there probably indeed lies a great deal of crypto-Muslim sentiment. Interestingly, however, García Pedraza has also uncovered many testaments of morisco men and women who consciously chose to depart from the notaries' standard invocational formulae in order to include mention of specific Christian devotions particularly dear to them, including above all the Virgin Mary. In his 1564 testament, for example, the Granada morisco Daniel Sánchez el Zinety included a uniquely worded statement of his devotion to Mary found in no other testament recorded by the notary, referring to the Virgin specifically as "Mother of our Lord, whom we Christians all hold and invoke as protector and advocate in our tribulations."[51]

Thus, despite the obvious patterns of conflict that colored so much of Granada's postconquest history, it would be inaccurate to depict the city's "native" community entirely in terms of a stark and exclusive dichotomy between a collaborator elite and a working-class crypto-Muslim resistance. Instead, in the constantly changing society of the frontier city, the categories of "collaboration" and "resistance" are best understood as the extreme poles of a continuum along which the great majority of Granada's mudéjares and moriscos, wealthy and working-class alike, fell somewhere in between. A clear line between "collaborators" and "rebels" is at times difficult to draw, and an accurate understanding of Granada's "native" community must take into account the fact that continuous flux was as typical among the moriscos as it was among the city's Christian immigrant population.

Apparent collaborators could and sometimes did, for example, become rebels. As early as 1497, two mudéjar officeholders, identified in the documents as the *alguaciles* (constables) Mohammed Çaba and "[El] Tuerto" (literally "the one-eyed"), instigated a local Muslim riot against new royal taxes.[52] Even more dramatic was the case of the morisco collaborator-turned-renegade Don Hernando de Córdoba. Although a member of the wealthy and noble Córdoba family and the holder of a voting position on Granada's municipal council, Don Hernando's lavish personal spending habits and hot temper had made him by 1568 an unwelcome figure among the frontier city's elite. Already in great debt and embittered by the fact that his father had been sentenced to the galleys for a variety of crimes, Don Hernando deepened his troubles that year by pulling out a dagger against his rivals during a meeting of the municipal council. Placed under strict house arrest for this offense, he pledged to sell his spot on the council to the wealthy morisco Miguel de Palacios for sixteen hundred ducats (thereby alleviating his financial woes) and then move to Italy or Flanders. When local authorities seized the money from the transaction, however, Don Hernando was left penniless and powerless. Unable to leave the country, he fled instead to the Alpujarras on December 23, 1568—the eve of the second rebellion—and joined with morisco rebels, who elevated him to the position of "king" of the "restored" Muslim kingdom of Andalusia. As ruler, he resurrected his family's ancestral Muslim name "Aben Humeya" and led rebel forces until his assassination the following October by rivals from within the morisco rebellion.[53]

Although the outright rebellion of Aben Humeya was an exceptional case, other members of the supposed "collaborator" elite also at times risked their positions in local society by protesting or attempting to ameliorate and moderate oppressive church and state policies aimed at their less-powerful fellow moriscos. The influential morisco nobleman Don Alonso de Granada Venegas, the great-grandson of the mudéjar collaborator Yaya al-Nayyar, for example, spent the tense months preceding the outbreak of rebellion in 1568 at the court of Philip II as a spokesman for his people, unsuccessfully lobbying the crown for more lenient treatment of Granada's moriscos and the redress of a variety of morisco grievances.[54]

Conversely, those who expressed most eloquently the resentment and resistance of the morisco community against the oppressive policies of state and church officials could also profess openly, and perhaps even sincerely, their loyalty to the crown. The morisco leader Francisco Núñez Muley, for example, was a man whose life and career make particularly clear the inadequacy of the collaborator-versus-resistance dichotomy as a tool for understanding Granada's "native" community. We know little about Núñez Muley's early life other than his own claim that as a young man in the first decade of the sixteenth century he served three years as a page to Granada's first archbishop Hernando de Talavera, and he even accompanied the archbishop in 1502 on a tour of the Alpujarras. He rose to prominence in the 1510s and 1520s as a representative of the moriscos in the controversial negotiations with the crown concerning the persistence among Granada's native community of much of their ancestral culture, including the use of the Arabic language, their traditional dress, the festive *zambra* dance, and the custom of regular bathing at the bath houses along the city's Darro River. In

1526, Núñez Muley had a personal audience in Granada with Charles V in which the morisco leader expressed gratitude to his sovereign for suspending the prohibitions of the Royal Chapel Congregation.

When in 1566 the forty-year grace period granted by the emperor expired, the government of Charles's son, King Philip II, resuscitated many of these same prohibitions and ordered them enforced strictly by Granada's royal court. In response, the aging Núñez Muley, still a respected spokesman among the moriscos, wrote a lengthy letter to the new hard-line president of the royal court, Pedro de Deza, petitioning him to suspend enforcement of the provisions.[55] Núñez Muley's argumentation in his 1567 "Memorial" to Deza was at once both bitter and satirical as well as engaging and forceful. He asserted above all that the cultural practices in question were simply regional customs that bore no religious significance whatsoever. He pointed out, for example, that Christians in Jerusalem and on the isle of Malta both typically spoke Arabic and dressed in a manner that was quite different from that of Castile, yet no knowledgeable Christian questioned the sincerity of their faith. With regard to the *zambra,* moreover, Muley noted that it had always been a purely secular custom and that, under the rule of the sultans, the old *alfaquís* had ironically been just as suspicious of it as the Christian authorities had become in his own time. At a typical wedding in Muslim Granada before the conquest, he claimed, all *zambras* ceased whenever an *alfaquí* showed up. In addition, Núñez Muley ridiculed the authorities' suspicion of Granada's bath houses as sites of crypto-Muslim rites, pointing out not only that the baths were always frequented by immigrants as well as moriscos, but also that no good Muslim would ever use the dirty water of the baths for ritual ablution.

Despite its bitter edge, Núñez Muley's letter maintained throughout that he and his fellow moriscos were—and had always been—good Christians and loyal subjects of the crown of Castile. As "proof" of their supposed fealty, he pointed to the accomplishments of morisco military commanders (all from elite collaborator families) who had fought in the crown's service, including, ironically, Don Hernando de Córdoba—uncle of the future rebel "king" Aben Humeya—who had accompanied the count of Tendilla in the suppression of rebels in Baza during the Comuneros uprising of 1520–1521. Even while expressing his loyalty and sincere Christian belief, however, Núñez Muley interestingly chose in the opening sections of the letter to remind Deza and the Christian authorities explicitly that the "conversion of the natives of this kingdom was by force and in violation of the surrender terms agreed to by the Catholic Monarchs." Núñez Muley's stance of accommodation was thus coupled with unmistakable expressions of resentment and hostility toward the unjust treatment received by his people at the hands of church and state authorities.

Of course, simply to accept at face value Núñez Muley's assertion that Granada's moriscos were all good Christians and loyal subjects of the crown would be no less naive than accepting the similarly overgeneralized images of them by contemporaries such as Navagero as uniformly rebellious. To be sure, there clearly remained even among the urban morisco community many crypto-Muslims, and the city produced a fair share of violent resistance. On balance, however, both outright collaborators on the one hand and open rebels on the other were relatively rare in the frontier city's dynamic and evolving morisco community. If there is a voice in the documentary record that speaks for the frustrations of the majority of Granada's sixteenth-century morisco community, it is most likely that of Núñez Muley, whose greatest hope was to maintain an acceptable place for himself and his people in the midst of an unjust situation toward which he could not help but express a degree of indignation and open resentment.

CHAPTER THREE

A Divided City, A Shared City
Drawing and Crossing Ethnic Boundaries

The eventual expulsion of most of the city's "native" community in 1569–1570 at the height of the second rebellion casts
an imposing shadow over any examination of morisco-
Christian immigrant relations in postconquest Granada. Given the tragic
outcome, it is difficult to avoid the temptation to emphasize moments of
confrontation, ignoring in the process the mostly peaceable ways in which
the frontier city's two principal ethnic groups interacted with one another on
a daily basis for nearly eight decades. As recently as 1994, in fact, historian
Miguel Ángel Ladero Quesada characterized the nature of Christian
immigrant-morisco relations in postconquest Granada entirely in simplistic
terms of mutual hatred: "Their reciprocal rejection was profound—to accept
nothing, or almost nothing from each other, convinced as they were of the
superiority of their respective religions and their whole cultural worlds."[1]

While such gross overgeneralizations make it easy to cast the Granada
story as a central chapter in the master narrative of Spain's early modern
transformation into a closed, exclusionary society, they obscure a much more
complicated state of affairs revealed by detailed research in local archival
sources. As we have seen, both the immigrant and morisco communities were
complex and dynamic rather than monolithic and static. Moreover, despite
repeated efforts on the part of leaders from both communities to segregate the
city along ethnic lines, and despite the attempts by many moriscos to isolate
themselves from the immigrants, Granada's ever-changing urban landscape
continued throughout the period under study to provide ample opportunity
for daily interaction and various forms of exchange between morisco and immigrant men and women of all socioeconomic classes.

In exploring through the course of this chapter the complex ways in
which physical and social boundaries between the two communities were
both drawn and crossed, it is nonetheless critical to avoid painting too rosy
a picture of immigrant-morisco relations. To Muslims as well as Christians
throughout the peninsula, Granada had after all carried for more than two
centuries before the 1492 conquest enormous symbolic significance as the

very center of Iberian Islam. A triumphalist sense of a crusade brought to successful completion no doubt colored many immigrants' impressions of their morisco neighbors. Conversely, among the moriscos—especially those who privately clung to the faith of their ancestors—the legacy of conquest, broken treaty promises, and mandatory conversion embittered common attitudes toward the immigrants. One cannot ignore the obvious power relationships between conquerors and conquered. It is certainly not surprising under these circumstances that both the immigrants on the one hand and the moriscos on the other maintained a large degree of communal identity and sorlidarity vis à vis the other up until the expulsion. Although incidents of actual ethnic and/or religious violence in the postconquest city itself were rare, members of both groups frequently voiced overt and subtle expressions of hostility. In short, the physical and social landscapes that provided the context for the creation of Christian Granada were characterized by daily interaction and exchange as well as by religious and ethnic confrontation.

The general lack of intermarriage was the most visible evidence of the maintenance of boundaries between immigrants and moriscos.[2] On both sides of Granada's ethnic divide, reluctance to marry across ethnic lines appears to have been an unwritten rule and a primary means of maintaining community identity. As we have seen in cases such as the Hermes and Granada Venegas families, this rule was certainly not absolute; some socially prominent and ascendant morisco and immigrant families did, in fact, forge important social and political ties through intermarriage. Crown policy, moreover, strongly advocated such intermarriage at all social levels as a practice that fostered the assimilation of the newly converted, and royal letters even at times specifically referred to these elite intermarriages as a model that should be imitated throughout local society.[3] The broader morisco and immigrant communities, however, generally ignored such messages. Offspring of "mixed marriages" were thus rare, and most were born to families already well established in the local elite. Unlike early colonial societies in Mexico and Peru, in which the so-called *mestizos* constituted a large and visible component, frontier Granada produced no new perceived category or vocabulary of mixed ethnicity.[4]

Various factors from both sides of the morisco-immigrant divide contributed to this relative lack of miscegenation in Granada. First, as numerous studies have demonstrated, moriscos throughout sixteenth-century Spain maintained a strong mudéjar and Iberian Muslim tradition of agnatic kinship networks. These networks traditionally formed the basis of various forms of family interactions, from economic cooperation to interclan feuds, and they typically proved resilient to change, even in the face of conquest and conversion, all the way up to the final 1609 royal decree expelling all moriscos from the peninsula.[5] Second, Granada's Christian immigrant society from a very early stage included large numbers of Castilian women as well as men, and the opportunity to marry within the immigrant community was thus much greater in Granada than in the New World, where European women were much less common among the earliest settler groups.

Finally, Granada's moriscos and immigrants alike were heirs to a medieval Iberian tradition in which sexual politics had long played an important role in interfaith relations and in the definition and maintenance of group identity. As David Nirenberg has argued in an insightful article based on his research on Muslim-Christian-Jewish relations in the Aragonese kingdoms, the protection of Christian women from the "stain" of sex with a man of another faith was a pervasive concern among Christian political authorities in the later Middle Ages. Nirenberg goes on to show that the firm maintenance of the Christian female body as the defining and inviolable boundary between religious communities through strict and explicit laws and their rigorous enforcement ironically made other forms of daily cultural and economic interaction appear less threatening and less dangerous to members of all groups.[6] Sixteenth-century Granada, of course, was very different from fourteenth-century Aragon in that there was no openly practicing Muslim (or Jewish) community. It therefore had no formal laws against sexual relations between morisco men and immigrant women and, as noted above, crown policy actually favored intermarriage. Nonetheless, various ordinances passed by Granada's Christian immigrant-majority municipal council after 1500 demonstrate a continuing concern with controlling what they portrayed to be the sexual licentiousness of morisco men, particularly with regard to immigrant women. In 1501, for example, they explicitly prohibited the presence of morisco men in the city's baths while women were bathing.[7] Even as late as 1537, the council passed an ordinance banning morisco and Muslim slave men from going to the spot on the Genil River where immigrant women regularly washed clothes, claiming that the moriscos and slaves went there only "to make bad women" of the clothes-washers.[8] As we will see, sixteenth-century Granada, like Nirenberg's medieval crown of Aragon, was characterized by a great deal of interaction between groups, but it should not be forgotten that this always took place within a social context in which both groups, with the exception of a few elite families, maintained a high degree of community solidarity through the maintenance of sexual boundaries and refusal to intermarry.

Less well defended than the city's sexual boundaries, by contrast, were the physical lines of residential segregation that separated Granada's two principal ethnic communities. In 1498, only six years after the conquest, Granada's mudéjar and Christian immigrant leadership reached an agreement concerning the strict segregation of the city along religious lines. Despite its obvious significance, the segregation accord has received scant attention in previous histories of Granada,[9] probably because of the very complexity of questions regarding its production and problematic legacy.[10] Examination of the production of this treaty and the incomplete application of its terms provides critical insight into the nature of interethnic relations in postconquest Granada. Specifically, I will illustrate here some of the complex ways in which patterns of ethnic segregation and distribution of space within the urban landscape helped to shape and influence not only Granada's endemic ethnic hostilities, but also, ironically, patterns of exchange and interaction between immigrants and moriscos.

Previous scholarship on Granada's urban development has been largely impressionistic. In particular, José Luis Orozco Pardo's book *Christianópolis* mistakenly describes the city's divided ethnic landscape as the result of a careful and deliberate policy of urban planning and segregation on the part of the crown and its local functionaries. Such privileging of royal policy as the guiding determinant of urban change is typical of recent trends in the historiography of early modern urbanism. Whether as an exaltation of the power of the Renaissance monarch, or later, as the sacralization of public spaces in the interest of the Counter-Reformation church, explanations of early modern urban change are often subordinated to grand narratives concerning the growth of state or ecclesiastical authority.[11] Orozco Pardo in particular claims that the reorganization of urban space in postconquest Granada reflected the sort of rational urban theory espoused by Italian Renaissance thinkers such as Leon Battista Alberti, which were in turn applied to Granada by the Catholic Monarchs Ferdinand and Isabella and their grandson Charles V. The eventual result, according to Orozco Pardo, was a Renaissance city par excellence, characterized by what he calls the "orderly distribution of classes and ethnicities."[12]

Close scrutiny of available sources, however, reveals that Orozco Pardo's tidy summary of sixteenth-century Granada's urban development is only partly accurate. It is true that Ferdinand and Isabella played a critical role in the physical transformation of the city in the years immediately after the conquest, ordering, for example, the clearing of specific spaces in the city for Castilian-style plazas and the widening and straightening of many of the formerly Muslim city's dark, narrow and curving streets.[13] As Helen Nader has argued, however, there was nothing necessarily new nor Italian about such approaches to urban development; Spaniards from antiquity through the Middle Ages had always attempted when possible to develop towns with rectangular plazas and rectilinear street designs.[14] With regard to the specific issue of religious and ethnic segregation, moreover, I contend that Orozco Pardo's analysis falls short on two counts. First, the driving forces behind efforts to segregate Granada into distinct religious and ethnic zones came not from crown mandates, but from the actions and aims of specific members of Granada's local population itself, native and immigrant alike. Second, all efforts to create strictly segregated Christian immigrant and morisco zones in postconquest Granada ultimately failed. As a result, sixteenth-century Granada was a city in which ethnic separation was neither "orderly" nor absolute. Instead, the physical lines that separated Granada's moriscos and Christian immigrants were blurred, permeable, and constantly revised and renegotiated over the decades leading up to the expulsion of the moriscos from the city in 1569.

Like the surrender treaty of 1492, the surviving summary of the terms of the 1498 segregation accord reveals that it was by nature explicitly a bilateral agreement of the sort that was frequently negotiated with political authorities by religious minorities in some Spanish cities, Muslim and Christian alike, in the high and later Middle Ages.[15] It was not, that is to say, an arrangement that was unilaterally imposed by the dominant powers, as was the case, for example, in the forced segregation of Jews into ghettos in sixteenth-century Italian cities such as Venice and Rome or of local Jewish and Muslim minorities in some medieval Castilian cities.[16] The bilateral character of the agreement does not imply, however, that the segregation was entirely "voluntary," nor does it mean that all of the city's mudéjares were necessarily pleased by the new arrangement. The key to making sense of the segregation treaty lies in understanding exactly who negotiated the agreement on each side and what they sought to gain from it. Answers to these complicated questions are in fact suggested by the terms of the accord itself.

The treaty's provisions were strict and explicit. They stipulated that the city's Muslims concentrate themselves in the Albaicín—a neighborhood of serpentine streets spread over two hills on the city's northeastern edge. In addition to the city's principal *morería* (mudéjar quarter) in the Albaicín, the Muslims also retained a small enclave in the commercial heart of the lower city near the great mosque. The terms of the treaty required all Muslims who owned properties in the remaining areas of the "lower city" to sell at a fair price to prominent Christians, who in turn were required to sell these houses at no more than a just profit to future Christian immigrants.

A quick glance at map 1 reveals the apparent inequity of this arrangement. For royal secretary Hernando de Zafra and other leaders in the by-then predominantly immigrant municipal council, the advantages were obvious. Above all, the treaty represented the opening of the vast majority of space in the lower city for Christian purchase, making possible the subsequent growth of a large and vibrant Christian immigrant community over the next few decades. Moreover, the document itself also describes the advantages perceived by the Christian immigrants in maintaining a small mudéjar enclave in the city center. Specifically, the accord stipulated that it was to house a total of some five hundred men, women, and children—some from the most prominent Muslim families and others from the much-needed construction professions—who would function as "hostages" (*rehenes*) far removed from the bulk of their coreligionists in the Albaicín, thus curbing the possibility of a local mudéjar rebellion.

By contrast, the Muslims—represented in the negotiations by the prominent *alfaquí* Mohammed el Pequeñí and his translator Yuça de Mora—received only a small fraction of the city's surface area, despite the fact that at that point they still comprised the vast majority of the city's population. Moreover, compliance with the treaty would involve the massive upheaval of mudéjar families from their homes in the lower city and their transferral

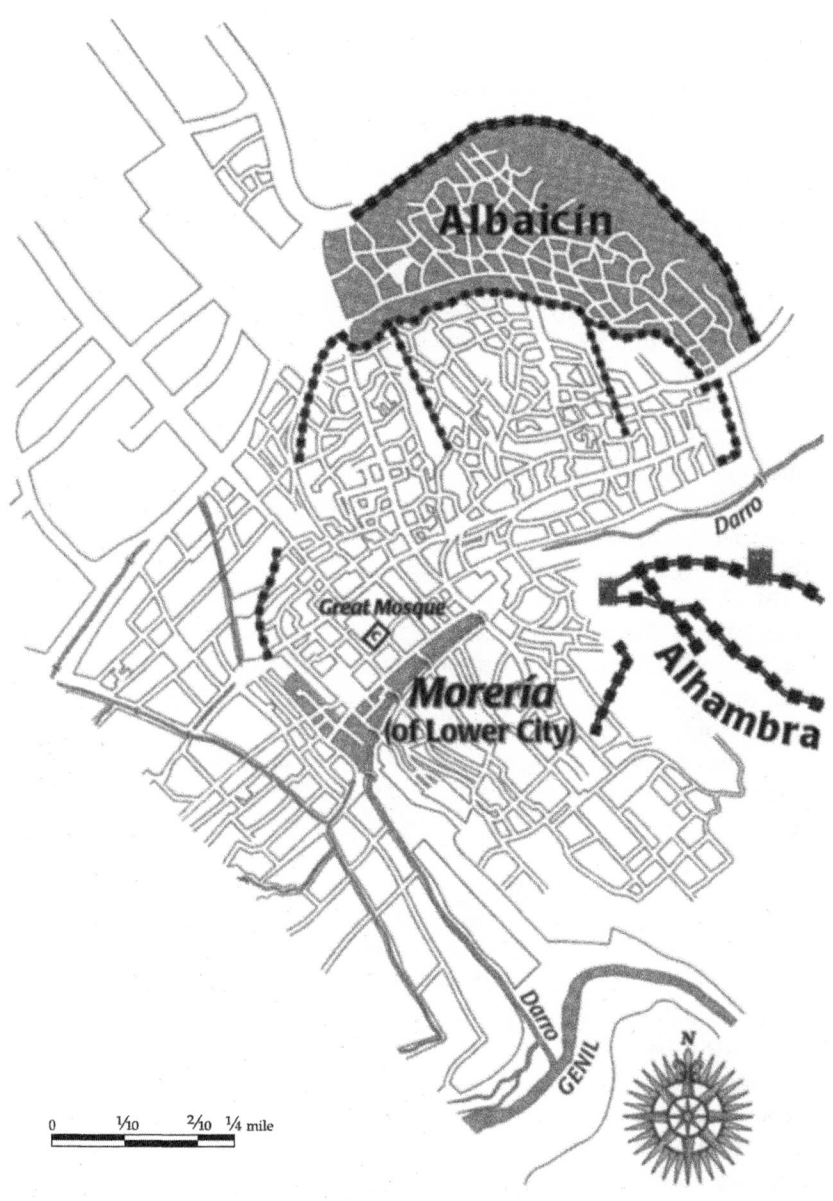

Albaicín

Darro

Great Mosque

Morería
(of Lower City)

Alhambra

N

0   1/10   2/10   1/4 mile

Darro

GENIL

Map prepared by Dick Gilbreath at the University of Kentucky Cartography Lab

MAP 1. 1498 Segregation Accord

to the hundreds of houses left vacant by emigrants that the treaty indicated were then available in the Albaicín. Finally, the Muslims' allotted zone in the Albaicín was a hilly, isolated, and in many ways undesirable part of the city. What led el Pequeñí and other Muslim leaders to accept such an apparently lopsided deal?

Part of the answer, of course, may lie in the politics of collaboration—the effort on the part of el Pequeñí and some of Granada's other prominent Muslims to ingratiate themselves with crown authorities in order to secure a place in the city's newly emerging Christian local power structure. We know, for example, that within a year of signing the segregation treaty (and months before the mass baptisms of January and February 1500) el Pequeñí himself converted to Christianity and received a number of new titles and offices from the crown.[17] Explaining the agreement entirely as an expression of elite collaboration with the conquerors, however, would be misleading for a variety of reasons. As we saw earlier, el Pequeñí never exploited his positions in order to become a wealthy man, and despite his central role in the negotiation of the segregation agreement, he appears to have remained a respected leader among the bulk of Granada's morisco community well into the early decades of the sixteenth century.

In addition to the explicitly bilateral character of the treaty itself, moreover, related documents concerning its implementation illustrate that many among Granada's mudéjar community in 1498 actually desired the segregation of the city along religious lines in order to maintain some form of protected isolation from the city's growing number of Christian immigrants. A 1499 letter from the Catholic Monarchs to captain general of Granada Iñigo López de Mendoza, for example, suggests not only that the segregation agreement itself had been negotiated in the first place at the request of the mudéjares, but also that it was the Muslim leadership led by el Pequeñí, and not the Christian authorities, who demanded that the old walls and gates separating the Albaicín from the rest of the city be tightly guarded and that access be strictly limited to resident Muslims: "Know that *at the request of the Muslims of the city* we have ordered that they be given *morerías* to which they can come in order to be separated from the Christians, and know also that the said Muslims have now petitioned that we appoint an official to be responsible for guarding the gates and keys and insuring the protection of the said *morerías.*"[18] The letter went on to appoint the captain general himself, who as we will see was generally trusted by the mudéjares (and later moriscos) as an honest broker and protector, to the task of overseeing the protection of the Albaicín's walls and gates.

The experiences of the moriscos in frontier Granada were certainly far too diverse to admit blanket generalizations, and many members of Granada's "native" community from various backgrounds successfully integrated themselves into the economic, social, and even political structures of the increasingly immigrant-dominated sixteenth-century city. Nonetheless, it is also clear that many local moriscos—and probably a majority of them, if subsequent development of the city's "native" community up until the 1569–1570 expulsions is any reliable indication—sought for various reasons to isolate themselves as much as possible from the burgeoning immigrant community. Among the moriscos, of course, there remained many individuals and families who were self-consciously "crypto-Muslim." To these religious nonconformists, isolation from the Christian immigrants and their authorities meant above all the opportunity to continue secretly to practice the faith of their ancestors while feigning allegiance to the religion of the conquerors. Yet morisco efforts to maintain protected isolation in the Albaicín did not necessarily imply in all cases a defense of formal Islam. The Albaicín also represented a protected zone in which many of Granada's moriscos maintained elements of their culture that may or—if one follows Nuñez Muley's reasoning—may *not* have borne religious significance, including the use of the Arabic language, traditional dress, and traditional local festive dances such as the *zambra*.

More to the point, many traditionalist members of Granada's morisco community, whether self-consciously crypto-Muslim or not, defended the Albaicín as a zone in which they could remain free of what they considered the immoral practices of a Christian immigrant community that was widely viewed among the moriscos as particularly rowdy and roguish, and frequently drunk. Wine, of course, symbolized both the cultural and religious chasms that separated the city's two principal ethnic communities. While municipal ordinances and local court documents make it clear that many moriscos did in fact drink wine, and some of them quite heavily,[19] there remained among Granada's morisco community a significant and strong lobby that sought to maintain the Albaicín as an alcohol-free zone. As late as 1508—eight years after the forced conversions of 1500—pressure from morisco *regidores* resulted in the passage by the city's mostly Christian immigrant municipal council of an ordinance banning the establishment of taverns and the sale of wine in the Albaicín, except in a tiny Christian immigrant enclave that had by that point already grown in the central Albaicín parish of San Salvador.[20]

For a variety of reasons, the sort of protected isolation from Christian immigrant society desired by many of the city's moriscos proved impossible to maintain in the constantly shifting landscape of sixteenth-century Granada. Through the first seven decades of the sixteenth century, the incursions of Christian immigrants increasingly brought the culture of the conquerors right to the doorsteps and into the homes of even the most traditionalist moriscos of the city. The religious reshuffling of Granada's urban space mandated by the 1498 segregation agreement had only just begun when the treaty's strict terms, along with all other previous agreements between the two communities, were annulled by the Muslim rebellion and royal conversion order. (These ethnic divisions are shown in map 2 and table 3.1. The numbers on map 2 correspond to the locations of the numbered parishes listed in table 3.1.)

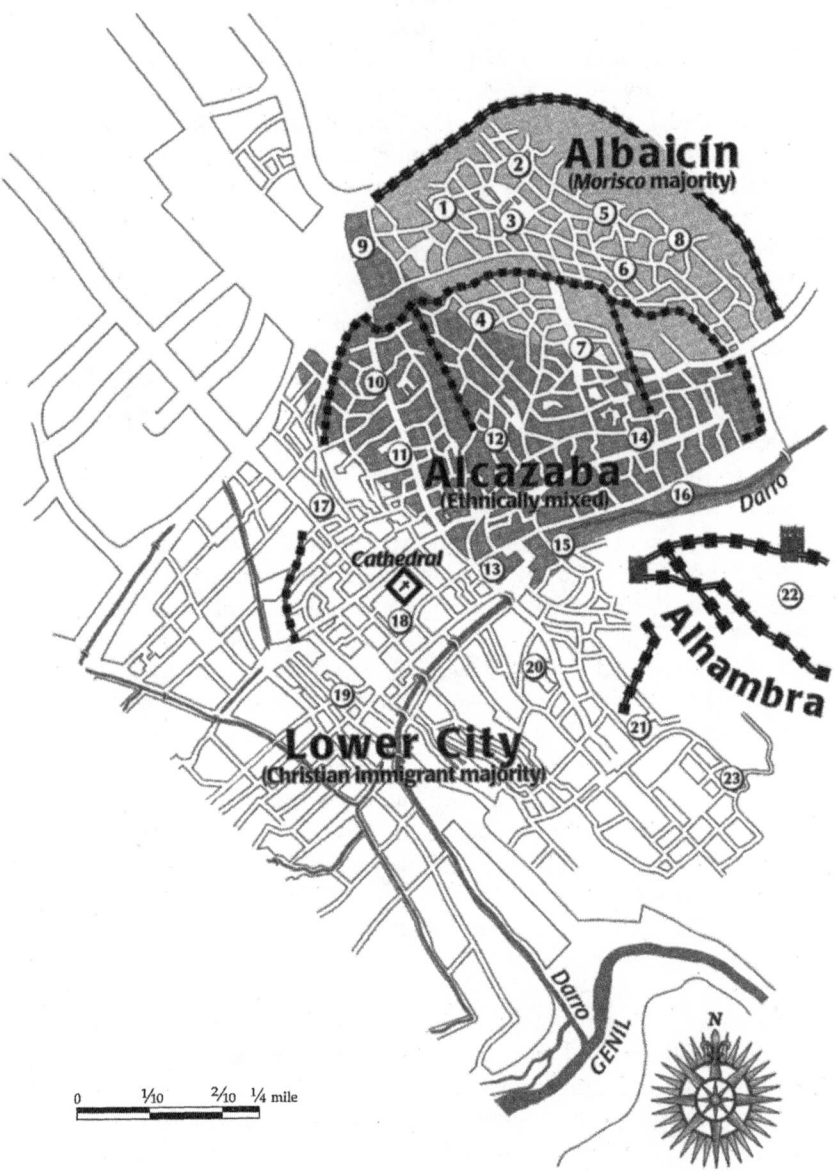

Map prepared by Dick Gilbreath at the University of Kentucky Cartography Lab

MAP 2. Ethnic division in Granada circa 1561. Numbers on map correspond with
the locations of the numbered parish churches listed on Table 3.1.

TABLE 3.1 Population of Granada, 1561, by Parish

Albaicín: Morisco Majority Parishes		Lower City: Immigrant Majority Parishes	
1. San Cristóbal	2,230	17. San Justo y Pastor	1,593
2. San Gregorio	834	18. Sagrario/ Iglesia Mayor	3,935
3. San Bartólome/San Lorenzo	656	19. Santa María Magdalena	2,079
4. San Miguel	1,322	20. San Matías	2,918
5. San Luis	1,037	21. Santa Escolástica	3,269
6. San Salvador	2,927	22. Santa María/Alhambra	1,010
7. San Nicolás	1,876	23. San Cecilio	1,720
8. Santa Isabel	1,007	TOTAL	16,524
* San Martín	674		
* San Blas	757		
TOTAL	13,320		

Alcazaba: Ethnically Mixed		Regular Clergy	
9. San Ildefonso	2092	1207 (see below)	
10. San Andrés	2234		
11. Santiago	2501		
12. San José	1718		
13. San Gil	1604		
14. San Juan de los Reyes	2125	GRAND TOTAL FOR CITY: 46,794	
15. Santa Ana	2094	(roughly 2/3 immigrant, 1/3 morisco)	
16. San Pedro	1375		
TOTAL	15,743		

* Precise locations of San Martín and San Blas parishes unknown. Both were located in the far eastern portion of the Albaicín.

Source: Archivo General de Simancas, Cámara de Castilla, caja 2150, lists by household each individual resident (male and female, young and old) of nearly every parish in Granada in 1561, but three clarifications are necessary. First, unlike the other parish reports, that of the Sagrario/Iglesia Mayor lists only the head of each household. The total number of heads of household in the parish report has thus been multiplied by the average number of residents listed per household in the other immigrant majority parishes of the city (4.04) to produce the Sagrario/Iglesia Mayor figure provided here. Second, Santa María de la Alhambra parish is not included at all in the 1561 census. A 1548 archiepiscopal visitation of the parish (Archivo Parroquial de San Cecilio, Libro de Visitaciones de Santa María de la Alhambra), however, noted that at that date the parish had 250 *vecinos*—a figure that has been multiplied here by the same coefficient of 4.04 to obtain this estimate. Third and finally, the 1561 census data did not include Granada's regular clergy. To the total of 45,087 listed in this table I have thus added 1,207—the number of regular clergy resident in the city according to the 1591 census (Cortés Peña and Vincent, *Historia de Granada*, 177)—to arrive at the final total.

As a result, sixteenth-century Granada became a city of limited ethnic segregation—a city in which the physical lines dividing the immigrant and morisco communities were blurred and continually renegotiated. The legacy of the 1498 segregation agreement for the history of the city was critical in that it set up a general pattern according to which the hilly northeastern portions of the city, and in particular the Albaicín, were considered the moriscos' zone, while the lower city would remain throughout the period under study primarily Christian immigrant. Yet the spatial boundaries that separated the two communities were neither absolute nor static. Local vocabulary revealed by documents such as municipal ordinances and trial testimony suggest that even as early as 1500—the year of the mass conversions—Granada was understood by its residents to be divided into three conceptual "zones"[21] as represented in map 2: the predominantly morisco Albaicín; the predominantly Christian immigrant lower city (ciudad baja); and the ethnically mixed areas of the border parishes, located mostly in a district called by locals the Alcazaba. Even these lines, however, were far from the impermeable divisions envisioned in the 1498 segregation treaty. The 1561 census, the results of which are summarized in table 3.1, reveal several morisco families in all parts of the lower city, including the parish of Magdalena—the immigrant parish furthest removed from the Albaicín. Also, nearly every neighborhood in the Albaicín listed Christian immigrant residents in the 1561 census, with only the remote parish of San Cristóbal reported as "inhabited entirely by moriscos."

In interpreting these data, it must be recognized that the 1561 census represents the state of affairs a full sixty years after the royal conversion order of 1500. These figures were, in short, the result of decades-long processes of emigration and immigration by which the Muslim-majority city of the 1490s was transformed into an immigrant-majority city. Understanding precisely how this transformation occurred within the context of the changing spatial and geographic relationships between the two communities provides critical insight not only into the nature of interaction and exchange between the two groups, but also into some of the causes and conditions of the city's enduring patterns of religious and ethnic hostility.

Specifically, as Christian immigrants poured into the city through the first half of the sixteenth century, the data indicate that they did not as a rule cordon themselves off in separate neighborhoods isolated from the city's morisco population. If we remember that a small minority of the Albaicín's population was immigrant and, similarly, that all lower city parishes included a morisco minority, in fact, we see that the data summarized in table 3.1 suggest that the Christian immigrant population of the ethnically mixed Alcazaba border parishes and lower Albaicín had grown at a rate roughly equal to or perhaps slightly greater than that of the more solidly immigrant-majority parishes of the lower city. Between 1500 and 1561, all of the border parishes experienced a transition from a morisco majority to an immigrant majority, and in some of the parishes the change was quite dramatic.

In at least one of these formerly morisco parishes, the influx of Christian immigrants was in fact by royal design. Ferdinand and Isabella themselves targeted the Alcazaba parish of San José as an area for Christian immigrant expansion into a traditionally morisco zone. In a 1505 letter to Archbishop Hernando de Talavera, Ferdinand explained that one of the reasons he and his late wife chose to place Granada's new royal appellate court on this edge of the Alcazaba was to encourage "Old Christian" migration into that nearly entirely morisco district of the city.[22] Christian immigrants, especially the bureaucrats, judges, and lawyers of the royal appellate court, responded to the crown's initiative by buying houses and sharing the space of San José parish with their morisco neighbors.

In other border parishes, however, the Christian immigrant takeover appears to have been more gradual and often a matter of circumstance. The parish of San Ildefonso, just outside the city walls on Granada's northern edge, straddling some of the poorer regions of the immigrant and morisco communities, exemplifies this sort of demographic pressure. Parish registers show that, around 1520, the moriscos of the parish solidly outnumbered the immigrants. Of ninety-four baptisms conducted in San Ildefonso from 1519 to 1522, forty-five, or slightly fewer than half, were of children born to parents whose names clearly indicate that they were morisco.[23] Because a large number of moriscos had adopted Christian names by that point, and because it is likely that at least some crypto-Muslims among the parish's morisco populace avoided having their children baptized, one may conclude that well over half the births in San Ildefonso parish in those years were to morisco parents. Also, especially in light of the studies by Bernard Vincent that demonstrate that birthrates among Granada's Christian immigrants tended to be higher than those of the city's morisco community, these numbers clearly show that, in the years around 1520, San Ildefonso was a parish with a heavily morisco majority population. Four decades later, in 1561, however, when in the royal census San Ildefonso was one of only two local parishes to report its Christian immigrant and morisco residents in separate lists, moriscos numbered only 359 out of 2,092 inhabitants—a mere 17 percent of the total.[24]

Alongside illustrating the ongoing immigrant influx into the border parishes, the San Ildefonso data also strongly suggest a simultaneous large-scale withdrawal of most, though not all, of the local morisco community away from those portions of the city that may have appeared to them to be becoming too saturated with the newcomers. As the morisco population of San Ildefonso dwindled through the middle decades of the century, in fact, those of the more solidly morisco neighborhoods of the Albaicín appear to have grown significantly. High atop the hill near the old wall separating the Alcazaba from the Albaicín, for example, the parish of San Nicolás retained until the expulsions of 1569–1570 a heavily morisco-majority populace. That parish's baptismal records, moreover, paint a dramatic picture of mid-century demographic growth: from a mere 33 baptisms in 1545, the total more than doubled to at least 68 in 1565.[25] Especially given Vincent's data on the relatively low birthrate among the frontier city's native community, the most plausible explanation for this growth is, of course, that the parish was receiving many moriscos who were fleeing from San Ildefonso and other increasingly immigrant-dominated border parishes. From this data emerges a fairly strong image of social cohesion among Granada's morisco populace, most of which appears actively to have sought isolation—although admittedly to varying degrees—from the frontier city's rapidly growing immigrant community.

All such efforts, however, were ultimately doomed to failure. The demographic pressure exerted by the ever-growing Christian immigrant community, as it continued to spread into the border parishes and even into the Albaicín itself, continuously eroded the spatial division between the city's two principal ethnic groups. For the great majority of Granada's moriscos and immigrants alike, this meant that daily life in their neighborhood streets and plazas involved regular interethnic contact and provided numerous opportunities for expressions of ethnic hostility as well as interaction and exchange. While the reactions of members of both communities to living under such circumstances varied widely, some moriscos continued to express resentment at the penetration of their district by the immigrants. For example, Luis de Mármol Carvajal, the historian of the second rebellion, reported having seen an intercepted letter from an anonymous morisco of the Albaicín soliciting support from potential North African allies in the 1568 uprising. Among the writer's complaints about the oppression under which the city's moriscos lived was, in fact, the mere presence of the immigrants and their "immoral" cultural traditions in the morisco districts of the Albaicín and Alcazaba. Mármol reported that in this letter the morisco angrily lamented that the Christian authorities had "opened our gates in order that there be greater sin and evil among us."[26]

The introduction of taverns and wine shops into the Albaicín despite the 1508 ordinance against them provides a clear example of the sorts of incursions to which the morisco author of this letter was referring. As early as 1511, a group of three Christian immigrants who had moved into the heart of the Albaicín petitioned the crown to annul the local ordinance passed three years earlier forbidding the establishment of taverns and wine shops in the Albaicín. Despite stiff opposition from local morisco leaders, the crown granted the local request, overturned the local ordinance, and allowed the immigrants to sell alcohol in the Albaicín.[27] The cultural traditions of the morisco community, then, were threatened not only by the oppressive policies of church and state, but also by the pressure of the growing local Christian immigrant community itself.

In short, the evolution of Granada's ethnic landscape through the first two-thirds of the sixteenth century was a complicated historical process that involved many competing voices and interests. The result was a city of limited ethnic segregation in which there remained abundant space for both daily, peaceable interaction on the one hand and expressions of ethnic hostility on the other. The role of the crown in guiding Granadan urban development was important, but it was not, as Orozco Pardo claimed, in itself determining, and it was most often responsive to local interests rather than directive. In addition, ironically, the very fluidity of spatial boundaries that allowed for daily interaction and exchange itself contributed significantly to the escalation of tensions leading up to the 1569–1570 expulsions of the moriscos from the city. As they streamed into Granada, Christian immigrants brought with them their own traditions and applied them indiscriminately in their new city, even in the Albaicín, where such activities were neither welcome nor acceptable among many of their morisco neighbors.

The aggressiveness of the immigrants in imposing their own customs by no means implies, however, that they were unwilling to embrace many Granadan mudéjar/morisco traditions as well. The adoption by conquerors of certain desirable aspects of conquered peoples' cultures is certainly not uncommon in history—particularly among the peoples and civilizations of the Mediterranean basin—and in no way should such "borrowing" necessarily be interpreted as a sign of good will or good intentions toward the moriscos. Still, the level of immigrant acculturation to what many of them found to be the exotic and intriguing traditions of their new home city, especially in the early decades after the conquest, is somewhat shocking given the simultaneous persistence of overt ethnic tensions. According to the morisco leader Núñez Muley, Archbishop Talavera himself even condoned the apparently common use of henna for cosmetic and medical purposes among Christian immigrant women—practices that they had learned from their Morisca neighbors.[28] Yet those early settlers who chose to adopt local traditions also found that even the usually tolerant old archbishop's patience with such cultural borrowing had its limits. As early as 1498, Talavera announced that Christian residents of the city were no longer to bathe in the Muslims' bath houses, nor eat poultry slaughtered and cleaned by local mudéjar butchers according to their traditional rites, nor walk about publicly in "moorish" dress—all of which had apparently become commonplace among the immigrants, men and women alike.[29] Talavera's sanctions concerning clothing apparently had little effect, at least among immigrant women. A new royal provision of 1513 explicitly denounced what it called the "custom" among Christian immigrant women in Granada of continuing to wear the *almalafa*—the draping overgarment traditionally worn in public by Morisca women, which covered much of the head and could also be worn in such a way as to cover part of the face as well.[30] Again, this seems to have had little effect. Ten years later, in 1523, the municipal council once more issued the same mandate to the Christian immigrant women of the city and ordered that for a second offense a delinquent woman would be whipped.[31]

FIGURE 3.1a & 3.1b. Morisca woman wearing an *almalafa*. Source: Christoph Weiditz, *Authentic Everyday Dress of the Renaissance: All 154 Plates from the "Trachtenbuch"* (New York: Dover Publications, 1994). Courtesy of Dover Publications.

Also gand die Edeln frawen morgen
auf der gassen In granada seytlen
genant dasse hun

The persistence of a staunch isolationist lobby among the moriscos should not be taken to mean that similar acculturation was not equally common among the city's "native" community. Even the most traditionalist moriscos tucked away in the most remote parishes of the Albaicín could hardly have remained untouched by the customs of the conquerors. In many ways, "Castilianization" among Granada's native population was in fact a process already well underway during the late Nasrid period, even a century or more before the conquest. As Angus MacKay has shown, the cultural frontier between late medieval Castile and Nasrid Granada had long been highly permeable to transcultural exchange. Such preconquest acculturation is visible, he argues, in a variety of ways, including the appearance of Franco-Gothic influences in Nasrid pottery beginning around 1370, and especially in the "frontier ballads" written and sung by Christians as well as Muslims celebrating on both sides of the political boundary the deeds of great warriors.[32] The conquest and ensuing waves of Christian immigration to the city accelerated the process, despite the reservations of traditionalist moriscos.

Linguistically, for example, there were few moriscos in the city—especially by the mid sixteenth century—who could not manage at least a simple conversation in a broken and heavily accented Castilian. It is true that Núñez Muley argued in his 1567 *Memorial* that many older moriscos had still never managed to learn to speak Castilian and that any royal mandate prohibiting spoken Arabic would thus prove impossible to implement. He was referring primarily, however, to the moriscos of the Alpujarras villages and other rural areas of the archdiocese, where, unlike the case in the city of Granada, there were very few Christian immigrants.[33] If for practical reasons most of the city's "native" men and women generally learned at least some Castilian, it should not be assumed that they forgot their ancestral Hipano-Arabic tongue in the process. Although repeated royal prohibitions of the use of Arabic in written correspondence and official documents effectively eliminated at least the public use of written Arabic in the city by mid-century, the streets and stores of Granada's Albaicín and Alcazaba districts continued until the expulsion to be filled by Arabic as well as Castilian conversation. The survival of Arabic among sixteenth-century Granada's moriscos stands in direct contrast to the nearly complete disappearance of their ancestral tongue among the moriscos of Castile and Aragon, who after centuries of Christian rule had developed a unique written language called Aljamía, which was comprised mostly of Castilian words and structures, but written in Arabic script. Some anonymous Castilian and Aragonese crypto-Muslim religious polemics written in Aljamía lamented that moriscos throughout sixteenth-century Spain had become so thoroughly *Aljamiado* that they had entirely forgotten their Arabic, written and spoken alike.[34] Yet as Juan Martínez Ruiz has demonstrated, sixteenth-century Granada's largely bilingual "native" community never used the Aljamía of the northern moriscos, preserving instead their traditional Arabic in everyday speech among themselves and even in clandestine writings until the local expulsions of 1569–1570.[35]

Along with learning to speak Castilian, there were, as we have seen, many members of Granada's morisco community who actively sought to integrate themselves into the social and economic mainstream of the increasingly immigrant-dominated city. Under these circumstances it is perhaps not surprising that many openly adopted other aspects of the conquerors' culture as well. By 1567, for example, nearly all of the city's morisco men, Núñez Muley claimed, had long since abandoned their traditional clothing and begun to dress in the Castilian manner.[36]

Alongside such examples of mutual exchange, however, there also endured unmistakable patterns of confrontation and expressions of ethnic hostility on both sides. Among the Christian immigrants, for example, public use of the ethnic slur "moorish dogs" (*perros moros*) toward their morisco neighbors remained common up until the expulsions, despite a strong royal rebuke issued by Charles V against the use of such epithets.[37] Even certain members of the local clergy used the term often enough to warrant a 1565 reprimand from the archbishop.[38] In addition, open hostility toward moriscos in the streets of the city was often matched by more covert efforts to exclude them from the community. When writing her last will and testament in 1537, for example, the wealthy immigrant Catalina Hernández charitably provided for the foundation of a house for orphaned girls in Granada, but explicitly prohibited the acceptance of morisca girls in the new orphanage.[39]

Historians from Julio Caro Baroja to Enrique Soria Mesa have typically argued that Christian immigrant attitudes toward Granada's "native" population varied along distinct class lines.[40] Many of the landholders who held seats on Granada's municipal council—above all the Mendoza—stood firmly as the principal defenders of morisco property and rights. Hostility toward the moriscos, by contrast, emerged principally from among the city's working-class immigrants and local royal bureaucrats of middle-class origin—particularly those of the Chancery. According to this formulation, the reasons for the landed elite's defense of the moriscos were primarily economic. Their calls for toleration and moderation, it is argued, must be understood in light of their interest in maintaining peace and order on their lucrative seigneurial holdings in the nearby villages and countryside of the former Nasrid sultanate—holdings which were populated almost entirely by morisco peasants who industriously farmed small parcels of land and/or raised silkworms. As a popular maxim in sixteenth-century Granada stated: "A man with a moor is never poor" (*Quién tiene moro, tiene oro*).[41] In this sense, the "liberal" attitude of the landed elite was rooted in a conservative desire to maintain peace and stability within a system from which they profited enormously.

This scheme for making sense of immigrant attitudes toward the moriscos is mostly accurate. The Mendoza, who always maintained close friendships and family alliances with the Granada Venegas and other elite "native" families, were in fact always at the forefront of efforts to moderate royal prohibitions of various aspects of morisco culture and curb the excesses of Granada's Inquisition tribunal and Chancery.[42] Yet as we have seen, working and middle-class immigrant men and women were by no means incapable of reaching across ethnic boundaries culturally, economically and residentially, nor were the landed elite families of the municipal council entirely innocent of expressions of ethnic hostility.

The few well-documented incidents of massive and open ethnic violence against the moriscos in the city illustrate the complexity of the question. On Easter eve 1568, in the midst of the increasing tensions that would eventually lead to the outbreak of the second rebellion, soldiers of the Alhambra garrison mistakenly rang a bell used to warn the city of impending danger. Rumors of a potential morisco uprising had been current for months, and in response to the warning, the Christian immigrants of the city rose up in a riot against the moriscos of the Albaicín. Luis de Mármol Carvajal, an eyewitness to the events of that night, noted that the crowd that gathered to confront the moriscos was comprised largely of working-class immigrants. He explained that the "fury of the plebeians" would have resulted in a massacre of the moriscos had the *corregidor* and various nobles not quickly blockaded the streets leading up into the Albaicín. Still, according to Mármol Carvajal's report, the immigrant commoners of the city were not the only ones who came armed and ready to kill moriscos that night. Armed friars from the Franciscan house of the lower city joined in their muster, and ironically, the municipal council itself provided weapons to the citizens. Also ironically, President Pedro de Deza of the Royal Chancery, whose harsh persecution of the moriscos is often blamed in large measure for the eventual outbreak of the second rebellion, showed up that evening to calm the crowds and protect the moriscos.[43]

Fear of the "other" community as a potential threat to life and property was, of course, mutual among Granada's two principal ethnic groups, and expressions of active hostility and passive exclusion toward the immigrants were equally common among the moriscos. From the early sixteenth century, armed squadrons of morisco bandits called *monfíes* proved a constant danger to immigrant traders and commerce in the countryside around the city. Some of these gangs even apparently operated covertly out of the bases in the isolated upper parishes of the Albaicín itself, where they enjoyed either the support or at least the tacit complicity of many of their fellow morisco neighbors.[44]

At a less dramatic level, some of the city's morisco merchants simply refused to do business with immigrants. On April 9, 1522, apparently for reasons of sanitation and public health, Granada's municipal council passed a controversial ordinance banning the sale of tongues, tripe, and internal organs at the city's butcher shops. The reactions to this ban by immigrants and moriscos alike provide a particularly poignant glimpse into the complexity of cultural and religious politics in sixteenth-century Granada. Tripe apparently constituted an important part of the moriscos' traditional diet. Unlike the introduction of wine sales into the Albaicín, however, it was not an issue of explicit religious significance. Nonetheless, the prohibition met with strong resistance among the residents of the Albaicín. One week after the initial ban, pressure from the morisco community forced the municipal council to clarify that the prohibition applied only to the immigrant butchers of the lower city and not to the morisco butchers of the Albaicín.[45] The existence of two sets of rules—one for the Albaicín and another for the lower city—was common in sixteenth-century Granada, especially with regard to issues of public sanitation. In 1537, for example, the municipal council passed new ordinances requiring that the city's residents keep their property clean and then specified that the rule did not apply to the Albaicín, where cleanliness had never been a problem and where, the council explained, "there does not seem to be the same necessity as in the lower city."[46] Despite the ban on tripe and organs in the lower city's butcher shops, moreover, many Christian immigrants continued in the mid-1520s to purchase and eat them, and the only place where they could buy such goods was in the supposedly more sanitary markets of the Albaicín. In 1524, two years after the initial ban, the municipal council passed a new ordinance mandating that those butchers who sold tripe and organs (namely, the morisco butchers of the Albaicín) must sell these goods publicly to all who entered their shops requesting them and not to hide them from certain customers.[47] To whom were the morisco butchers refusing to sell, and why? Because sale of such products was prohibited in the lower city, and because this ordinance came so soon after the lower-city ban, it is reasonably clear that the targets of the morisco butchers' exclusionary practices were Christian immigrants who were walking up into the Albaicín to buy the morisco butchers' supplies of tripe and organs. In strictly economic terms, the butchers' refusal to do business with the immigrants appears on the surface to make little sense, especially since the consumption of beef tripe was not in itself an issue of traditional religious division. In order to serve their "regular" customers (many of whom were, of course, faithful crypto-Muslims), however, most if not all of the Albaicín's butchers continued to observe in their markets the traditional slaughter rituals of Islam. Simply having potential Christian immigrant "witnesses" to such rites anywhere near their shops represented a threat to their security. In short, this incident illustrates that mutual acculturation at a variety of levels between moriscos and immigrants did not imply social or religious assimilation, nor did it necessarily prevent hostility. Physical, social, and cultural boundaries were frequently crossed, but community identity and ethnic conflict endured.

The changing physical face of the city, nonetheless, continued throughout the sixteenth century to reflect both cultural traditions, and nowhere more, ironically, than in the city's ecclesiastical architecture—particularly the new parish churches. Architectural *mudejarismo*, characterized by a combination of the intricate brickwork, use of colored tiles, and exquisitely detailed wooden ceilings typical of Iberian Muslim architecture with various Christian features, was by no means invented in frontier Granada. Such hybrid styles of architecture had been popular on the Castilian and Aragonese frontiers in the high Middle Ages, and numerous surviving medieval examples of the mudéjar style can be found today in Toledo and other cities in Castile, Andalusia, and Aragon.[48] What is most interesting about the sixteenth-century revival of architectural *mudejarismo* in Granada and other towns in the old Nasrid sultanate is that such styles had all but vanished in the construction of new churches elsewhere in Spain by the fourteenth century.[49] Orozco Pardo argues that the use of traditionally Muslim architectural styles in Granada waned after an initial fascination, pointing especially to the construction of Diego Siloé's Renaissance-style high altar of Granada's cathedral in the 1540s and 1550s as the key turning point away from the locally inspired mudéjar style.[50] Sixteenth-century parish documents concerning church construction, housed today in the archive of Granada's archiepiscopal curia, make clear, however, that the ongoing construction and expansion of local parish churches in the mudéjar style continued through the 1560s and even after the expulsion of the local morisco community in 1569.[51] The parish church of Santa Ana pictured here in figure 3.2—one of the most eloquent examples of this mixed style with its clearly mudéjar tower and Renaissance façade—was completed in 1561. These new churches, moreover, were in most cases the handiwork of morisco architects and craftsmen, especially in the border parishes and Albaicín. The parish of San Pedro and San Pablo, located like Santa Ana on the banks of the Darro River in a border district of mixed ethnicity, employed for much of the work on its new church building in the 1560s a local morisco named Hernando el Feri.[52] In at least one small way, then, the creation of Christian Granada might be said to have been very much a morisco project.

Many residents of sixteenth-century Granada thus heard mass and received sacraments in church buildings that embodied (or, perhaps better, appropriated) rather than rejected the city's distinct historical legacy. Moreover, as the Christian immigrants sat or stood in these churches listening to a sermon or the mass, they could look around them and see not only the faces of fellow immigrants, but also those of their morisco neighbors, especially in the border parishes and Albaicín. Though such conditions were by no means unique in sixteenth-century Spain, the degree to which the "Old

FIGURE 3.2. Parish Church of Santa Ana, Granada, **completed** circa 1561. Photo by author.

Christian"-morisco encounter was a part of daily life for all of the city's residents was certainly far greater in Granada than in any other part of the peninsula (with the possible exception of some heavily morisco towns and villages near Valencia). These conditions themselves were enough to bring to the practice of Christianity in Granada a somewhat unique flavor and an atmosphere distinct from those of the towns and villages from which the immigrants had come.

CHAPTER FOUR

The Emergence of a New Order
Granada's Governing Institutions

Thc conquest of Granada had been a royal project, and in theory, crown authority over the conquered city was absolute. With the exception of the Alhambra palace and its environs—placed by Ferdinand and Isabella under the seigneurial authority of the count of Tendilla—Granada was a royal city, subject to the crown's direct authority rather than to that of a noble lord. The Catholic Monarchs and their successors held complete control, for example, over the naming not only of the members of the city's royal appellate court, but also of the officials of the municipal council. Through a papal grant of royal patronage over Granada's church (*Real Patronato*) that previewed a similar patronage that the crown would enjoy over the church in the Americas, the crown also held direct control over all major ecclesiastical appointments in the city and kingdom of Granada.[1] In no other Spanish city, in short, did the crown enjoy the degree of direct authority that it officially possessed in postconquest Granada.

In practice, however, the role of the crown in shaping the institutional structures and political life of frontier Granada was limited and indirect. Historians of colonial Latin America have long recognized that royal mandates, while significant, were often reconfigured to fit local conditions or simply ignored by viceregal and local authorities who exercised a great degree of practical autonomy in their remote American settings. More recently, historians of Spain itself have revealed a vibrant medieval tradition of municipal autonomy that endured and even grew alongside the consolidation of monarchical power in the late Middle Ages and early modern period.[2] One of the most important effects of this line of inquiry has been to focus scholars' attention on the critical roles played by local governments and municipal elites in shaping the political cultures of Spain and its empire in the early modern period.[3]

The case of frontier Granada is of particular interest in this regard because it provides a glimpse at the construction of an entirely new system of administrative institutions in the absence of longstanding local medieval

73

traditions and long-established local oligarchies. To be sure, there were a handful of selected administrative practices inherited from the Nasrid period that were for practical reasons carried over into the institutional framework of Christian Granada—above all through the traditional incomes of the sultans, many of which were appropriated by the crown and applied to new purposes such as the financing of the city's new parish churches and municipal council.[4] Though exotic and intriguing, such vestiges of Nasrid administrative tradition were on balance few and relatively superficial in frontier Granada. In contrast to the persistently Muslim character of the appearance and architecture of much of the city, the story of postconquest Granada's governing institutions is much more one of rapid and radical transformation than of continuity.

The role played by the Catholic Monarchs and their officials in the elaboration of new administrative structures for the conquered city was both critical and foundational. Once established, however, Granada's secular and ecclesiastical institutions and the officials who staffed them began to create their own policies and patterns of interaction that constituted the most significant determinants of the city's political life. This is not to say that crown initiatives ceased entirely to play an important role in local politics. Royal mandates affecting local matters, however, were most often issued in response to specific petitions made by groups and/or individuals within Granada itself. The development of crown policy toward Granada customarily depended more on which members of the local community held royal favor at any given moment than on independent royal initiatives.

As one of Iberia's largest cities, a commercial hub, and the former capital of the Nasrid sultanate, Granada, not surprisingly, was transformed in the decades after 1492 into an administrative center of not only regional but also national significance. This transformation involved the introduction into the city of a wide array of new institutions. In addition to a municipal council and *audiencia* (royal court of first instance) of the sort that could be found in any of Spain's major cities, for example, Granada also housed after 1505 one of only two royal appellate courts (*Real Chancillería*) in the crown of Castile, as well as a royal mint and the military officers and staff of the powerful Captaincy General. Granada's new ecclesiastical establishment included not only the standard cathedral chapter, archiepiscopal court, and after 1526, Inquisition tribunal, but also a prestigious corps of clergy to staff the city's Royal Chapel—the burial site chosen and endowed by the Catholic Monarchs Isabella and Ferdinand. As a result, postconquest Granada became, like other more established administrative centers such as Seville and Valladolid in the kingdom of Castile or Barcelona in the crown of Aragon, a city whose local political stage was particularly crowded with large numbers of ambitious individuals seeking wealth and influence.[5]

Moreover, the local administrative mechanisms planted in Granada—both secular and ecclesiastical—grew in ways that reflected the relative fluidity of Granada's frontier society. The sheer quantity and complexity of local governing institutions meant that literally hundreds of individuals and families, including not only "Old Christian" immigrants but also judeoconverso immigrants and even some moriscos, had access in varying degrees to the city's power structures. In addition, because the development of the city's church and state institutions remained throughout the period an ongoing work in progress, jurisdictional conflicts and power struggles among and within the city's various institutions were endemic. It is thus inappropriate in the case of sixteenth-century Granada to speak of a monolithic local oligarchical "elite" of the sort that dominated the political life of many sixteenth-century Spanish cities such as Ávila and Córdoba.[6] The constant tensions within and among the various groups and individuals who vied for places and voices in the city's power structures influenced in profound ways the principal topic of this study: the development of the conquered city's nascent local religious customs and traditions.

ACCESS TO POWER: GRANADA'S SECULAR GOVERNMENT INSTITUTIONS

Alongside the city's archbishop, the single most influential official in the city and kingdom of Granada in the early postconquest period was the captain general. Bestowed by the Catholic Monarchs in 1492 upon Don Iñigo López de Mendoza, marqués of Mondéjar and count of Tendilla, in return for his military leadership during the wars of conquest against the Nasrid sultanate, the office of captain general remained in the hands of the powerful Mendoza family for generations. On Don Iñigo's death in 1515, the position passed to his son Luis Hurtado de Mendoza (1515–1543), who was in turn succeeded by his son, also named Iñigo López de Mendoza (1543–1580). Essentially a military officer, the captain general was charged with overseeing the soldiers of the kingdom and the construction and maintenance of coastal defense fortifications. In addition to their military duties, the Mendozas also received the title *alcaide* (governor) of the Alhambra, which gave them complete civil and criminal jurisdiction over the approximately one thousand immigrant residents who lived and worked in the Alhambra complex.

Beyond their seigneurial control over the Alhambra, the Mendozas also long remained a powerful force in the political life of the city as a whole. For more than a century, Granada's municipal council included a large bloc of Mendoza family members and political clients (*criados*). One of many families to benefit from Mendoza patronage in this regard was the influential and socially ascendant Trillo lineage, whose members for years had served the Mendozas not only in Granada but also in their common ancestral homeland in the Castilian diocese of Guadalajara. Born and raised in Granada in the first two decades of the sixteenth century, for example, Juan de Trillo went back to the Guadalajara region and served for a number of years as governor of the Mendozas' seigneurial estate of Mondéjar. Sometime before 1525, he returned to Granada and occupied a nonvoting position previously held by his father on the municipal council, and in 1542 his ascent under Mendoza patronage culminated in his acquisition of a voting position as *regidor*.[7]

Though the Mendozas had many friends and allies in the frontier city, their wealth and influence, as well as their ongoing defense of Granada's moriscos against exploitation at the hands of church and state officials, also made them the objects of scorn among many in Granada's immigrant community. In a 1518 civil court trial, the municipal councilman Gómez de Santillán, a perennial enemy of the count of Tendilla,[8] charged that officials hired by the city council to assess property values and plan the expansion of the city's central Bibarrambla plaza were political creatures of the Mendoza family. The assessors' reports to the council, claimed Santillán, protected Mendoza property around the plaza at the expense of the others and went against the public interest. His accusations were confirmed by a variety of witnesses. The royal court ruled in favor of Santillán and ordered that new assessors be appointed.[9]

Santillán's suggestion that the count of Tendilla was far overstepping the boundaries of his official post as captain general was in many ways accurate. Especially in the first few decades after the conquest, Iñigo López de Mendoza acted almost as if he were viceroy of the city and kingdom.[10] At times he even criticized the policies of the crown and its officials. In a letter to a royal secretary dated July 30, 1508, for example, Tendilla openly berated King Ferdinand for the inappropriate appointment of two unqualified officials to positions of influence in Granada: "Sir, I have said many times and continue to say each day that the King our lord should fast and do penance for having appointed a man who knows no grammar to a position as judge (in Granada's Chancery), and the judge's brother—a man who does not even know how to read—to a prebend in our cathedral church."[11]

One the most honored lineages among the Spanish high nobility, the Mendoza family numbered among its members some of the most influential soldiers, scholars, statesmen, and clergymen in fifteenth- and sixteenth-century Spain.[12] Like many grandees, they frequently expressed resentment against those whom they perceived as self-serving upstarts from relatively humble social backgrounds who were increasingly finding their way into positions of power in the expanding bureaucracies of Spain under the Catholic Monarchs and early Habsburgs. Over time, in fact, the growth and consolidation of other local administrative institutions in frontier Granada, staffed in large part by precisely such social climbers, gradually diluted the political influence of the captains general.

Particularly confrontational was the relationship between the Mendoza faction and one of Granada's other principal administrative institutions— the jurists and bureaucrats of Granada's Chancery, or royal appellate court.

Initially established by Ferdinand and Isabella in 1494 in the town of Ciudad Real in La Mancha, the Chancery was moved by order of the Catholic Monarchs to Granada in 1505. One of only two such tribunals in the Iberian possessions of the crown of Castile (the other was in Valladolid), Granada's Chancery held appellate jurisdiction over all cities and towns south of the Tagus River.[13] With a staff of more than two dozen crown-appointed judges and administrators and a small army of lawyers and scribes, the Chancery brought to the frontier city large numbers of well-educated, multitalented, and often ambitious men. Within the local social and political arena, the officials of Granada's Chancery proved a highly confrontational and assertive group greatly concerned with outward displays of status. They frequently became involved in conflicts, sometimes violent ones, with various other local institutions over the issue of precedence in seating arrangements at public festivities and observances such as autos de fe, processions, and masses at the cathedral. In 1563, in fact, court officials even placed the future captain general Luis Hurtado de Mendoza himself under house arrest and threw members of his entourage into jail after a violent scuffle over seating precedence at services in Granada's Royal Chapel.[14]

More important than either the Mendoza family or the Chancery in determining the tone of local politics was Granada's municipal council (*ayuntamiento*). As in other Spanish cities, Granada's municipal council carried a variety of responsibilities, from the upkeep of the city's public works and regulation of local trade and commerce, to maintaining law and order and issuing and enforcing local ordinances. The officeholders of the municipal council included not only "Old Christians," but also many judeoconversos and some moriscos, and newly wealthy men as well as nobles from established families. Many relatives and allies of the counts of Tendilla sat on the council, as did a number of their bitter enemies from the Chancery. As such, Granada's municipal council was a focal point in which various interests and groups within the community met and often clashed.

The form of the municipal council developed slowly in the decades after the 1492 Christian conquest of the city. In accordance with the terms of the surrender treaty, the city's local government initially remained in the hands of a municipal council that consisted of twenty-one mudéjar voting members appointed by the crown, supplemented by the Catholic Monarchs' four most important local officials: royal secretary Hernando de Zafra, Archbishop Hernando de Talavera, *corregidor* Andrés Calderón, and the captain general. As historian Ángel Galán Sánchez has shown, this earliest mudéjar municipal council was no mere formality. For the first three or four years after the conquest, Mohammed el Pequeñí and his fellow Muslim councilmen actively administered the commerce, public works, and laws of the city.[15]

As the legal protections guaranteed by the surrender treaty eroded through the course of the 1490s, and as Christian immigrants in ever-larger numbers streamed into the city, however, Muslim dominance of local politics quickly faded. By 1497, the date of the earliest surviving minutes of council meetings preserved in Granada's municipal archive, the council's semiweekly gatherings were regularly attended by only seven men—all of them Christian immigrants. For some unknown reason, the Muslim municipal councilors, who at this point at least officially retained their titles, had apparently stopped attending. On October 3, 1497, in fact, the immigrant municipal councilmen changed the days of regular council meetings from Tuesday and Saturday evenings to Tuesday and Friday, offering only the curiously phrased rationale that, for religious reasons, their mudéjar colleagues "cannot come on Friday evenings, and nowadays the Muslims no longer come."[16]

The trend toward the exclusion of Granada's still-majority "native" population from municipal politics was interrupted only briefly in the years surrounding the first rebellion. The morisco collaborator Don Alonso de Granada Venegas, for example, gained a voting position on the council in 1499, and more newly converted moriscos soon followed. After the suppression of the December 1499 uprising in the city, and with rebellion still raging in the nearby Alpujarras, a royal decree dated September 20, 1500, gave Granada's municipal council a formal structure similar to those of other cities in the crown of Castile.[17] This decree placed at the top of Granada's local government twenty-four crown-appointed councilmen, called *veinticuatros* or *regidores*, who held votes on the municipal council. Beneath the voting members, the decree provided for twenty posts for nonvoting aldermen (*jurados*), as well as a variety of scribes and bureaucrats to be appointed directly by the voting councilmen. Of the original twenty-four appointees to the powerful *regidor* positions, seven, including Alonso de Granada Venegas and el Pequeñí, were moriscos, and an eighth morisco was added before the end of 1501.[18]

Many of these early morisco appointees appear to have received their posts as political rewards for their conversions before the mass baptisms of 1500, or for specific services to the crown. On their deaths their seats often passed to Christian immigrants. In 1511, for example, Francisco de los Cobos, an ascendant bureaucrat from Úbeda and future royal secretary to Charles V, occupied the seat previously held by the morisco Francisco Jiménez Xama.[19] Through the course of the sixteenth century, the morisco presence on Granada's municipal council continued to decline. By 1566, the council included only three morisco *regidores*—one each from the powerful Granada Venegas, Zegrí, and Córdoba families, each of which had through the decades (despite the declining political fortunes of the Córdoba family in the later 1560s) become well-integrated into the upper echelons of Christian immigrant society through marriage and political connections.

For the Christian immigrants who attained them, as well as the handful of morisco families who managed to hold them, seats as voting members on Granada's municipal council were sources of and expressions of a family's political power. As in many other cities, positions as *regidores,* once obtained, usually passed from fathers to sons or to other relatives in a way that perpetuated the power of specific families. Granada's city council, however, also remained open to penetration by a number of newly ascendant families such as the Pérez de Herrasti and the judeoconverso de la Torre. This relatively high degree of accessibility was in part a function of Granada's distinct frontier setting as a new local society under construction, and in part a reflection of the fact that in Granada, as in a number of other Spanish cities in the early Habsburg era, the quantity of *regidor* positions increased over the years as the crown sold new positions as a way of raising revenue.[20] In fact, though the 1500 royal decree establishing the municipal council limited the number of *regidores* to twenty-four (hence the title *veinticuatros*), the actual number of voting members on the council rose to thirty-five by 1556.[21]

From 1501 to 1571, a total of at least 136 different men held voting seats on Granada's municipal council.[22] Of these, 101, or roughly three-quarters, came from a group of thirty-one families who placed at least two of their members on the municipal council as *regidores* during the period under study—a set of families that together constituted the core of Granada's developing and ever-changing political elite. Background information is available for nineteen of these thirty-one families (sixteen Christian immigrant families plus the three morisco lineages).[23] The heterogeneity of this group is the most striking feature to emerge from close study of this data, as families from a variety of religious, geographical, and professional backgrounds maneuvered into positions in Granada's evolving local elite through the first half of the sixteenth century.

With regard to religious background, for example, hereditary places in frontier Granada's ruling class were by no means the exclusive preserve of "Old Christians." In addition to the three prominent morisco families mentioned above, the municipal council also included a considerable number of judeoconversos. Of the nineteen lineages for whom data are available, four (Álvarez Zapata, Bobadilla, de la Torre, and Rengifo) have been reasonably clearly identified as families of certain or near-certain converso origin, and this total will certainly continue to rise with further research on the subject.[24] To be sure, Granada was by no means unique among Spanish cities in this regard. Through the fifteenth and sixteenth centuries, conversos managed to gain a significant number of seats on municipal councils in Seville, Toledo, and many other Castilian cities.[25] Still—perhaps because of the lack of a local Inquisition tribunal for more than three decades, and/or because of the city's relatively anonymous frontier immigrant society in which one's ancestry was generally not a matter of public knowledge—judeoconversos generally found access to such positions to be much easier in Granada than in most Castilian cities, and their presence on the council was generally less controversial in Granada than elsewhere.[26]

In terms of geographic origins, Granada's *regidor* families represented roughly the same range as the immigrant community as a whole, which drew heavily, though not exclusively, from Spain's south. The three prominent morisco families, of course, traced their recent family roots to the city and kingdom of Granada itself. Of the remaining sixteen lineages whose residence before coming to Granada is known, one came from Galicia, one from the Basque country, five from Old Castile, seven from New Castile, and two from Andalusia. Moreover, among these sixteen lineages, only two pairs shared a common point of origin: the Toledan judeoconverso tax-collector and merchant Álvarez Zapata and de la Torre families, and the Mendoza and their Trillo clients from the Guadalajara region. In short, while preexisting interfamily relationships transplanted from specific localities in Castile appear to have played an appreciable role in local politics, on balance the city's emerging political elite is best understood as the coming together in a frontier setting of a new set of elite families and the ongoing construction among them of new systems of relations, intermarriages, alliances, and rivalries.

Further complicating frontier Granada's local political scene was the wide range of social and professional backgrounds from which these prominent lineages came. Among the postconquest city's earliest *regidor* families, only the Mendozas were members of Spain's old titled aristocracy. Some came from military families whose local influence began in the form of lesser political offices granted by the crown in return for service as soldiers during the wars of conquest (such as the Pérez de Herrasti and Arias de Mansilla), while others, by contrast, came from merchant backgrounds (including the de la Torre and Álvarez Zapata). Many were well-educated bureaucrats and administrators, some of whom came to Granada originally to take positions in the Chancery (such as the Mexía, Pisa, and Obregón), while others had previously occupied powerful offices in the direct service of the crown (including the Zafra and Agreda). In short, paths to local political power in frontier Granada were various.

One important thread linking the overwhelming majority of these otherwise diverse families, and one that distinguishes them from the broader Christian immigrant community as a whole, was their common presence in the city from the very earliest years after the 1492 conquest. Of the sixteen elite Christian immigrant lineages, thirteen had family members present among Granada's small, nascent immigrant community in the 1490s. Moreover, even the three families whose first Granada resident came to the city after 1500—all of whom were associated with the Chancery—arrived at relatively early dates: the Mexía and Pisa in or shortly after 1505 with the transfer of the appellate court from Ciudad Real to Granada, and the Obregón in or around 1514. As was often the case in Spain's New World colonies, presence in the early postconquest settler community appears to have conferred a considerable degree of prestige that helped many immigrant families from a variety of backgrounds vault into positions of authority in the evolving local hierarchy.

Such ascents, however, generally did not occur overnight. Although Dr. Gracian de Mexía first came to Granada from Ciudad Real as a royal court judge around 1505, for example, the rise of the Mexía family to the top of the local political scene culminated only in 1532 with the acquisition of voting position on the municipal council by his son Alonso de Mexía. Similarly gradual was the emergence of many of these families, including the Álvarez Zapata, whose first *reguiduría* was obtained in 1512, the Osorio (1526), the Pérez de Herrasti (1541), the Trillo (1542), the Ávila (1546), the Agreda (1549), the Obregón (1552), and the Arias de Mansilla (1557). In addition, approximately one-quarter of the men who served as *regidores* in Granada during this period came from outside of the core group of thirty-one families, including even one merchant of Genoese origin.[27] Clearly underscored by these data is the fact that postconquest Granada's municipal elite was not a closed and self-perpetuating elite of the sort that dominated politics in many Castilian cities, particularly in the north. Instead, in a way that reflected the general fluidity of the frontier city's immigrant community as a whole, it remained throughout the period remarkably open to penetration by socially ascendant families of means.

For many of these upwardly mobile immigrant families and individuals, the office of *jurado,* or nonvoting alderman, often provided a springboard to the more influential voting positions on the council. According to the 1500 royal decree that established the council's structure, there were to be twenty *jurados,* each representing one of the city's parishes. All of the initial group of *jurados* were crown appointees, but a 1505 royal decree clarified that when a holder of one of these seats died, his successor was to be determined by an election among the residents of the parish that he represented. Yet, in practice, this apparently democratic provision meant little. As was the case with the *regidores, jurados* were allowed before dying or moving to other offices to renounce their posts in favor of specific family members or political allies. Parish elections were thus rare, generally occurring only in the case of the sudden death of the officeholder. Of at least 112 men who held *jurado* posts in Granada between 1501 and 1571, only six are mentioned in surviving documentation to have received their positions via election.[28]

Although allowed to attend municipal council meetings, the *jurados* could neither vote nor speak. They were, however, allowed to present petitions on behalf of the city's residents, and they managed frequently in the sixteenth century to play an active role in city politics. No doubt many *jurados,* like the Mendoza ally Juan de Trillo, were tied politically to specific factions and patronage networks among the *regidores.* Yet groups of *jura-*

dos at times challenged the local power of the *regidores* and the city's more established families. For example, in 1532, a group of *jurados* petitioned the Chancery to annul that year's elections of local judges, public works administrators, and other city officials by the *regidores*. The *jurados* accused some of the more powerful *veinticuatros* of having rigged the election in such a way as to place their own followers and servants in key regulatory positions. The judges of the Chancery found in favor of the *jurados*, canceled the election, and called for a new one.[29] In 1558, when the *regidores* announced plans to spend a great deal of money from the municipal treasury on public mourning rites for the deceased Charles V, one of the *jurados* protested that the city's common funds should not be spent on such extravagant ceremonies.[30]

Despite constant factionalism and conflict within the municipal council, it remained the city's most powerful institution and the most important determinant of the political direction of the city. Nonetheless, its authority was not limitless. The city's residents could and sometimes did challenge the policies of the *regidores*. In 1531, for example, Francisco de Montpellier—a Granada resident who owned a few houses that had been seized by the city five years earlier in order to widen one of Granada's central plazas—filed a lawsuit against the municipal council. In his lawsuit, Montpellier charged that the city had not yet destroyed the houses nor carried out its plans to widen the corresponding portion of the plaza. Instead, he argued, the city was simply renting out the houses and enjoying the incomes that were rightfully his. The Chancery ruled in Montpellier's favor, ordered the city to pay him for the houses, and added that if the buildings were not destroyed within a year, they would revert automatically to Montpellier.[31]

In short, political authority in frontier Granada was above all diffuse. The power of each of Granada's principal secular administrative institutions was limited by the presence and strength of other institutions within the city, and numerous groups and individuals within the community found in this complexity avenues for the expression and pursuit of their interests.

HERNANDO DE TALAVERA AND THE ESTABLISHMENT OF GRANADA'S CHURCH INSTITUTIONS

"I will not be a bishop except in Granada." As personal confessor to Queen Isabella of Castile since 1475, the Hieronymite friar Hernando de Talavera (1430?–1507) reportedly used these words often in response to the queen's repeated requests that he accept an episcopal appointment. Talavera's refrain became something of a joke between the queen and her confessor,[32] as the conquest of Granada remained in the 1470s a distant and unclear goal. Though perhaps spoken with tongue-in-cheek, Talavera's words also reflected the idealism with which he envisioned the future possibilities of a Christian Granada. Like many reform-minded clergymen of the era,

Talavera often spoke of the pristine, primitive church of the apostles as a model to which Christendom should aspire to return, and the construction of a new local church in Granada would provide a theater in which such ambitions might be acted out. Shortly after entering the Nasrid capital in triumph in 1492, Queen Isabella held her Hieronymite confessor to his old promise and appointed him first archbishop of the newly conquered city.[33]

Although the rapid proliferation of church institutions would eventually make Christian Granada's ecclesiastical establishment just as multivocal, dynamic, and contentious as the city's secular elite, Talavera alone dominated the earliest history of Granada's postconquest church. Officially, the new archdiocese of Granada was the creation of two foundational documents authorized by the pope, the first dated May 21, 1492, establishing the archiepiscopacy and the offices of the cathedral chapter, and the second dated October 15, 1501—after the first rebellion and mass baptisms—outlining the archdiocese's network of parish churches. The Holy See entrusted the composition of these two documents to the archbishops of Toledo and Seville, respectively. With regard to the 1492 foundation, however, it was clearly left to Talavera himself to implement its provisions and adjust them to fit local circumstances, which he clearly did. He reduced, for example, the number of canons in Granada's cathedral chapter from the forty demanded by the foundation to a more practical twelve because of the archdiocese's financial constraints.[34] The 1501 foundation of the parishes, moreover, simply gave formal recognition and staffing details to a parish structure that had already effectively emerged under Talavera's direction in the wake of the mass baptisms of January and February 1500. Jesús Suberviola Martínez even argues that its actual text was most likely authored by the old Hieronymite friar himself and not by the archbishop of Seville.[35]

To the job of creating a new church on the Granada frontier, Talavera brought the experience of a lengthy and prestigious career working both as a trusted royal servant and an influential if controversial reform-minded clergyman. Despite the fact that he is universally recognized as one of the most eminent figures in the political and religious life of late-fifteenth-century Spain, scholars still have not managed to find a conclusive answer to the puzzling question of Talavera's family origins. It has become a commonplace among prominent scholars of the past century, from Americo Castro and Marcel Bataillon onward, to assert the "near certainty" of Talavera's Jewish ancestry.[36] In the historiography of early modern Spain, moreover, this is not simply a matter of minor genealogical detail. Talavera's supposed judeoconverso roots provide to some historians sufficient rationale to explain the high value he placed on the ideals of religious toleration, reasonable persuasion rather than forced conversion, and respect for the faith of former Jews and Muslims newly converted to Christianity.[37] Yet as Henry Kamen has pointed out, the evidence offered thus far for Talavera's converso roots is hardly conclusive.[38] Various theories have been offered concerning exactly who the archbishop's parents were, the most common claims insisting on the close connections between Talavera and the family of the well-known converso general of the Hieronymite order Fray Alonso de Oropesa—ties that were in fact more likely ones of friendship and service rather than lineage.[39] The other main source of evidence comes from the controversial and highly publicized 1505–1507 inquisition trial in which Talavera and his sister, along with various friends and family members, were accused of crypto-Judaism. In the trial, the inquisitors squarely asserted that Talavera was widely known to be of judeoconverso origin. Though the pope acquitted Talavera on all charges of religious infidelity, the archbishop never during the course of the trial explicitly denied that he was of Jewish ancestry. On balance, the available evidence strongly suggests, although it by no means proves, that Granada's first archbishop was from a family of recently converted Jews.

Whether of Jewish descent or not, Talavera has long been regarded as one of early modern Spain's most prominent defenders of the ideals of religious liberty and toleration. Throughout his years of service to the crown before coming to Granada, Talavera had repeatedly criticized the persecution faced by Castile's judeoconversos. He also argued, most notably in his controversial 1480 book *Católica impugnación,* that the best way to attract backsliding converts and even outright infidels to the true Catholic faith was through example, reason, and persuasion rather than by force or threat. Talavera's behavior in the earliest years of his archiepiscopacy in Granada is often cited as testimony to the sincerity of his convictions on these matters. His wisdom and his respect for Muslim Granada's culture and traditions earned him, according to all contemporary accounts, the lasting admiration of the city's mudéjar community, who commonly called him the *santo alfaquí* of the Christians.[40] By that point past sixty years of age, Talavera tried—although by all accounts he mostly failed—to learn at least rudimentary Arabic, and he ordered the translation into Arabic of his own simple Castilian vernacular catechism and its publication in Granada for the instruction of new converts.[41] Unlike later ecclesiastics in Granada, moreover, Archbishop Talavera actually embraced many of Muslim Granada's secular customs, including the traditional *zambra* dance, which he allowed to be performed in the churches of the city and archdiocese, and he even incorporated it into Granada's earliest Corpus Christi celebrations.[42] Although a respected and even beloved figure among Granada's mudéjares, Talavera managed by persuasion to convert to the Catholic faith no more than a few hundred of them.

In recent years, troubling questions raised by some scholars have begun to tarnish the heroic reputation traditionally enjoyed by Archbishop Talavera as a man of unswerving patience and toleration. The near silence in the documentary record concerning Talavera's role in the critical events leading up to the mass baptisms of January and February 1500, for example, has led Ladero Quesada and other scholars to speculate that the failure of his peaceable missionary efforts may have frustrated the archbishop to the point that he eventually abandoned his long-held ideal of persuasion over coercion. Ladero Quesada, in fact, has argued that the archbishop must have been at least a tacit accomplice in the plans put into action by Cisneros in November 1499.[43] Moreover, the image of Talavera that emerges from Surviola Martínez's study of the royal patronage of the church in Granada is much more one of a subservient political operative of the crown than that of an assertive and independent religious idealist and reformer.[44]

For Talavera and his new church in Granada, the royal patronage indeed proved to be a mixed blessing. On the one hand, it provided a remarkable opportunity to create new ecclesiastical structures in line with the most progressive and reform-minded ideals of the day, free from the tangled webs of lay-sponsored benefices and ancient local institutional customs that frustrated reform efforts in so many dioceses across Europe. On the other hand, it also imposed many constraints on Granada's archbishops, above all because the royal patronage gave the crown complete control over local church finances. As a result, Granada's archiepiscopacy remained throughout the period by far the least lucrative of the four archbishoprics of the crown of Castile, since much of its income was siphoned off to help meet the ever-growing financial needs of the monarchy. In 1525, for example, while the archbishop of Toledo enjoyed sixty thousand ducats of income each year, the archbishop of Seville twenty-two thousand, and the archbishop of Santiago sixteen thousand, the incomes of the archbishop of Granada amounted to only seven thousand ducats each year.[45] In addition, the royal patronage gave to the crown the right to appoint directly all of the major ecclesiastical officials in the archdiocese. As was the case with the city's secular institutions, however, crown control over Granada's church, though in theory nearly complete, was in practice only limited and indirect. In a manner resembling what John Frederick Schwaller found in his study of the clergy in early colonial Mexico where the crown also enjoyed royal patronage,[46] ecclesiastical appointments in frontier Granada almost always went to men who had been recommended to the crown by authorities in Granada itself, including most often the city's archbishops, but also in some cases local secular powers such as the captain general.[47] Despite the royal patronage, that is to say, individuals who were most familiar with local conditions nearly always made the key decisions regarding the staffing of local church positions.

During the early years of Talavera's archiepiscopacy, there remained little distinction between secular and ecclesiastical authority in the city of Granada. Archbishop Talavera served at the same time as the city's principal Christian religious authority and one of the most powerful and influential voices in municipal government. The crown charged Talavera, as a member of Granada's municipal council in the 1490s, with the duty of receiving and responding to citizens' petitions and complaints regarding city government.[48] Moreover, the archbishop and his officials also acted as something of a police force among the early Christian immigrant community. However gentle and tolerant Talavera was in his interactions with the city's Muslim population, he was exceptionally stringent in the enforcement of morality among Granada's small early Christian immigrant community. In a 1530 biography of the archbishop, Talavera's student and follower Alonso Fernández de Madrid reported that Talavera's ecclesiastical court and jail were generally busier and more heavily populated than the secular tribunals and the city jail.[49]

In his governance of Granada's early church, however, Talavera proved in many ways to be an innovative visionary. Attempting to infuse his clergy with the spiritual energy of the scriptural church of the apostles, the archbishop initiated a number of local institutions and traditions that would help to shape the reform visions of later clergymen both locally and in the Roman Catholic church as a whole. Soon after arriving in Granada, for example, Talavera began the practice of regularly calling the clergymen of the city and archdiocese to meet once each month in his house to discuss solutions to the common problems they all faced. Although Talavera's immediate successors discontinued these "minisynods," Granada's archbishops Gaspar de Avalos (1529–1541) and Pedro Guerrero (1546–1576) later resuscitated this tradition.

More significantly, Talavera established in Granada in 1492 a highly influential school—later called the Colegio Eclesiástico de San Cecilio—for the education of future clergymen.[50] This "proto-seminary," as it is sometimes called, provided grammatical, theological, and moral training for twenty-five young men between the ages of fifteen and twenty-five. Though small, Talavera's school produced among its students some of Spain's most important church leaders of the early sixteenth century, including Granada's future archbishop Avalos and the noted reformer and future bishop of Málaga and Cuenca, Diego Ramírez de Villaescusa.[51] Like the regular meetings of the clergy, however, Talavera's school declined through neglect and a lack of adequate funding in the two decades after his 1507 death. It was not until the archiepiscopal tenure of the school's alumnus Avalos in the 1530s that it again received sufficient funds to restore it to the level it had reached under Talavera in the decade after the 1492 conquest of the city.

Despite the precedent set by Talavera in the 1490s for strong and innovative leadership, the archiepiscopal office in Granada declined dramatically in prestige and influence in the early sixteenth century. This decline was already noticeable in the closing years of Talavera's tenure. In the final years of his life 1505–1507, the aging archbishop, now in his seventies, had to direct most of his energies toward clearing his own name and those of his friends and colleagues who faced persecution at the hands of the Inquisition. The decline continued under Talavera's immediate successor Antonio de Rojas (1509–1524), who was for the most part a nonresident prelate who paid greater attention to his duties as president of the Royal Council of Castile (particularly during the crisis years of the Comuneros uprising 1520–1521) than to the spiritual guidance of his flock in Granada. Rojas appears to have been especially disliked by the city's parish clergy, who later accused him of diverting an enormous sum of more than thirty thousand ducats from Granada's parish churches to the archiepiscopal treasury.[52] Following Rojas, Granada's archiepiscopal see passed quickly through the hands of three men who died shortly after taking office: Francisco de Herrera (1524), Pedro Portocarrero (1526), and Talavera's student and fellow Hieronymite Pedro Ramiro de Alva (1527–1528). Not until the arrival of Gaspar de Avalos would the city again have a lasting resident prelate, but even his leadership was consistently undermined by bitter opposition from local clergymen and the animosity that his policies and personality engendered among the moriscos of the city and archdiocese. Only with the arrival of Archbishop Pedro Guerrero (1546–1576) would Granada again have a prelate who approached the stature and authority enjoyed by Talavera in the early years after the conquest.

Throughout the critical and formative four decades that separated the beginning of Talavera's Inquisition trial in 1505 from the arrival of Archbishop Guerrero in 1546, the creation of Christian Granada thus proceeded with little or no effective archiepiscopal guidance. Episcopal absenteeism was, of course, an endemic problem in many Spanish dioceses in the first half of the sixteenth century, and Granada was by no means unique in this regard. In a newly created archdiocese still building even its most basic institutional structures and public traditions, however, the consequences of ineffective episcopal direction were especially profound.

During those times when there was no archbishop in Granada, the city's most powerful ecclesiastical institution was, at least in theory, the cathedral chapter. For various reasons, however, Granada's chapter was significantly weaker than those of other cities in the crown of Castile. Above all, like the city's archbishops, Granada's chapter suffered financial weakness because of crown control of its incomes through the royal patronage. The shortage of money that had led Archbishop Talavera to reduce significantly the number of offices and prebends ordered by the 1492 papal foundation document meant that Granada's cathedral chapter was much smaller than those elsewhere in Castile. In the fairly typical northern diocese of Burgos, for example, the chapter consisted of eighteen upper officeholders called "dignitaries," forty-four canons, and twenty prebend-holders, and an additional twenty men who held half-prebends, for a total staff of 104.[53] Frontier

Granada's cathedral chapter, by contrast, included only six dignitaries, twelve canons, and twelve prebends, comprising a total of only thirty members.

Even with the reduction of offices, moreover, incomes of chapter officials remained relatively low—generally too low to attract members from the city's wealthiest and most powerful families. Thus, unlike the situation in Castilian cities such as Avila and Burgos, where the same closed oligarchy of families dominated both the municipal council and the cathedral chapter, there is very little overlap in Granada between the names of chapter members and those of the city's emerging secular elite.[54] Granada's sixteenth-century cathedral chapter was thus a social world unto itself, staffed largely by clergymen of middle- or even working-class backgrounds.

Judging by the staunch local resistance to the crown-mandated 1554 imposition of purity of blood (*limpieza de sangre*) requirements for chapter positions,[55] Granada's canons and prebend-holders also likely included at least some judeoconversos. Of the thirty men who held positions in the chapter from 1560 to 1564, only eleven appear to have been subjected to official *limpieza* inquiries, and all eleven were indeed ruled to be "Old Christian." Still, the testimony gathered in these *limpieza* checks provides fascinating testimony to the relatively humble social backgrounds from which many of Granada's chapter officials came. One, for example—the canon and future chapter secretary Martín de Maldonado—was from a family of day laborers in a village near the Old Castilian city of Soria.[56] Another—the canon Diego Romano—was the grandson of a silversmith and son of a royal scribe from Valladolid.[57] None of the eleven were from prominent noble lineages. Moreover, even at this late date—six decades after the conquest—only two appear to have grown up in Granada itself. Of the remainder, four were recent immigrants from Old Castile, four from cities and towns in northern and western Andalusia, and the other one from the nearby formerly Nasrid town of Loja.[58] Granada's cathedral chapter, in short, represented a point of access to some degree of influence and prestige to men from a wide variety of middle- and working-class backgrounds.

The chapter's most important and time-consuming job was the oversight of the construction of the conquered city's new cathedral. Under Talavera's direction, Granada's first cathedral chapter was installed in 1492 in the recently founded Franciscan friary inside the Alhambra complex. It then moved shortly afterward to share the space of the new, larger Franciscan friary and church then under construction on the lower city's southern edge, where it remained for the rest of the 1490s. In 1501, after the mass baptisms of the previous year, Granada's great mosque in the city's center was consecrated as a church and turned into the city's new cathedral. It was from this impressive monument to the city's Islamic past that the chapter over the next five decades directed the construction of a new building next door that would eventually dwarf its Muslim predecessor—Granada's enormous Renaissance-style cathedral designed by Diego Siloé and finally consecrated by Archbishop Guerrero on August 17, 1561.[59]

Like the jurists of the Chancery, the canons of the cathedral chapter proved to be a contentious group greatly concerned with matters of social prestige and protocol. Conflicts with the municipal council over seating precedence at Inquisition autos de fe and other observances were common.[60] Even more virulent were the ongoing struggles between the cathedral chapter and its not-so-friendly neighbor—the equally confrontational chaplains of Granada's Royal Chapel. In 1504, in the final year of her life, Queen Isabella herself provided for the construction of a burial chapel in Granada, the site of her greatest victory. The site chosen was nestled uncomfortably between the old main mosque on one side and the site where the new cathedral was to be constructed on the other, and the Royal Chapel would, in fact, eventually share a wall with each. Upon completion of the awkward late Gothic structure in 1521, the remains of Ferdinand and Isabella were interred there, and their grandson Charles V ordered that the original chapter of thirteen chaplains requested by Isabella be increased to twenty-five. As Siloé's new cathedral structure next door soared ever higher into the air through the 1540s, fears of being overshadowed, both figuratively and literally, led the Royal Chapel clergy to file a series of lawsuits against the cathedral. Endemic conflicts led eventually to a 1564 proposal by one of the cathedral canons that the Royal Chapel be abolished as an independent entity and that the chapel be incorporated into the fabric of the cathedral. The attempt failed and conflicts persisted.[61]

Amidst its constant bickering with rival institutions, the cathedral chapter through the first half of the new century appears to have played only a minor role in the broader public religious life of the city outside of the construction of the cathedral building. As we will see, the cathedral officials in the early decades of the new century repeatedly refused lay immigrant requests that they participate actively in a wide array of religious displays and processions in the nascent Christian public religious life of the frontier city. In addition, archiepiscopal investigations reveal that Granada's chapter was often guilty of the same abuses characteristic of chapters elsewhere, including everything from chatting or sleeping in the choir during masses to outright absenteeism.[62] In short, Granada's cathedral chapter played no more than a secondary role in the city's broader religious and civic life for most of the sixteenth century.

Especially in the critical formative decades between the beginning of the Inquisition's campaign against Talavera in 1505 and the arrival of Archbishop Guerrero in 1546, then, frontier Granada's new ecclesiastical establishment lacked effective central leadership from its two principal administrative institutions—the archiepiscopacy and the cathedral chapter. A striking emblem of this lack of effective guidance in the local ecclesiastical hierarchy was the fact that Granada remained through the first two-thirds of the sixteenth century one of only three dioceses in Spain (along with its nearby suffragan dioceses of Almería and Guadix), and the only archdiocese, that lacked a standard set of synodal constitutions to govern the local administration of the faith.[63] No genuine and formal synodal assembly would be held in Granada until Archbishop Guerrero's 1565 Provincial Council, and Granada finally would receive its first published and official synodal constitutions in 1572—three years after the morisco expulsion and a full eight decades after the conquest. In the absence of effective archiepiscopal guidance, the forces that shaped Christian Granada's developing religious culture emerged primarily from various lay groups among Granada's Christian immigrant community, and from their interactions with the friars and parish clergymen who, unlike most of the city's archbishops and cathedral chapter dignitaries, were in fact a daily presence in the plazas, pulpits, and festive processions of the newly conquered frontier city.

CHAPTER FIVE

Creating Christian Granada

Lay Initiative and the Invention of Local Religious Traditions, 1492–1550

Granada's earliest immigrant community in the 1490s included a small group of laborers from Asturias and Spain's other mountainous northern coastal regions. On arrival, most of these Asturian immigrants, prohibited by the surrender agreement from residing within the city itself, concentrated themselves in a marginal neighborhood outside the city walls, in an area stretching out from the lower city toward the plains to the west. Within the first few years after the conquest, the Asturians had constructed within their new neighborhood a small chapel dedicated to Our Lady and San Roque—the cult of San Roque being a devotion typically strong in the far northern regions of Spain from which they had come. Around this chapel there grew also a confraternity, or lay religious brotherhood, dedicated to the Virgin and San Roque. In implementing the 1501 foundation document establishing Granada's parishes, Archbishop Talavera took advantage of the existence of this new chapel, converting it into the neighborhood's parish church of Santa María Magdalena. Through the early decades of the new century, nonetheless, the cult and confraternity of the Virgin and San Roque still provided the devotional, organizational, and social focus of the religious life of the new parish. It was the confraternity itself, in fact, that undertook and paid for the work necessary to expand the parish church structure between the years 1508 and 1520 to meet the needs of the growing neighborhood as new immigrants continued to arrive.[1]

Postconquest Granada presents a unique opportunity to observe the creation of a new, local, urban Christian religious culture within the Iberian Peninsula. In the cities, towns, and villages of late-fifteenth- and early-sixteenth-century Castile from which the vast majority of the immigrants came, local religious cultures reflected centuries of development stretching back into the poorly documented mists of the Reconquest period. Because conquered Granada had no longstanding local Christian tradition, the comparably well-documented growth of Christian culture in the city during the period under study was quite literally a continuous process of creation and innovation.

Bearing in mind the particularly dynamic nature of frontier Granada's social and institutional landscapes outlined thus far, this chapter returns to some of the central questions raised in the introduction to this book: who created Christian Granada, how, and to what ends? Answers to these questions are predictably complex, but the example of the relatively humble Asturian immigrants, who shaped and developed their own parish church with little apparent guidance from archbishops or parish clergymen, is emblematic of a general trend. In the absence of strong leadership from either the upper echelons of the local church hierarchy or the parish clergy through the first half of the sixteenth century, local Christian culture in Granada grew in ways shaped primarily by the lay residents of the city itself. Local clergymen—especially the mendicant friars who established local foundations very quickly in the years after the conquest—must certainly be counted among the creators. Many of the most important and enduring religious institutions and traditions that comprised Granada's local Christian culture, however, grew from lay initiatives and lay-initiated dialogue with local clergy. Not surprisingly, the vast majority of these initiatives came from the Christian immigrant community. Though not entirely excluded from this process, the role of the moriscos in the creation of the frontier city's developing Christian religious culture was, by contrast, extremely limited.

Although the religious life of the postconquest frontier city involved the introduction of customs and traditions that were entirely new to Granadan soil, it would be an exaggeration to say that the city's religious life was created entirely ex nihilo. Obviously, religious beliefs and activities among much of Granada's "native" community continued to reflect their particular spiritual inheritance, as many of the city's supposedly Christian moriscos still rested their hope for salvation on the secret practice of the faith of their ancestors. Granada's immigrants also brought with them to the frontier city their own religious legacies, including not only myriad local devotions and practices specific to the hundreds of hometowns from which they had come, but also customs and controversies common to cities and villages across early modern Catholic Europe. The creation of Christian Granada, in fact, coincided with an era that was for all of Spain and most of Europe remarkable because of its creativity, vitality, and growing conflict in matters of religion. Throughout the reign of Charles V (1518–1556), controversial devotional and intellectual currents of both domestic and international origin continued to flow relatively freely among Spanish clergymen, academics, and even common lay people, and some of these broader developments were of fundamental significance in understanding the nature of the religious culture that developed in postconquest Granada.

From outside Spain, for example, came the influence of northern European spiritual movements such as the *devotio moderna,* as well as intellectual fashions such as Christian humanism, championed by the Dutch writer Erasmus of Rotterdam. Thousands of copies of Castilian translations of Erasmus's devotional works as well as his biting satires of church corruption, along with various spiritual guides by Spanish and foreign authors and devotional Books of Hours, sold rapidly at bookstores in Granada and across Spain to an increasingly literate Spanish laity.[2] Among Spanish intellectuals and clergymen, the Dutch humanist's more sophisticated theological works and scriptural philology also remained popular and influential throughout the first half of the sixteenth century, even in the wake of a controversial 1527 ecclesiastical assembly in Valladolid at which various churchmen raised concerns about the possible heterodoxy of some of his ideas.[3]

Meanwhile, from within Spain itself came a variety of innovative spiritual and mystical movements. Some, such as that of the Franciscan friar Francisco de Osuna and other writers who promoted what they termed *recogimiento* as a method of purposeful, prayerful, and contemplative contact with God, at times inched dangerously close to the edge of acceptable Catholic orthodoxy—an edge that remained very murky and poorly defined in the decades preceding the promulgation of the landmark doctrinal canons of the first convocation of the Council of Trent (1545–1547). Although often controversial, the *recogido* movement exerted fundamental influence on future Spanish saints such as Teresa of Avila, Ignatius Loyola, and—of particular importance from the point of view of this study—the "apostle of Andalusia," Juan de Avila.[4] Other groups, such as the *alumbrados* (or illuminati) led in the 1520s by the visionary Isabel de la Cruz, crossed nearly everyone's boundaries of acceptable orthodoxy in their emphasis on personal religious liberation through a passive spiritual union with God. Numbering among their adherents large numbers of common laboring-class lay women and men, many of them judeoconversos, the *alumbrados* proved mostly defenseless in the face of an onslaught of Inquisitorial persecution that gutted the original movement by the 1530s.[5] In frontier Granada, the *alumbrado* Juan López de Celaín—formerly a close friend and confidant of Isabel de la Cruz—actually managed in the relative anonymity of the frontier city in the 1520s to rise to the powerful positions of provisor of the archiepiscopal court and chaplain in the Royal Chapel before finally being prosecuted and burned at the stake as one of the first victims of Granada's newly established Inquisition tribunal in 1529.[6] Meanwhile, in the decades surrounding the failed Comuneros (1520–1521) and Germanías (1519–1522) rebellions, political protest and religious fervor merged in a wave of egalitarian, apocalyptic millenarianism that swept across Valencia and central Castile. Fueled by a group of socially radical Franciscan authors and preachers, these ideas were particularly popular among judeoconverso men and women.[7]

Setting aside the singular case of the illuminist López de Celaín, Granada's immigrant community was never a hotbed for these most radical forms of protest. Nonetheless, the general spiritual and intellectual ferment of the early sixteenth century that contributed to various transformations in the religious life of Spain and all of Europe also affected frontier Granada in profound and tangible ways. A 1544 inventory of the small bookstore owned by the immigrant Pedro de Torres reveals, for example, that Granada's residents, like most Spaniards of the era, had easy access to the works of all the leading Catholic theological and spiritual writers of the day. At the time of the inventory, Torres's store stocked more than 500 total volumes of 161 listed titles, including 14 different Books of Hours, devotional classics by foreign and native authors such as Thomas à Kempis and Francisco de Osuna, and various works of Erasmus of Rotterdam. More than half of its stock was dedicated to explicitly religious materials, including not only spiritual guides for lay people, but also more sophisticated theological works for the scholars and students of the university and pastoral manuals for parish clergymen. Torres's Granada bookstore resembled in its religious focus most Castilian bookshops of the era, and reflected the demands of a local market, at least among the immigrant community, whose devotional reading tastes appear to have differed little from those of Spain's other major cities.[8]

The creation of Christian Granada thus constitutes one episode in a much larger story of sixteenth-century religious change in Spain and Europe as a whole. Readers familiar with the wave of recent studies of "local religion" and reform in sixteenth-century Spain will not be surprised to read in the following pages several common storylines: poorly trained and morally wayward priests; endemic rivalry and legal wrangling between parish clergymen and regular religious orders; pervasive anticlericalism coupled ironically with devotional fervor among many of the immigrants; and bitter confrontations over attempts by some archbishops and humanist-trained churchmen to impose new, "reformed" standards of Christian education and behavior on clergy and laity alike.[9]

Yet for all the similarities, frontier Granada's local religious scene also remained fundamentally distinct from those of Spain's other major cities, and not only in terms of its enduring "morisco problem." The sheer quantity of new religious institutions established in Granada during the period under study, for example, was not only unique among Spanish cities, but it also must have proven bewildering to many of the city's immigrants and moriscos alike. Between 1492 and 1570, Granada witnessed the emergence of twenty-five new parishes, twenty-two monasteries and other houses pertaining to the religious orders, at least fifty lay religious brotherhoods (cofradías, or confraternities), eight major hospitals, and more than a dozen small shrines and chapels. Along with the ethnic division between immigrants and moriscos, the most significant condition that distinguished Granada's public religious culture from those of most other contemporary

Castilian cities was that each and every one of these institutions was a brand-new creation whose founders, staff, and promoters—lay and ecclesiastical alike—had above all to define an entirely new place for themselves in the emerging social, cultural, and institutional life of the postconquest city. The result of this was a particularly dynamic marketplace of local religious institutions and organizations that fostered innovative approaches to meeting the spiritual and social demands of the laity, particularly the Christian immigrants. Out of this volatile and creative milieu would emerge not only tensions that would contribute to the outbreak of the second morisco rebellion in 1568, but also reform-minded programs and ideas such as those of Juan de Dios and Juan de Avila that would exert profound influence on broader changes in Catholic Christendom as a whole in the era of the Council of Trent.

PARISH, MONASTERY, AND COMMUNITY

In the competition among local religious institutions for the devotional attention, time, and resources of the community as a whole, frontier Granada's parish clergy were the clear losers. Directing the religious life of the laity toward the parish—rather than to monasteries, private chapels, or shrines—had been a primary concern of the Roman Catholic church hierarchy since the reform era of the high Middle Ages. Pope Innocent III and the Fourth Lateran Council of 1215 ordered that each member of the Christian flock have his or her own parish in which to attend mass, confess, and receive the sacraments. In urban areas of Spain, as in much of Europe, however, the development of both parish organization and personal identification with the parish among the laity had been very slow and incomplete. The parish, intended to be the principal focal point of lay religious practice and the sole venue for the regular distribution of the sacraments to the laity, remained in early sixteenth-century Spanish cities only one of a variety of devotional and sacramental centers.

While parish organization was fairly weak in cities throughout early-sixteenth-century Spain, it was exceptionally so in frontier Granada. In other cities in the kingdom of Castile, for example, the number of sixteenth-century testators who requested burial in their parish churches rather than in a monastery was as high as 80 percent.[10] In Granada, however, only 45 percent of Christian immigrant testators requested burial in their parish churches. In addition, many of Granada's immigrants openly identified themselves as "parishioners" of local churches that were not parishes at all, but rather sanctuaries that pertained to local houses of the religious orders. In 1552, for example, day laborer Andrés Godínez testified in a civil trial that he was a parishioner of the "parish" of Los Mártires—at the time a house of Franciscan tertiaries.[11] Why was personal identification with parishes so weak among Granada's Christian immigrants?

As in many other cities in Catholic Europe, the weakness of the parish as a devotional center owed at least in part to the generally negative reputation of parish clergymen. In Granada, parish clergy were particularly prone, for example, to bickering about the size and distribution of incomes. Archbishop Avalos's proposed synodal constitutions of 1530 accused local parish priests of exploiting their positions by charging exorbitant amounts for the administration of the sacraments.[12] Moreover, the same decrees ordered that the priests (*curas*) and beneficed clergy (*beneficiados*) of the parishes put an end to their incessant arguing over who held the rights to various parish incomes, as such in-fighting greatly damaged the image of the clergy in the eyes of the laity.[13] Also harmful to the parish clergy's reputation was the ongoing struggle with their parishioners over control of parish purse strings. The 1501 foundation document placed parish account books squarely in the hands of a lay-elected churchwarden, or accounts-keeper (*mayordomo*), as was the custom in many areas of Spain.[14] In 1527, however, a royal letter accused the archbishops, cathedral chapter, and local clergy of ignoring these provisions of the foundation and simply allowing parish clergymen themselves to keep the accounts—an abuse that the crown ordered to cease.[15] The wording of the document leaves unclear exactly who petitioned the crown for such action against the clergy, but it is evident that at least some sectors of the lay community were upset by what they saw as greedy clergymen usurping the financial oversight of the parish that pertained legally to a lay-elected official.

Such stock images of greedy and parasitic parish clergymen were by no means unique to Granada. An understanding of the particular lack of personal identification with parish churches among Granada's Christian immigrants relative to those of other communities in Spain must therefore be based in other factors more specific to Granada's frontier society. First, for example, the institution of the parish itself depended in large measure on having a stable resident population of the sort that was difficult to find among the city's particularly mobile Christian immigrants. Granada's upper-level clergy, in fact, explicitly pointed to the transient nature of the local Old Christian population as an obstacle to parish identification among the laity. In 1548, the newly arrived archbishop Pedro Guerrero observed that the city's Christian immigrants seemed to change residences even within the city itself very frequently. Guerrero suspected that they did so with the conscious intent of avoiding the obligation of paying tithes in that parish: "Some Old Christians customarily move from one residence to another in order to prevent the parish clergy from having any record of them."[16]

Second, in recently conquered Granada, parish church edifices simply remained either unbuilt or under construction for much of the period under study. Initially, with the exception of Santa María Magdalena, all of Granada's new parishes were in fact installed in the recently consecrated mosques of the former Nasrid capital. Archbishop Talavera had in fact, already transformed some local mosques into Christian churches well before the official parish foundation document of 1501. One—the parish church of San José in the Alcazaba district—had been in operation in the consecrated Al Murabitin (Almoravid) mosque as early as 1494.[17] The great majority of the mosques, however, were converted into churches during and immediately after the mass baptisms of January and February 1500.[18] For at least the first four decades of the new century, parish-level worship in frontier Granada occurred almost exclusively in these former mosques—in physical settings that were distinctly Islamic in architectural style, décor, and character. As the century progressed, parish after parish gradually began to replace the old mosques with new church buildings. The process of construction of most of the churches that one can see today in Granada began in the 1520s and 1530s and continued off and on for the remainder of the century. Most of these new churches were built on the foundations of the old mosques themselves, and often in the distinctive mudéjar architectural style. Moreover, the construction process itself often interrupted religious services from time to time in most of the city's parishes throughout the sixteenth century. In short, although officially established in years around 1500, the actual infrastructure of Granada's new parishes remained very much a work in progress throughout the early postconquest period.

Compared with the parishes, some of the city's most popular religious orders—especially the mendicant friars—had a considerable head start in this regard. With the help of substantial crown endowments, the Franciscans, Dominicans, Hieronymites, and Mercedarians all established local houses immediately after the conquest. The Franciscans completed their new friary and church in the lower city by 1507, and the Dominicans finished construction of their new building in the same neighborhood shortly thereafter.[19] Other monasteries, convents, and friaries soon followed.[20] Those established in the crucial early years carried a distinct advantage. Some of them—especially, as we will see, the Franciscans' church—were among the city's principal centers of lay religious practice in the early sixteenth century.

In frontier Granada, the regular orders and secular clergy competed for the devotional lives of the laity in ways that paralleled similar struggles on Christian Spain's medieval reconquest frontiers on the one hand as well as its early modern empire in the Americas on the other. As had often been true on the *reconquista* frontiers of the thirteenth century, and as would again be the case in much of the New World, the balance in Granada tipped in favor of the friars, and especially the Franciscans, for much of the sixteenth century.[21] The nature of this conflict was largely economic, as parishes and religious orders alike depended heavily on the offerings, gifts, and bequests of the laity for their sustained success. In fundamental ways, local religious institutions—parishes and monasteries alike—were in fact creations of the laity. International religious orders could establish local houses, and the secular church hierarchy could mandate the foundation of parishes and even endow them with certain incomes and tithes to be paid by the laity. Ultimately, however, the growth and lasting success of most religious foundations depended on the goodwill and generosity of local laity, or at least some sector thereof.[22] The absence of long-standing traditions in frontier Granada, combined with the ongoing establishment of scores of new foundations throughout the period under study, meant that the city had a particularly open marketplace of religious institutions.

On what bases did lay people make choices between and among competing religious institutions as foci of their religious lives and recipients of their offerings and pious gifts? A lengthy court case in the late 1550s between the local Dominican friary of Santa Cruz and the secular clergy of the nearby parishes of San Matías, Santa Escolástica, and San Cecilio includes explicit testimony from numerous typical Granadan lay people regarding the relative popularity and roles in the community of the regular and secular clergy.[23] At issue in this case was the "funeral fourth" (*cuarta funeral*)—the right traditionally claimed by the parishes to collect from a monastery one-fourth of all the incomes from bequests and masses ordered by testators from their parishes who requested burial in and/or left such gifts to that monastery.[24] The Dominicans contended that Pope Sixtus IV's 1474 bull *Mare magnum* explicitly exempted their order from the obligation to pay the cuarta, while the parishes insisted that such payments were obligatory in all cases.

Both the Dominicans and the parish clergymen called a variety of witnesses to testify regarding their good reputation and relative poverty and the poor character and undeserved wealth of their opponents. For their part, the Dominicans had little trouble finding witnesses willing to tell specific stories about misbehavior on the part of the *curas* and *beneficiados* of the concerned parishes. Hernando López, a parishioner of Santa Escolástica, testified that the clergy of Santa Escolástica had recently kept possession for nearly two weeks of the rotting corpse of a woman who had requested burial in Santa Cruz, because her husband refused, on the Dominicans' advice, to pay the *cuarta*. The parish clergy's strong-arm technique worked, as the distraught widower eventually gave in and simply paid the *cuarta* in order to proceed with his wife's burial.[25] Three other witnesses testified that the parish clergy of San Matías extorted a gold ring and cash from Luis de Buentalmente in a similar scheme in which they refused to transfer the body of Buentalmente's mother-in-law to Santa Cruz for burial as she had requested. When news of this scandal spread to the archiepiscopal curia, an ecclesiastical judge quickly ordered the clergy of San Matías to return the gold ring to Buentalmente.[26]

Still, the testimony in this trial hardly supports simple characterizations of the laity's views of the friars as positive and of the secular clergy as negative. Although the Dominicans were theoretically a "mendicant" order, the Spanish popular imagination generally associated them more with the intellectual life of the universities and the rigorous defense of orthodoxy through the Inquisition than with any ideals of Christian humility or impoverished service.[27] Not surprisingly, the Dominicans could not find a single witness who would agree with their characterization of their house as impoverished and in desperate need of their exemption from paying the *cuarta*.[28] For their part, the parish clergy also tried to find witnesses to testify concerning their poverty. Not surprisingly, they found little sympathy among the laity, even among those whom they called as "friendly" witnesses. One of the witnesses for the parish clergy, Antón Sánchez, a ropemaker and resident of the parish of San Andrés, seemed surprised to hear that either of the two sides in this trial would claim to be poor. He testified along with nearly all of the other witnesses that the Dominicans, who had received a wealthy royal endowment during the time of Ferdinand and Isabella, were generally regarded as wealthy. The court then asked Sánchez about the poverty of the parish *beneficiados* who had called him to testify in their favor. The court scribe recorded his testimony:

> What the witness claims to know about this subject is that he holds all of the *beneficiados* to be wealthy men, and that there are certainly a number of monasteries and convents in this city that are poorer than they are, and that the said *beneficiados* eat quite well, and would continue to do so whether or not they were paid the *cuarta*."[29]

Had they known that he would give such testimony, the *beneficiados* probably would not have summoned him to answer this question in the first place. In testifying against the parish clergy, though, Sánchez also points us beyond the specific institutions involved in this case, none of which seems to have been held in the highest regard even by the lay witnesses whom they themselves chose to call. Though such information was not solicited by the question itself, Sánchez volunteered the idea that there were certain monasteries and convents in Granada that might be considered poor, or at least poorer than the *beneficiados*. Unfortunately, he did not specify the local institutions to which he was referring. Still, his testimony suggests that we should not take this case as evidence of a simple, cynical anticlericalism among Granada's Christian immigrants. Like Sánchez, most of the lay immigrants seem to have believed that there were, in fact, some religious institutions in the city that were not filled with greedy, parasitic clergymen, and some that were worthy of both their respect and their pious offerings.

Used cautiously, last wills and testaments provide one means of measuring the relative levels of respect and popularity among the laity enjoyed by the city's various religious institutions. Nearing death, each testator usually specified in his or her will for masses to be said in specific churches and/or for certain charitable gifts to ecclesiastical institutions or pious causes. Care must be taken, of course, in reading these testaments as evidence. The choices made by testators were not in all cases completely free ones. Certain formulaic or mandatory bequests (alternatively termed the *mandas acostumbradas* or *mandas forzosas*), for example, were either imposed on the testator or at least strongly encouraged by the notaries who recorded the testaments.[30] Also, certain nonmandatory bequests sometimes show up often in testaments written by certain notaries, suggesting that some notaries perhaps recommended certain institutions or causes to their testators, in which case the bequest may tell us more about the religious life of the notary than about that of the testator.

Bearing in mind these precautions, I have compiled a database of 163 Christian immigrant last wills and testaments written in the city of Granada from the 1520s to the 1570s. In constructing such a database, one must also take care to insure that the sample is as representative as possible of the community under study. In terms of sex, the data include the testaments of eighty-three women and eighty men. With regard to socioeconomic class, the data are also reasonably representative. Sixty-three of the 163 testaments (39 percent) provided specific information concerning the professions of the testator and/or of family members, and of these sixty-three, thirty-five (56 percent) came from families of laborers or artisans—numbers that correspond fairly well with the economic contours of the Christian immigrant community as a whole summarized earlier in table 1.2. In terms of age, one might expect in any database of last wills and testaments a strong bias toward older men and women. Although such is true to a degree with the numbers presented here, it should be noted that the testators also included several younger men and women in their twenties and thirties. Such testaments are surprisingly common in sixteenth-century notarial records, since young women frequently wrote wills while preparing for the perils of childbirth and young men often did so before going off to war. Of the 163 testators in the database, seven (three soldiers and four pregnant women) gave clear indication that they were young. Several other testators, moreover, mentioned living parents either as executors or heirs, suggesting that they were not terribly old. Finally, the data are also chronologically balanced across the period under study, including twenty-eight wills from the 1520s, twenty-eight from the 1530s, twenty-four from the 1540s, twenty from the 1550s, thirty-two from the 1560s, and thirty-one from the 1570s.

With regard to the ordering of requiem and memorial masses and mass cycles, Granada's Christian immigrant testaments follow patterns similar but not identical to those revealed by studies of wills in other sixteenth-century Spanish locales. As in the Castilian cities of Madrid and Cuenca, for example, virtually all of Granada's immigrant testators made specific provisions for the saying of masses for the benefit of their own souls and often for those of deceased family members and/or other souls in purgatory. As in these other cities, moreover, the quantity of masses requested by Granada's testators increased dramatically through the course of the sixteenth century. From an average of 28 masses per testator in the 1520s, the mean nearly tripled to 83 in the 1570s—a rate of growth that virtually mirrored similarly rapid increases in Cuenca and Madrid. In terms of total numbers of masses, however, Granada's testators appear to have remained somewhat restrained compared with those of these two Castilian cities. In Madrid, the average quantity of masses requested was especially high, rising from 90 per will in the 1520s to 476 in the 1570s [31] In Cuenca, the numbers were not nearly as large as those of Madrid, but they were still substantially higher than Granada's, increasing from approximately 60–70 masses per testator before 1535 to 136 in 1545, and to 173 in 1585.[32]

Concerning provision in their wills for charitable bequests to ecclesiastical institutions and pious causes, by contrast, Granada's immigrant community was distinguished by a rate of giving that was strikingly higher than those of the other sixteenth-century Spanish cities that have been studied. In Madrid, for example, only about 10 percent of sixteenth-century wills included provisions for any charitable giving beyond the prescribed *mandas acostumbradas,* and in Cuenca the figure appears not to have been much higher.[33] In Granada, a remarkable 106 of 163 testaments (65 percent) included specific provisions for pious giving outside of the context of the *mandas forzosas.* This tendency among Granada's wills to direct a higher proportion of available resources toward charitable bequests, and less toward masses, likely reflects at least in part the specific needs of the frontier city, where, as we have seen, the expensive physical infrastructure of local churches, monasteries, and beneficent institutions such as hospitals and schools remained very much under construction for the bulk of the period under study.

Analysis of testators' choices concerning which local religious institutions to make recipients of their bequests and mass orders reveals a clear preference for the city's mendicant orders and hospitals over the secular clergy and the parishes. It is true that the vast majority of testators (137 of 163) made some mention of their own parishes as recipients of mass orders and/or pious bequests. In most cases, however, mention of the parish appears to have been just a matter of custom. Bequests to parishes, for example, were typically very small, ranging from only one *maravedí* to one or two *reales* (1 real equaled 34 maravedís) and were almost always accompanied in the texts of testaments by the formulaic statement that such money was given "in honor and reverence of sacraments received," all in accordance with common notarial practice. The frequency with which the parishes were mentioned in the testaments should thus not necessarily be interpreted as an indication of their centrality in the religious lives of Granada's Christian immigrants. This becomes especially clear when one compares the amounts of money left by testators to their parishes with the amounts they left to Granada's monasteries, hospitals, and other local religious institutions. Excluding the seventeen wealthier testators whose total pious gifts exceeded two ducats (1 ducat equaled 375 *maravedís*) and whose data, if included, would skew significantly the image of a "normal" giver,[34] the average immigrant testator in Granada between 1520 and 1569 gave 50.72 *maravedís* to his or her parish, compared with 122.85 *maravedís* to other local ecclesiastical and charitable institutions.[35] If we factor back in the seventeen wealthy testators and examine the total amount of bequests in order to gauge the overall income from testamentary giving of the city's parishes relative to that of Granada's regular orders and other local religious institutions, the disparity becomes even more dramatic. The 132 testaments covering the period 1520–1569, for example, include a grand total of only 12,064 *maravedís* in gifts to the parishes (or 92 per testator), compared with 137,428 *maravedís* to hospitals, monasteries, or other local religious institutions (or 1049 per testator).[36]

Of course, pious bequests represent only a fraction of the total revenues of parishes and parish clergymen, and the city's *curas* and *beneficiados* were by no means impoverished as a result of the laity's tendency to favor the regular orders in their testamentary giving. In addition to receiving a cut of parishioners' regular tithes and specific charges for administration of sacraments as dictated by the terms of the parishes' 1501 foundation document,[37] a potentially large source of money for clergymen lay in the regular saying of weekly, monthly, or annual memorial masses richly and "perpetually" endowed by some testators for the benefit of own souls as well as, customarily, those of departed family members (past, present, and future) in purgatory.[38] Of the 163 testators under study, only 25 endowed such foundations. Of the 25, moreover, only 8 went to the testator's parish church in Granada, with the remaining 17 being directed to the city's regular orders. Most individual testators, then, obviously could not afford such foundations, and those who did usually chose the friars over their parish clergy as custodians. Nonetheless, even a handful of these foundations could help to raise parish clergymen's incomes well above those of skilled artisans. By 1569, for example, the two *beneficados* of the Alcazaba parish of San José near Granada's Royal Chancery—a large parish that at the time housed more than seventeen hundred parishioners— regularly fulfilled the provisions of only fourteen such foundations, but they earned in return for these services an extra 32,231 *maravedís* in annual incomes.[39]

Unlike the parishes, whose inclusion in lists of pious bequests was largely a matter of custom and notarial convention, the mention of other local religious institutions seems to have been much more a matter of personal choice. Table 5.1 summarizes the total number of testators in this study's database who included each of the listed local religious institutions as the recipient of pious bequests or mass orders. Among the city's regular-order houses, the Franciscans' main local foundation—called simply "San Francisco"—was clearly preferred, with 40 percent (66 of 163) of testators either leaving a bequest to or ordering masses from it. Moreover, the Franciscans' popularity cut across all lines of gender and class. The apparent popularity of the next three most-mentioned monastic houses—the Trinitarian foundation Santísima Trinidad, the Observant Franciscan house Nuestra Señora de la Victoria, and the Mercedarians' Nuestra Señora de la Merced—is in part illusory. All three were included at various times in the lists of customary bequests suggested by the notaries. Sometimes, especially in the earliest periods covered by the database, they were listed separately in testaments, with no explicit indication of their status as customary bequests. Still, all three are frequently mentioned outside of the context of the *mandas acostumbradas,* and they remained throughout the period among the city's most popular recipients of mass orders and charitable gifts. As "redemptive" orders who took as a major duty the ransoming of Christian captives from Muslim lands, the Mercedarians and Trinitarians were popular recipients of bequests throughout Spain,[40] and especially so in frontier Granada. Perhaps not surprisingly given the testimony cited in the *cuarta funeral* trial discussed above, the local Dominican foundation of Santa Cruz was relatively unpopular, being mentioned by only 7 percent of testators.

One additional caution should be inserted concerning the interpretation of these data. Obscured somewhat in the summary provided by this table is the fact that some of the institutions mentioned were established fairly late in the period covered by the database, and their popularity relative to other institutions is thus masked to a degree by the fact that they could not have been mentioned by earlier testators. This is especially true in the case of the Hospital of Juan de Dios, which became a genuine sensation among charitable givers in Granada after the death of its founder in 1550. Counting only the data after 1550, Juan de Dios's hospital was mentioned by twenty-three of eighty-three testators (27 percent)—a figure which places it squarely among the city's most popular recipients of pious bequests from the 1550s to the 1570s. Moreover, the amounts of money given by testators to the hospital were often extremely large. Those who chose to give to Juan de Dios's foundation in most cases made it their largest recipient of pious bequests, and many gave more money to the hospital than to all other recipients of their gifts combined.[41]

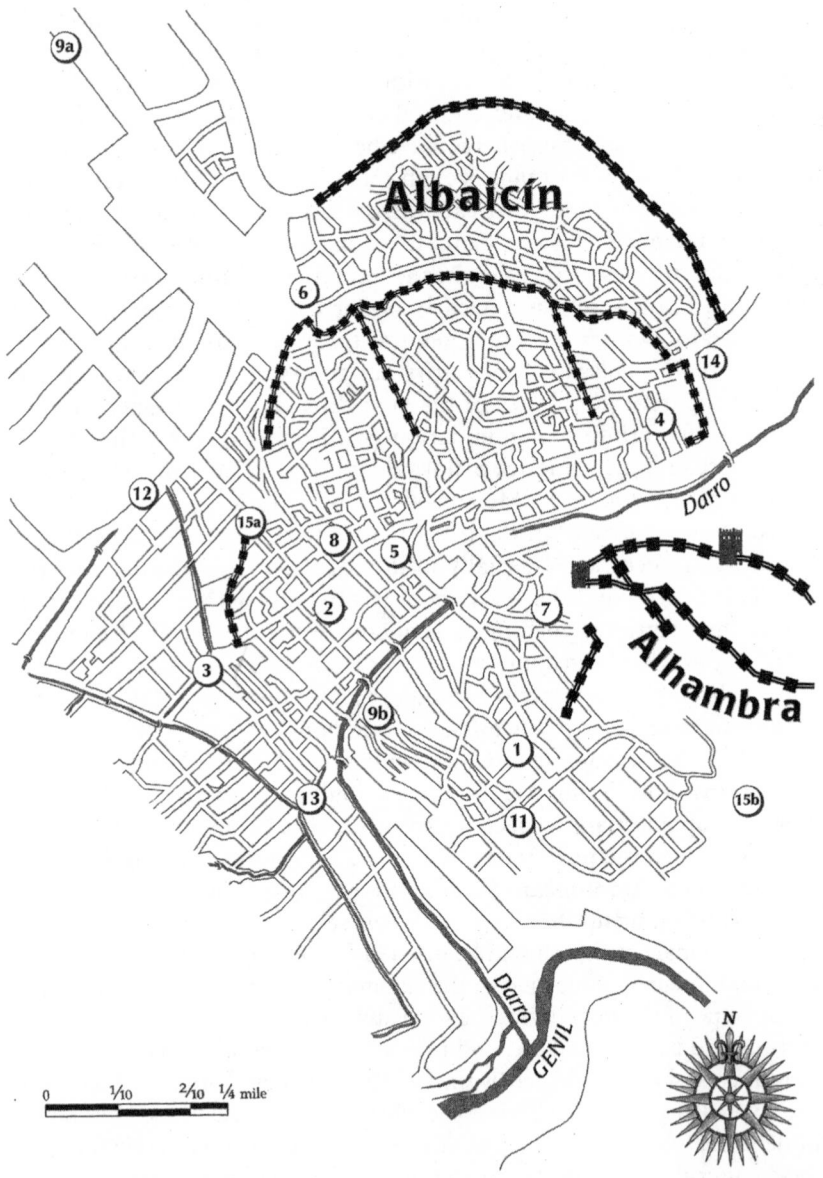

9a

Albaicín

6

14

4

Darro

12

15a

8

5

Alhambra

2

7

3

9b

1

13

15b

11

Darro

GENIL

N

0   1/10   2/10   1/4 mile

Map prepared by Dick Gilbreath at the University of Kentucky Cartography Lab

MAP 3. Numbers on Map 3 correspond with the locations of the numbered religious institutions listed in Table 5.1.

TABLE 5.1 Local Religious and Beneficent Institutions Most Frequently Mentioned by Christian Immigrant Lay Testators in Granada as Recipients of Mass Orders and or Pious Bequests 1520–1570s

Institution and Date Founded	Women (n=83)	Men (n=80)	Total (n=163)
1. San Francisco (Franciscans), 1492	33	33	66 (40%)
2. Obra of the Cathedral	31	28	59 (36%)
3. Santísima Trinidad (Trinitarians), ca. 1517	25	21	46 (28%)
4. Nuestra Señora de la Victoria (Observant Franciscans), 1509	26	16	42 (26%)
5. Hospital of Corpus Christi, ca. 1520	22	14	36 (22%)
6. Nuestra Señora de la Merced (Mercedarians), 1492	16	9	25 (15%)
7. Hospital of Juan de Dios, 1537	14	9	23 (14%)
8. San Agustín (Augustinians), 1513	13	7	20 (12%)
9a. Hospital of San Lázaro, ca. 1492 (Leper Hospital)	10	8	18 (11%)
9b. Nuestra Señora de la Cabeza (Carmelites), 1508	13	5	18 (11%)
11. Santa Cruz la Real (Dominicans), 1492	9	3	12 (7%)
12. San Jerónimo (Hieronymites), 1492	5	5	10 (6%)
13. San Antón (Franciscan Tertiaries), ca. 1492	5	4	9 (6%)
14. San Antonio (Observant Franciscans), 1534	7	1	8 (5%)
15a. La Encarnación (Poor Clares), 1524	5	1	6 (4%)
15b. Los Mártires (Franciscan Tertiaries), ca. 1492	4	2	6 (4%)

What do testators' choices reveal about the values of the Christian immigrants and about the nature of the local religious culture they were creating? What was it that made institutions and groups such as the Franciscan friars and the hospital of Juan de Dios so popular among the frontier city's immigrant laity? A 1565 letter from a *beneficiado* of Santa Escolástica parish to Archbishop Pedro Guerrero suggesting reforms needed in the archdiocese provides a voice from the losers' side in the competition among religious institutions: "The friars of the monasteries should not be allowed go out to peoples' houses to conduct confessions among the sick, because this practice encourages the laity to disregard their parish clergy and flee from their parishes, and thus the priests do not know each member of their flocks. From this situation comes the general damnation of the community."[42]

The *beneficiado*'s inflammatory rhetoric is typical of the state of relations between the friars and the secular clergy of Granada's parishes. By identifying the practice of venturing out into the community to administer sacraments to the sick inside their homes as a source of the friars' popularity among the laity, he points toward an important difference in lay perceptions of the regular and secular clergy. What the Franciscans, the brothers of the Hospital of Juan de Dios, and other locally popular institutions offered that the parish clergy often did not was a high level of participation in a wide range of religious, social, and charitable activities that transcended the walls of the church buildings themselves. Various lay groups—especially through the vehicle of the lay religious brotherhoods (or confraternities) that will be discussed momentarily—were constructing a vibrant public religious culture in Granada in the first half of the sixteenth century. Often, these groups issued calls for the city's clergy to join in their activities. Although Granada's secular clergy balked, many of the city's noncloistered regular orders participated actively in lay-initiated public religious activities. Friars, most often Franciscans, almost always gave sermons at public religious festivities organized by lay groups and institutions such as confraternities and the municipal council.[43]

Franciscan popularity among Granada's immigrant laity, moreover, extended beyond the order's principal local foundation. Besides San Francisco, most of the other ten local Franciscan foundations (five male houses and five female convents) were also frequent recipients of lay bequests and mass orders.[44] Importantly, various local Franciscan foundations had received critical support from Queen Isabella and King Ferdinand in the early years after the conquest. In addition to the large endowment granted by the Catholic Monarchs to the main house of San Francisco, Isabella also provided for the rapid construction of a new Franciscan Poor Clares convent, called Santa Isabel la Real, which opened in the heart of the Albaicín in 1504.[45]

As the data in table 5.1 clearly indicate, women were more likely than men to include pious bequests and mass orders in their testaments, and Franciscan foundations were particularly popular among female testators. In addition to the broader roles played by the regular orders in the religious life of the community as a whole, they provided services and opportunities of particular significance to many women. To women facing poverty, widows, and beaten or abandoned wives, for example, convents throughout Catholic Europe often provided shelter and refuge.[46] In Granada, the Franciscan Poor Clare foundation of Nuestra Señora de la Encarnación, founded in 1524, was particularly important in this regard. Doña Isabel de Avalos (known locally as Isabel de la Cruz), the sister of Archbishop Avalos and abbess of the convent, refused to turn away any woman who came to the house in need. The house thus became extremely crowded and often faced financial insolvency in its early years. Largely because of the pious reputation of its abbess, who was treated locally as a saint after her death, however, La Encarnación became the most popular recipient of lay gifts among local female houses (although in Granada as elsewhere, convents of nuns generally received far fewer pious gifts than did male houses).[47] Moreover, as María del Mar Graña Cid has argued, female Franciscanism among the religious orders offered women the greatest range of options, as they could choose to take vows either as Poor Clares or in the observant Franciscan order of the Immaculate Conception, or not take vows at all and remain in a house as a lay sister of the Franciscan Third Order of Penitence.[48] Granada's various Franciscan institutions, that is to say, served well a variety of social needs among the women and men of the immigrant community.

Finally, the main Franciscan friary of the lower city also housed many of the city's most active and influential lay religious brotherhoods, connecting the friars to some of the groups that proved most important in shaping the city's nascent public religious traditions and customs. Of the four local confraternities most frequently requested by testators for accompaniment in funeral processions, three were based in San Francisco: the penitential brotherhood of Santa Vera Cruz (10 percent of testators), the confraternity of Nuestra Señora de la Concepción (6 percent), and notably, the brotherhood of San Sebastián (7 percent), whose annual procession and feast each January was a centerpiece of Granada's local festive calendar.[49]

CONFRATERNITIES AND COMMUNITY TRADITIONS

Because the merchant community figured so prominently among Granada's early Christian immigrants, it is not surprising that they were the moving force in the creation of some of the conquered city's earliest public religious rituals and traditions. A local shrine dedicated to San Sebastián provided the focal point for the devotion of the confraternity of San Sebastián, whose membership consisted primarily of wealthy merchants.[50] This shrine was located on the banks of the Genil River, on the southern edge of town next to the main bridge over the river, near the spot where Boabdil surrendered the city to the Catholic Monarchs on January 2, 1492. The exact date of construction of this shrine is unknown, but it was located on a site formerly used by Muslims as a place of prayer, and it became a Christian devotional center shortly after the conquest. The date of the foundation of the confraternity is unclear. A brief eighteenth-century manuscript history of the confraternity explained that the brotherhood originated as a "simple congregation," with no official church approval or written bylaws (constituciones) whatsoever.[51] The confraternity was initially based in the shrine of San Sebastián next to the Genil River bridge just outside of town, from which it moved to a chapel that it founded, also dedicated to San Sebastián, in the nearby newly constructed Franciscan friary of the lower city. Meanwhile, the members, or cofrades, maintained their control over the shrine.

By 1531, when it received official approval of its constitutions from Archbishop Gaspar de Avalos, the confraternity of San Sebastián had already become an important and highly visible element of local religious culture. Part of the confraternity's prestige within the community stemmed from the procession it organized for the feast of San Sebastián each January to its shrine by the Genil bridge. It is unclear when this procession was instituted—perhaps during the 1521 local outbreak of the plague, against which Catholics universally regarded San Sebastián as a protector. Judging by the obvious wealth of the confraternity and its members, the procession was certainly a visually spectacular event. In 1540, the confraternity for the first time petitioned the cathedral chapter to join in the celebration by accompanying them on this procession each year.[52] The cathedral chapter declined to participate in the entire procession, explaining that custom allowed them only to lend certain ornaments to the confraternity, to permit the procession to begin inside the cathedral (at the time still housed in the old main mosque), and to accompany the procession only as far as the cathedral's doors. However, they could not, they explained, leave the cathedral.[53] As we will see, this was neither the first nor the only occasion when the cathedral chapter declined lay invitations to take to the streets to participate in the nascent public ritual and ceremonial life of the city.

Confraternities such as those of San Sebastián and the Asturian immigrants' brotherhood of the Virgin and San Roque constituted one of the principal means for the organization and expression of lay piety and community religious activity throughout late medieval and early modern Catholic Europe.[54] Recent scholarly interpretation of the confraternities and their role in pre-Tridentine Catholic society has emphasized two principal themes. First, such religious brotherhoods were lay-controlled means of organizing local religious life, often filling spiritual and social voids created by the inadequacies of the parish-level clergy and other local church institutions. The confraternities usually had their own religious images, chapels, and shrines, and they even employed their own ordained chaplains who administered the sacraments. Moreover, these organizations were in many cases independent of the direct oversight of the local clergy. As such, the confraternities in many localities of fifteenth- and early-sixteenth-century Catholic Europe played a more decisive role in defining local religious practice than did the clergy. In Toledo, one parish priest complained that, "with so many brotherhoods, the laymen are in such firm control that they order the priests around as if they were day laborers."[55]

Second, recent scholarship has shed light on the ways in which confraternities functioned to alleviate social and economic tensions within communities. Through charitable activities both among their own members and throughout the community, the brotherhoods helped to forge vertical bonds of solidarity in local societies. Their festive banquets and celebrations often brought together men and women, cofrades and non-cofrades alike, from across the local social spectrum. Moreover, confraternities served to police the behavior of their own members and to provide a forum in which disputes among cofrades could be resolved without recourse to official authorities. In many confraternities, members were forbidden to file lawsuits against one another; instead, all disputes were to be settled within the context of the brotherhood.

In addition to their critical roles in harmonizing social relations, confraternities could also serve as vehicles for the social and economic advancement of particular groups. This was especially true in frontier Granada. The invention of new confraternities and new religious traditions in the post-conquest city occurred alongside the gradual and irregular development of the city's social, economic, and political power structures. Authority and its symbolic expressions were largely open and undetermined issues in the dynamic social landscape of frontier Granada—matters to be defined by those who had the means and took the initiative to do so. Confraternities provided an important avenue by which such initiatives were taken. The invention and/or promotion of a particular devotion, public ritual, or tradition could bring to a confraternity and its members not only social prestige, but also economic strength through the offerings and bequests of the laity of the broader community. On the cynical side, especially before greater archiepiscopal regulation of the confraternities was imposed in the 1560s in the wake of the Tridentine reforms, such pious offerings were easily and apparently frequently embezzled for personal use by cofrades in some brotherhoods. Writing as an "interested citizen" in 1565, for example, Granada resident Pero Sánchez Toledano implored Granada's archbishop Guerrero to take strong action against the cofrades of three local brotherhoods who regularly collected alms at the city's public executions for the purpose of ordering masses for the soul of the condemned, but actually used only a small fraction of the money for masses and pocketed the rest for themselves.[56]

Frontier Granada's confraternities grew gradually in the years after the conquest. From surviving last wills and testaments, parish registers, municipal council proceedings, cathedral chapter records, and recent studies by Miguel Luis López Muñoz and Amalia García Pedraza, I have compiled what I believe to be a very nearly complete list of fifty confraternities established in the city in the period 1492–1569, although there may have been a few others that have escaped notice. Of the city's immigrant population as a whole, moreover, roughly one-third participated actively in the brotherhoods as cofrades.[57] Although fewer than half of Granada's immigrants were active cofrades, the importance of the brotherhoods in the broader public religious life of the community is made evident by a variety of sources. Of the 163 testators sampled for this study, for example, 129 (nearly 80 percent) named at least one local confraternity to accompany their funeral processions. Some of the brotherhoods, moreover, played critical roles in shaping a number of the frontier city's most visible and most popular new local religious institutions and traditions—including, for example, the hospital endowed and operated by the cofrades of San Sebastián, as well as the brotherhood's annual procession and festival.

What sorts of factors determined the relative success or failure of

Granada's various new confraternities as contributors to the development of local Christian culture? How did confraternal activities relate to the social, economic, and political structures and tensions of the community as a whole? Membership in confraternities appears to have been fairly uniform across class lines in Granada, with the city's laborers and artisans, if anything, somewhat more likely to be *cofrades* than their wealthier neighbors. Of the testators who identified themselves as laborers or artisans, 42 percent were members of confraternities—a total slightly higher than that of the community as a whole. Still, one might expect that those confraternities having the most impact on local religious culture would be those with the most resources, and hence those with the highest proportions of members drawn from the wealthier classes of the city—especially the merchants and well-educated royal bureaucrats. The wealth of its merchant *cofrades*, for example, must certainly be considered a contributing factor to the success of the confraternity of San Sebastián.

Most of Granada's confraternities, however, were not composed of wealthy members, nor were the richest brotherhoods necessarily the most influential. Unlike the confraternity of San Sebastián, that of Nuestra Señora de las Angustias (Our Lady of Anguishes) did not consist primarily of wealthy *cofrades*. Instead, its membership consisted almost entirely of artisans and skilled laborers.[58] Though certainly not destitute, the members of this confraternity did not have the same level of resources available to a wealthier brotherhood such as that of San Sebastián. The original constitutions of the confraternity of las Angustias, for example, included a provision by which two brothers were regularly selected to go out into the streets to beg alms from the community, a practice they justified on the grounds that "the confraternity is poor, and its expenses are great."[59] Moreover, the confraternity did not even have its own image of Christ for its processions, and it regularly had to borrow one from a church or another confraternity until it finally found the funds to commission its own statue in 1582.[60]

Still, from the foundation of this brotherhood through the end of the sixteenth century, these artisans successfully promoted devotion to their image to the degree that the Virgin of las Angustias became universally regarded as patron of the city, and it has been an enduring, if at times controversial, symbol of the city ever since. In the troubled civil war–era Granada of Federico García Lorca, the image served as a rallying symbol for local fascists, whose request for a special procession of the Angustias image to celebrate General Francisco Franco's entry into Madrid was flatly refused by Granada's largely republican municipal council.[61] Even in the mostly secularized and generally socialist-voting society of Granada today, one can hardly find a business, restaurant, or bar that does not prominently display a cheap gift-store replica or picture of the Virgin of Angustias. Given the central and lasting role that it attained so quickly in Granada's cultural history, local historians traditionally assumed that its earliest promoters must have been among Granada's wealthy elite. As recently as 1989, Miguel Luis López Muñoz, the leading historian of Granada's confraternities, speculated that the founders of the brotherhood must have been prominent citizens of the city.[62] Although written in a difficult sixteenth-century script, the detailed records of the confraternity's activities in the 1580s and 1590s make it clear, however, that as the confraternity developed into the city's most prestigious brotherhood, its membership never strayed, at least not through the end of the sixteenth century, from its roots among the immigrant artisans and skilled laborers of the city.

How were these otherwise average residents of the city able to attract to their cause the devotion and gifts of the broader community? Like that of San Sebastián, the confraternity of las Angustias began in the early years of the sixteenth century as an unofficial group of lay devotees to a particular image. The image in this case was a small painting of the Virgin, reputedly brought to Granada by Queen Isabella herself and installed in an outdoor public shrine just inside one of the city gates on Granada's southern side. Local oral tradition, recorded in the eighteenth century, held that

> the people of that neighborhood held great devotion toward this image, which moved all of them to pay homage to her with such zeal that it could not be contained within their general and separate gifts and honors. Rather, the devotees united themselves in a confraternity, and this brotherhood multiplied the cult, celebration, and attendance of this Virgin to the degree that it became necessary for them to establish their own chapel. And, as the devotion and zeal of the brotherhood increased, it moved in 1545 to obtain official approval of its constitutions.[63]

Among other things, these 1545 constitutions outlined a variety of masses, annual festivals, and sermons commissioned by the confraternity in its small shrine.[64]

Sometime shortly after 1545, the sacred painting of the Virgin that had served as the primary object of the confraternity's devotion was replaced, in a mysterious and reputedly miraculous way, by a sculpted image of the Virgin. The legend surrounding the appearance of the new Virgin maintained that some silkworkers who were members of the confraternity visited Toledo and were enraptured by the beauty of an image of Our Lady of Sorrows (*Nuestra Señora de los Dolores*) in one of Toledo's monasteries. They asked members of the Toledan confraternity dedicated to that image to seek out a craftsman there in Toledo who could produce a similar image for the Granada's confraternity. Some months or years later, the Granada *cofrades,* having never received notice or indication of price from Toledo, assumed that their request had been forgotten. However, one day two elderly men showed up at the confraternity's chapel in Granada with a beautiful new statue of the grieving Virgin and the lifeless body of her son. After adoring the new image for a while, the *cofrades* turned around to thank the bearers of the beautiful gift, only to see that the two elderly men had disappeared. The confraternity then ordered some of its members to go to Toledo to offer formal thanks. Upon arriving in Toledo, however, the commission was told that no such image had been ordered or sent by the Toledan brotherhood and that no one in Toledo had ever heard of or seen anyone matching the description of the two old men who had delivered the statue to Granada.[65] The true origins of the statue of the Virgin of las Angustias were thus shrouded in mystery—mystery that was quickly publicized as a miracle for the benefit of the budding confraternity. The miraculous image gained a large local following in Granada, so large that the confraternity reaped sufficient financial benefit to transform itself from an average confraternity into one of the city's wealthiest.

Additions to the confraternity's constitutions made in 1556 indicate that the brotherhood had become by that point a penitential confraternity—one that engaged in disciplinary acts such as flagellation during their Holy Thursday night procession each year.[66] Such penitential confraternities were often considered especially dangerous by many clergymen throughout Catholic Europe, who feared that the laity regarded such self-mortification as a particularly powerful means of obtaining divine grace without recourse to the church and its sacraments. Such brotherhoods tended, in fact, to be well respected among laymen of all social classes, even though their *cofrades* generally came from working-class backgrounds.[67] In the years after the Council of Trent, archbishops Guerrero and Méndez de Salvatierra would take various measures to obstruct the growth of the popularity of the Angustias brotherhood, perhaps because it represented in the eyes of the laity such a powerful alternative means to grace.

In the 1550s and early 1560s, however, little impeded the confraternity's rise. It not only sought and received papal approval of its activities and constitutions,[68] but also began forging alliances with other powerful forces both inside and outside the community of Granada. Among the new members attracted to the confraternity in this period were the cloth-shearer Pablo Cabrera, the town crier Alonso Rodríguez, and the steward of the Hospital of San Sebastián Hernando Mexía. Cabrera, who was to remain an active *cofrade* until his death in 1587, served as president of the confraternity in 1556, when the new bylaws concerning the disciplinary procession were added. In 1584, when King Philip II personally requested from the confraternity information regarding its nature and history, Cabrera was apparently the only one of the generation of *cofrades* that produced the constitutions of 1545 and 1556 still alive, or at least the only one still active. The confraternity's brief report to the king, certainly written or at least informed by Cabrera, is among the few surviving firsthand accounts of the confraternity's activities in its early years.[69] Rodríguez, who died in 1558, was heavily in debt and was unable to leave monetary bequests to any religious cause, but he did choose to be buried in his confraternal tunic. Though he could not have been of much financial help to the confraternity, he did have connections both with the municipal councilors, for whom he worked, and with Archbishop Guerrero, for whom he had conducted numerous auctions.[70] Mexía, who was also a *cofrade* of the brotherhood of San Sebastián, may have been related to the powerful Mexía members of the municipal council, and thus may have provided the confraternity with further connections among the city's emerging political elite.[71]

Taking advantage of these and other avenues into the broader community, the otherwise humble *cofrades* of Angustias succeeded in promoting devotion to the Virgin of Angustias at all levels of the immigrant community. The confraternity received bequests, mass orders, and requests for funeral accompaniment not only from the poor of the city such as Leonor Juarez,[72] the widow of a day laborer, but also from wealthy devotees such as the noblewoman Doña María de Camacho.[73] Such gifts could be quite large. Doña Felipa de Córdoba, for example, granted the confraternity rental properties that earned 130 ducats per year.[74]

The confraternity also reached outside the community to attract the attention of the two men who became the brotherhood's most powerful allies—King Philip II and his half-brother Don Juan de Austria. In 1567, Philip granted the confraternity a number of properties surrounding its tiny chapel in order that the structure might be expanded to meet the needs created by the city's growing devotion to the image.[75] In 1569, when Don Juan de Austria came to Granada on his way to put down the morisco rebellion in the Alpujarras, he chose to pray in front of the Virgin of Angustias and to entrust the success of his campaign to her. Such was his devotion to this image that he became a *cofrade* of the brotherhood. Upon his victorious return from the Alpujarras campaign, he went back to the chapel to pray and give thanks to the Virgin of Angustias.[76] Today, a large portrait of the brotherhood's most famous *cofrade* still hangs in the confraternity's chapter hall.

Decades later, in 1638, local chronicler Francisco Henríquez de Jorquera described the confraternity of Angustias as one of the city's most prestigious—a status toward which it had already made significant steps by 1570:

> It is one of the wealthiest confraternities in Granada, and the alms and
> gifts that it receives are very large due to the great devotion that can be
> found throughout Granada for its miraculous image. . . . The gifts received
> by this confraternity are indeed wondrous, so much so that after having
> met all of its expenses, which are themselves great, much money remains.
> This money is then taken and invested in rent-bearing properties and other
> possessions such that incomes continue to increase year after year.[77]

All the while, the confraternity continued to draw its members from the artisans and skilled laborers of the city. In the minutes of the meetings of the brotherhood in the 1580s and 1590s, the professions of thirteen *cofrades* are noted. Included among them are two cloth-shearers, two bar-bers, two ropemakers, two tailors, one armorer, one clothes-seller, one tan-ner, and one shopkeeper.[78] From relatively humble origins, and often against the opposition of the city's high clergy, this confraternity con-structed one of the city's most important and enduring cultural symbols and enjoyed the financial and social benefits that came with it. As the case of the brotherhood of las Angustias illustrates, the active roles played by Granada's confraternities in the creation of the public religious traditions of the newly conquered city spanned the class divisions of the Christian immi-grant community.

Among the moriscos, by contrast, confraternal activity appears to have been rare at all social levels. The sources provide evidence of only two morisco confraternities in the Albaicín, both of which were founded in the 1560s: the male confraternity of La Resurrección based in San Salvador parish and the female sisterhood of La Concepción de Nuestra Señora. Re-garding the specific activities of the morisca sisterhood, we know next to nothing. The men's confraternity, however, was a matter of some contro-versy in the city. In his history of the second rebellion, Diego Hurtado de Mendoza asserted that the brotherhood of La Resurrección had been noth-ing more than an elaborate subterfuge beneath the cover of which the most embittered members of the city's morisco community met regularly to dis-cuss and plan rebellion. According to Hurtado de Mendoza, the morisco *cofrades* of La Resurrección often traveled throughout the towns and vil-lages of the Alpujarras under the guise of collecting alms, while their true mission was to coordinate plans with their armed brethren of the rural *monfíes*.[79] In her study of morisco testaments, however, García Pedraza has demonstrated that, at least in terms of its daily activities in the city, the brotherhood functioned in much the same way as a traditional Spanish con-fraternity, providing funeral procession accompaniment, organizing reli-gious festivities, and even operating its own hospital for the care of the poor and the sick in the Albaicín.[80]

Morisco membership in lay religious brotherhoods, moreover, was not strictly limited to the two Albaicín confraternities. Some moriscos also be-longed to Christian immigrant-majority brotherhoods, including Lorenzo Albeytar, who noted in his 1564 testament that he was simultaneously a *cofrade* of La Resurrección and of the predominantly Christian immigrant confraternity of El Santísimo Sacramento (the Most Blessed Sacrament) in the parish of San Pedro y San Pablo.[81] Overall, however, few such cases have been discovered, and the role of the moriscos in the broader confrater-nal life of the city as a whole appears to have been minimal.

Under the direction of Archbishop Talavera, by contrast, Granada's morisco community appears to have played an appreciable and somewhat ironic role in the early development of one of the city's most important pub-lic religious observances—the festival of Corpus Christi. Of course, the importance of Corpus celebrations was by no means unique to Granada; the festival of Corpus Christi had grown dramatically in communities throughout late medieval Europe since its establishment as an official church observance in Pope Urban IV's 1264 bull *Transiturus*.[82] Though popular throughout Spain and all of Catholic Europe, eucharistic devotion took on a special meaning in the context of the religious and ethnic divisions of postconquest Granada. As a triumphant symbol of Catholic truth, the eucharist served as a potentially powerful symbolic tool in the struggle to extirpate the vestiges of Islam.[83] For their part, Muslim theologians had, of course, long regarded the eucharist and the doctrine of transubstantiation as objects of scorn and ridicule.

In Granada's earliest Corpus celebrations under Archbishop Talavera, however, the divisive potential of the host with respect to the city's two distinct ethnic communities was in fact scarcely noticeable. Talavera actively promoted mudéjar, and later morisco, participation in the festivities, and as noted earlier, even encouraged the incorporation into the Corpus procession itself of traditional local festive customs such as the *zambra* dance,[84] although the formal use of the *zambra* in Corpus observances likely did not survive for long after the archbishop's death in 1507. There are some indications of individual morisco hostility toward the parading of the host through the city. In 1569, for example, the Inquisition arrested nineteen-year-old Gaspar Pacheco, a morisco resident of Granada, for refusing to kneel as the sacrament passed by him in the streets. According to witnesses, friends nearby immediately encouraged the young man to conform to this custom, imploring him "Look, it is our Lord," to which Pacheco reportedly responded boldly and simply, "I do not believe it."[85] On the whole, however, such incidents appear to have been much less common in frontier Granada than one might expect, and in any case there is no record of Corpus celebrations ever providing an occasion for large-scale interethnic violence in frontier Granada.

Although Granada's earliest Corpus celebrations incorporated some traditional morisco elements, their structure derived principally from common traditions brought by the immigrants from their Castilian hometowns. Most important of these was the citywide Corpus Christi procession itself. Accompanying the host in this procession was a veritable cross-section of local society: the municipal council, confraternities, guilds, municipal leaders from the nearby villages, and at least when one was present in the city, the archbishop. Interspersed among these groups were various demons and giants causing mischief, and the *tarasca*, or dragon, whose symbolic power would eventually be broken by the overwhelming power of the host as it was carried through the city's streets.[86] Granada's immigrants also included among the Corpus festivities other typically Castilian traditions such as *autos sacramentales*, popular religious plays about the sacrament, which were acted out both by amateurs in the streets and by professionals in more organized settings such as the city's Corral de Carbón–the old Nasrid-era wheat exchange.[87] In addition, until 1515, bulls were run in the city's central plaza of Bibarrambla as part of the celebration.[88] The atmosphere was, at least in the early years, carnivalesque. Nearly forgotten amidst all of the outdoor religious spectacle and secular fun in the streets were the more solemn religious observances and masses said within the cathedral and other churches to honor the sacrament. In 1543, the cathedral chapter decided that the high mass normally said in the cathedral after the procession should be moved to the time period just before the procession, apparently because no one came to mass once the celebration had taken to the streets.[89]

In addition to the general, communitywide Corpus festivities, residents of each parish organized certain neighborhood observances of their own in honor of the eucharist. Often, initiative in these matters was taken by the parishes' Cofradías del Santísimo Sacramento (Confraternities of the Most Blessed Sacrament). Such parish-level brotherhoods of eucharistic devotion became customary throughout Spain during the sixteenth century, and they seem to have had a particularly early start in Granada. Impetus for the foundation of such confraternities in many Spanish communities came from a papal bull of 1542 granting certain indulgences for the creation of eucharistic brotherhoods such as that which had been founded in 1538 by Tommaso Stella in Rome's church of Santa Maria della Minerva.[90] However, Granada's earliest such foundations, which predate these developments, illustrate that neither indulgences nor Stella's Roman model were necessary to stoke the Granadan immigrants' eucharistic devotion.

By 1538, the date of the foundation of the Roman brotherhood, confraternities of the Most Blessed Sacrament had already been established in at least one of Granada's Christian immigrant parishes—that of Magdalena—and perhaps two others, Santiago and San Justo.[91] In the parish of the cathedral, moreover, a eucharistic confraternity of sorts had existed since the 1520s. Founded as the "confraternity of the Holy Name of Jesus," its original constitutions were written and approved in or before 1529.[92] In addition to provisions for masses and observances in honor of the name of Jesus, the cofrades included in these original constitutions the practice, later universal among the eucharistic brotherhoods, of ceremonially accompanying the sacrament at those times when it was taken out of a church to be administered to the sick in their homes.[93] Sometime between 1529 and 1548, the brotherhood officially changed its name to the confraternity of "the Most Blessed Sacrament and the Holy Name of Jesus," explicitly recognizing the eucharistic devotion that it had practiced since its official formation.[94] By 1547, in addition to the cathedral parish, those of San Andrés and Santa Ana had eucharistic confraternities. By 1557, at least one more had been founded in Santa Escolástica, and before the end of the century, all of Granada's parishes housed one.

Initiative in the creation of these confraternities, moreover, often came from the laity. The brotherhood in San Justo parish, for example, was created as the result of a bequest of parishioner Catalina Hernández. In her testament, dated April 21, 1537, she left six hundred *maravedís* per year in fixed annuities "in order that a confraternity be formed to accompany the Most Blessed Sacrament of the church of San Justo of this city, or if this cannot be done, the said 600 *maravedís* go to the priest of San Justo."[95] The priest never received the money. In a July 20, 1539, testament, Catalina González requested the accompaniment in her funeral procession of the confraternity of the Most Blessed Sacrament of San Justo parish, of which her husband was a member. Hernández's deathbed wish to found such a brotherhood in her parish had thus been fulfilled.[96]

Besides the confraternities, the city's municipal council also acted as a key source of local lay initiatives in the creation of the city's developing religious culture. For example, the *regidores* took various measures to regulate and shape the Corpus procession, including mandating the order in which the guilds would march.[97] Even more emblematic of their role as initiators of new traditions was the annual memorial celebration established by the municipal councilors in honor of Queen Isabella. In 1514, the council established and endowed this festival to be held each May 7—the day of Saint John the Evangelist—which had been the day when Isabella's body arrived in Granada after her death in 1504.[98] After Ferdinand's death in 1516, the observance was converted into a memorial celebration for both of the Catholic Monarchs. Like Corpus, this celebration mixed religious observances with secular festivities. The running of bulls in the Bibarrambla plaza on Corpus Christi day, for example, was moved by the municipal council to the day of Saint John in 1515 to coincide with their own memorial celebration in honor of Isabella.[99] All of the city's other governing institutions—including the royal appellate court officials, the titled nobility, the cathedral chapter, the friars, the clergy of the Royal Chapel, and the archbishop—were invited, as were all of the city's residents. However, the festival was clearly orchestrated, promoted, and paid for by the municipal council.

In typical fashion, the cathedral chapter strongly resisted the *regidores'* call to participate in the public festivities and masses in the Royal Chapel ordered by the municipal councilors, arguing that the municipal council had to pay them for their presence at such observances. The municipal council's representatives in the Cortes of Castile complained to the crown of the chapter's refusal to take part, and in 1523 Charles V responded with a royal decree directly ordering the chapter to attend the memorial observances with no payment whatsoever from the city.[100] Despite the royal order, the cathedral clergy continued to resist. Again the city's representatives at the Cortes took their case to the crown, and in 1542 Charles V repeated his admonition to the chapter, angrily adding, "I am amazed that you have not complied with my written orders."[101]

The cathedral chapter's reluctance to participate in this celebration is emblematic of the relative passivity of the city's secular clergy at all levels in the processes by which Granada's new public religious traditions were created, especially through the first half of the sixteenth century. Various lay individuals and groups within the Christian immigrant community actively engaged in the definition of that culture, and their initiatives often called explicitly for greater public participation on the part of the city's clergy. Through the first half of the sixteenth century, Granada's archbishops, cathedral chapter, and parish clergy proved largely unresponsive to such lay invitations. By contrast, many of the city's regular clergy (especially the Franciscan friars) were highly active participants in the growing public religious life of the immigrant community.

In short, the men and women of frontier Granada's Christian immigrant community demanded from the city's clergy and ecclesiastical institutions extensive participation in a broad range of civic, social, and charitable functions, and responded most favorably to those local religious institutions which best met these expectations. Under these conditions, it is not surprising that frontier Granada proved to be fertile ground for broadly influential reformers—above all the future saints Juan de Dios and Juan de Avila—who promoted highly public, active, and apostolic notions of the role of the clergy and church institutions in the life of the community.

CHAPTER SIX

Defining Reform

New Directions in Granada's
Religious Life, 1526–1546

Arguably the most powerful ruler Europe had seen since the days of the ancient Roman Empire, the young Habsburg Holy Roman emperor, duke of Burgundy and king of Castile and Aragon, Charles V, entered Granada on June 4, 1526, for what would be his first and only visit to the frontier city.[1] According to royal chronicler Prudencio de Sandoval, the emperor had brought his enormous entourage to Granada simply to see the sights of the old Nasrid capital and flee the brutal summertime heat and humidity of Seville, where he had spent the spring with his new Portuguese bride, Empress Isabella.[2] Within days of his arrival, however, local morisco leaders began to pepper the emperor with reports of administrative abuses endured by Granada's "native" population at the hands of local church and state authorities.[3] The disturbed Charles immediately commissioned a team of clergymen to undertake an investigative tour of the old Nasrid sultanate and report to him on the validity of the charges. The visitation team included, importantly, Gaspar de Avalos, the man whom Charles would appoint archbishop of Granada three years later and who, as archbishop, would be Granada's first active, long-lasting, and resident prelate since Hernando de Talavera.[4] Avalos and his fellow visitors returned weeks later with a report not only confirming many of the moriscos' accusations, but also, much to the morisco leadership's chagrin, condemning the religious lives of the moriscos themselves who, they charged, remained fundamentally Muslim in belief and practice. Thus drawn into local politics, Charles convened an assembly of many of Spain's most prominent clergymen—including once again the future Archbishop Avalos—and charged them with two tasks: first, to identify what did and did not constitute crypto-Muslim practice among his morisco subjects; and second, to eliminate the endemic corruption among church and state officials whose abuse of power he believed inhibited the moriscos' effective assimilation.[5] The efforts of Avalos and his fellow commissioners culminated in November and December 1526 in the landmark decrees of the Royal

Chapel Congregation, held in the newly completed royal mausoleum adjacent to the frontier city's old main mosque, and presided over by the emperor himself only steps away from the crypt in which his grandparents Isabella and Ferdinand lay entombed.

Had they been implemented, the twenty-five mandates issued by the Royal Chapel Congregation would have demanded a far-reaching overhaul not only of the social and cultural lives of many of Granada's moriscos, but also of the administrative practices of various local church and state authorities. With regard to the moriscos, the congregation repeated and gave new emphasis to previous royal prohibitions flatly condemning a variety of customs that were clearly vestiges of Islamic religious practices, including traditional slaughter rites, the circumcision of boys, and the wearing of amulets with Muslim symbols such as the crescent moon—all of which reportedly remained common among many of the "native" inhabitants of the city and archdiocese.[6] The congregation's prohibitions—again in many cases repeating previous royal orders—also conflated with such explicitly religious observances a variety of local cultural traditions that may or may not have carried religious significance to those moriscos who engaged in them, including, for example, the wearing by morisca women of the traditional almalafa.[7] Even more fundamentally, the congregation strictly prohibited the use of spoken or written Arabic and demanded that all remaining Arabic administrative documents be immediately translated into Castilian.[8] The congregation's mandates also targeted with similar resolve various abuses committed by local church and state authorities, including, for example, the forcing of moriscos by some clergymen to purchase indulgences or bulls of Crusade, and the appropriation by seigneurial landowners of incomes designated for parish churches in the mostly morisco rural areas of the archdiocese.[9]

On the vital twin issues of morisco assimilation and administrative reform, however, neither the drama of the emperor's 1526 visit and Royal Chapel Congregation nor the troubled twelve-year archiepiscopate of Gaspar de Avalos (1529–1541) that soon followed brought significant or lasting alteration to the local situation in Granada. For his part, the emperor personally gutted the efforts of his 1526 ecclesiastical congregation by accepting an enormous morisco bribe in exchange for suspending for forty years the implementation of nearly all of the Royal Chapel decrees. Although frustrated by the emperor's nullification of the 1526 mandates, to which he had been among the key contributors, Gaspar de Avalos soon had a chance to renew the spirit of the Royal Chapel Congregation when he became Granada's archbishop in 1529. Unlike Charles himself, Avalos did not lack the resolve to confront aggressively the "morisco problem" and administrative corruption with the full force, attention, and authority of his office. In the end, however, Avalos's archiepiscopacy would prove no more successful than the Royal Chapel Congregation in bringing significant change to the city and archdiocese. His brow-beating style of leadership and the heavy-handed imposition of his reform measures provoked the bitter and eventually fatal opposition to his proposals not only of Granada's morisco elites, but also, more powerfully, of all the city's other major governing institutions, including the municipal council, the captain general, Royal Chancery, and even much of his own local ecclesiastical establishment. When Avalos left Granada in 1541 to assume the wealthier see of Santiago de Compostela, few in the frontier city were sad to see him go.

By the time of Archbishop Avalos's departure, however, new devotional currents had already begun to transform significantly Granada's religious landscape—currents that from their origins in Granada in the 1530s would also eventually contribute in profound ways to critical transformations in the Roman Catholic church as a whole in the era leading up to the ecumenical Council of Trent (1545–1563). Ironically, the unexpected sources of these new developments were not the high-profile, controversial, and ultimately failed campaigns of emperor and archbishop, but rather two fairly humble and in many ways typical members of Granada's Christian immigrant community. One, in fact, was not a clergyman at all, but rather a layman—the poor book peddler and former soldier João Cidade, who under his better-known adopted name Juan de Dios (John of God) would become postconquest Granada's first locally produced, officially canonized saint, despite persistent rumors of his probable insanity. The other, although a priest, was an equally unlikely candidate for broad influence on the future direction of the Roman Catholic church and eventual sainthood—the judeoconverso itinerant preacher Juan de Avila, who had in fact received an acquittal from Seville's Inquisition tribunal on charges of heresy only three years before first coming to Granada in 1536.

An emperor, an archbishop, a judeoconverso preacher, and a reputed madman—this chapter explores the new directions in Granada's religious history represented by these four individuals during the two transitional decades between the Royal Chapel Congregation in 1526 and the beginning of another new era in Granada coinciding with the arrival of Archbishop Pedro Guerrero in 1546. The focus is primarily on comparing and contrasting the reform-minded ideals and programs of Archbishop Avalos, Juan de Dios, and Juan de Avila. The three men all knew and interacted with one another, and they appear to have understood their efforts mostly in complementary rather than competitive terms. Yet while Avalos's policies and programs floundered as he became the object of scorn among much of Granada's immigrant and morisco communities alike, those of Juan de Dios and Juan de Avila prospered in the unique social, cultural, and religious circumstances of the frontier city, and quickly spread outside Granada to affect reform movements throughout Iberia and beyond. The local success of Juan de Dios and Juan de Avila owed much to the ways in which their innovative programs responded directly to and indeed even grew largely from the sorts of spiritual and civic concerns characteristic among much of frontier Granada's lay immigrant community. The notions of Christian practice espoused by both men also carried strong potential for reaching across the city's and archdiocese's ethnic boundaries and providing new devotional ground, doctrinally Roman Catholic and socially integrative, on which at least some of Granada's immigrants and moriscos might build common purpose. For various reasons that remain to be discussed in chapters 7 and 8, however, the potential for a harmonious local Christian community independent of distinctions between "Old Christians" and "New Christians" represented by the ideals of these two men would go mostly unrealized in the subsequent decades leading up to the outbreak of rebellion in 1568.

CHARLES V AND GASPAR DE AVALOS: FROM THE ROYAL CHAPEL CONGREGATION TO A TUMULTUOUS ARCHIEPISCOPACY

On the afternoon of Charles V's arrival on June 4, 1526, Granada's residents welcomed their king and his new bride with more than just the standard, expensive pomp and celebration demanded by such occasions. Politics and ceremony merged when a group of local morisca women daringly entertained the newlywed royal couple with a particularly enthusiastic wedding dance that formed part of a traditional Granadan morisco wedding-night festival known as the *leylas*.[10] Surviving records do not specify exactly who made the decision to include this local custom in the city's reception ceremonies—possibly the powerful morisco municipal councilmen who would only days later present their king with the aforementioned lists of grievances concerning the administrative abuses regularly endured by the kingdom's moriscos. The *leylas* dances, of course, represented exactly the sort of controversy that Charles would order the Royal Chapel Congregation to resolve: did Granada's moriscos associate such customs with their supposedly discarded ancestral religion in a way that inhibited their development of genuine Christian faith?

The different reactions of the emperor and the future Archbishop Avalos to such morisco customs reveal that the two men likely disagreed on this question. For his part, although only twenty-six years old, the Flemish emperor was already a well-traveled and reasonably well-educated man of highly cosmopolitan tastes. Like many immigrants and visitors to the frontier city, he appears to have been captivated by many of what appeared to him the exotic customs of Granada's "native" population, and he even seems to have become something of an aficionado of morisco dances such as the *leylas*. On the night of December 11, at the end of his seven-month stay, Charles in fact invited fellow northerner and fellow traveler, the Elector Palatine, Archduke Friedrich von Wittelsbach, to the gardens of the Alhambra to spend their final night in Granada enjoying an evening of morisco dance performances.[11] Interestingly, too, despite claims to the con-

FIGURE 6.1. Morisco dance. Source: Christoph Weiditz, *Authentic Everyday Dress of the Renaissance: All 154 Plates from the "Trachtenbuch"* (New York: Dover Publications, 1994). Courtesy of Dover Publications.

trary by later historians,[12] the Royal Chapel Congregation over which Charles had presided during his final weeks in Granada did not include among its list of prohibited morisco cultural traditions any explicit mention of specific controversial morisco dance traditions such as the *leylas* and the *zambra*.[13] Sandoval's eyewitness account of Charles's visit, moreover, suggests that it was precisely such enduring legacies of the former sultanate's preconquest culture that may have made Granada the emperor's favorite city in all of his Spanish kingdoms: "He resided during his stay in the Alhambra, and he so marveled at the old palaces, the Moorish art, the ingenious fountains and use of water, the sheer force of the place and the greatness of the town, that although he was pleased by all of the cities of his kingdom, from this one he derived particular pleasure."[14]

To be sure, the emperor remained throughout his stay steadfastly committed to the goal of insuring that Granada's moriscos become good Roman Catholics, as evidenced by his insistence on the introduction of a local Inquisition tribunal notwithstanding the morisco bribe. His willingness to accept the morisco deal may indicate, however, that Charles associated traditional cultural customs much less strongly with religious loyalty than did his commissioners who produced the Royal Chapel mandates. That is to say, in accordance with the arguments always made by the morisco leader Francisco Núñez Muley, who was among the principal negotiators in 1526, Charles seems to have agreed that the use of *almalafas* and the Arabic language did not necessarily imply religious infidelity.[15] Formal Islam was certainly not to be allowed, but the secular customs of his morisco subjects were to be tolerated and perhaps even in some cases embraced. In this way, Charles was at least to some degree heir the cultural *mudejarismo* of an Archbishop Talavera.

Perhaps more important, the emperor's suspension of the Royal Chapel mandates also reflected a legacy of political pragmatism of the sort practiced by his grandfather Ferdinand in his treatment of the mudéjares of the crown of Aragon. Although his very presence testifies to the importance he placed on Granada and the effective evangelization of its "native" population, the emperor's most urgent political concerns always lay elsewhere. From his arrival in June until his departure for Valladolid on December 12, the sultans' old Alhambra palace where Charles resided remained the epicenter of European diplomacy and power politics.[16] It was there, for example, that the emperor received a constant flow of dispatches and embassies from French king Francis I, whose armies Charles had so crushingly defeated the previous year at the Battle of Pavia, cementing in the process his status as hegemon of European affairs. During his stay in Granada, Charles was particularly distracted from local issues by tricky negotiations concerning Francis's abrogation of the Treaty of Madrid, despite the fact that the emperor still held the French king's two sons (including future king Henry II) hostage to insure French compliance with the treaty's terms.[17] It was also in Granada that he continued to receive news concerning his burgeoning empire in the New World in the wake of the conquests of Hernando Cortés. In 1526, Charles was perhaps the most powerful ruler in the world, with the possible exception only of the Chinese and Ottoman emperors. The victories and advances of the latter, however, stand as a powerful reminder that, for all his strength, Charles also faced many serious threats. During his time in Granada news arrived of Suleyman the Magnificent's annihilation of the imperial forces at the Battle of Mohács and the consequent Ottoman conquest of Hungary—a victory that left Suleyman poised to lay siege to Charles's ancestral Habsburg capital of Vienna three years later.[18] Even within his own realms, the emperor faced dangerous challenges—none greater, of course, than the religious fragmentation of Germany occasioned by Martin Luther and the coming of the Protestant Reformation. In order to face such crises, Charles needed not only diplomatic skill, but also new sources of revenue. The morisco effort to bribe the emperor was thus well-timed. With all of these challenges elsewhere, now was certainly not the time for Charles to risk a morisco rebellion by insisting on the sort of hard-line policy represented by the Royal Chapel mandates.

Unlike the emperor and local morisco defenders such as the count of Tendilla, others in attendance at Granada's royal entry ceremonies that sweltering June afternoon in 1526 must have regarded the inclusion of the *leylas* dances an abomination. Judging by his actions after becoming archbishop,

Gaspar de Avalos clearly held such traditions to be blatant hypocrisy and a living vestige of Muslim loyalty among the moriscos. If the emperor was heir to the traditions of King Ferdinand and Archbishop Talavera, Avalos by contrast is best understood as heir to the legacies of Queen Isabella and Archbishop Cisneros. In 1535, for example, he initiated a harsh and controversial campaign of repression against morisco dances and other local customs by ordering the arrest of those moriscos in the nearby village of Güéjar Sierra who dared to participate in *leylas* or wear traditional clothing such as the *almalafa*.[19] Riots ensued in Güéjar Sierra, and the resulting storm of controversy in the city of Granada itself would leave Avalos a virtual pariah in his own archdiocese.

Avalos had ironically come to his new job as archbishop of Granada in 1529 better prepared than any of his predecessors to face the unique challenges of governing the archdiocese. Although originally a native of Murcia, he had a longstanding relationship and deep familiarity with the frontier city that began when he as a young man attended Hernando de Talavera's famous "proto-seminary," the Colegio Eclesiástico de San Cecilio. One of the school's most accomplished alumni, Avalos went on to study theology in Paris, Salamanca, and Valladolid.[20] After a brief stay in the Hieronymite monastery in Guadalupe, he then returned to the old Nasrid sultanate in 1524, becoming bishop of Granada's nearby suffragan diocese of Guadix, where he would serve until 1528 as prelate of a flock that was even more overwhelmingly morisco-majority than that of Granada proper. It was during his tenure in Guadix that the emperor commissioned Avalos to conduct the extensive visitation of the archdiocese of Granada that occasioned the 1526 Royal Chapel Congregation. When Avalos took possession of the Granadan see three years later, he was thus already very familiar with the particular problems facing his new archdiocese.

The breadth of the response to the archbishop's daring 1535 crusade against morisco customs, however, reveals that such extensive local experience did not necessarily translate into local political savvy. With the support of the capital city's morisco elites, the riotous moriscos of Güéjar Sierra called on the captain general, the Royal Chancery, and Granada's municipal council to intervene on their behalf and restrain the archbishop from his aggressive policies. Attempting to maintain the cultural status quo and uneasy peace in the former sultanate, the municipal council responded by commissioning three of its members—the *corregidor* Hernán de Arias Saavedra, the Toledan judeoconverso tax collector Hernando Álvarez Zapata, and the Mendoza ally and political client Juan de Trillo—to lobby the archbishop to moderate his stance. When Avalos rebuffed the *regidores'* efforts at gentle persuasion, the city's secular government institutions teamed up to escalate the growing feud against what they considered a clear overstepping of archiepiscopal authority. First, town criers were ordered to announce throughout the city, and in a particularly loud fashion in the small plaza outside the windows of the archiepiscopal palace, that no citizen of Granada was to obey the orders of the archbishop in any matter that did not pertain directly to the governance of the church.[21] Second, the Royal Chancery sent one of its judges, Licenciado Luzón, to remind the archbishop firmly that officials of the royal court had the authority to hang a prelate who contravened the will of the crown. Luzón's threat was a clear reference to the royal execution a decade earlier of the bishop of Zamora and former Comuneros leader Antonio de Acuña. Lúzon may or may not have known that it carried particular significance to Archbishop Avalos, whose extended family included many former Comuneros, above all the rebellion's leading figure Juan de Padilla.[22] The alignment of the morisco community and all of the frontier city's major secular powers against him compelled Avalos grudgingly to accept for the time being the crown-endorsed narrow definitions of what exactly constituted genuine vestiges of Muslim practice among his morisco flock. Yet his leadership role in the formulation of the suspended 1526 Royal Chapel mandates against morisco cultural customs, together with his failed attempt as archbishop to eradicate traditional dress and dance, continued to make him the object of suspicion and even open derision among the moriscos for the remainder of his tenure in the frontier city.[23]

The moriscos and local secular elites, moreover, were not the only enemies Avalos made in his early years as archbishop. Even before the mid-1530s Güéjar Sierra controversy, the archbishop had already alienated much of the city's ecclesiastical establishment through rigorous efforts at reforming many of the abuses he and his fellow visitors and commissioners had identified in the months leading up to the 1526 Royal Chapel Congregation. If he had learned little from his former teacher Talavera in the way of respect for local customs, he was by contrast very much the old Hieronymite's heir in his aggressive pursuit of ecclesiastical reform. Yet in these matters as well, Avalos's strongest efforts ultimately failed because of strong local opposition to his authoritarian methods.

Among the official recommendations made by the emperor at the end of his 1526 visit was that an official synod be held within two years and that the archdiocese finally receive what it lacked and what every other major diocese in Spain had—a formal set of synodal constitutions to govern the local administration of the faith.[24] Even at the time of Avalos's accession to the Granadan see three years later, however, no such decrees had yet been issued, and it fell to him to do so. In a manner typical of his leadership style in the early years of his archiepiscopacy, Avalos attempted to impose on his new archdiocese a new set of administrative constitutions of his own design with little or no consultation with or input from his cathedral chapter or lower secular clergy—a set of synodal decrees, that is to say, that did not have the backing of a formal, consultative synodal assembly. Shortly after his arrival, he composed a reasonably comprehensive set of constitutions that he clearly intended to stand as the equivalent of and with the authority of an archdiocesan synod. The surviving copies, however, are all undated, and the earliest existing dated reference to them is in a November 12, 1532, ruling by the judges of Granada's royal court.[25] Avalos wrote the constitutions, then, sometime between his arrival in Granada in 1529 and the 1532 court ruling, probably in 1530.[26] Unfortunately for the archbishop, years of legal bickering prevented him from ever publishing and officially enacting the constitutions. Even if their long-term impact was negligible, however, the proposed constitutions reveal a great deal about the religious life of the city and archdiocese around 1530, as well as the ideals and agenda of Archbishop Avalos himself.

On the one hand, Avalos's idealistic constitutions show that the new archbishop was squarely grounded in a peninsulawide tradition of reform synods and councils that by 1530 was already two generations old, dating back at least to the landmark 1473 Provincial Council of Aranda and 1478 National Council of Seville. Synods in nearly all of Spain's dioceses over the intervening decades had not only set up strong standards for the improvement of the educational quality of parish clergy and the elimination of rampant corruption and absenteeism, but also established firm expectations concerning the duties of all lay men and women to learn basic Christian doctrine, to attend mass every Sunday and festival day, and to confess and receive communion at least once each year.[27] A renewed wave of synods throughout Spain in the 1530s (including Avalos's proposed Granada constitutions), however, repeated and elaborated many of the orders of previous councils and synods, testifying to a general failure to enforce effectively most of the earlier mandates.[28] On a wide variety of issues, the constitutions written by Avalos were thus very much in line with what other reform-minded prelates across Spain were doing in their dioceses in the years around 1530. With regard to his parish clergy, Avalos, like many bishops across the peninsula, demanded not only regular residence in the parish, but also frequent study, appropriate standards of dress, and a strict code of exemplary moral conduct that required among other things that his priests abandon the apparently still-common practice of concubinage.[29] Similarly, Avalos adopted a common late-fifteenth- and early-sixteenth-century Spanish approach to episcopal regulation of lay sacramental participation by ordering each of his parish priests to keep detailed records of all of their parishioners who dutifully came to confession each Lenten season and subsequently received communion, and to use those lists to identify, fine, and eventually excommunicate those men and women who refused or otherwise failed to do so.[30]

On the other hand, despite the fact that he was still new to Granada's archiepiscopal post in 1530–1531, Avalos also infused his proposed synodal constitutions with various unique and innovative proposals that reflected the intimate personal knowledge of local conditions he had gained through years of experience in the frontier city. In the text of the decrees themselves, for example, the archbishop acknowledged explicitly that his new flock consisted mostly of new converts to Christianity, not only from Islam but also from Judaism.[31] Even more important, he recognized and responded to this fact by acknowledging that the unique conditions of the archdiocese required innovative and effective educational strategies aimed above all at the indoctrination of "New Christians." To this end, he ordered each of his parish priests in predominantly "New Christian" parishes to set aside at every mass an amount of time after the offering during which they were carefully and deliberately to instruct their entire flocks in the basic doctrine of the church (including the basic prayers, the Creed, the Ten Commandments, the mortal sins, and how to confess). Avalos further specified that such instruction was to be done in simple vernacular Castilian, spoken slowly, clearly, and without technical theological terms or concepts. Also to be included in the priest's teaching during each mass was a concrete and simple lesson concerning specific rites, practices, and beliefs that were vestiges of Islam or Judaism and were thus to be avoided.[32]

In addition to these weekly lessons by the priest, Avalos designed a complex system that required the priests and/or sacristans of each parish to meet with a different segment of their local morisco communities each day of the week for age-appropriate and sex-appropriate doctrinal instruction. Boys, for example, received special instruction on Sundays and Tuesdays, unmarried girls ages nine and up on Saturdays and younger girls from five to eight years old every weekday morning.[33] Interestingly, the archbishop required married women and widows to gather for such instruction on Friday afternoon—keeping these Moriscas, who were in many cases probably correctly viewed by church officials as the most important transmitters of Islamic doctrine to their children,[34] in Christian church buildings at what had been in their ancestral faith a critical time of prayer, religious services, and religious education.[35] Although Avalos recognized the need for intensive religious indoctrination, he also acknowledged the difficulty of the process for the instructors and the neophyte Christians alike. The otherwise often hard-line archbishop's constitutions explicitly specified, for example, that those moriscos who refused annual communion on the grounds that they had not yet received sufficient instruction on matters of the Christian faith to accept so holy a sacrament should not necessarily be considered apostates, nor should they incur the standard penalties imposed upon "Old Christians" for such behavior.[36] Alongside such specific provisions concerning the newly converted, the archbishop also demonstrated in the constitutions a keen awareness of certain problems created by the particularly mobile and transient nature of much of Granada's growing Christian immigrant community as a whole. In the decrees concerning the sacrament of marriage, for example, Avalos acknowledged that immigrants often came to Granada to start new lives, and some, despite the fact that they were still married to spouses whom they had abandoned in their hometowns, claimed on arrival in Granada to be single and subsequently married again. Although such problems were not necessarily unique to Granada, the distinct social conditions of Granada may have facilitated such bigamy, Avalos recognized, because in a newly formed society of immigrants, one's personal and family past was easily kept secret, and in many cases no one knew to raise an objection. In response to this problem, the archbishop ordered in his constitutions that no priest allow any newly arrived stranger to marry without first obtaining either a written statement from the priest of his or her home parish that he or she was indeed single, or direct permission from the archbishop's court and provisor.[37]

Although clearly in keeping with the reform-minded ideals of many Spanish prelates of the day and in many ways carefully gauged to fit local circumstances, Avalos's synodal decrees certainly did not please everyone. In particular, Avalos's proposed reforms refocused authority and ecclesiastical incomes at the parish level squarely on the office of the parish priest (*cura*) at the expense of each parish's other beneficed clergymen (*beneficiados*).[38] In response, Granada's *beneficiados* protested loudly and filed a lawsuit against the archbishop in Granada's royal court in or before 1532.[39] Similar measures to streamline parish administration and combat the negative image of the secular clergy caused by constant bickering between *beneficiados* and *curas* over incomes were common throughout Spain in the reform era. Elsewhere in Spain, however, the office of *beneficiado* was often simply a sinecure held by an absentee clergyman who rarely if ever saw the parishioners.[40] At least in the capital city, by contrast, frontier Granada's *beneficiados* were generally not only resident, but also active participants in the daily parochial duties of distributing the sacraments to the laity. In their lawsuit against the archbishop, the *beneficiados* portrayed themselves as the backbone of Granada's parishes, complaining that, in general, "the *curas* appointed by the archbishop are not as capable as the said *beneficiados*."[41]

Because of the royal patronage of Granada's church, the *beneficiados* contended, the crown's courts held clear jurisdiction over this matter—a point that was never challenged by Archbishop Avalos.[42] In their case, the *beneficiados* argued that Avalos's proposals undermined their position and incomes within the parishes as defined both by custom and by the official provisions of the crown-endorsed provisions of the 1501 foundation of the archdiocese's parishes. In addition to their complaints against the constitutions themselves, the *beneficiados* listed specific grievances in which they portrayed the archbishop as a heavy-handed and unjust prelate who had, among other things, imprisoned without reason many *beneficiados* who had expressed open opposition to his plans and prevented them from holding meetings as a group to discuss their case.[43] They also argued that Avalos had tried to issue the constitutions illegally—without due consultation and participation of either the *beneficiados* themselves or of the cathedral chapter as demanded by standard synodal custom.[44] For their part, Avalos and his lawyer politely expressed some doubts about the sincerity of some of the *beneficiados* involved in the lawsuit: "The zeal and good intention of the [*beneficiados*] is understood, except three or four of them who pursue this case more out of desire to live in liberty [from archiepiscopal authority] than for the reasons that they have stated."[45]

After three years of legal bickering, the royal judges in 1535 issued a definitive ruling in favor of the *beneficiados,* declaring that Avalos had in fact improperly silenced opposition and failed to formulate his synodal decrees with all due "solemnities."[46] Avalos did not convene another synod, nor did he revise his constitutions. His decrees were never published, and they never took effect as the official governing constitutions of the archdiocese.

Despite the ongoing frustration of the *beneficiados'* lawsuit and the failure to implement his synodal decrees, the reform-minded archbishop continued to work through other channels to improve the quality of his local secular clergy. He provided new funding and renewed life, for example, to the innovative school that he himself had attended decades earlier—Archbishop Talavera's Colegio Eclesiástico de San Cecilio.[47] He also founded in Granada with the help of his friend and fellow reformer Juan de Avila another similar institution for the moral and theological training of future priests, the Colegio de Santa Catalina.[48] Even more significantly, Avalos fostered the growth of Granada's new university from its opening in 1532.[49] In 1536, he conducted a rigorous visitation of the city's cathedral chapter, ordering that the canons enact a number of reforms in order to improve their image in the eyes of the laity.[50] Finally, Avalos, unlike most of his predecessors, also took it upon himself to play a highly visible role in the religious life of the city by preaching publicly on all festival days.[51]

In short, despite his numerous failures and shortcomings, Avalos brought to the frontier city a reform zeal and a lasting, active archiepiscopal presence of the sort that it had not seen since Talavera. His twelve-year stay in Granada produced not only a great deal of controversy, but also a new official concern with the reform of the local secular clergy. Still, at the end of Avalos's tenure in Granada, little had changed at a practical level as a result of his policies. His synodal reforms had been overturned. The morisco community and rival local governing institutions alike generally viewed him with either suspicion or disdain. Outside of the local ecclesiastical hierarchy, however, Granada in the 1530s saw other developments that not only reshaped the religious life of the city but also influenced the direction of sixteenth-century Catholic reform worldwide.

PUBLIC CHARITY AND SPIRITUAL RENEWAL: THE CASE OF SAN JUAN DE DIOS

João Cidade was in many ways a typical member of Granada's Christian immigrant community. Like most of his neighbors in the frontier city, he had grown up somewhere else.[52] Also like many of his neighbors, Juan had been a soldier and had traveled extensively. He served, for example, in the armies of Charles V in campaigns against the French and the Turks, and he had also spent time in the Portuguese garrison of Ceuta on the North African coast.[53] After returning to Spain from Africa, Juan made a poor living by traveling and peddling small, cheap devotional books, chivalric romances, and religious images in the cities and villages of Andalusia. Sometime in the mid-1530s, he brought his business to Granada, where he rented a tiny house on the city's northern edge to serve as his bookstore. During his time in Granada, Juan, like many other immigrants, also created for himself an entirely new identity.

This poor bookseller was an unlikely candidate to become postconquest Granada's first saint. His earliest biographer, Francisco de Castro, reported that during his time in Africa, in fact, João had very nearly converted to Islam, only to be dissuaded after a long talk with a Franciscan friar.[54] This experience may have instilled in the young soldier a level of understanding and familiarity with Muslim tradition and practice that would serve him well later among the moriscos of frontier Granada. A seventeenth-century account of his life reported that he had also considered becoming a priest a number of times, but had always shied away.[55] Still, by the time of his death in 1550, he was apparently already considered a saint among the residents of the city, and there are local textual references to him as a "saint" as early as 1577,[56] though in Rome he was officially beatified only in 1630, and canonized in 1690.[57]

João Cidade became Juan de Dios ("John of God") as a result of a dramatic conversion experience in Granada during the city's Saint Sebastian's day festivities on January 20, 1537. That day the humble bookseller went to a sermon at the chapel of los Mártires. The preacher was the famous "apostle of Andalusia" Juan de Avila, himself also later canonized.[58] After hearing Avila's powerful sermon, João was overcome with grief over the sinful life that he had led, and he immediately began a convulsive fit of public penitence that convinced most of the city that he was insane: "[He] left the church so remorseful that he confessed his sins aloud, and begged God's mercy. He then proceeded to his bookstore, where he gave away all of the devotional books, ripped apart with his teeth all of the chivalric romances, and gave all of his money to the poor. He gave away everything in Christ's name, and he left himself nearly completely undressed He was barefoot and dressed only in a shirt, and some boys in the street tossed him about and proclaimed him crazy."[59]

The apparent madman then went to talk with Juan de Avila, who comforted him for a while. But after taking leave of the preacher he began his public fits again: "Just as he had earlier, he went through the principal streets of Granada, doing flips and giving other signs of a man who had lost all judgment; and thus believing him to be insane, the boys screamed at him and mistreated him. They threw dirt, mud, and other filth at him, which he endured with great patience and happiness, wanting through this to make amends for some of the offenses that he had committed against his maker."[60] He was finally taken to the Royal Hospital, which treated the insane. His "treatment" there involved being lashed repeatedly with a whip.[61] Despite the hospital's harsh prescription, he recovered quickly, and upon his release went on a pilgrimage to the shrine of the Virgin of Guadalupe in Extremadura in search of spiritual comfort.[62]

On returning to Granada, and after further consultation with his spiritual mentor, Juan de Avila, Juan de Dios committed himself to a life of tireless service to the poor. He initially gathered firewood, which he brought each day to the Plaza of Bibarrambla to distribute among the needy. His return was greeted with great ridicule by many of the city's citizens, who well remembered his fits of apparent insanity.[63] In 1537, Juan de Dios rented a house in the fish market district of the city and opened its doors to receive all classes of the sick and poor. He supported his new hospital by continuing to gather firewood to sell in the city. The hospital grew rapidly, and Juan was forced to find additional finances. After gathering and selling firewood each day, he began to take to the streets each night with a large basket strapped to his back to beg for alms with cries that became the recognized signature of Juan de Dios and his followers among the city's residents: "Is there anyone who will do something good for his own brothers?" and "Who will do something good for himself?"[64]

Through his unique style in begging alms and his heroic acts of charity, the reputed madman gained the attention, respect, and support of much of the frontier city's populace, morisco and immigrant alike.[65] Many of the specific stories of his bravery and selflessness, of course, come to us only from early biographies and histories whose hagiographic intent must be taken into account. Whether or not one accepts their literal veracity, the dramatic stories nonetheless tell a great deal about the religious culture of sixteenth-century Granada and the especially pious reputation enjoyed by its first recognized saint. On a cold December night when his own hospital was low on firewood, for example, he was reported to have swum out into the frigid waters of the Genil River to collect wood that had been carried down the river from the mountains.[66] Another evening, when a fire at the Royal Hospital threatened to kill many of the sick and injured who could not escape by themselves, Juan reportedly risked his own life to enter the building repeatedly and carry out the endangered. One account says that he was at one point trapped by the flames and doomed to certain death. Miraculously, according to the report, the flames then simply parted, allowing him to escape and to continue his life of service to the poor.[67] As his own hospital grew, Juan had to move to a larger building on the *cuesta de Gómeres*—a narrow street on the steep hill leading up to the Alhambra. Many of the hospital's infirm residents could not make the climb, and Juan is said to have carried each of them up the hill on his own shoulders.

Juan's heroic acts attracted a number of men who pledged to follow his example and to attend the poor and sick of the new hospital. These "brothers" of Juan de Dios tended to come from humble origins themselves, though there were some wealthy exceptions.[68] Moreover, after Juan's death, an auxiliary confraternity, that of *las cinco plagas de Jesús* ("the five wounds of Jesus"), was founded to provide additional regular workers for the hospital. Unlike the official Brothers of Juan de Dios, however, most members of the auxiliary confraternity appear to have been upwardly mobile men of money and means. At least four of them were well-educated bureaucrats, and there are indications that such social climbers may have comprised the backbone of the brotherhood. Active participation in and support for the new hospital, that is to say, came from across Granada's social spectrum and even included many members of the local morisco community.[69]

When Juan de Dios died on March 8, 1550, virtually the entire city attended his funeral. It was the largest public religious gathering in the city's sixteenth-century history. Representatives of all of the city's governing institutions, both civil and ecclesiastical, came, as did all of the religious orders, confraternities, and nearly all of Granada's residents, morisco and Christian immigrant alike: "Such an infinity of people came that they did not fit in the streets, and all who came, even the moriscos, cried and spoke of his great charity and the great example that he had provided them. . . . So many people came to touch the medals and rosaries on his body, or to take away some relic, that it took a very long time to bury him."[70]

Among the immigrant testaments summarized in table 5.1 (see chapter 5), the popularity of Juan's new house was exceeded only by that of one other local hospital—that of Corpus Christi, an institution which enjoyed the advantage of a papal grant of indulgence to anyone who ordered masses there.[71] The particularly strong local appeal of Juan de Dios and his hospital, moreover, appears to have crossed all of the frontier city's class and ethnic boundaries.[72] The count of Tendilla and the duke and duchess of Sesa, for example, were among Juan de Dios's greatest benefactors,[73] as were the elite morisco Zegrí and Granada Venegas families.[74] In his 1563 testament, the noted architect and designer of the high altar of Granada's cathedral Diego de Siloé made the hospital of Juan de Dios his sole heir.[75] Even the local Genoese merchant community charitably extended to him much-needed credit to support the nascent hospital.[76]

The wealthy and powerful Toledan judeoconverso tax collector Juan de la Torre was also a friend and admirer. One story reports that Juan de Dios was walking down the street one afternoon when he accidentally bumped into a nonlocal nobleman who was visiting Granada on business. Juan de Dios apologized, but the insulted gentleman, who thought the apology insincere, punched him. Ever humble, Juan de Dios responded that he deserved such treatment and asked the nobleman to hit him again. The noble then told some of his men, who were standing nearby, to give Juan a good beating. As they began to fulfill their master's order, Juan de la Torre happened to walk by. Appalled by what he saw, he immediately intervened. After Juan de la Torre exclaimed that the man to whom they were giving such a beating was Juan de Dios, the noble called his men away and kneeled at the poor, beaten man's feet to ask forgiveness.[77]

The heroic early biographies, of course, tend to exaggerate Juan's local popularity. Juan de Dios certainly had many friends throughout frontier Granadan society, but a careful look at all available evidence suggests that he likely had at least some local detractors as well. Juan himself seems to have understood that not all Granadans were as charitable as he was. He wrote to a friend in Málaga: "Often I do not leave the house because of all the debts I owe."[78] Also, for all the generosity he found among Granada's residents, local alms were still insufficient for the maintenance of his ambitious project. He had to supplement local charity, for example, by wandering throughout Andalusia in search of wealthy nobles who would give additional support.[79] Also, Juan insisted that his hospital indiscriminately accept all the poor and sick who asked for comfort, and the resulting mass of people that collected at his house was considered by some a threat to the community. When Archbishop Pedro Guerrero arrived in Granada in 1547, one of his first actions was to order a visitation of the hospital of Juan de Dios, which he had heard was filled with idle, dissolute, and wicked people.[80]

Despite such problems, Juan de Dios and his hospital enjoyed a virtually unrivaled degree of communitywide support. No other institution in the city was so successful at bringing together the efforts of men and women—"Old Christian," judeoconverso, and morisco alike—[81] from across Granada's ethnic and social spectrum. How did such a man, initially thought to be insane, pull together such diverse and otherwise largely irreconcilable interests toward a common cause? What was unique about his program and message?

In cities throughout late-fifteenth- and early- sixteenth-century Spain, population growth was accompanied by increases in the number of urban poor, and there was a great deal of debate about how best to cope with the problem. In many cities during this era a variety of new institutions were established to help the needy.[82] The problem, some complained, was that the multiplication of institutions did not necessarily imply greater efficacy in alleviating the problems of urban poverty. Consolidation of services into a smaller number of hospitals would allow for more efficient use of resources, they argued. Hospital foundation, however, was often a highly particularist matter of personal piety. Those who founded or patronized hospitals often did so with the expectation of personal or familial spiritual benefit, and they strongly resisted efforts to consolidate their funds with those of other hospitals to forge a more efficient community poor-relief effort.[83]

In this regard, Granada before Juan de Dios was no exception. Most of the city's charitable institutions were bound by the conditions set by a specific donor, patron, or testator. For example, in his 1501 testament, Juan Muñoz provided for the foundation of a hospital and mandated that it never be absorbed into another institution: "Because it is my determined will that this *my* hospital should remain forever dedicated to the advocation of the Mother of Christ, I order that neither the house nor the rents or properties may be removed, transported, or absorbed into any other pious work in any manner by a king, queen, or prelate, on pain of falling under the damnation of the mother of Christ."[84]

Other Granadan hospitals were similarly tied to particular interests.[85] The only institution of sufficient size and resources to serve as a general community hospital was the Royal Hospital established and endowed by the Catholic Monarchs Ferdinand and Isabella. However, it suffered from extreme mismanagement, and Granada's archbishops siphoned off many of its funds to support the archiepiscopal hospital of Santa Ana.[86]

The hospital founded by Juan de Dios in 1537 was unlike any of the city's existing establishments. Most important, the hospital was itself founded in poverty and was thus not beholden to the interests or mandates of a single, specific patron. In addition, it did not limit itself to treating specific sorts of people. Instead, its doors were open to all varieties of poor and sick persons who requested assistance, including, it appears, local moriscos.[87] In clever satire of the locally popular epithet *quién tiene moro tiene oro* ("a man with a moor is never poor"), for example, Juan wrote to the duchess of Sesa, "Give here, give there, it's all profitable; where there are more moors, there's more profit."[88] In a similar spirit of cooperation, people from all sectors of Granadan society, from nobles to laborers, immigrants and moriscos alike, participated as apparent equals in the day-to-day distribution of food and assistance to the hospital's poor and sick. Regardless of social status, for example, all who assisted were required to perform certain specified ritual signs of humility as they served the patients and residents of the hospital.[89] In short, the Hospital of Juan de Dios appealed to a ideal of charity that transcended particularist or corporate interests, and in so doing it found a surprisingly enthusiastic following that spanned not only the frontier city's class boundaries, but also, most shockingly, its ethnic divisions as well.

Such idealistic considerations alone, however, were not the only factors contributing to the hospital's popularity and success. On a more practical level, Granada's municipal council had for years searched in vain for a way to remove the city's beggars and vagabonds from the streets. In 1520, they issued an ordinance requiring that each vagabond be apprehended and placed in the custody of a "señor" for whom he or she would be required to work as a servant.[90] In 1532, the municipal council reported that there were still many beggars on the streets and ordered that all of them who were not native to Granada be expelled.[91] As a house that took in all poor indiscriminately, the Hospital of Juan de Dios provided the municipal council with a convenient wastebasket where they could dispose of what they considered the city's undesirable elements. Juan's follower and biographer Francisco de Castro reported that the city often brought vagabonds and beggars by force to the hospital, "so that public squares were cleansed of these lost persons."[92]

Beyond these idealistic and practical considerations, perhaps the most important contributing factor to the success and popularity of Juan de Dios and his followers was the public presence that they assumed in the religious life of the city. Many individuals and groups within the Granadan immigrant community actively solicited increased participation of the city's clergy in the religious observances of the streets and public spaces of the city. Moreover, as we have seen, the Christian immigrants tended to respond favorably to such civic-minded institutions by making them the beneficiaries of their pious offerings and bequests. While other hospitals depended on specific patrons and/or alms-box collections, Juan and his followers were a regular presence in the streets of Granada, begging alms with the standard exclamations of the founder: "Do something good for the poor of the Hospital of Juan de Dios!" and "Do something good for yourselves!"[93] Some brothers apparently even used these regular alms-gathering excursions as opportunities for informal street-preaching. Such preaching by laymen, even if just informal evangelization, naturally drew the ire and suspicion of church authorities,[94] but it fit well with the sorts of public religious activity solicited and supported by local immigrant laity. In addition to public begging, the brothers of the Hospital of Juan de Dios and the members of the confraternity that assisted them engaged in a wide variety of other activities beyond the care of the poor and sick within the walls of the hospital itself. Among these activities were the care of the city's orphans and widows, the counseling of married couples who were having problems, the visitation and spiritual guidance of prostitutes, and service as tutors, executors of testaments, and godfathers to children.[95]

Perhaps the most powerful testimony to the impact of Juan de Dios on the other religious institutions of the community came through imitation. In 1552, two years after Juan's death, the cathedral chapter began to break its seclusion from the city's public religious life, ordering for the first time that its own canons and dignitaries themselves take to the streets to beg alms for the completion of the new cathedral.[96] It is not unreasonable to surmise that the success of Juan de Dios and his followers constituted at least part of the chapter's inspiration to undertake such activities. In any case, Juan and his followers were just the first of a variety of new groups to take religious causes into Granada's public spaces in the middle decades of the century, including the Jesuits after 1554.

After Juan's death in 1550, his hospital and followers faced debts that threatened the survival of the institution itself. Archbishop Pedro Guerrero saved the hospital by paying off these debts, and the local Hieronymite friars donated a plot of land on which the brothers could build a new and larger hospital.[97] Such generosity, however, came at the price of subjecting the hospital to stricter archiepiscopal control and the direct oversight of a rector appointed by the prior of the Hieronymite monastery. The brothers of Juan de Dios spent the remainder of the century trying to disentangle themselves from these ties.[98] After numerous legal struggles with the Hieronymites, the brothers in 1571 persuaded Pope Pius V to grant them the status of an independent religious "congregation," thus freeing them from the supervision of the Hieronymites.[99] Later, in 1586, Pope Sixtus V declared the brothers of Juan de Dios an independent "order," thus liberating them from archiepiscopal supervision.[100]

Meanwhile, the movement begun by the seemingly mad Granadan immigrant bookseller spread beyond the city of its origin to become an international phenomenon. Juan's followers founded new hospitals after the Granadan model in Seville, Córdoba, Lucena, and Madrid.[101] Then, in 1584, the brothers took over the old Ospedale di San Giovanni Calibita in Rome, and their capable management of that institution may have played a role in Pope Sixtus V's decision to grant them status as an independent order.[102] Forged amidst the unique circumstances of Granada's frontier society, the Brothers Hospitallers of San Juan de Dios found a receptive audience throughout early modern Catholic Christendom for their unique brand of charity.

THE "APOSTLE OF ANDALUSIA": SAN JUAN DE AVILA AND HIS FOLLOWERS IN GRANADA

The man whose preaching ignited Juan de Dios's transformation was also in many ways a typical member of Granada's immigrant community. Juan de Avila, like Juan de la Torre and so many other Granadan immigrants, came from a family of Jewish converts to Christianity.[103] Also like Juan de la Torre, Avila was a transient, rather than a permanent, resident of the city. He first came to Granada in 1536, and remained in the city on that occasion for three years. He returned to Granada for a short stay in 1542, and did so again in 1543 and 1548.[104] Though he spent a total of fewer than five years in Granada, Avila was the most important and most influential figure among local religious reformers. He also developed a personal attachment to Granada and its residents, among whom he found so many followers that he reportedly took to calling the city "my Granada."[105]

Juan de Avila was not only the central figure in Granada's various religious reform movements, but he was also among the most important shapers of sixteenth-century churchwide Catholic reform. As Marcel Bataillon once wrote: "Either directly or through Luis de Granada, Avila's influence was as long-lasting as anyone's, and perhaps was not equaled in all of the European Counter-Reformation. . . . Few authors deserve the title 'Father of the Modern Church' as much as Avila."[106] The historical figure of Juan de Avila thus connects local Granadan Christian culture with broader Spanish and international reform currents and ideas. However, Avila's success in attracting support in Granada should not be understood simply as the successful "implementation" of prepackaged ideas that he brought into the community from outside. Rather, his ideas on reform grew in response to local conditions as much as they reshaped local practices. Specifically, Juan de Avila's views on Christian education and missionary evangelization developed through a combination of his own humanist educational background, his exposure to the works of Francisco de Osuna and other Spanish spiritual writers, and the practical experience drawn from years of apostolic activity in the communities of Andalusia—including, perhaps most importantly, Granada. Avila's specific ideas on reform, forged in response to the conditions and demands of the communities in which he worked, were in turn summarized in three reform treatises that he submitted to the ecumenical Council of Trent (1545–1563).[107] These reform treatises were among the most important influences on the formulation of Trent's landmark reform decrees. Avila's ideas on reform thus became institutionalized within long-lasting structures of the early modern church. In short, his career is emblematic of the process of dialogue between local demands and universal institutional concerns that gave shape to Catholic reform in the early modern era.

Avila was born in 1499 to a judeoconverso father and an Old Christian mother in Almodóvar del Campo, a small town in La Mancha.[108] From 1520 to 1526, he studied arts and later theology at the University of Alcalá—at the time the center of a flowering of Erasmian humanist thought in Spain. On completion of his studies, Avila went to Seville and requested that he be allowed to preach as a missionary in the New World. His request was denied, possibly because of his Jewish heritage. He instead became an itinerant preacher in the cities and towns of Andalusia, where he quickly built a reputation as one of the most powerful orators of his day. His friend, confidant, and biographer Luis de Granada spoke admiringly of his rousing sermons, and the bishop of León, Francisco de Terrones, wrote that those who heard Avila preach "went away with their heads lowered, silent, not speaking to one another, self-reflective, and full of remorse—all because of the pure force and virtue of the great preacher."[109] He typically preached not only in churches, but also in the plazas, streets, and other public spaces of the cities and towns in which he worked.[110] His emphatic style found not only a large following, but also many critics—especially in the town of Écija, where he preached in 1531. Some of Écija's residents denounced him to the Inquisition's Seville tribunal for statements that they thought bordered on Illuminism and Lutheranism. After enduring a one-year imprisonment and trial, he was acquitted on nearly all charges, receiving from the

Holy Office only a mild reprimand and suggestions that he moderate his tone and style.[111] In Granada, Avila experienced no such difficulties with the Inquisition. Instead, he found a community in which his powerful and highly public apostolic style enjoyed nearly universal praise.

Juan de Avila's 1551 and 1561 *Memoriales* to the Council of Trent provide a systematic summary of his educational and missionary program as it had developed over his decades of missionary work in Andalusia. As outlined in these reform treatises, Avila's message was one that emphasized the moral training of the Christian flock over behavioral regulation, and personal internalization of faith over external observance of rules. As he explained in his 1551 treatise to the Council of Trent:

> The means used by many to achieve reformation of common customs is to make good laws and order that they be enforced under great penalties; this done, they hold that they have completed their business. But impatient subjects lack the fundamental virtue to comply with these good laws; therefore the laws appear burdensome, and those subject to them will seek out mischief in order to undermine them, will flee from them, or will openly break them. And since punishment is bothersome to both the punisher and the punished, such enterprises usually fail, and they usually culminate in the type of situation that we have now: much evil despite many good laws.[112]

Avila compared this enforcement model of reform to the "old law" of the authoritarian Old Testament and contrasted it with a program aimed at cultivating the fundamentals of "virtue" among Christians—a program that, to Avila, better reflected the "new law" of the gospels.[113]

To teach basic Christian doctrine in such a way that lay people internalized the moral lessons that it contained was thus Avila's principal goal. The achievement of this goal required among other things that the laity understand the message. He repeatedly called, for example, for the use of the vernacular rather than the traditional Latin in the teaching of basic doctrine and prayers.[114] Avila himself wrote a vernacular catechism in rhyming couplets, titled simply *Doctrina cristiana*, which became one of the most broadly used catechisms in sixteenth-century Spain.[115]

In addition, Avila held that lay acceptance of the gospel similarly required that the clergymen who taught the message be held in high regard among the laity. He thus called for the observance and enforcement of the strictest moral standards among the secular clergy. Central to his program of moral formation, in fact, was an active, apostolic notion of the role of the secular clergy, who were to assume primary responsibility for the spiritual guidance of each and every member of their flocks. Such immense responsibility required that they, too, undergo intensive moral training in preparation for their jobs.[116] Toward this end, Avila established many schools in cities and towns throughout Andalusia, and even a university in Baeza, for the doctrinal and moral training of clergymen.[117]

Such ideas were hardly unique to Juan de Avila. His calls for moral training and a more personal faith had, of course, been anticipated by a generation of Christian humanists from Erasmus to Juan de Valdés. Humanist thinkers had long argued for Christian education aimed at the cultivation of internalized virtue and a responsive conscience rather than a simple external adherence to rules and officially authorized observances. Exposed to the work of Erasmus and other Christian humanists during his years at Alcalá, Avila took their pleas for a more internalized Christian faith and applied them in his pastoral and educational work. Specific manifestations of humanist influence are numerous both in his writings and in his practical educational projects.[118] Avila even recommended Erasmus's writings to his followers, despite the growing suspicion of the great Dutch humanist in Spanish ecclesiastical circles.[119] The significance of Avila's missionary philosophy, then, lies less in its originality than in his application of these ideas to a wide variety of pastoral and educational situations.[120]

In communities such as Granada, Avila's humanist background bred an active pastoral style characterized above all by versatility. The goal of individual moral training allowed a broad range of approaches to his work that would not have been possible had he understood his job simply as the teaching and enforcement of rules. As he wrote in a letter to a noblewoman: "There are many ways to see God and to serve him, some more appealing to some people, and others to other people, according to the sensibilities of each individual."[121] To Avila, in fact, the goal of moral formation inherently required a great deal of flexibility in educational practice. Avila often metaphorically equated the roles of clergymen and surgeons. In order to be a good "surgeon of souls," he claimed, one must be able to diagnose, adjust to, and heal the specific spiritual ailments of each individual student, penitent, or advisee.[122] Such versatility enabled him to adjust his message to fit the unique social contingencies of each community in which he preached and each individual whom he advised.

Juan first arrived in Granada in 1536 as a little-known itinerant preacher with his Inquisition ordeal a recent memory. His style and message resonated at all levels of Granadan immigrant society, and he quickly became a local sensation. His frequent preaching brought about many dramatic conversions to the religious life. Luis de Granada wrote that Avila's sermons "were like a gun with much ammunition, that when fired wounded many birds."[123] Along with Juan de Dios, Granada residents so "wounded" by Avila's sermons included the wealthy noblewoman Doña María de la Paz. After hearing one of Avila's sermons, she reportedly went home immediately, destroyed her boutique, gave away all of her expensive clothing and other "vanities," and became a *beata* (lay holy woman).[124] Doña María de Mendoza made a vow of virginity after placing herself under Avila's spiritual direction.[125] Juan de Avila also converted Francisco de Borgia, later elected as the third general of the Society of Jesus, to the religious life during Borgia's 1539 trip to Granada for the funeral of the Empress Isabella.[126]

In addition to instruction of the laity through preaching and spiritual counseling, Avila, like his friend and spiritual advisee Archbishop Avalos, regularly insisted on the need to reform the local secular clergy, even if his preferred methods for doing so were at times at odds with those of the less flexible and more authoritarian archbishop. In this aspect of his reform program, Avila's experience in the city of Granada was particularly formative. Unlike the mostly morisco rural areas of the archdiocese, the city of Granada itself did not suffer from a shortage of clergymen, but the perceived poor moral quality of the city's priests seriously damaged the image of the church in the eyes of the laity. Avila later wrote in his reform treatises to the Council of Trent that he would in truth prefer to have fewer clergymen, as long as those ordained would maintain themselves as shining examples of Christian virtue within their communities.[127] On this issue, at least, Avalos could not have agreed more. In Juan de Avila, Avalos found at least one locally popular ally in the struggle he had begun with his proposed synodal constitutions, although Avila was less concerned with imposing strict synodal decrees than he was with moral education. The two men worked together to establish in 1537 the Colegio de Santa Catalina—a school aimed at the training of future priests in morality, theology, and the liberal arts.[128] Avila's influence is also manifest in the 1547 reformed constitutions given by one of Avalos's successors, Archbishop Pedro Guerrero, to Granada's Colegio Eclesiástico de San Cecilio—the archdiocesan school established originally by Talavera in 1492.[129] Both schools emphasized the moral training of priests, and their curricula prefigured and informed Avila's later educational foundations in other cities, as well the educational recommendations outlined in his reform treatises to the Council of Trent.

However, if the quality of Granada's parish clergy is used as a yardstick by which to measure Juan de Avila's impact on local ecclesiastical institutions and religious practice, then he appears to have had no more impact than his friend Archbishop Avalos. Locally, the two men's attempts to improve the education and public image of parish clergymen had little immediate practical impact. Lay images of the city's beneficed secular clergy remained, as they did in many Spanish cities, largely negative throughout the period.

Avila's failure to bring about the rapid wholesale reform of Granada's secular clergy was nonetheless balanced by success in other local endeavors. In addition to his personal popularity among the laity as a preacher, Avila built around himself in Granada a network of allies and followers who later exerted great influence on the direction and shape of religious reform locally and internationally. Though most *curas* and *beneficiados* in Granada's parishes remained unresponsive, Avila's flexible and highly public apostolic style matched well the sorts of religious activity popular among the larger Granadan immigrant community.

Who specifically were Avila's local supporters, and how did his program respond to their interests? His most fervent disciples in Granada were a group of young students and unbeneficed minor clergy that came to be known throughout Andalusia and across Spain as Avila's "sacerdotal school." An informal group of followers who swore loyalty to the aims of their leader, Avila's sacerdotal team originated in Granada in the late 1530s and spread over the next two decades to other communities throughout the kingdom of Castile.[130] Many of these disciples, at the urging of their master, later became Jesuits, and through them Juan de Avila's ideas greatly influenced the development of the Jesuit educational and missionary program in Europe and overseas.[131]

Among the Granadans who comprised this earliest apostolic team, a number were, like Avila himself, from families of recently converted Jews. Granadan judeoconversos drawn to the sacerdotal school included Diego de Santa Cruz and Cristóbal Sánchez—two brothers who had immigrated to Granada from Medina del Campo. Another judeoconverso immigrant from Baeza, Diego Pérez de Valdivia, also joined. Also among Avila's most important local judeoconverso followers was Pedro Navarro, who later became the rector of Granada's Jesuit house.[132]

As Juan de Avila's movement spread to other cities in the crown of Castile, it continued to prove particularly attractive to judeoconverso adherents. In the city of Avila, for example, a reform-minded group that included a number of judeoconversos applied the ideas of Juan de Avila and his Granadan sacerdotal school to reform efforts in their city in the 1540s and 1550s.[133] Jodi Bilinkoff explains the popularity of Juan de Avila's ideas among the formerly Jewish converts of the city of Avila largely as an expression of local social conflicts. Conversos in that Castilian city were generally excluded from local political authority as well as local religious institutions and traditions dominated by a closed oligarchy of entrenched Old Christian families. Juan de Avila's calls for a more personal faith and an active clergy dedicated to a more broadly defined public service therefore appealed to them.[134] In Granada, unlike Avila, judeoconversos had comprised a significant portion of the local elite ever since the conquest. Moreover, they had consistently been among the most important shapers of local religious customs and traditions. Despite the differences between the two cities, Granada's numerous judeoconversos may have been attracted to Juan de Avila's program for similar reasons, as well as the fact that Juan de Avila himself shared their stigmatized social status.

For many of the same reasons that it appealed so strongly to formerly Jewish converts, Avila's general message, and especially his emphasis on moral education over behavioral regulation and substantial personal faith over concern with "Old Christian" lineage, obviously carried strong potential for reaching out to at least some among Granada's morisco community as well. Although Avila made occasional references to the possible application of his ideas to the evangelization of the moriscos,[135] however, he never personally traveled to the heavily morisco rural towns and villages of the Alpujarras or the rest of the archdiocese, nor did he ever make it a point to focus his efforts in the city on the morisco parishes of the Albaicín. Perhaps his affiliation with the despised Archbishop Avalos limited his appeal to moriscos of all classes, although his role as spiritual guide to the almost universally admired Juan de Dios may have compensated for this in the eyes of some moriscos. It should also be remembered, however, that some of Granada's most rebellious moriscos expressed resentment at the prominent roles of judeoconversos in Granada's state and ecclesiastical institutions.[136] In the absence of better evidence, explaining Juan de Avila's personal failure to affect the morisco community in any noticeable way remains a matter of speculation. In any case, the clear potential for Avila's program to reach across the frontier city's endemic ethnic and religious division between moriscos and immigrants was largely unrealized at the time of Avila's final departure from Granada in 1548. In the 1550s, however, Pedro Navarro and other former "sacerdotal school" disciples who had entered the Society of Jesus would in fact take their mentor's message and techniques directly into the heart of the Albaicín to establish the Jesuit Casa de la Doctrina, which will be discussed in the next chapter.

Among the immigrants, by contrast, Avila's popularity was nearly universal. His local following ranged from the highest-born and most powerful sectors of Granadan immigrant society to the most destitute. Along with Juan de Dios, for example, two other Granadans originally from the lower end of Spain's social scale also became disciples of the "Apostle of Andalusia," taking his ideas and applying them in ways that significantly transformed early modern Catholicism worldwide: the Dominican author Fray Luis de Granada and archbishop of Granada Pedro Guerrero.

Luis de Sarria was born in the frontier city in 1504 to an impoverished woman who made her way by begging alms at the door of the city's Dominican monastery of Santa Cruz.[137] Orphaned at age five, Luis benefited from the charity of the family of the count of Tendilla, into whose house he was eventually taken to be raised and educated. At age twenty, Luis became a Dominican, professing at the same monastery by whose doors he had spent his earliest years learning to beg alongside his destitute mother. In 1529, the local Dominicans sent Luis to study at the Colegio de San Gregorio in Valladolid. At about this time, he changed his name to the one by which he would become well-known throughout Spain and the Catholic world—Luis de Granada. After adopting the name of his hometown, he almost never returned to it, coming back only for a brief stay in the mid-1530s. So, although his books were immensely popular in his native city, Fray Luis was not an active physical presence in Granada's religious life.

Still, as an internationally influential preacher and author who spent most of his formative years in Granada and who was an avowed disciple of Juan de Avila, Fray Luis's work merits some explanation.

In 1535, while in Córdoba, Fray Luis met Juan de Avila—one year before Avila's arrival in Granada.[138] The young Dominican would later call Avila his "spiritual master."[139] The paths of the two traveling preachers often crossed in the cities and towns of Andalusia in the 1540s, and they continued to correspond regularly until Avila's death in 1569.[140] After settling down in Portugal in the 1550s, Fray Luis published a number of highly influential devotional books. In particular, his 1554 *Libro de la oración y meditación* was by a wide margin Golden Age Spain's best-selling book.[141] Moreover, through the course of the sixteenth century, the popularity of Fray Luis's prayer-guide spread throughout the Catholic world. In addition to the major Western European languages, sixteenth-century editions of the *Libro de la oración* appeared in Greek and Polish, and the Jesuit followers of Francis Xavier even produced a Japanese translation for the benefit of new converts in that Far Eastern island kingdom.[142] Like his "spiritual master," Luis de Granada repeatedly stressed in his works the necessity of training and "formation" over regulation, and his statements to this effect often appear to be drawn almost directly from the words of Juan de Avila.[143]

Back in Fray Luis's frontier hometown, another self-professed disciple of Juan de Avila—Pedro Guerrero—became archbishop of Granada in 1546. Guerrero and Avila had met and become friends while both were students at Alcalá in the early 1520s.[144] The emperor, in fact, first offered the Granada see to the nearly universally respected Maestro Avila himself. For reasons of health, however, Avila refused the appointment and recommended that the post be given to his until then relatively obscure friend Guerrero.[145] Unlike any of his predecessors, Guerrero went on to enjoy an extremely long tenure as archbishop of Granada, holding the position for thirty years before his death in 1576. In addition to being an active and influential prelate within his own archdiocese, moreover, Guerrero also twice served as president of the powerful Spanish delegation at the Council of Trent, first in 1551–1552, and then again at the council's final convocation in 1562–1563. To the ecumenical council he carried not only Avila's celebrated reform treatises, but also years of experience working in the frontier archdiocese of Granada.

CHAPTER SEVEN

Negotiating Reform

Pedro Guerrero, Granada, and the Council of Trent, 1546–1563

By all accounts, Pedro Guerrero was among the most significant and influential figures at both the second (1551–1552) and third (1562–1563) meetings of the ecumenical Council of Trent. The Guerrero of the council's 1562–1563 final convocation, however, was a very different man from the one who had headed the Spanish delegation a decade earlier. In 1551–1552, the well-educated but still relatively inexperienced archbishop of Granada epitomized a spirit of cooperative effort and hard work, even if nearly all of his and Maestro Avila's reform goals remained unaccomplished when Maurice of Saxony's advancing armies hastened the fathers at Trent to disband prematurely. Cardinal Crescenzi, the papal legate selected by Pope Julius III to preside at second Trent, lavished praise on Guerrero for his work on decrees concerning the eucharist and confession, claiming explicitly that "nothing useful would have been accomplished without the Archbishop of Granada."[1]

Ten years later, by contrast, Pope Pius IV and his legates at third Trent had nothing kind to say about the now harshly confrontational archbishop who presided over a powerful and militantly reformist Spanish delegation. Of the nearly two hundred prelates from across Catholic Europe who descended on Trent in 1562–1563, none was a greater or more frequent source of controversy than frontier Granada's diminutive but boisterous Guerrero. Concerning his confrontational leadership style, the legates reported back to Pope Pius IV in Rome in 1562 that he was "harder and more obstinate than a rock."[2] Even Cardinal Carlo Borromeo—the pope's nephew who later as archbishop of Milan (1565–1584) became everyone's model of a reformed Tridentine prelate—voiced in 1563 a similar evaluation of his actions at Trent: "[S]ome of the Spaniards, and particularly the Archbishop of Granada, have a certain spirit of contradiction and singularity."[3] Guerrero himself acknowledged and even appeared to relish the common perception of him as the gadfly of the council. In January 1562, he wrote to King Philip II's ambassador in Rome: "I believe that I have made

FIGURE 7.1. Pedro Guerrero, archbishop of Granada 1546–1576. Photo courtesy of Miguel A. López and the Archdiocese of Granada.

myself a troublemaker in the eyes of these men, but this fact causes me no pain whatsoever."[4]

By that point in his career, involvement in bitter local controversies back in Granada had hardened the resolve of the appropriately named Archbishop Guerrero, whose surname in Spanish literally means "warrior." After a relatively peaceful first ten years, the archbishop struggled from 1556 until his death two decades later through a long series of confrontations involving various church officials and local lay leaders, immigrant and morisco alike, in the city and archdiocese of Granada. Of these conflicts, of course, none were more consequential for both the city and the Spanish kingdoms as a whole than the 1568 outbreak of the Second Rebellion of the Alpujarras and the consequent expulsion of the local morisco populace— developments to which the archbishop's own policies were an important contributing factor. Still, as a dedicated, reform-minded, and (except during his two stays at Trent) resident prelate whose thirty-year tenure from 1546 to 1576 remains even today the local record for archiepiscopal longevity, his was the most defining personality of a critical transitional period in the city's history.

Tracing the evolution of Guerrero's ideas and policies from the early years in Granada through the two trips to Trent and back again to the frontier city is important for two reasons. First, his career constitutes a particularly important prosopographical example of the hundreds of sixteenth-century ecclesiastics who brought local experience in their own cities, towns, and dioceses directly to bear on critical changes in the Roman Catholic church as a whole. In seeing the council from Guerrero's perspective as a clamorous agitator, one is reminded anew just how much was at stake at Trent and how broad a range of radical reform proposals actually came into play in the council's bitterly divisive debates. Trent was by no means a harmonious gathering of like-minded men who shared a uniform notion of what "official religion" should be. Instead, as the constant frustrations and occasional sense of triumph expressed by Guerrero and his reformist allies in the Spanish delegation bear witness, the council represented a hard-fought contest over the future course of the church—a contest into which the local reform experiences of prelates such as Guerrero figured significantly.

Second, the important role played by Guerrero in the frontier archdiocese's descent into rebellion in the years after his final return from Trent in 1564 cannot be fully understood without taking into account the course of the archbishop's career as a whole, including his experiences and actions at the ecumenical council. Nearly a decade of constant conflict, first with rival authorities in Granada 1556–1561, and then with reform opponents at Trent 1562–1563, stood behind the archbishop's 1565 renewal of aggressive campaigns against morisco culture. Moreover, Trent's decrees strengthening bishops' authority over the religious affairs of their dioceses—decrees to which Guerrero himself had been one of the key contributors—enabled the archbishop in the final decade of his life to abandon the versatile approach of his friend and advisor Juan de Avila and pursue instead the sorts of rigorous and inflexible policies that contributed to the outbreak of the morisco rebellion in 1568.

In locating Guerrero's place in the history of early modern Catholicism, one must on the one hand be careful not to overestimate the degree to which he was a "typical" reform-minded prelate of the era. To be sure, his own personality and the particularly volatile and innovative frontier character of Granada's religious landscape within which his policies and priorities evolved through the course of three decades in many ways distinguished his experiences from those of most other bishops. On the other hand, it would be similarly misleading either to overstate the frontier city's uniqueness or to attribute any of Trent's landmark reform decrees entirely or exclusively to Guerrero's hand. Hundreds of clergymen and lay people from all over Catholic Europe played critical roles in producing the sweeping package of reform mandates issued by the council's final sessions in the fall of 1563, and many of them shared similar educational backgrounds and reform concerns born of local circumstances often analogous to those faced by Guerrero in frontier Granada. Conscious of frontier Granada's distinctiveness and yet careful not to exaggerate either its singularity or the personal influence of its archbishop, this chapter demonstrates that the career of Pedro Guerrero encapsulates as well as anyone's the complex interplay of intellectual and devotional forces of both local and institutional origin that produced early modern Catholic reform.

A LIMITED AGENDA: THE NEW ARCHBISHOP, 1546–1554

For a man who would soon become well-known not only in Granada but also throughout Spain and indeed all of Catholic Christendom as a self-righteous and confrontational advocate of reform, Pedro Guerrero began his archiepiscopal tenure in the frontier city with what appears in retrospect a surprising degree of caution. Such deliberation was perhaps wise since, unlike Gaspar de Avalos, he arrived at the post woefully inexperienced and almost completely ignorant of local conditions. Like most of his new flock in Granada, Pedro Guerrero was an immigrant. As a native of a small village in Castile's far north where moriscos were a rare sight, moreover, Guerrero was a newcomer to whom the persistently Muslim appearance of the old Nasrid capital and the customs of its remaining "native" population must at first have appeared particularly foreign and exotic. He was born in 1501 in the village of Leza in La Rioja to "Old Christian" parents who, despite their apparent claim to noble descent, had fallen into relative poverty until the good fortune of their most successful son allowed the family to begin restoring its ancestral house and the repairing the coat of arms emblazoned above the main entrance.[5] Guerrero began his ascent from rural obscurity by studying liberal arts in the 1520s at the University of Alcalá, where he met and befriended his future collaborator in Granadan and churchwide reform, Juan de Avila. After Alcalá, Guerrero continued his schooling first in Sigüenza, and then in Salamanca, where he likely studied under the well-known Dominican theologian and political theorist Francisco de Vitoria. He then held a teaching post and a canonry in the cathedral of Sigüenza, where he apparently enjoyed modest success as a teacher and preacher.[6] Still, his career up to that point certainly did not predict future fame and influence. Having never been a bishop, and having spent most of his life in northern Castile far from the Granadan frontier, Guerrero was an unlikely choice in 1546 for Granada's vacant see.[7] Still, Juan de Avila's personal recommendation apparently carried great weight with the emperor, and the studious canon from Sigüenza was installed as archbishop of Granada on November 20, 1546.

In April 1547, less than six months after Guerrero's arrival, Juan de Avila wrote from Montilla a letter advising his old friend on the unique status and special needs of his new archdiocese. Maestro Avila, who by that point had spent a total of nearly four years in Granada, began his letter by insisting on the importance of constant preaching and public activity on the part of the archbishop: "Since the wolves never cease biting and killing, the prelate should never sleep nor shut up." In this regard, he pointed to the highly public style of Archbishop Gaspar de Avalos, despite his shortcomings, as a model for the new archbishop. Above all, Avila stressed in this letter the need to train morally exemplary secular clergymen to serve in both the city of Granada and the villages of the archdiocese, and the importance of providing capable preachers and teachers for the evangelization of the moriscos.[8] Guerrero welcomed his friend's advice, and he continued to consult Avila regularly until the future saint's death in 1569.[9]

Although in many ways responsive to Maestro Avila's call to be an active and publicly engaged prelate, Guerrero in the earliest years of his archiepiscopal tenure appears to have been even more concerned simply with avoiding the sorts of bitter controversy that had consistently undermined the authority of Archbishop Avalos before him. To be sure, Guerrero, like Avalos and most reform-minded clergymen of the era, shared the common goals of improving the quality of local clergy and bringing lay religious practice—immigrant and morisco alike—more into line with officially acceptable standards. Faced with a frontier city and archdiocese unaccustomed to strong resident prelates, however, the new archbishop in these earliest years of his long tenure chose to construct archiepiscopal authority and a modest local reform program cautiously rather than confrontationally. He did so, moreover, not by destroying lay initiative and local tradition, but rather by accommodating them, using them, and patiently directing them toward his own ends. In this regard, Guerrero's approach in his first decade stands in direct contrast with the heavy-handed and authoritarian tone that he would later adopt in the governance of his archdiocese, particularly in the turbulent years between his return to the frontier city from Trent in 1564 and the outbreak of the morisco rebellion in 1568.

His leadership touch in these early years was especially soft with respect to the morisco residents of the city and archdiocese. Content at least for the moment to maintain the uneasy but relatively peaceful status quo that had endured since the emperor's suspension of the Royal Chapel mandates two decades earlier, the archbishop's policy toward the former sultanate's converted "native" population in this opening stage of his tenure is best characterized as one of benign neglect. Especially in the absence of well-trained and dedicated parish clergymen, Guerrero's initial reluctance to push for more rapid morisco assimilation owed at least in part to a perhaps realistic recognition that any aggressive plan would be doomed to failure. In a poignant 1551 letter to Charles V, he privately expressed deep pessimism concerning the question of whether or not most of his morisco flock could ever be expected to become good, practicing Catholic Christians: "Most of the residents of this archdiocese are New Christians who are so firm in resisting all that Christianity demands of them, that even with all possible diligence we cannot convince them to do those things that they are obliged to do."[10]

Effective change in the city and archdiocese of Granada thus had to begin not with the moriscos, but rather with the parish clergy who were to be the principal teachers and models of Christian faith and practice to both the immigrants and the moriscos alike. On this score, the new archbishop wasted little time. Within a year of his arrival in the frontier city, Guerrero enacted strong parish reform measures, but managed to do so in a way that avoided the sort of bitter controversy that had consistently plagued Avalos. Instead of attempting to issue synodal constitutions as Avalos had done and facing the inevitable legal challenges that would follow, Guerrero chose to mandate change through the more subtle but more direct device of parish visitations. Through a series of visitations begun no later than January 1548, he issued a set of sixteen reform mandates directly to each parish of his archdiocese.[11] Of course, Guerrero's decision to conduct parish visitations was in itself not innovative; Guerrero's predecessors had also sent archiepiscopal visitors to Granada's parishes. However, earlier visitations in Granada, as in many Spanish communities, seem to have been little more than simple and often superficial audits of parish finances.[12] Moreover, no formal records had been kept of the previous visitors' activities, as is attested by the text of the 1548 visitation of the parish of Santa María in the Alhambra.[13] For the remainder of his long tenure in Granada, Guerrero would continue to be vigilant in the oversight of the parishes. The records of the parish of Santa María, for example, reveal that it received detailed and

well-documented examinations by archiepiscopal visitors eleven times between 1550 and 1570.[14]

The sixteen mandates issued to each parish by Guerrero during the 1548
visitations actually resembled in many ways Avalos's proposed synodal decrees as a detailed formula for the redirection of lay religious life toward the
parish and the parish clergy. In fact, the principal difference between the reform mandates of Avalos and those of Guerrero was simply that Guerrero
did not publicize his as synodal constitutions. Like those of his predecessor,
Guerrero's reform constitutions required each priest to keep a comprehensive list of all of the residents of his parish, update it frequently, and use it
as a checklist to make sure that all parishioners confessed and took communion within the parish church each Lenten season.[15] The new archbishop
also balanced such authoritarian measures to control lay practice with a
clear recognition that the laity's mistrust of the parish clergy must also be
removed in order to strengthen the parish as the primary devotional center.
His constitutions included, for example, an order that each church post
publicly a table on which archdiocesan regulations regarding the amounts
and distribution of incomes among parish clergy were spelled out explicitly,
and that these regulations be observed without complaint.[16] In another constitution, Guerrero implemented tighter regulation to prevent corruption
among the secular clergy regarding incomes from funeral and memorial
masses.[17]

Following Juan de Avila, however, Guerrero also realized that imposing
strict regulations on his secular clergy was, by itself, an ineffective means of
implementing reform. Change at the parish level depended also on instilling
in all of Granada's clergymen a greater sense of professional ethics and responsibility. Again like Juan de Avila, Guerrero held that moral reform
among the clergy depended above all on the more judicious selection and
education of future priests. In his 1547 letter to the newly installed archbishop, Maestro Avila enjoined Guerrero to give special favor to the Colegio de Santa Catalina—the school that had been founded by Avalos and
Avila in 1537 for the moral training of future clergymen.[18] Guerrero accepted this advice, fostering the growth of the school through gifts and personal visits. In addition, among Guerrero's first acts as archbishop was his
1547 composition of new constitutions for the Colegio Eclesiástico de San
Cecilio—the "proto-seminary" that had been founded by Talavera. Like
Santa Catalina, the reformed San Cecilio was to focus on the moral training
of future clergy through the *studia humanitatis*. Of equal importance, the
archbishop ordered both institutions to take greater care to select only candidates of demonstrable moral rectitude.[19] In short, Guerrero in the opening years of his tenure in Granada moved quickly but cautiously to address
some of the long-standing and widely recognized problems plaguing his
new archdiocese.

The crown's 1551 nomination of Guerrero to preside over Spain's delegation at the second convocation of the Council of Trent interrupted the archbishop's local reform efforts. Still, even while he was away from his archdiocese in the years 1551–1553, he continued the push for reform back home. He wrote from Trent, for example, a lengthy questionnaire to be read publicly in parish churches throughout the archdiocese. The questions concerned the proper Christian behavior of both the clergy and the laity of each parish. All persons, both ecclesiastical and lay, were asked to denounce anyone who failed to meet these standards. The question list started with the misbehavior of parish clergymen. Importantly, Guerrero involved the laity in the surveillance of the clergy by asking whether or not the priests, "by their lives, customs, and conversations, made of themselves good examples in order that they serve as the light and mirror of the community." The archbishop listed a variety of specific faults and abuses to be denounced, including concubinage, misuse of church property for private gain, charging extraordinary fees for the administration of the sacraments, and failing to say the votive masses for which they had been paid by their parishioners.[20] This explicit appeal for lay participation in the oversight of Granada's parish clergy encapsulates much of Guerrero's committed but accommodating approach to local reform in his early years as archbishop.

Beyond battling against ecclesiastical abuses, the archbishop, unlike many of his predecessors, was also an active preacher and a regular participant in the public religious life of the city. Heeding Avila's 1547 advice to be a constant presence among his flock, Guerrero imitated members of the city's most popular religious institutions such as the Franciscans and the Brothers of Juan de Dios by adopting a highly visible and public approach to his work. The Jesuit Pedro Navarro wrote in his quarterly report to Ignatius Loyola in May 1555, for example, that "a great multitude of people" had come to hear a recent sermon Guerrero had given on the epistle to the Hebrews.[21]

In another quarterly report, Navarro spoke at greater length on the substance of Guerrero's frequent public sermons: "The doctrine that [Guerrero] preaches to his community is admirable, and it fits very well the particular needs of this kingdom; he greatly encourages them to pray, to read Catholic spiritual books, and to make frequent and proper use of the holy sacraments."[22] Alongside observance of the church's official sacramental requirements, then, the archbishop entreated lay people to take an active role in their own moral and spiritual development through private, personal prayer and reading.[23] In short, his approach to his work in his early years in Granada can hardly be characterized as the aggressive destruction of local tradition and lay initiative and their replacement by a narrowly defined official orthodoxy. As an active prelate who responded to local lay concerns, petitions, and traditions, Guerrero found numerous allies in Granada's

Christian immigrant community, and the bridges that he built in these open-ing years would serve him well in the more confrontational decades to come.

His popularity in the city and archdiocese, however, was not universal, nor was it unconditional. In time, Guerrero would face local crises and con-flicts even greater in scope and consequences than those that had beset Archbishop Avalos before him. However, during the first decade of his tenure in Granada, the archbishop enjoyed broad support and made fairly steady progress toward his goals. Already by 1554, Guerrero had not only established basic guidelines to govern the religious activities of both the clergy and the laity, but had also bolstered the moral and professional train-ing of Granada's secular clergymen.

Significant change, however, could not occur overnight. Improving the quality of the secular clergy, for example, meant to a great extent simply waiting for much of the present generation of priests to pass and replacing them gradually with the more carefully selected and better-trained students of the newly reformed *colegios* and the university. Patient though he was in these early years, Guerrero could not afford to wait that long. Quality cler-gymen were needed immediately—not only for work among the Christian immigrants, but also, more importantly, to preach and teach among the archdiocese's moriscos, many of whom remained only nominally converted to Christianity. As Juan de Avila wrote to Guerrero in 1547: "It would be useful to have devoted and zealous preachers who would wander through-out the archdiocese and win souls; but where will we find them?"[24] The ar-rival of the Jesuits in Granada in 1554 provided a partial answer to this question.

THE JESUITS IN GRANADA, 1554–1556

As an active, apostolic group of preachers, confessors, educators, and missionaries, the Society of Jesus emerged rapidly in the middle decades of the sixteenth century as one of the most important elements in the aggres-sive resurgence of the Roman Catholic church after its early sixteenth-century crisis. Under the leadership of their founder Ignatius Loyola, the Je-suits obtained official papal recognition in 1540. Over the next fourteen years, Loyola's followers spread throughout much of Europe and even as far away as Japan. Despite the great success that they enjoyed in frontier mis-sionary settings elsewhere, however, this earliest phase of Jesuit expansion did not include official activity in the city or archdiocese of Granada.

Still, even before the 1554 official establishment of a Jesuit community in Granada, a number of Granadan immigrants—mostly local disciples of Juan de Avila—had already begun to enter into and to influence the nascent Society of Jesus. Many early Jesuits in fact considered the work of Maestro Avila and his sacerdotal team, which by the 1540s had spread from its

Granadan origins to include preachers and teachers in communities throughout Andalusia, to be a model for the development of their own organization and missionary efforts. The importance of the historical figure of Juan de Avila to sixteenth-century Catholic renewal in general is underscored by the fact that the Jesuit program itself was infused at all levels with the influence of Avila and his followers.[25] Sixteenth-century Jesuit historian Pedro de Ribadeneira said of Avila that "by preparing the way, he had done for the Society what John the Baptist had done for Christ our Lord."[26] In his combination of personal spiritual discipline and the active apostolic life, Avila had certainly anticipated the Jesuits. Yet his relationship with the Society of Jesus went beyond the simple role of honored predecessor. For one thing, Avila handed over to the Jesuits control of many of the schools that he had founded throughout Andalusia, and these schools became model institutions within the Jesuit educational system.[27] Moreover, at least twenty-eight of Avila's disciples had on the recommendation of their spiritual leader entered the Society of Jesus.[28] Of these members of the sacerdotal team who became Jesuits, many were residents of Granada, including the brothers Gaspar and Baltasar Loarte—two judeoconverso immigrants from Medina del Campo who became followers of Avila in 1537 before entering the Society of Jesus in 1554. Gaspar López, a native of Jérez de la Frontera, had also lived in Granada as a member of Avila's sacerdotal school before his 1549 entry into Loyola's society. Another Avila disciple, Cristóbal de Mendoza—also from Jérez—spent time in Granada in 1548 after having joined the Jesuits in 1546.[29]

Frontier Granada's original Jesuit establishment, moreover, was in fact founded in an indirect way by yet another former Avila disciple, the Jesuit Father Diego de Santa Cruz.[30] Maestro Avila had received Santa Cruz as a disciple in Granada in the late 1530s, and then in 1547 sent him on a mission to Evora, Portugal, whose archbishop had requested that some members of the sacerdotal team be sent to found a new school for priests in his city. While in Portugal, Diego de Santa Cruz was exposed to and impressed by the work of the Jesuits, and he entered the Society in Coimbra.[31] From Portugal, Santa Cruz attempted to direct the foundation of a Jesuit community back in his own native city of Granada. He convinced his brother Cristóbal Sánchez, who still lived in Granada, to donate to the society a house owned by the family in the center of the city.[32]

Building on Santa Cruz's initiative, the head of the Jesuits' Andalusian province, Miguel de Torres, in the spring of 1554 sent Jesuit father Juan González to talk with Archbishop Guerrero about a possible Jesuit foundation in the frontier city.[33] The archbishop enthusiastically welcomed the idea. Guerrero had first come into contact with the Jesuits during his first trip to the Council of Trent in 1551–1552. There Guerrero had befriended the Jesuits Alfonso Salmerón and Diego Laínez—the judeoconverso father who would later succeed Loyola as the second general of the society. Back in frontier Granada, Guerrero's greatest need was for more preachers and missionaries, preferably ones who were well educated and well disciplined. Impressed in this regard by the Jesuits, who must have appeared to him similar to the smaller and more informal organization headed by his friend Juan de Avila, Guerrero became the sponsor, benefactor, and protector of the frontier city's nascent Jesuit community.

On September 7, 1554, the Jesuits officially took possession of the house donated to the society by Cristóbal Sánchez. Granada's new Jesuit foundation was headed initially by Pedro Navarro—yet another Avila disciple from Granada who had joined the Society of Jesus.[34] Granada's original Jesuit contingent was small; only three Jesuit novices accompanied Navarro in the first year of the new foundation.[35] The house grew quickly, however, such that by the end of 1556, Granada had eight Jesuit fathers and twenty trainees.[36]

A variety of favorable local circumstances fostered Jesuit growth in Granada—above all the favor of Archbishop Guerrero himself. The archbishop personally attended many public sermons by local Jesuits,[37] and he encouraged his parish priests to read Loyola's *Spiritual Exercises* and to invite the Jesuits to preach in their churches.[38] Not all Spanish prelates of that era welcomed the Jesuits into their communities. In Toledo, for example, Archbishop Juan Martínez Siliceo banned the Society of Jesus. Siliceo's objections were based primarily on the Jesuits' admission of judeoconversos into their ranks.[39] Guerrero, as an avowed follower of the "New Christian" Juan de Avila and a friend of many Jesuit judeoconversos such as Diego Laínez, held no such objections. In Granada, the society in the early years of its local ministry in fact attracted many New Christian adherents, including not only judeoconversos such as the Loarte brothers, but also the native Granadan morisco Jesuits Juan Albotodo, Jerónimo Benarcoma, and Ignacio de las Casas.[40] In short, Guerrero's Granada in the 1550s, unlike Archbishop Siliceo's Toledo, provided a particularly amenable atmosphere for the Jesuits, despite the presence of many New Christians among their numbers.

Granada was a city accustomed to the appearance of new and innovative religious groups and institutions. From the confraternity of Nuestra Señora de las Angustias to Juan de Avila's sacerdotal school and the brothers of Juan de Dios, Granada's Christian immigrant community had created and welcomed many new religious groups that played active, visible roles within the community. H. Outram Evennett once wrote that "it is difficult for the modern Catholic to appreciate to the full exactly how revolutionary—how modernist—the institute of the Society of Jesus must have appeared in 1540."[41] One wonders, however, how truly "revolutionary" the Jesuits would have appeared in Granada, where the creation of a new Christian culture over the previous half-century had been characterized by constant innovation—often in ways that prefigured and directly influenced the growth of Loyola's society.

Even if not altogether revolutionary in Granada, the Jesuits' highly active and versatile missionary style quickly made them one of the frontier city's most visible and important religious groups, above all in the serpentine streets of the Albaicín. Shortly after the establishment of Granada's Jesuit house in 1554, in fact, Pedro Navarro and his fellow local Jesuits launched the first major evangelism campaigns to penetrate the city's most heavily morisco parishes since the suspension of Franciscan efforts there after the disturbances of 1513. Daringly perching themselves on makeshift pulpits in the narrow plazas and street corners of even the most isolated Albaicín neighborhoods, Granada's earliest Jesuits preached loudly and regularly among the city's most traditionalist morisco residents.[42] The goal of turning frontier Granada's most embittered crypto-Muslims into genuinely devoted Christians remained elusive, but the Jesuits appear to have had at least modest success among certain sectors of the local morisco community, particularly the youth. At the request of some local morisco leaders unnamed by the Jesuit sources but obviously friendly toward the society's mission, the local Jesuits in 1559 opened in the heart of the Albaicín a large school for morisco boys called the Casa de la Doctrina.[43] Within its first year, the school grew quickly to provide basic instruction not only in the rudiments of the Catholic faith but also in Castilian reading and writing to more than five hundred morisco boys from the city and surrounding villages.[44] Like those religious institutions that proved most popular among the frontier city's Christian immigrants, moreover, the twelve Jesuit fathers who staffed the Casa de la Doctrina also went beyond their explicitly pedagogical mission by engaging in a wide array of civic and charitable functions in the community in which they worked. These included, for example, publicly begging alms for distribution to the Albaicín's poor and raising money to provide dowries for poor Morisca young women.[45]

Of all the Jesuits assigned to work at the Casa de la Doctrina, none was more important either practically or symbolically than one of the Society of Jesus' few morisco members, the Granada native Juan de Albotodo. Born in 1527 the son of an Albaicín blacksmith, he studied at Granada's Colegio de Santa Catalina in the late 1540s and was already one of the frontier city's few ordained morisco priests when the Jesuits opened their first local establishment in 1554.[46] He entered the society in 1557 and was soon put to use preaching not only in the streets of the Albaicín, but also on a number of missionary trips to the villages of the nearby Alpujarras. When the Casa de la Doctrina opened in 1559, he became its most important teacher, and he would remain a fixture there for the next decade until the outbreak of the rebellion in 1568 and the closing of the school after the first local morisco expulsion the next summer. Obviously, many moriscos considered Albotodo a traitor. When Fárax aben Fárax and his rebel squadron combed the streets of the Albaicín on the tense Christmas Eve night of 1568 hoping to raise the neighborhood in revolt, for example, they made it a point to descend on the Casa de la Doctrina in an attempt to seize the Jesuit. Mármol Carvajal reported that the armed rebels attempted to break down the heavy entrance door of the Jesuits' Albaicín residence, all the while lambasting Albotodo inside with cries of "renegade dog." Fortunately for Albotodo and the other Jesuits inside, however, their barricade held through the night.[47]

Only slightly less controversial than in the Albaicín, Jesuit activity in the immigrant-majority parishes of the lower city was no less intense. Soon after their arrival, Navarro and his fellow Jesuits quickly began to challenge the city's Franciscans as the immigrant community's most visible and popular preachers, targeting above all the city's busy streets and plazas.[48] In addition, they often preached in the patio of the Hospital of Juan de Dios, where they customarily found large audiences that cut across all of the city's major social groups and classes.[49] Outstanding among Granada's earliest Jesuit preachers was Alonso de Avila—known locally as "Padre Basilio" after Archbishop Guerrero compared his zeal to that of Saint Basil.[50] Padre Basilio arrived in Granada in 1555, when he accompanied the Jesuit provincial Miguel de Torres on a visitation of the society's new Granada foundation. Basilio then stayed on in Granada and took over from Navarro as head of the local Jesuit community.[51] Navarro's December 1555 report to Loyola nonetheless graciously made note of Padre Basilio's popularity as a preacher: "So many people attend his sermons that church and street merge together, such that he is only able to preach in very large churches or in plazas."[52] A powerful orator, his sermons were likened by Guerrero to "a column of fire,"[53] and one seventeenth-century historian compared his impact in the city to that of Granada's greatest preacher by calling him "a second Maestro [Juan de] Avila."[54] Like Juan de Avila, Padre Basilio's sermons inspired a number of dramatic conversion experiences in the city—most notably that of the cathedral canon Francisco de la Torre, who in 1555 renounced his office to become a Jesuit.[55]

In addition to the regular public preaching of Basilio and others, local Jesuits also engaged in a variety of urban missionary campaigns that targeted specific social ills and particular groups within the community. In December 1555, for example, they began an intensive evangelization campaign aimed at Granada's principal house of prostitution, located just outside of the city walls. On Christmas day, Padre Basilio personally went to the house to preach both to the prostitutes and to their customers. He reportedly managed to convince one of the women and a handful of the men to leave the house with him that day, and he marched them as a group back to the cathedral, leading them in the reciting of the basic Christian doctrine and prayers as they walked. Pedro Navarro reported that many other prostitutes were moved by Basilio's words that day, but they decided not to

leave because "they did not have the money at the time to free themselves."[56] Martín Sánchez and his wife, who as master and mistress of the
house had a particularly poor reputation locally for the inhumane treatment and exploitation of the women who worked for them, resisted the Jesuits' efforts.[57] Still, two Jesuits returned on each of the following four
days—one to preach to the prostitutes, the other to the men who solicited
their services. Every day a few more were convinced to leave, and each
group marched publicly into the city, led by a Jesuit in the saying of the
basic prayers. On one of these processions, Basilio was reported by Navarro
to have accompanied the penitents. In addition to leading the doctrine and
prayers, he encouraged many lay people who were standing in the streets
watching the spectacle to join the group, such that by the time the procession arrived at the cathedral, Navarro claimed, it numbered some four
hundred souls. Hardly a disinterested reporter, he probably exaggerated the
size of the group, but it appears clear that the Jesuits did attract a great deal
of local interest in this campaign.[58] Navarro's report explained further that,
on the very same day, "a servant of God" (it is unclear whether he is referring to a Jesuit or a lay person) returned to the house and gave each of the
prostitutes two reales in order that they not sin that night. Similarly, Padre
Basilio began a campaign to raise money through lay donations in order to
enable the prostitutes to leave the house.[59] It is unclear whether or not the
Jesuit campaign had any long-term impact on prostitution in Granada, and
their efforts probably created many enemies within the community besides
Martín Sánchez and his wife. Still, such dramatic public spectacle, combined with their regular public sermons, made Granada's Jesuits the city's
most visible clergymen.

In the more private and personal setting of confession, too, local Jesuits
very quickly made important inroads into the hearts and souls of many of
the frontier city's immigrants. Throughout Catholic Europe, the members
of the Society of Jesus had developed a reputation as excellent confessors,
above all because of their versatility in adjusting confessional practices to
the specific spiritual needs of each individual penitent.[60] Their rivals, in fact,
often accused the Jesuits of excessive leniency in confession.[61] In Granada,
Pedro Navarro and other local Jesuits frequently heard confessions in the
parish church of San Gil, between the Royal Chancery and the cathedral,
where they were especially popular as confessors among students, clergymen, and women of all social backgrounds.[62]

Like the Society of Jesus, Archbishop Guerrero explicitly held that confessors should be given wide latitude to assign penance in confession according to the specific needs of the penitent. Guerrero's adherence to this
idea even extended to the belief that confessors, whether secular or regular
clergymen, should have the capacity to assign penance for and absolve sins
of heresy. To a degree, the archbishop's stand on this issue was at least in
part simply a practical response to the specific needs of his frontier archdio-

cese, populated as it was largely by converted Muslims.[63] However, it was also an idea that correlated well with the heavy emphasis placed by Juan de Avila and his sacerdotal school on the personal relationship between the clergyman and each individual member of his lay flock as the most important bond within the Christian church. Local inquisitors, however, opposed Guerrero on this issue, arguing that all cases of heresy should be brought to their attention and subjected to their jurisdiction.[64] In light of the inquisitors' opposition, a general grant of such power to all clergymen in the archdiocese was unthinkable. The archbishop did choose, however, to bestow this power upon the frontier city's Jesuit confessors—testimony to society's influence on Guerrero himself as well as within the broader community.[65]

Only one year after the Jesuits' arrival in Granada, Navarro wrote a self-congratulatory and glowing report to Loyola in December 1555 claiming that "the devotion of this city to the Society is greater than I have ever seen elsewhere."[66] Jesuit success, however, predictably bred conflict with some of the city's other religious institutions with whom they competed for the devotional lives and attention of Granada's laity. By 1558, for example, conflict with local Franciscans and Hieronymites would erupt into bitter, open public confrontation and a crisis for local Jesuits. Through its first four years, however, Granada's new Jesuit community remained a local sensation among many of the immigrants and at least some of the moriscos.

Although many Granadans were receptive to the society, the sometimes excessive zeal of local Jesuits also frequently provided occasion for controversy. One Jesuit campaign begun in 1555, for example, targeted some open fields in the nearby countryside where many city residents went on Sunday afternoons to gamble and engage in various sports and games. Local Jesuits were dispatched each Sunday to go out among these groups to preach, teach doctrine, and convince the lay people there to give up swearing and other immoral habits.[67] Many of the participants probably resented such Jesuit attacks on their fun. As in the campaign against prostitution, however, the Jesuit fathers also frequently managed to convince some of the laity present at these gatherings to follow them back into town, publicly reciting basic doctrine and prayers in unison as they marched through the streets to one church or another.

In addition to their intrusions into such informal diversions, the Jesuits occasionally interrupted formal public celebrations with their missionary moralizing. Before the January 2, 1556, running of bulls in the Plaza Bibar-rambla for the annual commemoration of the conquest of the city, for example, Padre Basilio himself reportedly tried to stop the festivities by standing in the middle of the plaza with a crucifix. City leaders responded with complaints about Basilio's extremism.[68]

Though local Jesuits often roused controversy among the immigrant and morisco communities alike, incidents such as this should not necessarily be taken as indicative of a growing antagonism between the society and the laity. After all, Granadans of all classes continued to flock to Jesuit sermons. Still, such lay objection to Basilio's intrusion is particularly interesting when contrasted to the sorts of complaints registered by Granada's lay institutions against the city's secular clergy for most of the first half of the century. Earlier gripes about the lack of ecclesiastical participation had been replaced by the occasional complaint against excessive public involvement on the part of certain local clergymen—in this case those of the Society of Jesus. Archbishop Guerrero could not have been displeased by such a situation. To be sure, his aim of providing a corps of active, disciplined, and involved parish clergy for the city and archdiocese remained a distant goal. Moreover, Guerrero continued to be frustrated by the morisco problem that had plagued Granada's archbishops since Talavera. For the moment, however, the local Jesuits to whom he had given his constant support, together with the city's still-popular Franciscans, provided him with effective proxies for a "reformed" and active parish clergy. So, despite the enormous difficulties that continued to face his archdiocese, Guerrero in early 1556 had reason for optimism.

Later that year, however, the city faced a series of disasters. Springtime floods gave way to a food shortage and near-famine that summer.[69] In the midst of the hardship, Guerrero himself fell gravely ill. Expecting to die, Guerrero stepped up his charitable giving, awaited his fate, and called Jesuit provincial leader Bustamente from Córdoba to Granada to be his personal confessor and to administer last rites.[70] Despite his preparations for death, the archbishop survived the ordeal. The floods, famine, and Guerrero's near-fatal illness, however, were harbingers of further crises to come over the next few years.

CONFLICTING GOALS AND THE CRISIS OF LOCAL REFORM, 1556–1561

One afternoon in the early fall of 1556, an Old Christian immigrant woman returned to her house in Granada to find her husband strangled to death. She then left the house to search for information on the identity of the murderer. A neighbor informed her that he had witnessed Fray Diego de Niño of the city's Carmelite monastery of Nuestra Señora de la Cabeza leaving the house shortly before the discovery of the body. She then took this information to municipal authorities, who later apprehended the friar as he was trying to escape the city disguised as a coal merchant. The local judiciary quickly tried Niño, found him guilty, and sentenced him to be hanged publicly in the field near the Fuente Nueva—just outside the city walls on Granada's northern edge.

Archbishop Guerrero and the entire ecclesiastical establishment of the city were outraged at the judiciary's treatment of the accused, whose case fell under the jurisdiction, they argued, of the ecclesiastical courts rather than the secular tribunal.[71] The Jesuit Padre Basilio led the local clergy's protests against the royal court's alleged injustice and abuse of power. Basilio's rage was such that the secular judges banned him from attending the execution, though they agreed to allow the Jesuit Pedro Navarro to accompany the condemned friar to the scaffold.

In early October, on the day of the execution, Padre Basilio ignored the ban and awaited the procession of the judicial officials and the condemned at the city's Elvira gate, through which they would have to pass to reach the scaffold at the Fuente Nueva. Apparently expecting trouble, the procession arrived at the gate accompanied by a heavily armed company of harquebusiers and crossbowmen. When Basilio stepped up to confront and stop the procession, one of the secular court officials punched him, and the procession continued to the scaffold. In front of a large crowd that had gathered at Fuente Nueva, the friar was hanged. Padre Basilio, who had managed to recover from the blow in time to walk out to the execution, protested loudly. As Niño was dying, Basilio reportedly lifted his eyes and hands to the heavens, and in a voice that frightened many among the large crowd, proclaimed that the judges who had carried out this sentence would soon face divine judgment. The Jesuit further then uttered a shocking prayer that his own death might coincide with those of the judges in order that he might plead before God for retribution against those who had violated the jurisdictional privileges of the church.[72] On October 17, in apparent fulfillment of the prophecy, the most stringent of the three judges died suddenly. Padre Basilio himself died the very same day, and one of the other judges died within the month.[73]

Meanwhile, the outraged Archbishop Guerrero placed the entire city under interdict, suspending the distribution of all sacraments in Granada until such time as justice could be achieved.[74] He then retired to the Carthusian monastery outside the city, from which he threatened to go personally to Valladolid to present his grievances against the local judiciary directly to the regent. The stalemate between the local judges and the archbishop dragged on through the winter. The beginning of Lent passed with the ban on sacraments still in place, and a troubled cathedral chapter petitioned Guerrero to reinstate the distribution of the sacraments before Holy Week.[75] Finally, the remaining judges and officials involved in the execution backed down and begged for absolution on or before April 17, 1557, when Guerrero lifted the interdict.[76] On April 27, Guerrero ordered a variety of dramatic public observances to mark the end of the confrontation and to celebrate the jurisdictional victory of the church. Included among his mandates were instructions that the entire city undertake a fast, make a general confession (to make up for missed Lentan confessions), and participate in a procession from the cathedral to the parish church of San Gil and back.[77]

The available sources give few hints regarding the reactions of the broader lay community to this crisis. Doubtless many lay people resented the clergy's exemption from secular justice, and among such people sympathy for the accused friar would have been difficult to find. It is also likely that many pious lay people, innocent of any wrongdoing, could not understand why they had been denied the sacraments. However, indications are that there was a strong outcry from at least a large part of Granada's laity in favor of the church's position and against the royal court officials. For example, Bermúdez de Pedraza's history of the Granadan church states that, on the day the friar went to the gallows, "the death sentence was carried out despite the loud clamoring of the community, who cried out for the liberty of the church and its ministers."[78] Though Bermúdez de Pedraza was not an eyewitness to the events of that day, and his account was written decades after the fact and based probably on second- and thirdhand testimony, there is reason to take his claim seriously. For example, far from damaging the reputation of the accused murderer's monastery of Nuestra Señora de la Cabeza, the monastery actually appears to have received a boost in lay gifts and bequests in the years after the incident.[79] Padre Basilio's dramatic intervention and apparently miraculous prophecy and death also may have played an important role in mustering at least some public support for the church's position. Basilio's actions in this incident capped a brief but brilliant career in Granada. After his death, Basilio, like Juan de Dios six years earlier, appears to have been treated locally as a saint.[80] For his part, Archbishop Guerrero may have alienated some of the faithful through the suspension of sacraments, but he also managed in the process to bolster archiepiscopal power and prestige within the community by maintaining his firm stance and eventually forcing the judges to bow to his authority.

For the archbishop and city alike, however, further crises soon followed. After the floods and famine of 1556, an even deadlier menace arrived in Granada in the summer of 1557—an outbreak of the plague.[81] Then, in spring of 1558, Archbishop Guerrero and the local Jesuits became entangled in another bitter public dispute, and this time their prestige and place in the community would not emerge undamaged.

During Lent that year, a woman told her Jesuit confessor that a priest had solicited sexual favors from her during a previous confession.[82] The Jesuit, unsure of what to do in such a case, told her that he could not absolve her without first consulting the archbishop. The Jesuit then related the incident to Guerrero, who ordered him to hold another confession with the woman, in which she would be required to say the name of the priest who had committed this sin before she could be assigned penance. The delinquent priest would then face charges for his offense. However, the woman had meanwhile begun to complain to friends and family about what she considered the imprudent treatment afforded her by the Jesuit confessor. Rumors about the case began to spread throughout the city, and the Jesuits soon faced public accusations of failing to observe confessional secrecy.

The local Jesuit community was headed at the time by Padre Juan Ramírez—yet another former disciple of Juan de Avila—who had succeeded Padre Basilio as rector. Faced with a local crisis of public confidence in the society, Ramírez consulted both Juan de Avila and Archbishop Guerrero regarding the proper course of action. Ramírez then delivered a public sermon in defense of the Jesuit confessor. He chose to give the sermon in the parish church of Santiago—the seat of the local Inquisition tribunal—and the audience included not only the inquisitors themselves, but also a huge crowd of concerned lay people and clergymen from throughout the city. Ramírez argued that in certain cases it was incumbent on penitents to share the names of accomplices with whom they had committed sins, and that the Jesuit confessor had in no way violated the confidentiality of confession—neither by requiring the name of the wayward priest nor by consulting the archbishop.[83]

Ramírez's sermon did little to calm the growing storm of protest. The Jesuits' remarkable success since their arrival in Granada only four years earlier apparently had created a great deal of resentment among at least some of the city's other religious houses, and this incident provided an opportunity for the Jesuits' rivals to attack the society. Throughout Lent, numerous local preachers denounced Ramírez's arguments specifically and the Jesuit approach to confession in general as doctrinally unsound. Their invectives even went as far as targeting Archbishop Guerrero himself for supporting the Jesuit position.[84] Granada's Hieronymite preachers were the most vocal, and the Franciscans, Trinitarians, and others echoed their attacks on the Jesuits and Guerrero. Fray Gabriel de Santoyo, the prior of the local Dominican house, was a solitary voice preaching in favor of Ramírez and Guerrero.[85]

Now under personal attack, Guerrero acted decisively and authoritatively to put an end to the growing discord within the ecclesiastical establishment and the turmoil that it was creating among the laity. He called all of the city's preachers to a closed-door meeting in his own house—removed from the view of the laity. There he explained to the preachers his position in favor of the Jesuits and stated that he would no longer allow arguments to the contrary to be preached from Granada's pulpits.[86]

At first glance, Guerrero's position on this issue appears paradoxical. As explained earlier, the archbishop had previously emphasized the sanctity of the confessor-penitent relationship to such an extreme degree that he supported granting all confessors the power to absolve even sins of heresy or apostasy without passing the information to archiepiscopal authorities or to the Inquisition. However, solicitation in confession constituted, to Guerrero, a special case. It was among the most dangerous threats to the maintenance of the image of the clergy as moral examples for the lay community—an image stressed constantly in the words and work of both Pedro Guerrero and Juan de Avila. Moreover, Guerrero, with Ramírez, maintained that the passing of information regarding such priests to proper authorities in order to combat this abuse did not constitute a violation of confessional secrecy. Restoring peace within the city depended above all on convincing the laity that by helping to eliminate this abuse, the Jesuits did not, as their enemies charged, take lightly the trust between confessor and penitent.

Guerrero's job in this regard was made particularly difficult by the fact that his mandate to cease all public debate and preaching on the issue had little effect. The Sunday after his meeting with the city's preachers, a Hieronymite openly defied the archbishop by preaching a sermon in the cathedral itself against the positions of Guerrero and the Jesuits. Guerrero then called another meeting and angrily repeated his order. Again, the archbishop's explicit order was ignored.[87]

Having remained aloof from the public furor of the debate up to this point, Guerrero then resolved to present his case openly and directly to the community. On Palm Sunday, after weeks of open confrontation among the city's preachers, the archbishop himself ascended the pulpit of the cathedral to preach on the issue. Guerrero defended the arguments made earlier by Ramírez, and forcefully added: "To say that they [the Jesuits] reveal confessions is a joke and a lie. . . . Pray to God that those who have preached such a message do not pay for it in hell!"[88] He then repeated publicly his order that there be no further debate on the issue. In the wake of Guerrero's Palm Sunday sermon, the city began its Holy Week observances, and the tense atmosphere of open confrontation that had lasted throughout Lent appears to have calmed. Later, a letter from the papal nuncio in Spain confirmed the doctrinal validity of the position argued by Ramírez and Guerrero.[89]

Whether valid or not, the mere suggestion that the Jesuits failed to maintain confessional secrecy was sufficient to do serious damage to the society's reputation and popularity among Granada's laity. A number of Jesuits, including the future general of the society Francisco Borgia, wrote that lay suspicion of local Jesuits was such that it would be best to curtail public activities in Granada for a while.[90] Even five years after this conflict, the local Jesuits still had apparently not completely recovered from this blow. In 1563, for example, the cathedral chapter turned down a request from the Jesuits that they be allowed to preach in the cathedral each night during Lent.[91] The next year, the Jesuits again made the request, and were again refused. The cathedral chapter offered instead to allow them to preach in the cathedral on Sundays at one o'clock in the afternoon, during *siesta*—a time that the Jesuits found unacceptable because much of the community would be asleep.[92] Some Jesuit preachers continued to draw large audiences,[93] but in general the society played a much less important public role in Granada after the 1558 controversy than they had during their first four years in the city. Word of the Granadan case also spread across Catholic Europe, providing fuel for Jesuit critics elsewhere. Reports from Flanders, for example, note that the controversy in Granada was cited by a number of preachers there as evidence that Jesuits in general failed to maintain the confidentiality of confessions.[94]

Archbishop Guerrero also carried the issues raised by this controversy beyond the borders of his own archdiocese. Explicit confirmation of the doctrinal validity of the responsibility of confessors to refer to their prelates all cases of confessional solicitation was not enough. In order to combat this abuse more effectively, Guerrero wrote a letter to Pope Paul IV, asking for an explicit papal brief authorizing the assignment of jurisdiction over such wayward priests directly to the Inquisition.[95] The pope responded favorably, issuing a brief authorizing the intervention of Granada's Inquisition tribunal in order to root out the problem of solicitation in confession. Guerrero then wrote another letter, explaining that such action was necessary not only in Granada, but also throughout Castile and all of Catholic Christendom:

> Regarding the brief that arrived for the inquisitors, such action is just as necessary throughout this Kingdom of Castile and beyond as it is there in Granada, perhaps even more so in certain places. I thus petition Your Holiness to extend such power to all of the Inquisitions of Spain, as it is among the most pressing business of the Christian religion that in all such matters such sacrilege and abuse cease."[96]

Pope Paul IV died before the arrival of this letter, and the matter was left to Pope Pius IV. In a 1561 brief directed to Spain's inquisitor general Valdés, the new pope granted jurisdiction over all such cases throughout the Spanish kingdoms to the Inquisition.[97]

This papal action is one example of a variety of ways in which local conditions and events in Granada contributed to broader developments within the Catholic church. As with the international growth of Juan de Dios's congregation of Brothers Hospitallers, this case illustrates how the creation of Christian Granada not only coincided with, but also in significant ways helped to shape, the development of sixteenth-century Catholic reform initiatives. To be sure, the same could be said of many if not most cities in Catholic Europe. The processes by which local concerns and controversies became issues of broader debate and institutional change were by no means limited to Granada. However, Granada's contributions to churchwide reform were particularly privileged in two related ways. First, Granada's status as a frontier Christian community under construction fostered creativity and innovation. Second, the products of Granada's distinct religious milieu included specific individuals such as Juan de Dios, Juan de Avila, and Pedro Guerrero, who exerted profound influence on the direction of churchwide reform initiatives in the era leading up to and including the Council of Trent.

On August 17, 1561, Archbishop Guerrero presided over the festive consecration ceremonies of Granada's magnificent new Renaissance-style cathedral. For Guerrero, the celebrations marked the end of an exceptionally turbulent period in the city's religious life. The archbishop had by that time already been called by King Philip II to preside again over the Spanish delegation at Trent, and he planned to begin his journey on the next day. The city would once again be without a resident prelate, this time for nearly three years. On the evening before the consecration, Guerrero personally attended the meeting of the cathedral chapter, and there he exhorted the canons, prebendaries, and other clergymen present once again to maintain exemplary moral behavior in his absence.[98] On August 18, Guerrero was on the road to Trent, carrying with him not only the reform treatises of his friend and advisor Juan de Avila, but also the bitter memories of recent confrontations that had underscored to him above all the pressing need for moral and institutional renewal in the church.

GRANADA AND THE CATHOLIC WORLD: PEDRO GUERRERO AT THE COUNCIL OF TRENT, 1562–1563

Having returned to Trent in time for the opening session of the council's critical third convocation in January 1562, Guerrero found himself at the head of a Spanish delegation stacked by King Philip II with like-minded reform advocates. Although always outnumbered by the deeply divided Italian delegates, the thirty-seven Spanish prelates who attended third Trent[99] by contrast constituted with rare exceptions a solid voting bloc united behind Guerrero's leadership.[100] His confrontational championing of reform initiatives also attracted support from outside the Spanish delegation, particularly among the Portuguese and, after their late arrival on November 14, 1562, the French bishops led by Cardinal Guise.[101] The acts of the council are full of instances in which not only Spaniards, but also representatives from other nations are recorded as having voted *cum Granatensi* on specific reform proposals.[102] Just as often, however, Guerrero's caustic and accusative tone polarized the council to such a degree that by the time of the final sessions in the fall of 1563, he also faced a group of Italian delegates who opposed every one of his initiatives as a matter of course. In the words of the most moderate of the Spanish fathers, Salamanca's bishop Pedro González de Mendoza: "The Italians hate Guerrero so much that upon hearing that he wants one thing, they do the contrary."[103]

Guerrero's self-righteous obstinacy and sense of personal mission at the council grew from a variety of sources. None was more important, of course, than the urgency he and many of his Spanish colleagues attributed to matters of institutional reform—especially in his case in light of the recent crises back home in Granada that had so dramatically underscored to him the need to strengthen episcopal authority and improve the moral and educational quality of the clergy. His aggressive demeanor also owed much to his belief that most of the other prelates at Trent, above all the Italians, were corrupt men more interested in personal gain than in the well-being of the church. His anger over the corruption he saw at the council endured through the remainder of his life. Nearing death in 1576, the archbishop explained in his last will and testament that he, unlike most other fathers at Trent, had refused to accept papal bribes:

> I have no special permission from the Holy See to dispose freely of certain goods held through the Church, although I easily could have obtained such permission during my second stay at Trent [1562–1563], as did all of the other prelates who graciously accepted such grants. I was likewise invited to do so, but in order to remain free to conduct the business of the council, I neither asked for it nor accepted it.[104]

Guerrero's staunchest ally in the council, the bishop of Segovia and former theology professor at the University of Granada Martín Pérez de Ayala, echoed these accusations. His autobiography is filled with stinging invectives against the corruption he saw at Trent.[105]

Despite the opposition and constant frustration faced by Guerrero and his Spanish colleagues during the council itself, the archbishop wrote retrospectively after returning to Granada in 1564 that the attempt to create a meaningful reform package at Trent had been a qualified success: "The council concluded with complete conformity and agreement among all those present, having decreed so many things pertaining to the reformation of the Church, and some of them quite substantial."[106]

Although Guerrero in 1564 was able to praise the council's accomplishments in the sphere of institutional reform, the progress of the reform cause at Trent had been anything but constant and triumphant. From its origin back in 1545 to the close of the twenty-fifth and final session in 1563, the Council of Trent passed under the title of *de reformatione* a total of 156 decrees or "chapters." Of these, however, the vast majority—112, or more than 70 percent of the total—were issued only during the council's third and final convocation (1562–1563), when Guerrero and the Spanish delegation were strongest and most influential. During its first gathering (1545–1547), the council had concerned itself primarily with the task of defining official church doctrine on those issues upon which the Protestants based their rebellion against Rome—including justification (through both faith and works), the sources of Christian revelation (tradition as well as scripture), and the septenarium of sacraments. The principal achievements of the abbreviated second convocation at Trent (1551–1552) also centered on doctrinal issues rather than reform decrees. Of the 112 reform chapters issued by third Trent, moreover, 82 were passed only in the council's final seven months (July–December 1563) after nearly a year and a half of bitter procedural debate and delay among the assembled fathers and the papal legates. Throughout the mostly sterile first eighteen months of the 1562–1563 convocation, Guerrero remained Trent's most powerful and constant voice in favor of proceeding rapidly to a sweeping reform agenda of the sort that ultimately did pass in the council's final sessions in 1563. His leadership during the early stages of third Trent is especially well documented with regard to three critical issues of debate.

First, Guerrero spearheaded the Spanish delegation's campaign for a papal declaration that this meeting constituted a continuation of the two previous gatherings at Trent rather than a brand new council.[107] With the full support of Philip II, Guerrero and his Spanish allies maintained from their earliest informal meetings in Trent in January 1562 that an unequivocal statement to this effect was essential in order to make sure that old doctrinal controversies would not be revisited and that the council would be able instead to move directly to matters of institutional reform.[108] The principal opposition to the Spaniards in this case came not from the pope or his legates, but rather from the ambassadors of the Holy Roman Emperor Ferdinand I and the French regent Catherine de' Medici. Both sought to reopen debate on critical doctrinal issues such as transubstantiation and the nature of justification in hopes of forging compromises that might help heal the religious divisions between Protestants and Catholics that beset Germany and France. Ferdinand in particular feared that his Lutheran princes might take a papal statement of continuation as a direct affront on their teachings, thus upsetting the uneasy peace that had reigned in the empire since the 1555 Peace of Augsburg.[109] For their part, Pope Pius and the legates wanted no more than Guerrero to return to thorny theological questions that they regarded as having been settled definitively by the council's earlier meetings. In order to ensure German and French attendance at third Trent, however, the papal party crafted an ambiguously worded bull of convocation stating that the 1562 meeting would be held "under discontinuation of any suspension."[110] In the end, the council would in fact spend some time debating specific and as yet unsettled doctrinal questions such as whether to extend to the laity communion in both kinds, but Guerrero's leadership and the firmness of the Spanish delegation on the issue of continuation helped to guarantee that the council did not bog down over the old issues of transubstantiation and justification.

Second, Guerrero championed an extremely controversial campaign for a clear statement by the council of the apostolic nature of the office of bishop. He and his fellow Spanish prelates first broached the issue in April 1562 during debates concerning a proposed requirement that all prelates reside in their dioceses.[111] While no one at council openly disagreed with mandatory residence as an ideal, discussion of this matter raised perennial questions that had long vexed the Roman church: what was of the ultimate source of a bishop's authority? Did he hold his office through the pope or directly from God? Guerrero and the Spaniards made clear from the beginning their conviction that residence was required "by divine law" (*ius div-*

inum) in accordance with the character of the episcopacy as an office instituted by Christ himself, and not just by the discretionary mandate of a human institution. Led by papal legate Ludovico Simonetta, the almost entirely Italian opposition to the Spanish position responded that couching the residence requirement in terms of *ius divinum* would threaten the role of the pope through whom, by their interpretation of Matthew 16: 18–19, all episcopal authority flowed. Fearing that this issue could irreparably divide the council, the pope and his legates at the end of April tabled the question for the time being and forbad further debate. Meeting behind the closed doors of Guerrero's lodgings on May 23, however, the entire Spanish delegation with the dissent only of the bishop of Salamanca privately pledged that the issue of *ius divinum* was of such importance to the reformation of the church as a whole that they as a group would leave Trent in protest if the pope and legates refused to confirm it.[112]

The legates finally reopened discussion of the matter in November, opening the way for some of the most vocal and bitter confrontations in the council's entire eighteen-year history. On December 1, Guerrero's suffragan bishop of Guadix stunned everyone present when he rose and stated flatly, "Not only do bishop hold all that they have by *ius divinum*, but also, though they are confirmed by the Holy See, they do not by this confirmation cease to hold divine sanction, since neither St. John Chrysotom nor St. Basil nor other ancient prelates can be shown ever to have been confirmed by or even to have received anything from the Roman pontiff!" A near riot ensued as Bishop Giovanni Trevisano of Verona proclaimed the Spaniard a schismatic and demanded that he recant. Guerrero himself then joined the fray by retorting that it was in fact men such as Trevisano who were schismatic, trying as they were to undermine open debate at an ecumenical council.[113] Days later, tempers flared once again when the Spanish firebrand Pérez de Ayala asserted even more provocatively that "the bishop, after receiving ordination and consecration, is freed from the authority of the Holy See, and there remains in him only a filial obligation of obedience such as that of a grown son liberated from the power of a father."[114] The issue still unresolved, Guerrero himself a month later entered into a bitter vocal confrontation with the archbishop of Otranto, exclaiming that to argue that episcopal authority was not based on *ius divinum* was outright heresy. At the same meeting, the recently arrived Cardinal Guise as head of the French delegation publicly threw his support behind Guerrero and the Spaniards.[115]

The impasse over *ius divinum* stalled proceedings for eight full months, as the council failed to pass a single doctrinal canon or reform decree from September 1562 until July 1563. Only by skillful diplomatic maneuvering did Cardinal Giovanni Morone—the man whom Pope Pius named president of the council in March after the deaths of the original legates Cardinals Gonzaga and Seripando—manage in the words of Hubert Jedin to "save the council" from this stalemate.[116] His solution evaded the specific question of the nature of the relationship between papal and episcopal authority, but placated Guerrero, Guise, and their delegations by phrasing an episcopal residence requirement as a "divine commandment."

Third and finally, Guerrero was also the recognized leader of a bitter struggle at third Trent to wrest control over setting the council's reform agenda away from the pope and legates and to place it instead in the hands of the bishops themselves. Pope Pius's opening statement read to the fathers in the first general congregation on 18 January 1562 made it clear that, as had been the case at Trent's first two gatherings, the right of determining the council's daily agenda and proposing specific decrees and reform chapters for voting rested only with him through his legates according to the traditional formula of *proponentibus legatis*. At the end of the statement, Guerrero and many of his fellow Spanish delegates immediately protested, and within days Guerrero personally wrote to the legates a detailed tract arguing that the liberty of the council demanded the elimination of the exclusive right of *proponentibus legatis*.[117] The legates, however, refused to budge. As Guerrero and the other Spanish bishops at Trent noted three months later in a joint letter to King Philip II:

> We complain because we have been denied the right to propose and deal
> with highly necessary things that are appropriate to such councils, and
> very important to the well-being of the entire Church, especially regard-
> ing matters of reformation. It has been nearly twenty years now that
> such issues have been discussed here, but we have not yet been able to re-
> form even a single abuse at its root among the great quantity of abuses
> that exist.[118]

Although the entire Spanish delegation backed him, Guerrero realized that this was a fight he would probably lose. Disheartened, he wrote to Philip: "If this is the way it will be done, then it would be better if you simply ordered us to return to our churches, for nothing will be accomplished."[119] Continued pressure from Guerrero and his delegation as well as King Philip and his ambassadors in Rome nonetheless nearly convinced Pope Pius himself a year later in May 1563 to dispense with the *proponentibus legatis* and allow the prelates at Trent to submit specific reform proposals for debate and vote on the floor of the council itself. Horrified by the very real and practical possibility that such an open format might drag the assembled fathers through several years of tedious and divisive debate, Morone wrote to Rome that he would leave Trent before accepting such an arrangement. Pope Pius accepted Morone's argument and maintained the exclusive right of proposition.[120] If reform were to occur at all, then, it would have to come through Morone's chair at the head of the council.

Guerrero's public pessimism concerning the degree to which the *proponentibus legatis* would block genuine reform efforts, however, turned out to be overstated. Beneath the procedural rancor and apparent deadlock of the council's first eighteen months, Granada's archbishop and his allies had already managed informally and outside of the context of the council's general congregations to make considerable progress toward the design of a meaningful reform program. Although the legates maintained firm control over the formal agenda, a February 20, 1562, letter from Pope Pius authorized the prelates at Trent to begin holding unofficial meetings among themselves in order to compile specific reform petitions.[121] Out of these informal gatherings emerged a flood of proposals that provided the raw material from which the landmark reform package finally passed by the council in the summer and fall of 1563 was constructed.

It was through these informal channels that Juan de Avila's three reform treatises played an important role in defining the Tridentine program.[122] Under Guerrero's leadership and drawing heavily on Avila's texts, the Spanish delegation on or before April 6, 1562, presented to the pope two highly influential and detailed lists of reform proposals aimed above all at strengthening episcopal power and improving the educational and moral quality of the secular clergy—the first titled "Petitiones communes" and the second "Aliae petitiones Hispanicae."[123] Guerrero also circulated Avila's tracts among non-Spanish reform allies at the council such as the Portuguese archbishop of Braga, Bartolomeo de Martyris, whose lengthy list of reform proposals also reflected the influence of the "apostle of Andalusia."[124] Of course, Avila's were not the only such proposals available to the fathers at Trent, and many of the pastoral concerns expressed in them were in fact shared by earlier works such as the famous 1537 "Consilium de emendanda ecclesia," produced at the request of the reform-minded Pope Paul III by a commission of bishops, abbots, and Roman curial officials headed by the Venetian diplomat and later cardinal, Gasparo Contarini.[125] After their tardy arrival, the French delegation headed by Cardinal Guise also presented to the pope in January 1563 their own list of petitions, somewhat shorter and more moderate than those of the Spanish and Portuguese, that reflected little if any direct influence from Avila or Guerrero.[126]

Together, these various reform proposals and petitions, along with the reform debates that they occasioned at the council itself, represent intermediate steps through which one can trace the complicated processes by which local ideas and experiences were translated into general church policy. Still, because of the pope's and legates' reservation of the right of *proponentibus legatis*, the prelates' proposals could not be submitted directly to the council as reform decrees to be debated and voted upon. Instead, they first had to be reviewed and revised by the pope and his officials and legates, who drew on these petitions in formulating the wording of specific reform decrees presented back to the fathers at Trent. The president of the council, Cardinal Giovanni Morone, and his advisor, Gabriel Paleotti, were the critical figures in this process. These men took the lead in selection and compilation of certain points from the prelates' petitions and the conversion of these proposals into the sweeping reform program presented to the council July–December 1563.[127] Once formulated by the papal authorities, these official reform decrees were then presented to the council as a whole for debate, revision, and passage.

Each reform decree issued by the council, then, had its own specific and complex production history. Although individual proposals had to pass through many hands and numerous levels of debate and revision before their inclusion in the council's final reform decrees, each stemmed at least in part from the practical experiences of one or, in most cases, many of the council's prelates in the communities in which they worked. Avila and Guerrero were, again, only two among hundreds of individuals involved in this process. Their disproportionately heavy influence at Trent, however, provides particularly clear and visible case-study examples of the ways in which the council's landmark churchwide decrees reflected lessons learned locally. Their contributions to the council's decrees reflected not only their common educational backgrounds and the broader Spanish reform tradition of which they were a part, but also the distinct and particularly innovative circumstances of frontier Granada. An exhaustive study of all of the specific ways in which Avila's and Guerrero's proposals helped to shape the Tridentine reform program would require an entire book-length study unto itself, but two examples are of particular significance to the subsequent historical development of the church as a whole and the city of Granada.

First, Avila and Guerrero made important and direct contributions to the shaping of what many regard as the most consequential of all reforms issued by the Council of Trent—the mandatory establishment in each diocese of a seminary for the proper training of future priests.[128] The original text of the seminary decree that Morone presented to the council for debate was a virtual copy of Cardinal Reginald Pole's mandates on clerical education from his 1554 London synod, which Pole had in turn drawn mostly from the 1552 constitutions of the Jesuit Collegium Germanicum in Rome.[129] To be sure, Avila's presence behind those Jesuit regulations was considerable,[130] but that influence was still at least three steps removed from the text of the council's first draft. His most visible impact on the final decree came only through the debate process, in which Guerrero and the other Spaniards, along with the archbishop of Braga and his Portuguese delegation, played leading roles.[131] The Jesuit German College's constitutions, Pole's synod decrees, and the first draft of the seminary decree presented to the council all included brief prefaces explaining the rationale for new educational institutions for clergy. In all three, such action was deemed necessary due simply to the shortage of priests throughout Catholic Christendom.[132] This contrasted with Avila's conviction that the main problem among the secular clergy was not their small numbers, but rather their poor moral quality. He had in fact written that he would prefer to have fewer priests, so long as those ordained would maintain themselves as shining examples of Christian virtue within their communities.[133] The curricula of his schools throughout Andalusia, including that of Granada's Colegio de Santa Catalina, thus placed ethical training at the center of the educational process. Archbishop Guerrero's own 1547 reformed constitutions for Talavera's old Colegio Eclesiástico de San Cecilio—widely regarded at Trent and throughout Catholic Christendom as a model institution for effective pastoral training—also echoed Avila's moral focus by ordering that its rectors take great care to accept as students only young men of demonstrable moral quality.[134] In his 1551 first *Memorial* to the council, Maestro Avila had already proposed mandatory seminary education, explaining its necessity on grounds of moral formation:

> If the Church wants good ministers, it must create them; and, if it wants good 'surgeons of souls,' it must take the responsibility of raising them so, as well as the responsibility for the work involved; and if not, it will not achieve what it desires. . . . A tree, in order to realize its potential, needs, from an early age, to be directed and straightened. The horse and the mule, in order that they learn to take proper steps, must first be under the hand of the trainer. [And, similarly,] In all human offices, the good official is not born already made, but rather must be made.[135]

When the definitive decree on seminary education was issued by the fathers at Trent in reform chapter eighteen of session twenty-three, it adopted Avila's rationale over that of Pole's synod decrees and the council's first draft. Though less given to colorful metaphor than Avila's *Memorial*, the final Tridentine seminary decree reflected rather clearly his rhetoric of moral formation:

> Whereas the age of youth, unless it be rightly trained, is apt to follow after the pleasures of the world; and unless it be formed, from its tender years, unto piety and religion, before habits of vice have taken possession of the whole man, it never will perfectly, and without the greatest, and well-nigh special, help of almighty God persevere in ecclesiastical discipline; this Holy Synod ordains, that all cathedral, metropolitan, and other churches greater than these, shall be bound . . . to educate religiously, and to train in ecclesiastical discipline, a certain number of youths of the city.[136]

The council's final decree further stipulated, as was the case in Granada's Colegio Eclesiástico according to Guerrero's 1547 constitutions, that these seminaries were to accept as students only young men "whose character and inclination afford a hope that they will always serve in the ecclesiastical ministry."[137]

Second, Guerrero's and Avila's hands are also particularly evident in a series of decrees by which the council significantly strengthened the authority of bishops in the governance of their own dioceses, even in the absence of an absolutely clear statement on the issue of *ius divinum*. These decrees targeted a variety of nodes of authority that had long undermined the power of bishops, including the regular orders, lay patrons, confraternities, and to a degree, even the papacy itself. To be sure, because such calls for streamlining episcopal authority long predated both Avila's reform tracts and Guerrero's tenure as archbishop of Granada, insisting on a rigid and exclusive line of causation between Guerrero's and Avila's personal proposals and the council's final decrees on these matters would be unjustified. Already in the 1537 "Consilium de emendanda ecclesia," for example, Contarini and his reform commission had identified the inability of bishops to direct all aspects of the religious lives of their dioceses as one of the most important problems that the church needed to address, although their treatise did not elaborate in great detail specific means by which to do so.[138] Throughout Spain and indeed all over Catholic Europe, moreover, reform-minded prelates had long complained that the proliferation of papal grants of exemption from episcopal oversight, above all to the regular orders, made effective diocesan administration impossible.

Although by no means the exclusive sources, Avila's proposals and Guerrero actions at council nonetheless contributed significantly to the shaping of the specific reform packages by which the council addressed these problems. In frontier Granada, the Franciscans and other local regular clergymen had played exceptionally important roles in the creation of the postconquest city's developing religious culture. While Guerrero obviously appreciated the essential services provided by Granada's Franciscans and Jesuits as preachers and confessors, their relative autonomy from archiepiscopal oversight constituted one of the most significant obstacles he faced in the governance of the frontier archdiocese. In the 1558 controversy over confessional secrecy and solicitation, for example, Guerrero's explicit orders had proven powerless to stop local Hieronymite and Franciscan friars who preached against his position.

In his 1551 reform tracts, Juan de Avila had already proposed a variety of specific measures to subject the public activities of religious orders to stricter surveillance by the bishop, including episcopal examination and licensing of all regular clergy who preached and heard confessions.[139] The council took no action on this issue during its second convocation, and Avila repeated these points in his 1561 reform tract.[140] Archbishop Guerrero, of course, strongly supported Avila's position on these issues, and he and his followers in the Spanish delegation included similar proposals in the reform texts they submitted at Trent in 1562.[141] In addition, Guerrero's Portuguese ally Bartolomeo de Martyris also echoed in his reform petitions such calls for episcopal examination of the regular orders' confessors and preachers.[142] Trent's final reform decrees reflected clearly the purposes of these petitions. Regarding friars who served as confessors, for example, the council ordered in reform chapter fifteen of session twenty-three that they be subject in all instances to their bishop's approval: "No one, even though he be a regular, is able to hear the confessions of seculars, not even of priests, and he is not to be reputed fit thereunto, unless he either holds a parochial benefice, or is, by bishops, after an examination if they shall think it necessary, or in some other manner, judged capable."[143]

By contrast, the council did not explicitly require episcopal examination of friars who preached publicly. However, reform chapter four of session twenty-four served well the aims of Guerrero and the other reformers in this matter: "But no one, whether secular or regular, shall presume to preach, even in churches of his own order, in opposition to the will of the bishop."[144] Armed with such an explicit statement of official church policy, bishops and archbishops would have greater authority to regulate the preaching of the regular clergy, and they would thus better be able to avoid the sort of situation that Guerrero faced during the 1558 confessional secrecy controversy in Granada.

Both in Granada and elsewhere, moreover, the regular orders often based their claims to exemption from episcopal mandates on specific papal grants of immunity. In their 1555–1558 lawsuit concerning the traditional payment of the funeral fourth, for example, Granada's Dominicans appealed specifically to the 1474 papal bull *Mare magnum*, which exempted them from the customary payments that Archbishop Guerrero and the city's beneficiados claimed they owed to the parish churches.[145] At Trent, Guerrero and his delegation lobbied for the removal of such exemptions in general and the *Mare magnum* in particular.[146] In its final session in December 1563, the Council of Trent passed twenty-two reform chapters aimed squarely at the regular orders, and mandated that all of the reforms be observed by the orders regardless of previous exemptions, including specifically the *Mare magnum*:

> This holy synod enjoins, that all and singular the matters contained in the foregoing decrees be observed in all convents and monasteries, colleges, and houses of all monks and religious whatsoever, . . . any privileges, under whatsoever form of words expressed, even those called Mare magnum, even those obtained at their foundation, as also any constitutions and rules whatsoever, even though sworn to, and any customs or prescriptions whatsoever, even though immemorial, to the contrary notwithstanding.[147]

Moreover, in reform chapter thirteen of the general reform decrees passed in session twenty-five, the council specified that the *Mare magnum* no longer freed the Dominicans or other mendicant orders from paying the funeral fourth.[148] The *Mare magnum* was, of course, a papal grant, and by calling for its effective elimination, Guerrero's stand in the 1555–1558 local controversy in Granada as well as the reform decrees passed by the council as a whole represented attacks not only on special exemptions held by certain regular orders, but also on the pope's right to issue such exemptions. The passage of this reform decree illustrates the degree to which Guerrero and other prelates at Trent succeeded in pushing reform through the council, even when such reform undermined papal privileges, and despite the pope's and legates' reservation of the right of *proponentibus legatis*. To be sure, the papal party at Trent managed to insert as the council's final reform decree a qualification that guaranteed that, regardless of any mandates issued by the council, "the authority of the Apostolic See both is, and is understood to be, untouched thereby."[149] Nevertheless, through numerous decrees aimed at centralizing authority within each diocese in the hands of the bishop and impeding both appeals to Rome on the one hand and specific papal grants of exemption from episcopal authority on the other, the council had already by that point significantly curtailed papal authority on a variety of important issues.

His authority within his own archdiocese thus strengthened by the very Tridentine decrees to which he had contributed significantly, Guerrero began his journey home in January 1564. With a sense of urgent determination honed by nearly a decade of bitter confrontations in Granada and in Trent, the archbishop who returned to his frontier see that April was a man who proved increasingly willing to abandon the flexible and patient approaches long advocated by his friend and advisor Juan de Avila in favor of rigorous regulation and discipline. Guerrero's aggressive rhetoric and uncompromising policies in the mid-1560s provoked the opposition of many in his archdiocese, including not only much of Granada's ecclesiastical establishment and municipal council, but also, more importantly, the moriscos, who rose in rebellion in December 1568.

CHAPTER EIGHT

Rebellion, Retrenchment, and the Road to the Sacromonte, 1564–1600

Having spent at that point a total of less than five years in Granada, Pedro Guerrero was still a relative newcomer among the city's immigrant community when he returned from his first journey to Trent on January 17, 1553. On his arrival, he received from much of his flock a warm welcome complete with festive reception ceremonies similar to those with which the city customarily observed the entrance and installation of a new prelate. Despite frigid winter temperatures, the community and its archbishop that afternoon together enjoyed among other things a number of outdoor performances of religious dramas on a makeshift stage set up by the cathedral chapter in the city's central Bibarrambla plaza.[1] Eleven years later, by contrast, the travel-weary archbishop returned home from his final trip to Trent on May 2, 1564, to a reception characterized at best as lukewarm. On hearing that Guerrero and his entourage were near, the cathedral chapter simply appointed two of its members to ride out to greet him, kiss his hands, and accompany him to the cathedral itself, where a simple, solemn indoor procession of clergymen constituted the entirety of the archbishop's official greeting.[2]

The Granada to which Guerrero returned in 1564 was indeed a different city than the one that he had first seen eighteen years earlier in 1546, and not simply in terms of cooler relations between the archbishop and his cathedral chapter. Above all, a cluster of oppressive state and ecclesiastical policies on the one hand and growing popular fears and ethnic hostility among both the immigrant and morisco communities on the other gradually upset in the years around 1560 the delicate local peace that had reigned since the suspension of the 1526 Royal Chapel mandates. Internationally, Turkish ascendancy in the Mediterranean sharpened the worries of distant royal advisors and local immigrant residents alike concerning Granada's moriscos as a possible "fifth column" for a direct Ottoman attack on Iberia.[3] At the national level, the 1557 discoveries of secret Protestant groups in Seville and Valladolid increased the general religious paranoia of crown, church, and Inquisition officials.[4]

Also in 1557, King Philip II for the first time declared bankruptcy, and among the means he used to augment royal incomes over the next few years were dramatic increases in taxes on the production and sale of Granadan silk, including a jump of more than 60 percent in 1561, followed closely by another of more than 30 percent in 1564. Already suffering declining incomes, the tens of thousands of morisco men and women in the frontier city and archdiocese who depended on this locally critical industry then faced even further deprivation when adverse weather conditions made the 1567 silk harvest the worst since the city's conquest.[5] Meanwhile, King Philip had also appointed in 1559 a commission headed by Dr. Santiago—a judge from Valladolid's royal appellate court—to investigate royal land claims in the kingdom of Granada. Royal officials suspected that the crown had been illegally defrauded of much of the old Nasrid royal patrimony. Although this was probably true, the usurpers were most likely corrupt bureaucrats in the local royal administration itself. Those who actually had their land confiscated by Santiago's commission over the next few years, however, were almost entirely rural moriscos who failed to produce for the commissioners adequate documentary title for what was in many cases ancestral family land. Unlike royal bureaucrats, they knew little of Castilian legal procedures, and most lacked sufficient financial resources to mount effective defenses of their claims in the crown's courts.[6]

By the late 1560s, the position of Granada's moriscos in the dominant society of the conquerors had become nearly untenable, and mutual suspicion increasingly dominated morisco-immigrant relations throughout the former sultanate. The fears of the capital city's Christian immigrant community came to a head in the disturbances of April 1568, when a pervasive rumor of a morisco uprising planned for Easter combined with a accidental ringing of a warning bell in the Alhambra to initiate a near riot. Although local officials reacted quickly to prevent an immigrant mob from ascending into the Albaicín for a preemptive strike, the incident intensified even further the paranoia of their morisco neighbors.[7]

Like Granada itself, Pedro Guerrero by 1564 had also changed significantly through the course of an already eventful archiepiscopal tenure that by this time approached two decades in length. On the one hand he carried himself with an enormous self-confidence buttressed by frequent success in recent confrontations both locally and abroad. On the other hand, he was also driven at times by an almost angry determination born of his failures and frustrations in the cause of reform. In any case, the archbishop had become—as Pope Pius already knew and Granada's morisco leaders, religious orders, and cathedral chapter alike would soon learn—a difficult man with whom to negotiate. His administrative authority over the archdiocese bolstered and streamlined by the Tridentine decrees to which he had been a principal contributor, moreover, he no longer felt compelled to negotiate religious change. Instead, ignoring the gentler and more versatile approaches to pastoral work long advocated by his friend and advisor Juan de Avila, Guerrero increasingly attempted to govern the religious affairs of his archdiocese by personal decree.

Emerging conflicts among local church authorities converged with the frontier city's festering ethnic tensions in the proceedings of a 1565 provincial ecclesiastical council convened in Granada, as in each of Spain's metropolitan sees in the three years after the closing of the Council of Trent, for the purpose of officially accepting and implementing the Tridentine canons and decrees.[8] At this council, unlike Trent, Pedro Guerrero personally presided. Although his suffragan bishops of Almería and Guadix flanked him at the head of the large meeting room in his archiepiscopal palace, Guerrero clearly ran the council. Ironically, the very same man who had complained so bitterly and incessantly at Trent over the tight control of the agenda by the pope and his legates maintained equally strict archiepiscopal control over the proceedings of his own council, reserving to himself the exclusive right to present proposals and silencing all opposition.[9] Granada's cathedral chapter, of course, protested loudly, and even the frontier city's secular municipal councilors, fearing that the increasingly harsh line against the moriscos advocated by the archbishop might threaten local peace, asserted that they had the right to review and protest any provisions of the council that negatively affected city residents.[10] After the close of the council, the cathedral chapter filed a lawsuit in royal court against the official enactment of Guerrero's new constitutions, claiming that "in no way can [the archbishop] make statutes without our presence and our consent."[11] The legal wrangling would ultimately doom these council mandates to the same fate that had befallen those of Avalos more than three decades earlier: they were never published and never enacted as official statutes.[12]

With the earlier lawsuit still pending, however, the determined archbishop in 1572 called an archdiocesan synod and again issued constitutions without allowing the cathedral chapter either a significant voice or the right of proposal. When the chapter again protested, Guerrero, basing his case in Trent's firm decrees concerning a prelate's control over the religious affairs of his own diocese, responded sternly: "With regard to the claims made by the cathedral chapter concerning their rightful possession of a decisive vote in making statutes, and in other matters, it is well-known that such power belongs exclusively to the prelate, and, by right, he may make statutes without the consent of the chapter or of any other counsel." The archbishop, who customarily signed his letters simply "P. granatens," chose to sign this one, in upper-case script, "PETRUS granatens"—an unmistakable reference to the notion of the apostolic nature of episcopal authority for which he had lobbied so vehemently at Trent.[13] Facing no effective legal opposition, the 1572 decrees were published in 1573, and for the first time Granada had an official standard set of synodal constitutions.

Under the guidance of Guerrero and his archiepiscopal successors Juan

Méndez de Salvatierra (1577–1588) and Pedro Vaca de Castro y Quiñones (1589–1610), Granada's ecclesiastical establishment increasingly conformed to Tridentine ideals. Local implementation of Trent's program was facilitated by the unique circumstances of the city and archdiocese. The issues of lay-sponsored parishes and lay-nominated benefices that proved such an obstacle to reform elsewhere, for example, were made irrelevant in Granada by the royal patronage of the entire archdiocese. In his 1565 instructions to all of Spain's prelates concerning the upcoming provincial councils, King Philip II included specific mandates concerning the proper provision of benefices according to the Tridentine mandates. The copy of this letter that survives in Granada's cathedral archive includes in the margins responses, written in Guerrero's hand, to each of the king's orders. Next to each of Philip's directives concerning patronage of benefices, the archbishop wrote: "Does not pertain to this kingdom" (*no toca a este reino*), because of the Real Patronato.[14] In addition, many of Trent's reforms were simply redundant in Granada—a fact that is not surprising given the deep influence, both direct and indirect, of Granadan reformers from Talavera to Avila and Guerrero on the formulation of the council's decrees. Local institutions such as the Colegio Eclesiástico founded by Talavera and reformed in 1547 by Guerrero, as well as the Colegio de Santa Catalina established in 1537 by Juan de Avila and Archbishop Avalos, for example, had already begun to bear fruit in preparing prospective clergymen who would be more likely than the preceding generation of priests to earn university degrees. Of beneficed clergymen who took positions in Granada's parishes before 1550, only 22 percent held university degrees. Among those who assumed their positions between 1551 and 1575, the figure rose to 31 percent.[15]

Yet such successes in local reform efforts in Granada, as in many Spanish communities, did not come without resistance. Over the final decade of his life, Archbishop Guerrero faced staunch opposition among various sectors of Granada's clergy, above all the cathedral chapter, as well as lay people and lay organizations affected by his authoritarian archiepiscopal mandates. By the time of the publication of his synod decrees in 1573, moreover, the rebellion and expulsion of the moriscos had forever transformed the city and archdiocese, and the same firm hand of Guerrero that had proven so vital to local ecclesiastical reform efforts had also contributed significantly to the outbreak of hostilities.

REBELLION AND EXPULSION, 1568–1571

It would be too much to say that the archbishop by the mid-1560s had already lost all hope of genuine conversion and effective evangelization among the morisco members of his flock. Even as late as May 1568, for example, he took the initiative of writing to Jesuit general Francisco Borgia requesting that, in addition to the Casa de la Doctrina, the Jesuits also provide sufficient teachers and preachers to staff yet another local school for morisco indoctrination. Guerrero's letter optimistically added that "we should be able to expect [the school] to bear fruit in the near future."[16]

Yet years of experience in the frontier city had also served to convince him by this point that such efforts were useless in the absence of strong regulations to eradicate not only formal observance of the Muslim faith, but also those enduring elements of preconquest local culture that, as he saw it, cemented morisco identity as a community apart. In his 1565 provincial council constitutions, the archbishop took fresh aim at what he perceived to be the remaining vestiges of Islam, repeating earlier royal bans on certain local burial practices and the circumcision of boys, for example.[17] Although he opted to leave most nonreligious cultural issues out of the council's official constitutions, Guerrero during the meetings also composed and submitted jointly with his suffragan bishops a lengthy letter to the crown in which he listed all the traditions he believed it necessary to prohibit in order to make effective morisco indoctrination and assimilation possible.[18] The letter not only repeated many of the 1526 Royal Chapel mandates concerning issues such as the use of the Arabic language and traditional dress, but also added specific music and dance customs left unmentioned in the earlier bans. Interestingly, in apparent anticipation of the standard morisco counter-argument, the archbishop asserted explicitly in this letter that a ban on zambras and leylas was in fact justified on purely practical grounds even if they bore no necessary or inherent religious significance: "It should also be ordered that they not perform zambras or leylas nor even play music with traditional morisco instruments regardless of whether or not they in the process sing or say anything against the faith."[19]

In response to the archbishop's recommendations, and with the forty-year grace period purchased by the moriscos from Emperor Charles V back in 1526 soon set to expire, King Philip convened in Madrid the next year a high-profile conference of royal officials, clergymen, and scholars to discuss the situation in Granada. The resulting provisions of the 1566 junta of Madrid, endorsed by the King Philip himself, enacted as royal law all of the prohibitions recommended by Guerrero's letter and ordered their strict enforcement.[20] Philip II, moreover, proved far less pliable in 1566 than his father had been in 1526, and the desperate diplomatic efforts of Granadan morisco leaders such as Alonso de Granada Venegas and Francisco Núñez Muley among others all failed miserably. Shortly after the close of the Madrid junta, Philip appointed one of its most prominent participants— Pedro de Deza of the Council of the Inquisition—to the critical post of president of Granada's royal appellate court and ordered him to oversee the efficient implementation and enforcement of the new decrees. On New Year's Day 1567, Deza ordered them read aloud in streets and plazas throughout Granada, and his subsequent rigorous application of the bans reportedly led him to boast after the expulsion that he had "disciplined Granada with blood."[21]

In the face of such persecution, many of the city's morisco men and women likely sympathized in the early months of 1569 with their armed brethren who in the opening stage of the rebellion still dominated the Alpujarras. Living as they did alongside a by-now generally hostile local immigrant community that outnumbered them at least two to one, however, the urban moriscos remained mostly passive throughout the six months that separated Farax aben Farax's daring raid on the Albaicín on Christmas Eve night 1568 from the first crown-mandated expulsion from the city in June 1569. During that period, in fact, the only incident of large-scale violence in the city itself was a brutal massacre in March initiated not by morisco rebels, but rather by an angry mob of immigrants who, reacting to a rumor of an impending jailbreak and surprise assault on the Alhambra, stormed Granada's jail and slaughtered nearly all of the 150 moriscos they found inside.[22]

With the rebellion at its height in the mountains to the south, the king's half-brother Don Juan de Austria arrived in Granada in April 1569 to take command of royal forces. On April 22, he convened what would become a particularly portentous meeting with local leaders to discuss a plan of action. When asked for his input, Chancery president Pedro de Deza admitted that he knew little of military matters, but asserted strongly his opinion that the capital city's large morisco populace must be expelled and resettled elsewhere in the crown of Castile in order that they not provide a constant source of supplies and new recruits for rebel armies. The duke of Sesa agreed, but their opinion was by no means unanimous. Archbishop Guerrero, for example, contended on practical grounds that such action was logistically impossible and that the process of carrying it out would inevitably provoke unnecessary violence and bloodshed. The opposition of Captain General Iñigo López de Mendoza, who, like his grandfather and father before him was generally seen as a trusted friend and protector of the moriscos, was even firmer. Agreeing with Guerrero on the impracticality of the plan and predicting the economic ruin of the city and entire region if it were actually carried out, he pushed the argument even further to question the morality of such an expulsion of so many people, most of whom were innocent of any disloyalty to the crown. Although Don Juan de Austria initially leaned toward Guerrero's position, he eventually found Deza's and Sesa's reasoning compelling, and he wrote to the king a request for a royal order of expulsion.[23]

The royal order that arrived in June recognized the enormously complex logistical problems of dislodging forcibly from their homes and transferring to destinations hundreds of miles away an entire community that numbered between fifteen thousand and twenty thousand men, women, and children. The decree thus explicitly limited those to be expelled immediately to the

city's morisco boys and men between the ages of ten and sixty. It was assumed that city's morisca women, the children, and the elderly presented no
military risk, and that they would in most cases sooner or later by necessity
follow the expelled. Still, the practical dangers of staging even a limited expulsion were imposing. How would it be possible to maintain peace
throughout the process? Considering the scale of the project and the techno-
logical and communications limitations of the mid sixteenth century, a great
deal of chaos and confusion had to be expected. Setting aside only for a moment the cruelty, brutality, and human tragedy involved, however, perhaps
the most remarkable aspect of the June 1569 expulsion was that it was carried out as efficiently as it was. From the initial Granada expulsion, moreover, royal officials gained critical experience in the administrative workings
of a process that would be repeated many times over in the next two years,
not only in Granada itself, but also in village after village and town after
town in the former sultanate as crown troops subdued the rebellion.

The next Don Juan de Austria himself returned to the city in June from his campaigns in the Alpujarras in order to direct personally the expulsion's critical
first stages. On the afternoon of June 23, squadrons of royal soldiers ascended the hill into the Albaicín and went door-to-door with orders that all
morisco boys and men in the designated age range proceed immediately to
their parish churches, where they were to be housed overnight under barricade and armed guard. Fear gripped the city's "native" community, which
appears to have been caught by surprise and unprepared to resist, although
Diego Hurtado de Mendoza reported that he knew of some morisco men
who managed in the confusion of the moment to slip out of the city with
whatever they could carry in their hands and flee to the Alpujarras to join
rebel forces.[24] In the early hours of the process, the shocked and outraged
morisco Jesuit Juan de Albotodo hurried to the house of Pedro de Deza de-
manding to know what was happening, but Deza's simple reassurances that
his people would remain safe likely did not provide him much comfort.[25] To
help maintain order in the midst of this massive endeavor, those local authorities most trusted by the moriscos, including the captain general and the
morisco *regidor* Don Alonso de Granada Venegas, were dispatched to ride
all afternoon throughout the Albaicín's narrow streets and plazas offering
assurances to the displaced and their families that their lives were not in
danger.[26] Through a long and terrifying night, order held.

The next morning, Juan de Austria personally oversaw from horseback
the process by which parish building after parish building was emptied in
turn and the morisco inmates of each marched, with hands humiliatingly
bound and under the watchful eyes of a company of harquebusiers, out the
Puerta de Elvira and into the enormous confines of the Royal Hospital outside the city walls on Granada's northern edge. Frustration mounted, and a
few incidents of confrontation and violence erupted. Mármol Carvajal
wrote that one of his fellow soldiers in the company guarding the moriscos

that day, an infantry captain from Seville named Alonso de Arellano, provocatively stoked the crusading zeal of the moment by placing a small crucifix on the tip of his lance in plain view of the morisco prisoners. Horrified that this meant that the morisco men in the streets were about to be ritually massacred, a morisca woman cried out in Arabic: "Oh you poor wretched men, they drive you like lambs to the slaughter! Would it not be better to die fighting them in your own homes where you were born!" Soldiers quickly took the woman away, and violence was avoided for the moment.[27] Later, however, just outside the Royal Hospital itself, a young morisco who had hidden a brick underneath his arm managed to free his hands long enough to hurl it defiantly at a soldier, who sustained from the blow only a minor injury on the arm. A short riot ensued, and a number of unarmed moriscos were killed before some of the soldiers managed to restore order.[28]

On securing all the remaining prisoners in the Royal Hospital, each was questioned and an inventory made of their names and ages. Some were then released and allowed to stay in Granada: merchants who were to be given time to settle local accounts and liquidate their assets before leaving; artisans and craftsmen whose skills were deemed essential to the local economy; and a number whose friends in the immigrant community managed to convince royal authorities of their loyalty.[29] The rest were left in detention to pass the night contemplating their situation, still unsure what fate their captors had planned for them. Even the soldier Mármol Carvajal could not remain unmoved by the scene he saw there that day amidst his detained morisco neighbors: "It was a miserable spectacle to see so many men of such different ages, heads held low, hands crossed, faces bathed in tears, deeply saddened by the loss of their homes, their families, their patria, their legacy, their possessions, and all they had that to them was worthwhile, and still they did not know for certain what would be done with them."[30]

The next morning, the exiles began their long marches under armed escort to destinations chosen for them by crown officials. Many went to Córdoba and nearby villages, others to Écija, others to Jaén, and some to other towns throughout Andalusia.[31] Many died en route from exhaustion, and some were robbed or even killed by the soldiers sent to guard them.[32] Meanwhile, many married morisca women back in Granada scrambled to sell what they could for cash, gather their children, and proceed to wherever their husbands had been sent.[33]

By the end of June, the initial expulsion had drained the city of between four and five thousand of its morisco residents. Additional forced removals carried out in December 1569 and July 1570 diminished further Granada's native population,[34] and by the time the rebellion in the Alpujarras was definitively crushed in 1571, the capital city had lost the overwhelming majority of its morisco residents and about one-third of the city's total population. Of a total of between fifteen and twenty thousand moriscos who lived in the city at the beginning of the rebellion, only approximately three or four thousand remained in 1571, and most of those who were allowed to stay were already fairly well integrated into the dominant society and culture of the conquerors.[35]

THE CLOSING OF THE GRANADA FRONTIER: ECONOMY, SOCIETY, AND RELIGION, 1571–1600

The human and demographic disasters of the rebellion years precipitated a nearly complete economic collapse in the city. The effects were felt immediately. According to Hurtado de Mendoza, within days of the June 1569 expulsion, the distribution and availability of food, goods, and services in the city had been disrupted to the point that soldiers and citizens alike suffered greatly, and many regularly resorted to theft to meet their daily needs.[36] The hard times continued even after the rebellion was subdued. In nearly all sectors of Granada's economy over the next three decades, crisis was evident. Above all, Granada's vital silk industry, within which the moriscos of the city and kingdom had played important roles at all levels of production and sale, dramatically declined. A 1572 report informed crown authorities that the cost of spinning a pound of raw silk into thread had more than quadrupled since the departure over the preceding three years of most of the morisca women who did such work, and a 1574 report noted further that the number of operating looms in the city had fallen from approximately four thousand before the expulsion to fewer than four hundred only five years later.[37] Only after 1600 would the silk industry recover partially, but prerebellion levels of production were never again matched.[38] The crisis also left Granada's ecclesiastical institutions in a rather desperate financial situation. In a January 1571 letter to King Philip, Archbishop Guerrero reported that the inventories compiled by his staff estimated total losses to church property throughout the archdiocese as a result of the rebellion at 9,130,115 maravedís. Much of this figure, moreover, represented losses of recurring annual rents and incomes caused by the exile of moriscos from church-owned lands. The cathedral chapter alone, for example, suffered a net decline of nearly 400,000 maravedís in its yearly budget as a result of the expulsion.[39]

Meanwhile, in the midst of the economic decline, the lines of Granada's formerly fluid frontier society gradually became more and more rigid. The sons and grandsons of upwardly mobile men such as Juan de la Torre and Domingo Pérez de Herrasti consolidated their positions among the municipal elite, and especially in the hard times that followed the rebellion and expulsion, it became increasingly difficult for other families to follow their paths to local power and influence. Analysis of the changing composition of Granada's municipal council from 1570 to 1600 reveals that this tendency toward a somewhat more closed oligarchy of empowered families did not, however, imply a complete exclusion of newcomers from positions of authority. During those three decades, a total of at least forty-six men received new appointments as *regidores*.[40] Of these forty-six, twenty came from well-established families who had already placed one or more members in the *reguría* in the decades preceding the rebellion, and all twenty received appointment via "renunciation" of the posts to them by senior family members. The remaining twenty-six "new" appointees, moreover, included members of only six families whose placement of more than one *regidor* on the municipal council during the period indicates that they had clearly solidified a place among the upper echelons of Granada's political elite.[41] Of the twenty-six new appointees, moreover, many had previously held personally or had family members who had occupied the less powerful post of *jurado* on Granada's municipal council in the years preceding the rebellion,[42] and thus their ascents to the *reguría* in the years after the morisco expulsion cannot be said to represent the appearance of families entirely new to the local political scene. While some degree of advancement was still possible, access to positions of local authority in Granada was significantly more limited in the decades after 1570 than it had been in the early postconquest period.

The city remained in the period 1571–1600 a pole of attraction for new immigrants, but to a far smaller degree than it had been before. In 1561, the city's Christian immigrant community numbered approximately thirty thousand. By the time of the 1591 royal census it had grown by between five thousand and ten thousand. How much of this increase was attributable to post-1570 immigration (as opposed to 1561–1570 immigration on the one hand or shifting birth and/or death rates on the other) is unclear. Given the paucity of economic incentives offered by the city in the crisis years after the rebellion, however, immigration after 1570 likely accounted for only a small fraction of the growth. Still, it is clear that the city attracted at least some newcomers. Much of the immigration in the century's closing decades came in association with a large-scale royal promotional campaign of land distribution to attract Castilian settlers to those abandoned villages and regions of the former sultanate outside the capital city that had been left empty when their former, overwhelmingly morisco majority populations were expelled.[43] Although King Philip's highly publicized "repopulation" campaign managed in the end to bring in fewer than forty thousand new immigrants to a region that had lost a total of some eighty thousand moriscos, it did make for a ongoing flow of outsiders passing through the capital city. Similarly, the constant presence of litigants from all over Castile's south still attracted by the royal appellate court, along with the university's steady stream of students from other cities and towns, meant that Granada even after the expulsions remained a city whose residents were accustomed to seeing many new faces in their streets each day.

Still, despite a degree of continuity, Granada after 1570 was fundamentally a different place than it had been before. The Granada "frontier" was closing, at least with regard to the capital city. First, Granada's former character as a frontier meeting-point of distinct cultural and religious traditions had all but vanished along with exiles, although this generalization must be qualified to acknowledge the persistently Muslim appearance of much of the city and the continued presence even after the expulsion of a small local morisco community. Second, the expulsions, alongside the 1571 Spanish victory at Lepanto that decreased the immediate threat of Ottoman seaborne incursions into the western Mediterranean, eventually led local residents and crown officials alike to cease thinking of Granada as a frontier military outpost under constant peril of rebellion or foreign attack. Third and finally, Granada by that point had lost the relatively open frontier character of its society that had previously offered abundant opportunity for social and economic advancement to so many immigrant upstarts through the first two-thirds of the century.

In most respects, Granada after 1570 shared in rather than diverged from patterns of social, economic, political, and religious development that were typical among Spain's other major cities of that era. Elsewhere, for example, similar economic crises and the hardening of social lines in the late sixteenth century contributed to a decline in the sorts of energetic innovation that had characterized the public and private religious lives of many citizens of sixteenth-century Spanish cities. Of the religious culture of the Castilian city of Avila in the late sixteenth and early seventeenth centuries, for example, Jodi Bilinkoff concluded:

> With the economic decline and stagnation as a backdrop, religious life in Avila also underwent fundamental transformations of mood and expression. A return to the traditional, dynastic style of founding monastic institutions by members of Avila's oligarchy, an impressive gain in the power and influence of the city's bishops, and a deepening suspicion of claims to mystical experience and the exercise of private mental prayer, all signaled a sharp departure from the movements for religious autonomy of the mid-sixteenth century. By 1620, the majestic walls of Avila served as a cruel metaphor for a city closing ranks.[44]

Just as the city of Avila in this period produced no new Saint Teresa, Granada in the final decades of the sixteenth century produced no new Juan de Dios or Juan de Avila. Over the years after his final return from Trent, Archbishop Guerrero attempted to maintain particularly firm control over the religious life of the city and archdiocese, and his approach to the control of lay practices and lay-controlled religious institutions became increasingly authoritarian. For example, in a mandate issued through his 1568 parish visitations, Guerrero set aside local tradition by ordering that the mayordomo who oversaw the financial administration of each parish be a *beneficiado* rather than a parishioner elected from among the laity.[45] He also targeted a number of lay-controlled public religious displays and festivities for elimination. His 1565 provincial council mandates, for example, banned as morally inappropriate all nighttime processions, including the exceptionally popular Holy Thursday night processions of the flagellant penitents of disciplinary confraternities such as Nuestra Señora de las Angustias.[46]

Neither Granada's rival ecclesiastical institutions nor the affected lay people, however, readily accepted such controversial archiepiscopal mandates without resistance. With regard to processions of flagellants, for example, members of the penitential brotherhoods simply circumvented the will of the archbishop by staging supposedly spontaneous marches on Holy Thursday night without the official banners and accouterments of their confraternities. In 1587, Guerrero's successor, Archbishop Juan Méndez de Salvatierra, repeated the ban on night processions, noting that:

> Some of the brothers of the said confraternities, moved by their appetites, with no consideration or reason whatsoever, . . . have rebelled against authority and boasted that they do not have to go out in their confraternities; instead, they have formed squadrons of forty or fifty people, and they conduct their own processions on [Holy Thursday] night.[47]

Moreover, such lay resistance to archiepiscopal mandates also frequently found support from within the local ecclesiastical establishment itself. Specifically, Granada's cathedral chapter, largely inactive through the first two-thirds of the century, began to play an increasingly public role in the religious life of the city from the mid-1560s. Turning the tables on Guerrero, the cathedral chapter in the later decades of the sixteenth century frequently sought to portray itself as the ally of the laity against oppressive archiepiscopal policies. They lodged a formal complaint, for example, against the ban on nighttime processions.[48] In addition, it was likely no coincidence that in 1566—the same year that they began their lawsuit against the provisions of Guerrero's 1565 provincial council—the cathedral chapter finally accepted for the first time the longstanding invitation of the confraternity of San Sebastián to participate in the public procession to the brotherhood's shrine.[49] Thus, despite the efforts of Guerrero and his successors in the decades after the Council of Trent to consolidate archiepiscopal authority, Granada's religious life continued to change in ways that reflected not only official "high church" policies and the archbishops' mandates, but also particularly local conditions, concerns, and complex lay demands.

THE ROAD TO THE SACROMONTE, 1595–1600

Although by that time the city had lost much of what had previously distinguished it as a frontier community, Granada's hybrid cultural inheritance produced a final sixteenth-century surprise in the form of the unearthing of the remarkable "relics" and lead books (*plomos*) of the Sacromonte from 1595 to 1599. The discoveries quickly attracted attention across Spain and generated nearly a century of controversy throughout the Roman church hierarchy until Pope Innocent XI's ultimate condemnation of the *plomos* as a hoax in 1682. In historical retrospect, the fraudulent nature of the forged "antiquities" of the Sacromonte is clear enough to nearly all modern scholars, although a few die-hard local advocates continued to write polemical defenses of their validity even well into the twentieth century.[50] Yet despite the fact that its roots lay in nothing more than an elaborate subterfuge, the devotional hysteria that gripped a mostly credulous Granada in the immediate wake of the Sacromonte discoveries holds important lessons concerning the nature of the city's religious culture in the closing years of the sixteenth century. Specifically, detailed analysis of the immediate local impact of the Sacromonte finds, especially in the critical years 1595–1596, confirms that patterns of lay initiative that had played such vital roles in producing Granada's nascent local Christian culture ever since the conquest continued to do so even amidst the increasingly authoritarian atmosphere of Spanish Catholicism in the closing decades of the sixteenth century. It is as a part of this continuing century-long process of invention of local Christian culture—a process in which local ecclesiastical officials had so often played roles that were responsive to rather than directive of broader lay concerns and demands—that the birth of Granada's cult of the Sacromonte martyrs is best understood.

The Sacromonte story would culminate in the 1595–1599 excavations on the "Monte Valparaíso," a rocky and mostly barren hill about one kilometer east of Granada's Guadix gate. The saga actually began, however, a few years earlier in the very heart of the city itself with the 1588 discovery of a small and apparently very old lead box. The box had been found in a pile of rubble by laborers engaged in the demolition of the Torre Turpiana—the former minaret of the city's Great Mosque that had for nearly a century since the mosque's 1501 Christian consecration served as the provisional bell tower of Granada's cathedral.[51] Many Granadans believed that the tower itself actually long predated the Muslim conquest of A.D. 711, and some had even attributed its construction to the ancient Phoenicians.[52] The startling first-century A.D. Christian "relics" found inside the box were thus considered at least plausibly valid even by many of the most educated locals. The relics included a small triangular piece of cloth purportedly used by the Virgin Mary herself to dry her tears at the Crucifixion, a small image of the Virgin and Child, and a bone of the ancient martyr St. Stephen. Most interestingly, the box also contained a parchment on which was written what appeared to be a previously unknown brief work of St. John the Evangelist, composed in alternating checkerboard-patterned red and black Castilian and Greek letters and words, prophesying the coming of Mohammed, Martin Luther, and the end of the world. The parchment also in-

cluded a commentary on John's prophecy composed and signed by San Cecilio, Granada's first bishop, written in the Arabic language for the benefit
of his apparently Arabic-speaking early Christian flock in Granada. Finally,
an accompanying Latin commentary written on the parchment noted that
the items in the box had been gifts to Cecilio given to him in Athens by none
other than St. Dionysius the Areopagite, and that Cecilio had ordered (in
the mid first century A.D.!) that they be hidden in the walls of the Torre
Turpiana in order to insure that they would not one day fall into the hands
of the "Moors."[53]

The historical lessons and revisions suggested by the Turpiana parchment were stunning. Aside from the existence of a heretofore unknown
prophecy of John the Evangelist, this document also constituted the first
"concrete" evidence of the historical existence of San Cecilio outside of
vague mentions of him in lists of bishops contained in medieval Spanish ecclesiastical codices. Even more surprising to some scholars were the suggestions inferred by the languages used on the parchment: first, that an early
form of Castilian was already present at least in this area of the largely
Latin-speaking western fringe of the Roman Empire in the first century
A.D.; and second, that many if not most of the original Christians of the region were Arabic speakers (and presumably the ancestors of Granada's
modern morisco populace).[54]

As shocking as the revelations that emerged from the Turpiana finds
were, they were far surpassed seven years later by the discovery of the related, though much larger, complex of supposed relics and ancient writings
on the Monte Valparaíso. On February 21, 1595, a treasure hunter named
Sebastián López and some workers in his employ were searching there for a
lost gold mine. López, a native of Jaén, had speculated that the Monte Valparaíso was the most likely location of a rich lode that had purportedly be-
longed to the eighth-century Visigoth King Roderic, but had been sealed
and hidden by his followers shortly before the area fell to invading Muslim
armies in the year 711. The treasure seeker López had learned of the legend
of the lost mine and received a cryptic description of its location via a mysterious little morisco book written in Arabic that had recently come into his
possession on the death of a infantry captain from Seville, who in turn had
obtained the book in a morisco village in the Alpujarras where he had been
held captive by rebel forces during the 1568–1571 war.[55]

What López and his fellow prospectors unearthed that day, however,
was not lost Visigothic gold, but rather the first in a series of archaeological
discoveries that would potentially necessitate the wholesale rewriting of
Christian history and theology. The curious item they discovered was a lead
plaque inscribed in an ancient Latin script. Unable to read it himself, he and
his companions carried the strange and weighty artifact back into the city
and eventually found a linguist who could make sense of it—a local Jesuit
father named Isidoro García. García told him that the inscription spoke of

the martyrdom on that site during the reign of the ancient Roman emperor Nero of a Christian named Mesitón, who, the plaque noted, was buried nearby. Upon hearing news of the discovery, Granada's Archbishop Pedro Vaca de Castro y Quiñones immediately ordered further excavation and sent along three of his own archiepiscopal curia officials, including his vicar general Justino Antolínez de Burgos, to oversee and witness the work.[56]

Rapidly over the coming months and then continuing at a slower pace through the next four years, the craggy earth and shallow caverns of the Monte Valparaíso yielded dozens of archaeological treasures that immediately became the subject of enduring controversy and debate across Spain and throughout the Roman church hierarchy.[57] The early discoveries in March and April 1595 included more lead plaques that made it clear that Mesitón had been but one of many martyrs executed on that hillside. One of the markers, unearthed by a twelve-year-old local girl named Isabel, even spoke of the martyrdom in a nearby cave in the year A.D. 56 of San Cecilio himself.[58] Another plaque made reference to the martyr San Tesifón, whose body, the inscription read, could be found in a cave on this "Sacro Monte"—the name by which the hill henceforth came to be known among Granadans.[59] Even more curiously, excavations also gradually uncovered one by one a total of nineteen mysterious "books" made of circular lead pages (hence the name plomos), bound by leaden thread and covered with a strange proto-Arabic script and even stranger visual images in which stars of David, lines, and crosses were juxtaposed in cryptic patterns. Finally, in some of the caves not far from the plaques, moreover, workers also discovered many half-charred bones and even teeth that they concluded must have been the remains of the ancient martyrs' broken and scorched bodies.[60]

The archbishop put a team of translators led by Miguel de Luna and Alonso de Castillo—two local scholars of morisco descent—to the task of deciphering and translating the enigmatic Arabic of the plomos.[61] Taken together with information garnered from the Turpiana parchment and the other Sacromonte artifacts, the stories and prophecies that slowly emerged from their painstaking translation work gradually gelled over the next few years into a stunning image of the centrality not only of the city of Granada, but also of the Arabic-speaking peoples of the world, in the establishment and spread of the Christian faith in its critical earliest decades. According to the plomos and to Tesifón's memorial plaque, the future bishop Cecilio and his fellow martyr Tesifón were two brothers of Arab descent who had been converted to Christianity by Jesus of Nazareth himself. Shortly after the crucifixion, they purportedly accompanied Christ's disciple Saint James ("Santiago" in Castilian) on his first missionary trip to Hispania. After their arrival in the Iberian Peninsula, the brothers were among those present when James performed on Granada's "Sacromonte" itself the first Christian mass ever held on the European continent. After their return to the Holy Land and James' death in Jerusalem, Cecilio and Tesifón went back to

Spain. As bishop of Granada's earliest Christian community, the Arab Cecilio, along with his brother and ten others, then became the region's first Christian martyrs when they were put to death in a series of executions there on the very same Sacromonte in A.D. 56.[62]

In an April 3, 1595, site report to Philip II—a well-known collector of relics himself—one of the archbishop's appointed overseers of the excavation, Justino Antolínez de Burgos, described an almost mystical sense of being transported back to that horrible but heroic moment in A.D. 56 as he and the workers entered one of the caves in which martyrs' bones were interred:

> As they continued digging out the cavern, they found inside it a large caged enclosure, and in it they found human leg bones, vertebrae, a piece of a skull, various teeth, a thighbone and a foot, many of them half burned, as was the cell itself, and its walls were all scratched up. Smoke and ashes were spread all over the place, making it all seem so immediate that it felt as though the martyrdoms could have taken place there only the night before.[63]

Ironically, of course, Antolínez's senses and sensibilities were not far off the mark in estimating the genuine age of these "relics." The entire complex of bones, plomos, plaques, and prophecies constituted a sophisticated forgery transparent to some of the keenest minds of the era. Initial skeptics, including Granada's former soldier and historian of the second rebellion Luis de Mármol Carvajal and the bishop of Segorbe, Juan Bautista Pérez, had little difficulty identifying the anachronisms that made the stories told by the Turpiana parchment, the Sacromonte plomos, and their supporters implausible, above all the use of the Castilian and even Arabic languages in the Iberian Peninsula in the first century A.D.[64] It would take nearly a century of conferences, meetings, and debates, however, before Pope Innocent XI finally issued the official 1682 papal condemnation of the Granada plomos as "pure human fictions, fabricated for the ruin of the Catholic faith."[65]

The precise identities of those involved in the subterfuge remains even today only a matter of speculation. Nearly all agree, however, that the sheer scale of the enterprise demanded the participation of many individuals with various areas of expertise ranging from linguistics and history to theology and even metalwork. Blame for concocting the text and message of the plomos is traditionally placed in part or in whole on the morisco translators Miguel de Luna and Alonso de Castillo,[66] but the evidence is almost entirely circumstantial and alternative and/or additional suspects are certainly not lacking.[67] It nonetheless remains reasonably clear on the basis of available evidence that the forgers as a group were all or nearly all of morisco descent.

The initially skeptical Mármol Carvajal, for example, believed that the plot likely had deep roots in Granadan morisco culture—roots that predated even the rebellion of 1568–1571. In a 1593 letter attacking the Torre

Turpiana finds as a hoax, Mármol wrote to Archbishop Castro with the tale of a local morisco man known as "El Meriní," who had died during the first year of the rebellion. According to the story that Mármol alleged to have heard repeatedly from the translator Alonso de Castillo in the five years since the Turpiana discoveries, El Meriní had explicitly told Castillo as early as the mid-1560s that, when the Torre Turpiana was destroyed, it would yield a lost ancient prophecy that would vindicate the moriscos' faith.[68] It is also interesting that the odd physical form—lead plaques and *plomos*—of the 1595–1599 Valparaíso discoveries also had at least one documented antecedent in recent Granadan morisco history. In 1571, in the aftermath of the rebellion and expulsion, a morisco resident of Granada named Miguel Hernández Haganí had been penanced by the Inquisition and sentenced to six years in the galleys for having in his possession "some papers written in Arabic and a plaque of lead (*plancha de plomo*) with Arabic letters that included some of the sayings of Mohammed."[69]

With regard to the formal textual content of the *plomos*, moreover, the greatest beneficiaries were clearly the historical reputation and social standing of Granada's moriscos. Not only did the lead books place the Arab brothers Cecilio and Tesifón in the presence of Christ himself at the time of their conversions, but they also made the local moriscos, as descendants of Cecilio's earliest Granadan converts, appear to have Christian roots in Granada that were far deeper than those of the immigrants. One of the lead books even included sayings attributed to the Virgin Mary herself, as told to Saints Peter and James and recorded by Cecilio and Tesifón, according to which the mother of Jesus had prophesied the future greatness of the Arabic-speaking peoples and their language.[70] One of the principal subthemes of the *plomos*, moreover, was an attempt to revise traditional Catholic Christology by creating a sort of syncretistic doctrine acceptable to those moriscos who might still hold reservations concerning the Christian Trinity. The lead books referred to Jesus never as "God" or the "Son of God," for example, but rather as the "Spirit" of God.[71] One of the visual images in the *plomos* (a contemporary schematic sketch and Castilian translation of which, drawn for inclusion in a 1597 report to the king, is pictured here in figure 8.1) shows freely juxtaposed Christian and Jewish symbols with words from the *shahāda*, or profession of faith, of Islam—a religious tradition that originated nearly six centuries after the supposed martyrdoms on the Sacromonte![72]

To be sure, recent scholarly interpretation of the Sacromonte phenomenon and its impact on Granadan society has done a great deal to move beyond the simplistic, if still unanswerable, question of the identity of the forgers. Katie Harris, for example, has demonstrated the important roles played by the relics in discourses of civic identity developed over the decades after the discoveries by members of, and in the interests of, Granada's increasingly closed seventeenth-century circle of political and intellectual

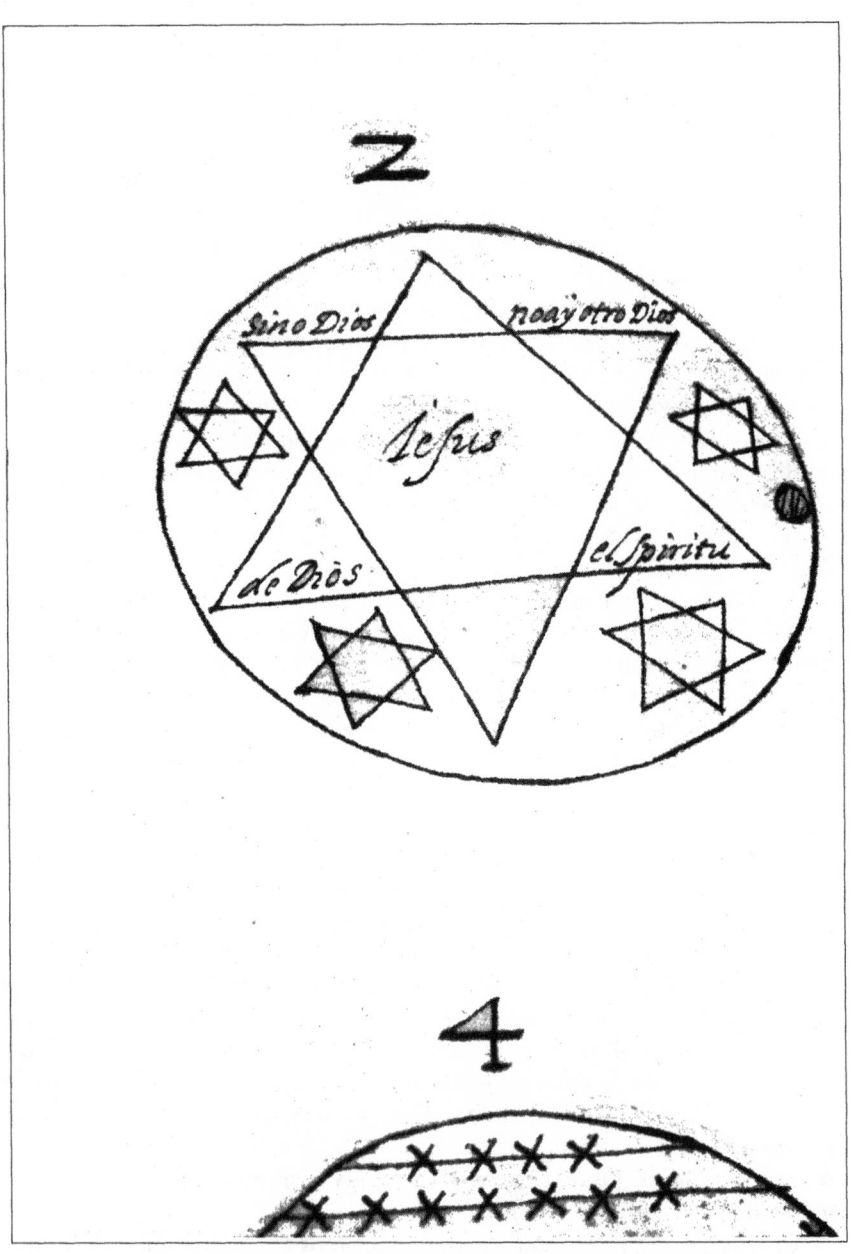

FIGURE 8.1. This image is a representation of the final page of one of the *plomos*—with the Arabic characters (which read right to left) translated into Castilian—drawn in a 1597 report on the findings to King Philip II. The words on the top of the star of David are the first half of the Muslim *shahāda*: "There is no God but God." The name of Jesus appears inside the star of David, and beneath the star are the words "Spirit of God." Source: Archivo y Biblioteca de Zabálburu, Madrid, carpeta 161, p. 126. Photo courtesy of the Archivo y Biblioteca de Zabálburu.

elites.[73] Yet at least one very troubling question remains: how could such an outlandish revision of so much of the early history of Christianity, especially one containing syncretistic theological elements so blatantly contrary to accepted (or acceptable) Catholic teachings, have been embraced initially by anyone, elite or not, in a late sixteenth-century Spanish context of rigidly enforced doctrinal orthodoxy?

Answering this question demands that we direct our attention squarely on the events of 1595–1596, because if the full extent of the *plomos'* challenge to acceptable orthodoxy had been made apparent immediately in the first few months after the initial discoveries, the entire complex of relics would no doubt have been quickly and completely dismissed by all authorities. Understanding why they were not rejected out of hand depends above all on recognizing that the martyrs and relics had *already* come to be seen locally as indispensable features of Granada's local religious culture in the spring and summer of 1595, long before the theological and historical details of the *plomos'* contents were fully revealed by their gradual discovery and the equally gradual appearance of Luna's and Castillo's translations. By the time the full range of challenges to accepted doctrine posed by the *plomos* became known and fully understood, Granadans of various social classes had already invested the relics with too much significance to dismiss them or to allow anyone else to do so without a struggle.

The local importance attached to the relics by most Granadans in 1595–1596, however, had ironically little or nothing to do with the apparent intentions of the forgers. However central the exaltation of the moriscos' heritage and the syncretistic theology had been in the forgers' designs, these elements of the story told by the *plomos* remained at first unknown (as the city waited months and in many cases even years for the translations) and later almost completely ignored in the Sacromonte craze that consumed Granada. Instead, other individuals and groups in the city symbolically appropriated the discoveries and endowed them with other meanings and interpretations that suited their own aims and purposes.

Focusing on these critical first two years, it is nonetheless difficult if not impossible to identify any specific element of the city's secular or ecclesiastical "elite" who provided constant enough support for the relics to justify an understanding of the process as a coordinated effort to bolster the social position of Granada's oligarchy. Instead, the cult of the Sacromonte martyrs spread rapidly in Granada precisely because its appeal, like that of the Hospital of Juan de Dios six decades earlier, spanned the city's economic, political, and ethnic divisions. To non-morisco Granadans of all social classes, the Sacromonte finds represented above all a tangible link to an uncommonly heroic Christian antiquity that all but erased the embarrassing historical stain of eight centuries of Muslim domination. It is true that the ancient and historically exalted character of Granada's Christianity and Christian institutions at least potentially provided strong symbolic support for the legitimacy of the city's late-sixteenth-century ruling classes. Yet the cathedral chapter, the municipal council, and even Archbishop Castro himself all appear in the key events of 1595–1596 to have acted in ways that were more responsive than directive, following rather than leading the broad-based devotional fervor.

The city's clergy, for example, certainly stood to gain from a community-wide boost in the veneration of saints.[74] Yet, for their part, the dignitaries and canons of the cathedral chapter proved remarkably slow and unenthusiastic in their response to early news of developments on the Sacromonte. The minutes of chapter meetings, in fact, make no mention whatsoever of events on the Monte Valparaíso until April 14, 1595—more than seven weeks after the discovery of the first lead plaque and a full month after the beginning of the archiepiscopal excavation team's work.[75] To be sure, the chapter from that date forward regularly designated one or more of its members to be present at the excavations.[76] It is also true that a pressing topic of discussion at chapter meetings over the next sixteen months was the question of whether or not the relics and *plomos* emerging from the Sacromonte would ultimately be housed, as the canons and dignitaries clearly wished, in an exalted (and likely quite lucrative) chapel within the cathedral itself. The chapter had for decades claimed as part of its corporate landholdings the "fuentes de Valparaíso,"[77] and the canons might reasonably have expected on this basis to stand a good chance of securing the transfer of the treasures to their own building. They formally petitioned the archbishop to do so in August 1596, but Castro rejected their request.[78] From that point on, the chapter remained noticeably lukewarm toward the Sacromonte cause. Although they instituted new festivities in 1601 in honor of San Cecilio as patron of the city, for example, they noted dryly three years later that they would continue the observance only so long as the archbishop paid for it.[79] On the whole, the chapter's actions with respect to the Sacromonte discoveries are best understood as an expression of their desire to protect the devotional "value" of the relics that they already housed in the cathedral relative to the increasingly popular Sacromonte finds over which they had no control. Of particular concern to the chapter in this regard were, of course, the recently discovered Torre Turpiana relics, which, since they had been found in a location that clearly pertained to the fabric of the cathedral, the archbishop explicitly recognized as part of the chapter's patrimony.[80]

The increasingly closed oligarchy of elite families that controlled the city's municipal council also appears to have played little or no role in the critical early development of the Sacromonte cult. In a November 1600 report to the crown, in fact, Archbishop Castro caustically attacked the *regidores* for their inattention to the Sacromonte martyrs, complaining that in nearly six years since the first discoveries on the Monte Valparaíso, the council "has not spent a *maravedí*, nor given even a drop of oil to the saints or to the caverns where they found them, nor in the [ceremonies of] authentication did it do or spend a thing."[81] While most Granada residents remained obsessed by their newfound devotion to Cecilio, Tesifón, and the other Valparaíso martyrs, the municipal council had instead spent a great deal of time and money in 1595–1600 continuing to promote the local cult of another of the region's ancient saints, Gregory of Betica.[82] Their relatively slow and unenthusiastic response to the 1595 discoveries certainly owed in large part to a desire to protect the local popularity of their own chosen devotion against the potential rival represented by the Sacromonte martyrs. During the first two decades of the seventeenth century, ironically, the municipal council shifted its position dramatically with regard to the Sacromonte cult. By the 1620s, for example, not only had the *regidores* appropriated from the archbishop primary control over the annual festivities in honor of San Cecilio, but they had also become one of the leading local voices in the fight against papal demands that the *plomos* be transferred to Rome.[83] Their enthusiastic championing of the Sacromonte cause, however, developed only after 1600, and there is scant evidence of their involvement in the critical developments of 1595–1596.[84]

Archbishop Castro, by contrast, was from a very early date an indispensable promoter of the Sacromonte cult. Yet even his support developed more in response to events around him than as a motive force. He certainly had compelling personal reasons to advance the cause. To him, the importance of the finds lay at least in part in their symbolic potential to bolster the strength and prestige of his office. If valid, the Sacromonte finds made him the episcopal successor to a man who, whatever his ethnic origins, had been converted by Jesus himself, had evangelized alongside Spain's patron saint James, and had heroically suffered a martyr's death on the Sacromonte. The *plomos*' stories also made him the prelate of the archdiocese that had been the site of Europe's first mass. All over Spain in the 1590s, moreover, many bishops enjoying the Tridentine resurgence of their positions were making extensive use of the remains and relics of their saintly predecessors to buttress the strength of the episcopacy. In 1593, for example, the body of Avila's first bishop, San Segundo, was ordered moved by the city's new Bishop Jerónimo Manrique de Lara from a small chapel operated by a confraternity to an exalted place in the cathedral via an enormously expensive public procession and ceremony aggrandizing his office.[85] A similar festival was ordered the next year in Cuenca in honor of the remains of that city's second bishop and first saint, Julián.[86]

Yet only the most cynical interpreter could attribute the archbishop's championing of the authenticity of the Sacromonte relics entirely to the self-serving promotion of a cause in which he as a well-educated man could not have genuinely believed. After some initial caution, Castro battled constantly to resist the orders first of the king and later of the pope to have the *plomos* transferred to Madrid or Rome for study, and he continued this struggle even after his transfer to the see of Seville in 1610.[87] Although one cannot necessarily be certain of his deepest convictions, he seems in the process to have become as genuine a believer as anyone. Like Justino Antolínez de Burgos, he may have developed through his personal visits to the caves a strong spiritual sense of connection to the martyrs. Among the arguments he repeatedly made against moving the *plomos* to Madrid or Rome, for example, was the idea that their proper evaluation could only be done in Granada, since only those who had actually visited the caves themselves and experienced their power could possibly interpret the finds properly.[88]

Castro's passionate devotion to the relics, however, did not follow immediately on their discovery in the spring of 1595. Perhaps not surprising given his training and background as a lawyer and former president of Granada's royal appellate court, Castro in the earliest days of the mania approached the finds not only with enthusiasm, but also with a healthy skepticism and careful efforts to gather and weigh appropriate evidence. Even well before the critical discoveries of 1595, the archbishop had already established his credentials as a man of caution and sober judgment through his handling of the ongoing controversy that still surrounded the 1588 Torre Turpiana finds. Shortly after his arrival in Granada in 1590, Castro resumed the official inquiries into the Turpiana relics that had been postponed on the death of Archbishop Méndez de Salvatierra two years earlier. After careful scrutiny of the arguments of proponents and detractors alike, the archbishop officially ruled in 1593 that the entire matter simply be tabled "until such time as God may grant more light."[89]

In his initial reactions to the 1595 Valparaíso discoveries, Castro demonstrated similar restraint. In one of his earliest letters to King Philip on the discoveries, dated April 7, 1595, the archbishop couched his report of events in the most cautious terms possible: "This is what has been done up to this point, and with all this I neither affirm nor approve anything, nor do I do more than simply relate the facts, because there remain many inquiries to be made."[90] Meanwhile, the investigations he ordered included the appointment of local silversmiths, apothecaries, and other skilled craftsmen to conduct experiments on and report on the likely age and composition of the *plomos*, the plaques, and the human remains, and the solicitation of the opinions of scholars from around Spain.[91] He also ordered his own staff to conduct interviews with elderly locals to find out if anyone had ever been seen living on the Monte Valparaíso or if anyone had previously known of the existence of the caves.[92] What was it, through all this careful analysis, that ultimately convinced the skeptical archbishop of the veracity of the finds, even in the face not only of his own initial caution, but also of the logical implausibility of the stories emerging from the caves and the apparently incontrovertible arguments of critics such as Mármol Carvajal and Bautista Pérez?

At least a significant part of the answer to this question lies in the early reactions of Castro's broader lay flock to the discoveries. As had been the case with the archbishop, the community at large was scarcely concerned with the *plomos'* syncretistic theology and new interpretation of morisco history. Unlike Castro, however, most Granadans appear immediately to have embraced the relics with open and unguarded enthusiasm. For Granada's "Old Christian" laity of all classes backgrounds, the simple notion that the martyrs and their remains constituted a tangible bridge to a glorious Christian antiquity, despite the intervening blemish of eight centuries of Islam, obviously served to bolster local pride and help cement civic identity.[93] Although the forgers aimed ultimately at much more fundamental transformations of doctrine and attitudes toward the moriscos, they were likely neither displeased nor surprised when as early as March and April 1595, as the archiepiscopal excavation team was just beginning its work, Granadans from across the city's social spectrum rapidly began to make the Monte Valparaíso the miraculous center of the city's spiritual life.

During those earliest months, Granadans of all classes flocked to the site to see the relics and to help in the hunt for more. Then, beginning that very same month and continuing at an accelerating pace through the course of the summer of 1595, a total of at least fourteen local residents from various backgrounds came forward with miraculous stories of the power of the Sacromonte and its relics to cure maladies ranging from old wounds to muteness and even paralysis. According to one report, the spiritual power of the site even inspired the immediate Christian conversion of a formerly staunchly Muslim slave named Fatima on her visit to the caves on the night of August 14. To the initial wave of fourteen "miracles" that first spring and summer there were added five more within the next eighteen months. In 1597, archiepiscopal curia officials compiled an inventory of these miracles and sent them to Madrid as part of the case to "prove" the legitimacy of the Sacromonte finds. Remarkable in the list of nineteen recipients of these miraculous interventions is the breadth of the local community they represented. The nineteen included thirteen women and only six men. Eight of the nineteen were clearly from the city's working classes, but of the six men, three held university degrees. None of them appear to have been associated with the elite lineages of the municipal council, but five were either officials or family members of officeholders in Granada's royal appellate court, of which Castro himself had recently served as president before becoming archbishop. On balance, the miracles provide testimony to the wide reach of early Sacromonte devotion across the city's class lines.[94] Might it also be possible that the string of miracle stories in the spring and summer of 1595, some of them involving people whom Castro no doubt knew personally, played a critical role in transforming the otherwise exceptionally cautious archbishop into such an ardent and passionate promoter of the cause?

In addition to these individual miracles, the reports of Castro and his curial officials to the crown also marshaled as evidence in support of the relics what they termed a communitywide "miracle" of spiritual revival and renewal that had accompanied the Sacromonte discoveries from the very beginning. Archbishop Castro, for example, ordered inquiries made with all of the city's confessors, who responded unanimously that the customs and religious lives of their penitents across the city had undergone a remarkable transformation since the relics were found. Nearly everyone, they claimed, confessed more regularly, especially since almost all of the city's residents went to the Sacromonte at one time or another, and no one dared enter the caverns without having first cleansed his or her conscience through confession and communion.[95]

The communitywide generalizations advanced by the archiepiscopal reports are, of course, highly impressionistic, and they almost certainly obscure what must have been a variety of lay reactions much more complex than the unanimity they suggest. Mármol Carvajal could not have been the only local lay skeptic. Nonetheless, a more concrete expression of exactly how broad and deep local lay enthusiasm for the relics actually was came in 1596 in the form of the rapid proliferation of ornate memorial crosses placed by Granadans along the road leading to Sacromonte caves. The first cross appeared on the hillside on May 4, 1596, although surviving evidence unfortunately does not tell us precisely who put it there. Over the next eight months, literally hundreds of processions organized and paid for by various individuals and organizations in the city carried crosses to the Sacromonte to honor Cecilio and the other martyrs. A particularly elaborate parade organized by the duchess of Sesa, for example, included more than a thousand local women and girls—some even dressed as angels—who at two o'clock in the morning streamed out of Granada's Puerta de Guadix on their way to place a richly decorated cross along the road near the caves. Such processions must have become regular nightly events in Granada through the summer and fall of 1596. By the end of the year, the total number of crosses exceeded twelve hundred—an average of five new crosses per day over an eight-month period! In the paradoxical words of one observer, the craze converted the Monte Valparaíso, into an "elegant jungle of crosses."[96] A handful of these monuments can still be seen today by the few tourists who bother to trace the early modern pilgrims' footsteps up the steep and winding road to the Sacromonte abbey and the martyrs' caves underneath.

In the end, the forgers themselves—whoever they were and assuming they were all still alive in 1595–1596—must have seen their initial excitement fade to dismay as the doctrinal and historical revisions suggested by their *plomos* remained almost entirely ignored amidst the broader devotional fervor that gripped the city. From the diverse threads of Granada's distinct cultural and religious legacies, they had fabricated a rich mythohistorical tapestry that might have provided the basis for a new society in Granada and perhaps all of Spain—a society that both honored and remained open to descendants of all of the "peoples of the book." On the one hand, they succeeded in launching a new and enduring local devotional craze, despite the radical nature of their message and the conservative mood of the times. On the other hand, however, they failed to plant their syncretistic vision of the true faith deeply enough in the hearts and souls of Granada's broader "Old Christian" community, let alone Spain as a whole, to accomplish their apparent goals of ethnic and religious reconciliation. In 1609, only fourteen years after the initial Sacromonte discoveries, King Philip III issued the final decree expelling the moriscos from all of his kingdoms. The forgers, in short, created the plaques and the *plomos,* but they did not in the process create the cult of the Sacromonte martyrs that would become one of the defining features of Granada's religious culture for nearly a century and beyond.

So who did? The Sacromonte phenomenon and its local impact from 1595 to 1600 raise yet again some of the central questions advanced in the introduction to this book, albeit now in the social, political, and economic contexts of a city that had changed dramatically since the "frontier days" of the first half of the century: who created Christian Granada, how and to what ends? For more than a century, the mandates of archbishops such as Talavera, Avalos, and Guerrero, as well as the reform efforts of "lesser" clergymen such as Juan de Avila, had certainly contributed significantly to change in the city's religious life. So too had the initiatives of local secular governing institutions such as the municipal council and royal appellate court. Yet can their efforts be said to have played a larger role in defining the tone of local religious culture than those of the mad bookseller Juan de Dios, the artisans of the confraternity of Nuestra Señora de las Angustias, the merchants of the brotherhood of San Sebastián, or the literally thousands of local men, women, and children who flocked to the Monte Valparaíso in 1595 and 1596 in search of relics or to plant a memorial cross in honor of the martyrs? The religious leaders, institutions, and reform programs that thrived in Granada were precisely those that responded best to the expectations, needs, and demands of broad sectors of the immigrant community. As the frontier character of the city faded in the wake of the rebellion, expulsion, and subsequent economic crisis, it is perhaps not surprising that Granada became much less productive of new and innovative ideas, lay organizations, and broadly influential religious reformers. Yet the Sacromonte phenomenon serves as a dramatic reminder that, even amidst the peninsulawide late-sixteenth-century conditions of deepening social conservatism on the one hand and Tridentine authoritarianism in the church on the other, local religious culture was still not simply prescribed to serve the interests of a presumably unitary secular or ecclesiastical "elite." By their visits, their prayers, and their crosses, Granadans from various social classes had already by the summer of 1596 made the caves and relics of Valparaíso their own in ways that the forgers had not foreseen and ecclesiastical authorities could not entirely control, even as the stories that continued to emerge from the *plomos* translations became more and more unbelievable.

Notes

INTRODUCTION

1. Jerónimo Münzer (Heironymus Münzer), *Viaje por España y Portugal: Reino de Granada (1494–1495),* ed. Fermín Camacho Evangelista (Granada: Ediciones TAT, 1987), 37.

2. I have chosen the term *Christian immigrants* to describe the Europeans who moved into the city in the decades following the conquest and their immediate descendants. It would be inappropriate to call them simply "the Christians," because the moriscos who remained in the city were also technically Christian following the mass baptisms of January and February 1500. Likewise, the term "Old Christians" would be inappropriate, because the immigrant community consisted in large part of *judeoconversos,* who, like the moriscos, were recent converts to Christianity (in their case, from Judaism) or the immediate descendants of such converts. Nor would the terms *Spaniards* or *Castilians* fit this group, which, though mostly from the crown of Castile, also included some Aragonese, Genoese, French, and Portuguese settlers among others. On the social and demographic composition of the immigrant community, see chapter 1.

3. See, for example, Antonio Garrido Aranda, *Organización de la iglesia en el reino de Granada y su proyección en Indias* (Seville: Escuela de Estudios Hispano-Americanos, 1979).

4. Gerard Delanty, "The Frontier and Identities of Exclusion in European History," *History of European Ideas* 22 (1996): 99; Howard Lamar and Leonard Thompson, eds., *The Frontier in History: North America and Southern Africa Compared* (New Haven: Yale University Press, 1981), 10.

5. Robert Ignatius Burns, *The Crusader Kingdom of Valencia: Reconstruction on a Thirteenth-Century Frontier* (Cambridge, Mass.: Harvard University Press, 1967), especially pp. vii–ix, in which he defines his concept of "frontier" as it applies to postconquest Valencia.

6. Andrew Hess, "The Moriscos: An Ottoman Fifth Column in Sixteenth-Century Spain," *American Historical Review* 74 (1968): 1–25.

7. Archivo Municipal de Granada (AMG), legajo 1930, año 1572.

8. Américo Castro, *España en su historia: cristianos, moros, y judíos,* 2d ed. (Barcelona: Editorial crítica, 1983), 200–209.

9. David Nirenberg, *Communities of Violence: Persecution of Minorities in the Middle Ages* (Princeton: Princeton University Press, 1996); Norman Roth, "Coexistence and Confrontation: Jews and Christians in Medieval Spain," in *The Jews of Spain and the Expulsion of 1492,* ed. Moshe Lazar and Stephen Haliczer (Lancaster, Calif.: Labyrinthos, 1997), 1–24.

10. Mark Meyerson, "Introduction," in *Christians, Muslims, and Jews in Medieval and Early Modern Spain: Interaction and Cultural Change,*" ed. Mark D. Meyerson and Edward D. English (Notre Dame: University of Notre Dame Press, 1999), xi–xxi.

11. The literature on this topic is vast. A few influential "classic" works include Antonio Domínguez Ortiz and Bernard Vincent, *Historia de los moriscos: vida y tragedia de una minoría,* 2d ed. (Madrid: Alianza editorial, 1993); Yitzhak Baer, *A History of the Jews in Christian Spain,* 2 vols., trans. Louis Schoffman (Philadelphia: Jewish Publication Society of America, 1966); Henry Kamen, *The Spanish Inquisition: A Historical Revision* (New Haven: Yale University Press, 1997).

12. Maurice Kriegel, "La prise d'une décision: l'expulsion des juifs d'Espagne," *Revue Historique* 260 (1978): 49–90. For an alternative interpretation that stresses popular pressure and especially the support of powerful judeoconverso members of Castilian municipal elites as critical factors contributing to the expulsion of the Jews, see Stephen Haliczer, "The Expulsion of the Jews as a Social Process," in *The Jews of Spain and the Expulsion of 1492*, eds. Moshe Lazar and Stephen Haliczer (Lancaster, Calif.: Labyrinthos, 1997), 237–251.

13. For a recent formulation of this argument, see Antonio Luis Cortés Peña, *Iglesia y cultura en la Andalucía moderna: Tendencias de la investigación, Estado de las cuestiones* (Granada: Proyecto Sur, 1996), 154–156.

14. Mark Meyerson, *The Muslims of Valencia in the Age of Fernando and Isabel: Between Coexistence and Crusade* (Berkeley: University of California Press, 1991), 5–6.

15. Ibid., 6–7; 10–12; 271–272.

16. Kenneth Garrad, "La industria sedera granadina en el siglo XVI y su conexión con el levantamiento de las Alpujarras," *Miscelánea de Estudios Árabes y Hebráicos* 5 (1956): 73–98.

17. Monumenta Historica Societatis Iesu (MHSI), *Litterae Quadrimestres,* 7 vols. (Madrid: A. Avrial, 1894–1932), 4:624–625.

18. Meyerson, *The Muslims of Valencia,* 57.

19. Enrique Soria Mesa, "De la conquista a la asimilación: La integración de la aristocracia nazarí en la oligarquía granadina, siglos XV-XVI," *Áreas* 74 (1992): 51–64; Amalia García Pedraza, "El otro morisco: Algunas reflexiones sobre el estudio de la religiosidad morisca a través de fuentes notariales," *Sharq al-Andalus* 12 (1995): 223–234. See also James B. Tueller, "Good and Faithful Christians: Moriscos and Catholicism in Early Modern Spain," Ph.D. diss.: Columbia University, 1997.

20. On the use and abuse of the terms *Catholic Reformation* and *Catholic Reform,* see John O'Malley, *Trent and All That: Renaming Catholicism in the Early Modern Era* (Cambridge: Harvard University Press, 2000), 130–134.

21. David Coleman, "Moral Formation and Social Control in the Catholic Reformation: The Case of San Juan de Avila," *Sixteenth Century Journal* 26 (1995):17–30.

22. Marc Forster, *The Counter-Reformation in the Villages: Religion and Reform in the Bishopric of Speyer, 1560–1720* (Ithaca: Cornell University Press, 1992); Sara T. Nalle, *God in La Mancha: Religious Reform and the People of Cuenca, 1500–1650* (Baltimore: The Johns Hopkins University Press, 1992).

23. Burns, *The Crusader Kingdom of Valencia,* esp. chapter 11.

24. John Frederick Schwaller, *The Church and Clergy in Sixteenth-Century Mexico* (Albuquerque: University of New Mexico Press, 1987).

25. Wilhelm Maurenbrecher, *Geschichte der katholischen Reformation* (Nördlingen: C. H. Beck, 1880); H. Outram Evennett, *The Spirit of the Counter-Reformation,* ed. John Bossy (Cambridge: Cambridge University Press, 1968), 11–12.

26. Elizabeth Gleason, *Gasparo Contarini: Venice, Rome, and Reform* (Berkeley: University of California Press, 1993).

27. Henry Kamen, *The Phoenix and the Flame: Catalonia and the Counter-Reformation* (New Haven: Yale University Press, 1993); Alyson Poska, *Regulating the People: The Catholic Reformation in Seventeenth-Century Spain* (London: E. J. Brill, 1998); Nalle, *God in La Mancha.*

28. For an example of how local concerns shaped another broadly influential reform movement—the one applied by Teresa of Avila to the Carmelite order—see Jodi Bilinkoff, *The Avila of Saint Teresa: Religious Reform in a Sixteenth-Century City* (Ithaca: Cornell University Press, 1989).

29. William Christian, *Local Religion in Sixteenth Century Spain* (Princeton: Princeton University Press, 1981). Christian's seminal book has fundamentally influenced nearly all subsequent studies of early modern Spanish Catholicism (including this one).

30. Craig Harline, "Official Religion-Popular Religion in Recent Historiography of the Catholic Reformation," *Archive for Reformation History* 81 (1990): 239–262. Harline and his colleague Eddy Put applied this approach in their recent book, *A Bishop's Tale: Mathias*

Hovius among his Flock in Seventeenth-Century Flanders (New Haven: Yale University Press, 2000).

31. For another recent example of this new approach to the institutional church in the post-Trent period, see Benjamin Ehlers's dissertation on Archbishop of Valencia Juan de Ribera, "Christians and Muslims in Valencia: The Archbishop Juan de Ribera (1532–1611) and the Formation of a *Communitas Christiana*," Ph.D. diss., The Johns Hopkins University, 1999.

1. A FRONTIER SOCIETY

1. Linda Martz, "Toledanos and the Kingdom of Granada, 1492–1560s," in *Spain, Europe and the Atlantic World. Essays in Honour of John H. Elliott,* ed. Richard L. Kagan and Geoffrey Parker (Cambridge: Cambridge University Press, 1995), 111.

2. *Colección de documentos inéditos para la historia de España* (CODOIN), 113 vols. (Madrid: Real Academia de la Historia, 1842–1898), 11: 516, 551; 14: 462; K. Garrad, "The Causes of the Second Rebellion of the Alpujarra (1568–1571)," Ph.D. diss., Cambridge University, 1955, 65–66.

3. AMG, legajo 1930, 1539 cédula.

4. Martz, "Toledanos and the Kingdom of Granada," 116–117.

5. Enrique Soria Mesa, "La familia Pérez de Herrasti: Un acercamiento al estudio de la élite local granadina en los siglos XV al XVII," *Chronica Nova* 19 (1991): 383–404.

6. Archivo de Protócolos de Granada (APG), 1577 protócolos of Bartólome Díaz, f. 125.

7. Cited in Jesús Luque Moreno, *Granada en el siglo XVI: Juan de Vilches y otros testimonios de la época* (Granada: Universidad de Granada, 1994), 237.

8. Miguel Angel Ladero Quesada, *Granada después de la conquista: Repobladores y moriscos,* 2d ed. (Granada: Diputación Provincial de Granada, 1993), 283.

9. Rafael Gerardo Peinado Santaella and José Enrique López de Coca Castañer, *Historia de Granada.* Vol. 2. *La época medieval, siglos VIII-XV* (Granada: Editorial Don Quijote, 1987), 312–313.

10. Archivo General de Simancas (AGS), Cámara de Castilla, leg. 2150. For details on the results of the 1561 royal census, see table 3.1 in chapter 3.

11. Antonio Luis Cortés Peña and Bernard Vincent, *Historia de Granada.* Vol. 3. *La época moderna, siglos XVI, XVII y XVIII* (Granada: Editorial Don Quixote, 1986), 61. Felipe Ruiz Martín, "Movimientos demográficos y económicos en el reino de Granada," *Anuario de Historia Económica y Social* 1 (1968): 144–145.

12. Antonio Domínguez Ortiz, *La sociedad española en el siglo XVII,* 2 vols. (Madrid: Consejo Superior de Investigaciones Científicas, 1963) 1:129–157.

13. Miguel Ángel Ladero Quesada, "La repoblación del reino de Granada anterior al año 1500," *Hispania* 28 (1968): 525–526.

14. Münzer, *Viaje por España,* 37.

15. Ladero Quesada, "La repoblación del reino de Granada," 526–527.

16. Archivo de la Real Chancillería de Granada (AChG), cabina 301, legajo 67, p. 5.

17. José Antonio López Nevot, *La organización institucional del municipio de Granada durante el siglo XVI* (Granada: Universidad de Granada, 1994), 111.

18. For detailed analysis of the development of Granada's governing classes, see chapter 4.

19. Ladero Quesada, *Granada después de la conquista,* 85–91; Bernard Vincent, *Andalucía en la edad moderna: Economía y sociedad* (Granada: Diputación Provincial de Granada, 1985), 197.

20. Ladero Quesada, "La repoblación del reino de Granada," 490.

21. Münzer, *Viaje por España,* 49.

22. Ladero Quesada, "La repoblación del reino de Granada," 526–527.

23. Luis de Mármol Carvajal, *Rebelión y castigo de los moriscos del reino de Granada* (Málaga, 1600; repr. Málaga: Editorial Arguval, 1991), 58.

24. Burns, *The Crusader Kingdom of Valencia,* 8–9.

25. Manuel González Jiménez, "Frontier and Settlement in the Kingdom of Castile (1085–1350)," in *Medieval Frontier Societies,* ed. Robert Bartlett and Angus MacKay (Oxford: Clarendon Press, 1989), 70–72.

26. Granada's municipal council listed the various *franquezas* granted by the crown in two separate entries in AMG, Libro 1 de actas, entries of December 15, 1497, and March 24, 1500. These incentives are also listed as an appendix in Ladero Quesada, "La repoblación del reino de Granada."

27. AMG, Libro 1 de actas, October 16, 1500.

28. AGS, Patronato Real, caja 10, p. 45.

29. The segregation agreement is discussed in greater detail in chapter 3.

30. The crown's violations of the treaty's terms are discussed in greater detail in chapter 2.

31. Peter Boyd Bowman, "Patterns of Spanish Emigration to the Indies until 1600," *Hispanic American Historical Review* 56 (1976): 580–604.

32. Thomas F. Glick, "Reading the *Repartimientos:* Modeling Settlement in the Wake of Conquest," in *Christians, Muslims, and Jews in Medieval and Early Modern Spain: Interaction and Cultural Change,* ed. Mark D. Meyerson and Edward D. English (Notre Dame: University of Notre Dame Press, 1999), 20–39.

33. Rafael G. Peinado Santaella, *La repoblación de la tierra de Granada: los montes orientales (1485–1515)* (Granada: Universidad de Granada, 1989); Ladero Quesada, "La repoblación del reino de Granada."

34. By supplementing her work in Seville's *Archivo General de las Indias* with precisely this sort of detailed research in local archives in both Spain and the Americas, Ida Altman has revolutionized our understanding of how early colonial settlement in the New World was orchestrated and experienced among Spaniards of various social backgrounds. See her two books: *Emigrants and Society: Extremadura and America in the Sixteenth Century* (Berkeley: University of California Press, 1989), and *Transatlantic Ties in the Spanish Empire: Brihuega, Spain, and Puebla, Mexico* (Stanford: Stanford University Press, 2000). For an example of how the "supply side" of immigration to frontier Granada can be explored in the archives of the cities and towns from which the immigrants came, see Martz, "Toledanos and the Kingdom of Granada."

35. Data drawn from: AChG, cabina 3, legajo 354, p. 3; cabina 3, legajo 884, p. 18; cabina 3, legajo 985, p. 9; cabina 3, legajo 1191, p. 1; cabina 3, legajo 1459, p. 10; cabina 302, legajo 341, p. 6; cabina 501, legajo 23, p. 5; cabina 507, legajo 1433, p. 1; cabina 511, legajo 2271, p. 3; and cabina 513, legajo 2527, p. 3.

36. Witnesses frequently responded to standard questions concerning their age and years of residence in the city with vague estimates, usually in multiples of ten, and they often contradicted themselves. As a result, I have chosen for this database only those individuals who testified more than once without contradiction, or those whose responses were not given in multiples of ten.

37. For a more detailed profile of the economic activities of the immigrant community, see table 1.2 below.

38. González Jiménez, "Frontier and Settlement," 64–73; Burns, *The Crusader Kingdom of Valencia,* 7–9; María Josefa Parejo Delgado, *Baeza y Úbeda en la baja edad media* (Granada: Editorial Don Quixote, 1988), 73; John Edwards, *Christian Córdoba: The City and Its Region in the Late Middle Ages* (Cambridge: Cambridge University Press, 1982), 7–8.

39. Cortés Peña and Vincent, *Historia de Granada,* 50.

40. Thomas Dandelet, "Spanish Conquest and Colonization at the Center of the Old World: The Spanish Nation in Rome, 1555–1625," *Journal of Modern History* 69 (1997): 479–511.

41. Boyd Bowman, "Patterns of Spanish Emigration," 582–590.

42. Cortés Peña and Vincent, *Historia de Granada,* 56–57.

43. Asunción Lavrin, "Women in Colonial Mexico," in *The Oxford History of Mexico,* ed. Michael C. Meyer and William H. Beezley (Oxford: Oxford University Press, 2000), 252; James Lockhart, *Spanish Peru 1532–1560: A Colonial Society* (Madison: University of Wisconsin Press, 1968), 169–170; Boyd Bowman, "Patterns of Spanish Emigration," 596–601.

44. The nature of this database is discussed in greater detail in chapter 5.

45. APG, 1539 *protócolos* of Martín de Olivares, f. 634.

46. APG, 1577 *protócolos* of Bartólome Díaz, f. 812–813.

47. Such legal restrictions, however, were not always strictly enforced: Altman, *Emigrants and Society,* 208.

48. Jaime Contreras, "Aldermen and Judaizers: Cryptojudaism, Counter-Reformation, and Local Power," trans. Susan Isabel Stein, in *Culture and Control in Counter-Reformation Spain,* ed. Anne J. Cruz and Mary Elizabeth Perry (Minneapolis: University of Minnesota Press, 1992), 95–99; Bilinkoff, *The Avila of St. Teresa,* 62–67.

49. Although it should be noted that, despite resistance, wealthy conversos had in fact managed by the early sixteenth century to attain powerful positions in many Castilian municipalities: Haliczer, "The Expulsion of the Jews as a Social Process," 245–249. The presence of conversos in Granada's governing institutions is discussed in greater detail in chapter 4.

50. AGS, Patronato Real, caja 10, p. 45; See also Stephen Gilman, "'Judea Pequenna:' Granada ante la Inquisición," *Nueva Revista de Filología Hispanica* 30 (1981): 586–593.

51. Cited in Jesús Luque Moreno, *Granada en el siglo XVI: Juan de Vilches y otros testimonios de la época* (Granada: Universidad de Granada, 1994), 237.

52. K. Garrad, "La inquisición y los moriscos granadinos," *Miscelánea de Estudios Árabes y Hebráicos* 9 (1960): 58.

53. Florencia García Ivars, *La represión en el tribunal inquisitorial de Granada, 1550–1819* (Madrid: Akal, 1991), 160.

54. Mármol Carvajal, *Rebelión y castigo,* 85–86.

55. Gilman, "'Judea Pequenna,'" 591.

56. James Amelang, *Honored Citizens of Barcelona: Patrician Culture and Class Relations, 1490–1714* (Princeton: Princeton University Press, 1986), 15–17.

57. Bilinkoff, *The Avila of Saint Teresa,* 62–77.

58. Edwards, *Christian Córdoba,* 189.

59. Cortés Peña and Vincent, *Historia de Granada,* 190.

60. AGS, Cámara de Castilla, leg. 2150. The data are arranged to summarize in a brief and manageable fashion the categories and classifications employed in the more detailed table found in Cortés Peña and Vincent, *Historia de Granada,* 120–126.

61. For comparison to similar data for Barcelona, see Teofilo Ruiz, *Spanish Society, 1400–1600* (New York: Longman, 2001), 62.

62. Peinado Santaella, and López de Coca Castañer, *Historia de Granada,* 288–304; 329–339.

63. The 1561 census data were collected in the months following the completion of the high altar of Granada's new cathedral—a project that had employed a small army of craftsmen and laborers. The number of construction industry workers represented in table 1.2 therefore likely represents a significant decline relative to preceding decades, since many workers had likely moved elsewhere in search of new jobs. On the construction of the cathedral, see Earl Rosenthal's classic study, *The Cathedral of Granada: A Study in the Spanish Renaissance* (Princeton: Princeton University Press, 1961).

64. See chapter 6's discussion of the Hospital of Juan de Dios.

65. Cortés Peña and Vincent, *Historia de Granada,* 128–129.

66. APG, 1548 protócolos de Martín de Olivares, October 20, 1548 testament of Alonso de Cuéllar.

67. Diego Hurtado de Mendoza, *Guerra de Granada* (Granada, 1610; repr. Granada: Impredisur, 1991), 109.

68. Münzer, *Viaje por España,* 55–56; CODOIN, 11: 537.

69. AMG, Libro de ordenanzas, 1672 recopilación, f. 123. All of this book's references to the municipal archive's Libro de ordenanzas are to the 1672 edition. An earlier 1551 edition is available at the archive, but because of its fragility, I was allowed to consult it only briefly, and I used my limited time simply to confirm that my transcriptions from the 1672 edition were accurate copies of the texts of the original ordinances.

70. AMG, legajo 1930, año 1572 (emphasis added).

71. Hurtado de Mendoza, *Guerra de Granada,* 109. On the medieval Spanish tradition of municipal militias, see James Powers, *A Society Organized for War: The Iberian Municipal*

Militias in the Central Middle Ages, 1000–1284 (Berkeley: University of California Press, 1988).

72. Lockhart, *Spanish Peru,* 251–252.

73. Cortés Peña and Vincent, *Historia de Granada,* 147. See also the September 21, 1539, testament of one such Genoese resident of Granada, the merchant known locally as "Miguel Lorcal:" APG, 1539 protócolos de Martín de Olivares, f. 786v.

74. APG, 1539 protócolos of Martín de Olivares, f. 317v. Mercury was a particularly important commodity at the time because it was considered by many to be effective in the treatment of syphilis, the spread of which had reached epidemic proportions at that time in Spain since its introduction to the Old World by sailors returning from the Indies.

75. Archivo de la Catedral de Granada (ACG), legajo 23, p. 17. Their names are listed in a 1573 crown-ordered investigation of the local book publishing industry in Granada. Besides the Frenchmen, the investigation notes that Granada's other printer was Antonio de Nebrija— the nephew of the great Spanish humanist grammarian of the same name.

76. APG, 1539 protócolos of Martín de Olivares, f. 573.

77. Altman, *Emigrants and Society,* 247–274.

78. David Vassberg, *The Village and the Outside World in Golden Age Castile: Mobility and Migration in Everyday Rural Life* (Cambridge: Cambridge University Press, 1996).

79. AChG, cabina 507, legajo 1433, p. 1.

80. Garrido Aranda, *Organización de la iglesia de Granada.*

81. ACG, legajo 506, p. 21, testimony of Benito de los Rios. Arevalo's name appears in the baptismal records of San Cecilio parish from the earliest surviving entries in 1521 until 1542: Archivo de la Parroquia de San Cecilio, Libro I de bautismos.

82. AChG, cabina 301, legajo 67, p. 5

2. MUDÉJARES AND MORISCOS

1. Enrique Soria Mesa, "La asimilación de la élite morisca en la Granada cristiana. El ejemplo de la familia Hermes," in *Mélanges Louis Cardaillac,* ed. Abdeljelil Temimi, 2 vols. (Zaghouan: Fondation Temimi, 1995), 2:649–658.

2. Cited in Luque Moreno, *Granada en el siglo XVI,* 236.

3. Mármol Carvajal, *Rebelión y castigo,* 63.

4. "Classic" studies include: Henry Charles Lea, *The Moriscos of Spain: Their Conversion and Expulsion* (Philadelphia, 1901; repr. New York: Burt Franklin, 1968); Julio Caro Baroja, *Los moriscos del reino de Granada: Ensayo de historia social,* 4th ed. (Madrid: Ediciones Istmo, 1991); Domínguez Ortiz and Vincent, *Historia de los moriscos.*

5. Galán Sánchez claims that Domínguez Ortiz was the first to use this term to describe Granada's "cooperative" mudéjar and morisco elites: Ángel Galán Sánchez, "Los vencidos: exilio, integración y resistencia," in *Historia del reino de Granada I: De los orígenes a la época mudéjar,* ed. Rafael G. Peinado Santaella (Granada: Universidad de Granada, 2000), 552.

6. Vincent, *Minorías y Marginados,* 126. This image of virtual unanimity continues to shape standard textbook accounts of the Moriscos: e.g., Ruiz, *Spanish Society,* 105–107.

7. Mercedes García Arenal, "El problema morisco: propuestas de discusión," *Al-Quantara* 13 (1992): 492.

8. One important exception to this trend is an excellent attempt by Javier Castillo Fernández to make some systematic sense of recent archival discoveries: "La asimilación de los moriscos granadinos: un modelo de análisis," in *Disidencias y exilios en la España moderna,* ed. Antonio Mestre Sanchís and Enrique Giménez López (Alicante: Universidad de Alicante, 1997), 347–361.

9. Cortés Peña and Vincent, *Historia de Granada,* 67. Vincent's findings for Granada's urban morisco population run counter to common contemporary stereotypes of moriscos throughout the Iberian Peninsula as particularly fecund: Ruiz, *Spanish Society,* 107.

10. Miguel Angel Ladero Quesada, *Los mudéjares de Castilla y otros estudios de historia medieval andaluza* (Granada: Universidad de Granada, 1989), 26–37; Meyerson, *The Muslims of Valencia,* 13–14.

11. For a published transcription of the entire surrender treaty, see Ladero Quesada, *Granada después de la conquista,* 435–445.

12. Ibid., 293.

13. Peinado Santaella and López de Coca Castañer, *Historia de Granada,* 361.

14. A *dobla* was worth 445 *maravedís.* Around the time of the conquest of Granada, a common laborer in Castile made about 15–20 *maravedís* per day, and an artisan, such as a carpenter, earned about 40 *maravedís* per day.

15. Ángel Galán Sánchez, *Los mudéjares del reino de Granada* (Granada: Universidad de Granada, 1991), 44.

16. Ladero Quesada, *Los mudéjares de Castilla,* 88.

17. Meyerson, *The Muslims of Valencia.*

18. Ladero Quesada, *Los mudéjares de Castilla.*

19. José Enrique López de Coca Castañer, "Las capitulaciones y la Granada mudéjar," in *La incorporación de Granada a la corona de Castilla,* ed. Miguel Ángel Ladero Quesada (Granada: Diputación Provincial de Granada, 1993), 266–267.

20. For a transcription of this royal proclamation, see Ladero Quesada, *Granada después de la conquista,* 447–450.

21. CODOIN, 11:490, 527, 555; 14:501.

22. Ladero Quesada, *Granada después de la conquista,* 340; Galán Sánchez, *Los mudéjares,* 51.

23. Ladero Quesada, *Los mudéjares de Castilla,* 147–148.

24. Galán Sánchez, *Los mudéjares,* 51.

25. Archivo Histórico Nacional, Madrid (AHN), Inquisición, legajo 1953, no. 2 (1563 auto), penitents #32 and 33; no. 3 (1566 auto), penitent #47; and no. 4 (1569 auto), penitent #100.

26. AHN, Inquisición, legajo 1953, no. 4 (1569 auto), penitents #75 and 76.

27. López de Coca Castañer, "Las capitulaciones y la Granada mudéjar," 272–273.

28. For a transcription of this document, see Ladero Quesada, *Granada después de la conquista,* 556–558.

29. Ángel Galán Sánchez, "Notas para una periodización de la historia de los moriscos granadinos. De las capitulaciones de la conversión a las medidas de la capilla real," *Actas III del Coloquio Histórico Medieval Andaluza* (Jaén, 1984): 95

30. Mármol Carvajal, *Rebelión y castigo,* 73.

31. Galán Sánchez, *Los mudéjares,* 271–273; López Nevot, *La organización institucional,* 187.

32. Galán Sánchez, *Los mudéjares,* 266–267.

33. For a detailed discussion of Granada's mudéjar bureaucracy during the period 1492–1499, see Galán Sánchez, *Los mudéjares,* 143–150.

34. Ibid., 275–276.

35. For discussion of the Granada Venegas family, see Soria Mesa, "De la conquista a la asimilación," and Galán Sánchez, *Los mudéjares,* 264–266.

36. Soria Mesa, "De la conquista a la asimilación," 54.

37. For discussion of the economic roles played by the moriscos, see Domínguez Ortiz and Vincent, *Historia de los moriscos,* 109–128.

38. Ibid., 43.

39. Garrad, "The Causes of the Second Rebellion of the Alpujarra," 180.

40. Mármol Carvajal, *Rebelión y castigo,* 91; Hurtado de Mendoza, *Guerra de Granada,* 25–29.

41. On the surviving archival resources of the Spanish Inquisition, see Gustav Henningsen, "The Archives and the Historiography of the Spanish Inquisition," in *The Inquisition in Early Modern Europe: Studies on Sources and Methods,* ed. Gustav Henningsen and John Tedeschi (De Kalb: Northern Illinois University Press, 1986), 54–78.

42. K. Garrad, "La inquisición y los moriscos granadinos, 1526–1580," *Miscelánea de Estudios Árabes y Hebráicos* 9 (1960): 55–72.

43. AHN, Inquisición, legajo 1953, no. 5, penitents #4, 5, 16, 24.

44. Ibid., no. 5, penitent #35

45. Ibid., no. 4, penitent #58.

46. Data drawn from Ibid., no. 1–5.

47. Darío Cabanelas Rodríguez, "Los moriscos: vida religiosa y evangelización," in *La incorporación de Granada a la Corona de Castilla,* ed. Miguel Ángel Ladero Quesada (Granada: Diputación Provincial, 1993), 505–506.

48. Domínguez Ortiz and Vincent, *Historia de los moriscos,* 97.

49. Amalia García Pedraza, "La asimilación del morisco Don Gonzalo Fernández el Zegrí: edición y análisis de su testamento," *Al-Quantara* 16 (1995): 45.

50. Domínguez Ortiz and Vincent, *Historia de los moriscos,* 96; see also Nalle, *God in La Mancha,* 128–129

51. García Pedraza, "El otro morisco," 231.

52. López de Coca Castañer, "Las capitulaciones y la Granada mudéjar," 296; Ladero Quesada, *Granada después de la conquista,* 470, document #75.

53. Mármol Carvajal, *Rebelión y castigo,* 93–94.

54. Erika Spivakovsky, "Some Notes on the Relations between Don Diego Hurtado de Mendoza and Don Alonso de Granada Venegas," *Archivum* 14 (1964): 212–232.

55. The complete text is transcribed in K. Garrad, "The Original Memorial of Don Francisco Núñez Muley," *Atlante* 2 (1954): 199–226.

3. A DIVIDED CITY, A SHARED CITY

1. Miguel Ángel Ladero Quesada, "Spain 1492: Social Values and Structures," in *Implicit Understandings: Observing, Reporting, and Reflecting on the Encounters Between Europeans and Other Peoples in the Early Modern Era,* ed. Stuart B. Schwartz (Cambridge: Cambridge University Press, 1994), 105.

2. Vincent, *Minorías y marginados,* 63.

3. ACG, Libro 3 de asuntos varios, f. 79v., chapter 25 of Emperor Charles V's 1526 instructions to Granada's new archbishop. Also ACG, Libro 11 de asuntos varios, f. 14v.–16v.: a 1530 royal provision encouraging intermarriage.

4. Lavrin, "Women in Colonial Mexico," 250–251. On the local politics of *mestizaje* in an early colonial Peruvian city, see Kathryn Burns, *Colonial Habits: Convents and the Spiritual Economy of Cuzco, Peru* (Durham: Duke University Press, 1999), 21–22, 32–36.

5. Meyerson, *The Muslims of Valencia,* 234–238.

6. David Nirenberg, "Religious and Sexual Boundaries in the Medieval Crown of Aragon," in *Christians, Muslims, and Jews in Medieval and Early Modern Spain: Interaction and Cultural Exchange,* ed. Mark D. Meyerson and Edward D. English (Notre Dame: University of Notre Dame Press, 1999), 141–160.

7. AMG, Libro I de actas, f. 190v.

8. Ibid., Libro de ordenanzas, f. 289.

9. Ladero Quesada, "La repoblación del reino de Granada," 527; Cortés Peña and Vincent, *Historia de Granada,* 60–61.

10. A summary of the specific provisions of the agreement survives in the Zafra family archive, and this document is transcribed in Miguel Garrido Atienza, *Las capitulaciones para la entrega del reino de Granada* (Granada: Paulino Ventura Travaset, 1910), 142–143.

11. Christopher Friedrichs, *The Early Modern City, 1450–1750* (London: Longman, 1995); Fernando Marías, "City Planning in Sixteenth-Century Spain," in *Spanish Cities of the Golden Age: The Views of Anton van den Wynegaerde,* ed. Richard L Kagan (Berkeley: University of California Press, 1989), 84–105.

12. José Luis Orozco Pardo, *Christianópolis: Urbanismo y contrarreforma en la Granada del 600* (Granada: Diputación Provincial de Granada, 1985), 70–87.

13. Münzer, *Viaje por España,* 48; Luque Moreno, *Granada en el siglo XVI,* 217; María J. Martínez Justicia, *La plaza pública como elemento urbanístico. Seis ejemplos en la ciudad de Granada* (Granada: Galería Virtual, 1996).

14. Helen Nader, "The Spain that Encountered Mexico," in *The Oxford History of Mex-*

ico, ed. Michael C. Meyer and William H. Beezley (Oxford: Oxford University Press, 2000): 42–43.

15. Ladero Quesada, *Los mudéjares de Castilla;* López de Coca Castañer, "Las capitulaciones y la Granada mudéjar," 263–265.

16. Benjamin C. I. Ravid, "From Geographical Realia to Historiographical Symbol: The Odyssey of the Word *Ghetto,*" and Kenneth R. Stow, "The Consciousness of Closure: Roman Jewry and Its *Ghet,*" both in *Essential Papers on Jewish Culture in Renaissance and Baroque Italy,* ed. David B. Ruderman (New York: New York University Press, 1992), 373–385 and 386–400; Ladero Quesada, *Los mudéjares de Castilla,* 65–68; 111–112.

17. Ladero Quesada, *Granada después de la conquista,* 329

18. AMG, legajo 1172, p. 62 (emphasis added).

19. On drunkenness among moriscos detained in Granada's city jail, for instance, see AMG, legajo 1905, p. 8.

20. Ibid., Libro de Ordenanzas, f. 123v.

21. Ibid., legajo 1253.

22. This letter is transcribed in Francisco Bermúdez de Pedraza, *Historia eclesiástica de Granada* (Granada, 1568; facs. ed., Granada: Editorial Don Quijote and Universidad de Granada, 1989), f. 201v.

23. Archivo de la Parroquia de San Ildefonso, Libro I de bautismos.

24. AGS, Cámara de Castilla, legajo 2150.

25. Archivo de la Parroquia de San José, Libro I de bautismos de San Nicolás. The 1565 total was probably even higher; the last entry in my database is dated October 23, 1565; Bernard Vincent, *Andalucía en la edad moderna: economía y sociedad* (Granada: Diputación Provincial, 1985): 162.

26. Mármol Carvajal, *Rebelión y castigo,* 85.

27. AMG, legajo 1858, p. 2.

28. Garrad, "The Original Memorial of Don Francisco Núñez Muley," 200.

29. AMG, Libro I de actas, f. 107v.–108.

30. Ibid., legajo 1929, p. 4.

31. Ibid., Libro de ordenanzas, f. 243 v.

32. Angus MacKay, "The Ballad and the Frontier in Late Medieval Spain," *Bulletin of Hispanic Studies* 53 (1976): 15–33.

33. Garrad, "The Original Memorial of Don Francisco Núñez Muley," 221–222.

34. Anwar Chejne, *Islam and the West: The Moriscos, A Cultural and Social History* (Albany: State University of New York Press, 1983).

35. Juan Martínez Ruiz, "Ausencia de literatura aljamiada y conservación del hispanoárabe y de la entidad arabo-musulmana en la Granada morisca (siglo XVI)," *Chronica Nova* 21 (1993–1994): 405–425.

36. Garrad, "The Original Memorial of Don Francisco Núñez Muley," 212.

37. ACG, Libro 3 de asuntos varios, f. 75v.–76.

38. Pedro Guerrero, *El concilio provincial de Granada en 1565. Edición crítica del malogrado concilio de Arzobispo Guerrero,* ed. Ignacio Pérez de Heredia y Valle (Rome: Instituto Español de Historia Eclesiástica, 1990).

39. APG, Protócolos de Martín de Olivares, 1537, f. 262.

40. Enrique Soria Mesa, *Señores y oligarcas: Los señoríos del Reino de Granada en la edad moderna* (Granada: Universidad de Granada, 1997), 107–109; Caro Baroja, *Los moriscos,* 56–57.

41. Caro Baroja, *Los moriscos,* 56.

42. Helen Nader, *The Mendoza Family in the Spanish Renaissance* (New Brunswick, N.J.: Rutgers University Press, 1979), 193–197.

43. Mármol Carvajal, *Rebelión y castigo,* 82–83.

44. Hurtado de Mendoza, *Guerra de Granada,* 10–11; Caro Baroja, *Los moriscos,* 169.

45. AMG, Libro de ordenanzas, f. 31v.–32.

46. Ibid., f. 289v.

47. Ibid., f. 34–34v.

48. Ignacio Henares Cuéllar and Rafael López Guzmán, *Architectura mudéjar granadina* (Granada: Caja General de Ahorros y Monte de Piedad, 1989); Ignacio Henares Cuéllar and Rafael López Guzmán, eds., *Mudéjar iberoamericano. Una expresión cultural de dos mundos* (Granada: Universidad de Granada, 1993).

49. J. N. Hillgarth, *The Spanish Kingdoms, 1250–1516*, 2 vols. (Oxford: Oxford University Press, 1978), 1:165.

50. Orozco Pardo, *Christianópolis*, 77.

51. Archivo de la Curia Arzobispal de Granada, uncatalogued *legajos* labeled by parish name. Especially detailed are the records concerning the construction of the *mudéjar*-style parish churches of Santa Ana and San Andrés.

52. Archivo de la parroquia de San Pedro y San Pablo, Libro III de bautismos, f. 112.

4. THE EMERGENCE OF A NEW ORDER

1. For a detailed overview of the origins and impact of the royal patronage of Granada's church, see Jesús Suberviola Martínez, *Real Patronato de Granada: El arzobispo Talavera, la iglesia, y el estado moderno (1486–1516), Estudio y documentos* (Granada: Caja General de Ahorros de Granada, 1985).

2. The definitive statement of this tradition is Helen Nader, *Liberty in Absolutist Castile: The Habsburg Sale of Towns, 1516–1700* (Baltimore: Johns Hopkins University Press, 1990).

3. Amelang, *Honored Citizens of Barcelona*; Mauro Hernández, *A la sombra de la corona: Poder local y oligarquía urbana (Madrid, 1606–1806)* (Madrid: Siglo Veintiuno, 1995).

4. The *hagüela* incomes that had constituted an important part of the Nasrid royal fisc, for instance, were applied in part by a 1495 royal grant to Granada's municipal council, and the *habices* rents that had traditionally funded charity and the provision of mosques in Nasrid Granada were after 1500 handed over to the Granada's new parish churches: Cortés Peña and Vincent, *Historia de Granada,* 166.

5. James Amelang, *Honored Citizens of Barcelona,* 18–21; Bartolomé Bennassar, *Valladolid au siècle d'or: une ville de Castille et sa campagne au XVIe siècle* (Paris: Mouton, 1967), 121–133; Ruth Pike, *Aristocrats and Traders: Sevillan Society in the Sixteenth Century* (Ithaca: Cornell University Press, 1972).

6. Bilinkoff, *The Avila of Saint Teresa,* 15–35; Edwards, *Christian Córdoba,* 189.

7. AChG, cabina 302, legajo 341, p. 6.

8. In various letters to family members, Iñigo López de Mendoza spoke of his ongoing rivalry with and personal distaste for Gómez de Santillán: *Correspondencia del Conde de Tendilla,* ed. Emilio Meneses García, 2 vols. (Madrid: Real Academia de la Historia, 1973), 1:313–314. See also María José Osorio Pérez, "Notas y documentos sobre un caballero veinticuatro granadino: Gómez de Santillán," in *Las ciudades andaluzas (siglos XIII–XVI): Actas del VI Coloquio Internacional de la Historia Medieval de Andalucía,* ed. José Enrique López de Coca Castañer y Ángel Galán Sánchez (Málaga: Universidad de Málaga, 1991), 483–493.

9. AChG, cabina 3, legajo 484, p. 8, *probanza* of Gómez de Santillán, question #8. Witnesses #4, 5, 8, and 9 explicitly confirm the accusation.

10. Cortes Peña and Vincent, *Historia de Granada,* 174.

11. *Correspondencia del Conde de Tendilla,* 1:359.

12. Nader, *The Mendoza Family.*

13. Antonio Ángel Ruiz Rodríguez, *La Real Chancillería de Granada en el siglo XVI* (Granada: Diputación Provincial de Granada, 1987).

14. AChG, cabina 504, legajo 760, Also see AMG, legajo 1930, a 1538 letter from Francisco de los Cobos to Granada's municipal council, which describes a 1538 violent confrontation between municipal councilmen and the Chancery officials over seating at the annual memorial mass for Isabella and Ferdinand.

15. Galán Sánchez, *Los mudéjares,* 150.

16. "No pueden entrar el viernes, e agora no entran ny vienen los moros": AMG, Libro I de actas, actas of October 3, 1497, f. 31v.

17. AMG, legajo 1253.

18. The seven moriscos included: Alonso de Granada Venegas, Pedro de Granada, Fran-

cisco Jiménez Xama, Pedro López Zaybona, Andrés de Granada el Basti, Fernando Enríquez el Pequeñí, and Fernando de Córdoba Abenhumeya. An eighth morisco, Miguel de León el Zaororí, was added by the end of 1501. See López Nevot, *La organización institucional*, 118, 143.

19. Ibid., 127.

20. Linda Martz, "Implementation of Pure-Blood Statutes in Sixteenth-Century Toledo," in *In Iberia and Beyond: Hispanic Jews Between Cultures,* ed. Bernard Dov Cooperman (Newark: University of Delaware Press, 1998), 245–271; Amelang, *Honored Citizens of Barcelona,* 34–35.

21. López Nevot, *La organización institucional*, 115.

22. Ibid., 108–112, although it should be mentioned that despite his extensive research, López Nevot was unable to overcome completely the large gaps that exist in surviving minutes of Granada's municipal council meetings during the periods 1502–1512 and 1522–1555. His list must therefore be considered incomplete.

23. The eighteen elite lineages about whom I have data include: Agreda, Álvarez Zapata, Arias de Mansilla, Ávila Ponce de León, Bobadilla, Córdoba y Válor, Fernández de Córdoba, Granada Venegas, Mendoza, Mexía, Obregón, Osorio, Pérez de Herrasti, Pisa, Rengifo, Santillán, de la Torre, Trillo y Figueroa, and Zegrí. The thirteen elite families about whom I have insufficient or no information include: Aguilar, Alarcón, Avalos, Bazán, Baeza Carvajal, Campo, Contreras, León, Medrano, Núñez de Toledo, Padi!la, and Peralta. Information on those families about whom I have data is drawn from the following: AChG, cabina 3, legajo 1088, p. 7; cabina 301, legajo 67, p. 5; cabina 302, legajo 207, p. 2; cabina 302, legajo 227, p. 7; cabina 302, legajo 330, p. 9; and cabina 303, legajo 423, p. 5; as well as in the articles of Enrique Soria Mesa, Linda Martz, Amalia García Pedraza, María José Osorio Pérez, and Andrés A. Vázquez Cano listed in the bibliography. Also see Maria Angustias Moreno Olmedo, *Heráldica y genealogía granadina* (Granada: Universidad de Granada, 1976).

24. Enrique Soria Mesa, "Crianza Real y clientelismo nobilario: Los Bobadilla, una familia de la oligarquía granadina," *Meridies* 1 (1994): 129–160; Martz, "Toledanos and the Kingdom of Granada." The Rengifo were relatives of Archbishop Talavera.

25. Haliczer, "The Expulsion of the Jews as a Social Process;" Pike, *Aristocrats and Traders,* 21–23.

26. Contrast Granada, for instance, to the cases discussed in the following: Contreras, "Aldermen and Judaizers," 95–97; Bilinkoff, *The Avila of Saint Teresa*; Martz, "Implementation of Pure Blood Statutes in Sixteenth-Century Toledo."

27. The Genoese merchant Esteban Lomelín (as his name appears in the Castilian-language documents) became a *regidor* in 1559: López Nevot, *La organización institucional,* 111.

28. López Nevot, *La organización institucional,* 187–190; 196–200.

29. AMG, Libro de ordenanzas, f. 8–8v. This was not the first time that such accusations had been leveled. In 1513, for instance, a royal decree had been issued which ordered that, because of voting irregularities, the *regidores* were to select municipal officials by lot from a list of nominated candidates rather than through elections which, through factional alliances, had often led to the placement of friends of powerful *regidores* in positions of administrative influence: Ibid., f. 7v–8. During his 1526 visit to the city, Charles V, on hearing similar complaints, repeated the 1513 order: Ibid., f. 9–9v. Continued corruption and failure to comply with these explicit royal mandates led to the 1532 complaints by the *jurados*.

30. AMG, legajo 1930, año 1558.

31. AChG, cabina 3, legajo 518, p. 9.

32. Alonso Fernández de Madrid, *Vida de Fray Fernando de Talavera, Primer arzobispo de Granada,* ed. Félix G. Olmedo (Granada: 1530; repr. Granada: Universidad de Granada, 1992), 430.

33. Talavera had in fact already given in to Isabella's requests to accept an episcopal appointment in 1485, when he became bishop of Ávila—a post which the professed reformer ironically served mostly in absentia until his appointment as archbishop of Granada in 1492.

34. Cortés Peña and Vincent, *Historia de Granada,* 77.

214 :: NOTES TO PAGES 83–90

35. Jesús Suberviola Martínez, "La erección parroquial granatense de 1501 y el reformismo cisneriano," *Cuaderno de Estudios Medievales* 14–15 (1985–1987), 120.

35. Jesús Suberviola Martínez, "La erección parroquial granatense de 1501 y el reformismo cisneriano," *Cuaderno de Estudios Medievales* 14–15 (1985–1987), 120.

36. Marcel Bataillon, *Erasmo y España: Estudios sobre la historia espiritual del siglo XVI,* 2d Spanish ed. (Mexico City: Fondo de cultura económica, 1966), 59; Francisco Javier Martínez Medina, "Estudio preliminar," in Alonso Fernández de Madrid, *Vida de Fray Fernando de Talavera, Primer arzobispo de Granada,* ed. Félix G. Olmedo (Granada, 1530; repr. Granada: University of Granada, 1992), xv–xvii.

37. Martínez Medina, "Estudio preliminar," xv–xvi.

38. Kamen, *The Spanish Inquisition,* 130.

39. In a 1562 *limpieza de sangre* inquiry into the background of Talavera's great-nephew Pedro de Acuña on the occasion of his candidacy for a prebend in Granada's cathedral, Granada cathedral canon Diego Romano reported having heard various stories among elderly men and women in Talavera de la Reina as to the family origins of Granada's first archbishop, the most common opinion being that he was the son of a squire who served the lord of Oropesa: ACG legajo 226, p. 29. For a summary of the various theories concerning Talavera's ancestry, see Martínez Medina, "Estudio preliminar," xv–xvii.

40. See especially the fond memories of Talavera discussed by the morisco leader Francisco Núñez Muley in Garrad, "The Original Memorial of Don Francisco Núñez Muley," 214–216.

41. Martínez Medina, "Estudio preliminar," li, lviii.

42. Garrad, "The Original Memorial of Don Francisco Núñez Muley," 214–215

43. Ladero Quesada, *Granada depués de la conquista,* 342–343.

44. Suberviola Martínez, *Real Patronato de Granada*

45. K. Garrad, "The Causes of the Second Rebellion of the Alpujarra," 74.

46. Schwaller, *The Church and Clergy in Sixteenth-Century Mexico,* 87.

47. *Correspondencia del Conde de Tendilla,* 1:342, 358.

48. AMG, Libro 1 de actas, actas of November 6, 1498.

49. Fernández de Madrid, *Vida de Fray Fernando de Talavera,* 108.

50. Francisco Martín Hernández, *Un seminario español pretridentino: El Real Colegio Eclesiástico de San Cecilio de Granada (1492–1842)* (Valladolid: Universidad de Valladolid, 1960).

51. On Ramírez de Villaescusa, see Nalle, *God in La Mancha,* 22–30.

52. ACG, Libro 3 de asuntos varios, f. 132v.

53. Constance Jones Mathers, "The Life of Canons in Sixteenth-Century Castile," in *Renaissance Society and Culture: Essays in Honor of Eugene F. Rice, Jr.,* ed. John Monfasani and Ronald G. Musto (New York: Italica Press, 1991), 161–162.

54. Pedro Gan Giménez, "Los prebendados de la iglesia granadina: Una bio-bibliografía," *Revista del Centro de Estudios Históricos de Granada y su Reino* 4 (1990), 139–171; Rafael Marín López, *El cabildo de la catedral de Granada en el siglo XVI* (Granada: Universidad de Granada, 1998), 151–153; Mathers, "The Life of Canons," 162; Bilinkoff, *The Avila of Saint Teresa,* 28–32.

55. ACG, Libro 3 de actas capitulares, f. 188v., actas of January 8, 1555.

56. Ibid., legajo 294, p. 49.

57. Ibid., legajo 519, p. 13.

58. The other nine surviving *limpieza* hearings include: ACG, legajo 220, p. 11 (Pedro Ordoñez de Castellanos); legajo 226, p. 18 (Juan de Salcedo); legajo 226, p. 6 (Alonso de Baena); legajo 226, p. 29 (Pedro de Acuña); legajo 226, p. 20 (Pedro de Aranda); legajo 509, p. 23 (Diego de Tello); legajo 519, p. 10 (Pedro de Magaña); legajo 519, p. 13 (Luis de Pedraza); legajo 519, p. 16 (Antonio de Frias);

59. ACG, Libro 4 de actas capitulares, f. 129 v.; Rafael Marín López, "El cabildo eclesiástico granadino y las obras de la catedral en el siglo XVI," *Chrónica Nova* 22 (1995): 211–241.

60. Marín López, *El cabildo de la catedral,* 135–149.

61. Ibid., 92–105.

62. See the 1536 visitation of the chapter by Archbishop Avalos: ACG, legajo 8, p. 19.

63. The 1501 foundation document served some of the typical functions of synodal constitutions, but it was not nearly as complete a guide to pastoral responsibilities, spiritual life, and

official diocesan festivities as were most contemporary synodal decrees in other Spanish dioceses. There exist some mentions of a set of constitutions written by Archbishop Talavera: e.g. ACG, Libro 3 de asuntos varios, f. 127; Antonio Marín Ocete, "El Concilio provincial de Granada en 1565," *Archivo Teológico Granadino* 25 (1962) 28–29. However, no surviving copy of such constitutions exist, and these allusions probably refer to a document called the *consueta*, which governed the activities of the cathedral and cathedral chapter. The *consueta*, however, was by no means a set of synodal constitutions. Talavera, or perhaps Archbishop Rojas, probably wrote it. The first mention of it that I have seen is from 1525: ACG, Libro 2 de actas capitulares, f. 136v., actas of February 25, 1525. Two copies survive in Granada's cathedral archive: ACG, Libro 3 de asuntos varios, f. 18–70v; ACG, Libro 13 de asuntos varios. The bishopric of Málaga, which was also part of the recently conquered kingdom of Granada, had held a synod in 1515 under Bishop Diego Ramírez de Villaescusa, who later became bishop of Cuenca and wrote the 1531 synodal constitutions of that diocese: Nalle, *God in La Mancha*, 22–30, 241 n. 72

5. CREATING CHRISTIAN GRANADA

1. Luis Miguel López Muñoz, *Las cofradías de la parroquia de Santa María Magdalena de Granada en los siglos XVII–XVIII* (Granada: Universidad de Granada, 1992), 63, 138; Juan Andrés Luna Díaz, "La parroquia de Santa María Magdalena de Granada, un barrio en expansión hacía la vega durante el siglo XVI," *Chrónica Nova* 11 (1980): 192–193.

2. Sara Nalle, "Literacy and Culture in Early Modern Castile," *Past and Present* 125 (1989): 65–96.

3. The older notion that the Valladolid Assembly represented the end of Erasmian influence in Spain has been convincingly dismissed by Lu Ann Homza, "Erasmus as Hero, or Heretic? Spanish Humanism and the Valladolid Assembly of 1527," *Renaissance Quarterly* 50 (1997): 78–118. See also her recent book, *Religious Authority in the Spanish Renaissance* (Baltimore: Johns Hopkins University Press, 2000).

4. Melquíades Andrés Martín, *Los recogidos: Nueva visión de la mística española (1500–1700)* (Madrid: Fundación Universitaria Española, 1976); Nancy E. Van Deusen, *Between the Sacred and the Worldly: The Institutional and Cultural Practice of Recogimiento in Colonial Lima* (Stanford: Stanford University Press, 2002).

5. Alastair Hamilton, *Heresy and Mysticism in Sixteenth-Century Spain: The Alumbrados* (Toronto: University of Toronto Press, 1992).

6. Antonio Marín Ocete, *El arzobispo Pedro Guerrero y la política conciliar española en el siglo XVI*, 2 vols. (Granada: Universidad de Granada, 1970), 1:142–143.

7. Sara Nalle, "The Millennial Moment: Revolution and Radical Religion in Sixteenth-Century Spain," in *Toward the Millennium: Messianic Expectations from the Bible to Waco*, ed. Peter Schäfer and Mark Cohen (Leiden: Brill, 1998), 153–173.

8. Religious works comprised 88 of the 161 different titles available in Torres's bookstore. Beside the religious books, Torres's inventory included fifteenth- and sixteenth-century Spanish and Italian Renaissance histories, poetry, and fiction (20 percent of titles), works by various classic ancient Latin authors (13 percent), legal and administrative texts and compilations (7 percent), and various cookbooks and popular broadsheets on specific topics (5 percent): APG, Libro 56, protócolos de Juan Tavera, f. 804–808v. For comparison to the 1545 inventory of Guillermo Ramón's larger but in many ways similar bookstore in Cuenca, see Nalle, "Literacy and Culture," 65–96.

9. William Christian, *Local Religion in Sixteenth-Century Spain;* Jodi Bilinkoff, *The Avila of Saint Teresa;* Sara Nalle, *God in La Mancha;* Henry Kamen, *The Phoenix and the Flame;* Alyson Poska, *Regulating the People.*

10. Nalle, *God in La Mancha,* 185, gives this figure for Cuenca 1505–1585. The percentage appears to have been somewhat lower in sixteenth-century Madrid, but the Madrid figures are still noticeably higher than those of Granada: Carlos Eire, *From Madrid to Purgatory: The Art and Craft of Dying in Sixteenth-Century Spain* (Cambridge: Cambridge University Press, 1995).

11. AChG, cabina 3, legajo 1583, p. 8. The house of los Mártires is discussed in Alonso de

Torres, *Crónica de la Provincia Franciscana de Granada,* ed. Rafael Mota Murillo (1683; repr., Madrid: Cisneros, 1984).

12. ACG, Libro 3 de asuntos varios, f. 92. This charge is repeated in the 1565 provincial council: Pedro Guerrero, *El Concilio Provincial de Granada en 1565,* 256.

13. ACG, Libro 3 de asuntos varios, f. 93.

14. Poska, *Regulating the People,* 55; Burns, *The Crusader Kingdom of Valencia,* 92.

15. ACG, Libro 11 de asuntos varios, f. 3v–5v.

16. Archivo de la Parroquia de San Cecilio, Libro de Visitas de Santa Maria Alhambra, 1548 visitation, constitution #15.

17. Münzer, *Viaje por Granada,* 42; Cortés Peña and Vincent, *Historia de Granada,* 28.

18. Ladero Quesada, *Los mudéjares de Castilla,* 135–142; Cortés Peña and Vincent, *Historia de Granada,* 28–29.

19. Cortés Peña and Vincent, *Historia de Granada,* 29; Torres, *Crónica de la Provincia Franciscana,* 18.

20. See Córtes Peña and Vincent, *Historia de Granada,* 29–30, for dates of construction of various monasteries and convents. See also María del Mar Graña Cid, "Reflexiones sobre la implantación del franciscanismo feminino en el reino de Granada (1492–1570)," in *I Congreso Internacional de Monacato Feminino en España, Portugal, y América 1492–1992,* 2 vols. (León: University of León, 1993), 2:523–538.

21. Burns, *The Crusader Kingdom of Valencia,* 197–198; Schwaller, *Church and Clergy in Sixteenth-Century Mexico,* 67–109.

22. Kamen, *The Phoenix and the Flame,* 158–159; Burns, *The Crusader Kingdom of Valencia,* 129–130.

23. The documents from this trial are contained in two separate *piezas* in the Chancery archive: AChG, cabina 3, legajo 1459, p. 10, and cabina 3, legajo 985, p. 9.

24. Roberto J. López López, *Comportamientos religiosos en Asturias durante el Antiguo Régimen* (Gijón: Silverio Cañada, 1989), 96–97.

25. AChG, cabina 3, legajo 1459, p. 10, second probanza, witness #7.

26. Ibid., second probanza, witnesses #8, #9, and #16.

27. Nalle, *Mad for God,* 67–68.

28. AChG, cabina 3, legajo 1459, p. 10. One lay witness did testify that the Dominicans were poor, but his testimony must be taken as partial, as he admitted that he was the brother of one of the friars.

29. AChG, cabina 3, legajo 985, p. 9, second probanza, witness #1.

30. For discussions of the legal and formulaic structures of sixteenth-century Castilian wills, see Eire, *From Madrid to Purgatory,* 34–44, 168–169, 236–237; Nalle, *God in La Mancha,* 182–183; López López, *Comportamientos religiosos en Asturias,* 161–163.

31. Eire, *From Madrid to Purgatory,* 178.

32. Nalle, *God in La Mancha,* 187–189.

33. The Madrid figure is based on a sample of 436 testaments ranging chronologically from the 1520s to the 1590s: Eire, *From Madrid to Purgatory,* 236. For Cuenca, Sara Nalle's database included 623 testaments covering the period 1505–1645. Over those 140-years as a whole, only 27 percent of testators included charitable provisions of any sort, although of the 214 wills covering the 1520s–1570s time period corresponding with this study's database, the total was 45 percent. Nalle does not, however, break down this data as Eire did to indicate what percentage of these arranged for charitable gifts beyond the *mandas acostumbradas: God in La Mancha,* 215.

34. See the 1558 testament of the Granada merchant Luis Moreno, a descendant of a wealthy Genoese merchant family: APG, Libro 107, 1558 protócolos of Hernando de Aguilar, f. 256 ff., 8 May 1558 testament of Luis Moreno. Moreno included in his testament a staggering total of 46,622 *maravedís* in pious bequests to various local religious causes, but not a single *maravedí* to Granada's Santiago parish church where he was a parishioner.

35. I have also chosen to exclude from this calculation the thirty-one testaments from the 1570s, because for a variety of reasons (above all inflation), their amounts of pious bequests are so much larger than those of previous decades as to make comparison meaningless.

36. It should be recognized, of course, that the single case of Luis Moreno's testament cited in note 34 above constitutes about one-third of the total 137,428 *maravedís* given to local religious institutions other than the parishes. Even if we exclude him, however, the disparity remains dramatic: 90,806 *maravedís* in pious gifts to local religious institutions other than the parishes in the remaining 131 testaments, or 693.18 *maravedís* per testator—still more than seven times the average gift per testator to the parishes.

37. According to the foundation document, charges for administration of sacraments were supposed to pertain exclusively to the *curas*, or parish priests, while the *beneficiados*, or other beneficed clergy, were to divide among themselves 25 percent of parish tithes as their main source of income: Suberviola Martínez, *Real Patronato de Granada*, 120. However, there was always in frontier Granada a great deal of confusion and controversy between and among *curas* and *beneficiados* over the division of responsibilities and incomes: see the discussion of the *beneficiados'* lawsuit against Archbishop Avalos in chapter 6.

38. Such foundations were often considered a symbol of family prestige: see Bilinkoff, *The Avila of Saint Teresa*, esp. chapter 2.

39. Data from a 1586 inventory of *memorias* and chapels that had been founded up to that point in San José parish, titled "Falda universal de memorias:" Archivo de la Parroquia de San José, legajo 16, p. 8. About one-third of this total appears to have gone to the parish's general fund, leaving the two *beneficiados* the remaining two-thirds to divide between themselves (for details on income distribution, see in the same book the specifications of the entry concerning the *memoria* established in 1548 by Hernando Díaz Valdepeñas). At this rate, each *beneficiado* would have earned from such foundations an *extra* 30 *maravedís*/day on top of all of his other regular incomes. In the 1560s, an average laborer in Castile made 40–50 *maravedís*/day.

40. Ellen Friedman, *Spanish Captives in North Africa in the Early Modern Age* (Madison: University of Wisconsin Press, 1983); Flynn, *Sacred Charity*, 341.

41. APG, Libro 171, 1569 protócolos of Juan de Padilla, f. 786–796v, November 30, 1569 testament of Juan López Macano; APG Libro 168, 1569 protócolos of Martín Dávila, f. 284–286, April 16, 1569 testament of Isabel de Ayllón; APG, Libro 210, 1577 protócolos de Luis Díaz, f. 657–659, August 16, 1577 testament of Alonso Castellano.

42. ACG, legajo 310, p. 3.

43. In October 1520 the cathedral chapter ordered that the local Franciscans, Dominicans, Augustinians, and Hieronymites provide preachers for certain occasions: ACG, Libro 2 de Actas, f. 31. In addition, at the funeral of the future saint Juan de Dios in 1550—reportedly the largest public religious gathering in the Granada's sixteenth-century history—a Franciscan was chosen to conduct the mass, and another Franciscan gave the sermon: Justino Antolínez de Burgos, *Historia eclesiástica de Granada*, ed. Manuel Sotomayor (Granada: Universidad de Granada, 1996), 353.

44. Besides San Francisco, the other ten local Franciscan foundations included the male houses of San Francisco de la Alhambra, Nuestra Señora de la Victoria (Observant Franciscans), San Antonio (Observant Franciscans), Los Santos Mártires (Franciscan tertiaries, or lay brothers), and San Antón Abad (also tertiaries), and the female houses Nuestra Señora de la Encarnación (Poor Clares), Nuestra Señora de los ángeles (Poor Clares), Nuestra Señora de la Concepción (Conceptionalist, or Observant), Santa Iñes (Minor Franciscans), and Santa Isabel la Real (Poor Clares). On the relationships between the Franciscan order and the various wings of female Franciscanism, see Graña Cid, "Reflexiones sobre la implantación," 523–538. The rapid proliferation of convents in postconquest Granada stands in direct contrast to the rather slow emergence of such institutions in many conquered regions of the New World. Even in the 1550s, two decades after the conquest of Peru, for example, Lima had only two female religious houses and Cuzco only one: K. Burns, *Colonial Habits*, 23.

45. Graña Cid, "Reflexiones sobre la implantación, 524.

46. P. Renée Baernstein, "In Widow's Habit: Women between Convent and Family in Sixteenth-Century Milan," *Sixteenth Century Journal* 25 (1994): 787–805.

47. Women's houses were generally perceived to have received large endowments from the families of each of the nuns who entered. For the local treatment of Isabel de la Cruz as a saint, see Antolínez de Burgos, *Historia eclesiástica*, 355–363.

48. Graña Cid, "Reflexiones sobre la implantación," 524.

49. The other was the brotherhood of Ánimas de Purgatorio (8%), housed in the parish of Sagrario/Iglesia Mayor.

50. Of 163 testators in the database of testaments compiled for this study, five were *cofrades* of the confraternity of San Sebastián, and four of these five were merchants. ACG, legajo 465, p. 3, contains a list of all members of this brotherhood in 1566, many of whom were merchants.

51. ACG, legajo 84, p. 6.

52. Ibid., Libro 2 de actas capitulares, f. 304.

53. Ibid., f. 319v.

54. Studies of confraternities include the essays in John Patrick Donelly, S.J., and Michael W. Maher, S.J., eds., *Confraternities and Catholic Reform in Italy, France and Spain* (Kirksville, Mo.: Truman State University Press, 1998); Christopher Black, *Italian Confraternities in the Sixteenth Century* (Cambridge: Cambridge University Press, 1989); Maureen Flynn, *Sacred Charity: Confraternities and Social Welfare in Spain, 1400–1700* (Ithaca: Cornell University Press, 1989).

55. Flynn, *Sacred Charity*, 117.

56. The three confraternities mentioned were Corpus Christi, Santa Caridad, and Santa Vera Cruz: ACG, legajo 310, p. 3.

57. Among the 163 Christian immigrant last wills and testaments sampled for this study, fifty-seven (35 percent) included indications that either the testator or the spouse of the testator was a member of at least one confraternity. In the testaments written before 1550, the total was 29 percent. After 1550, the total rose to 41 percent. These numbers are slightly higher than those of sixteenth-century Madrid: Eire, *From Madrid to Purgatory*, 137.

58. The twenty men who founded the confraternity are listed in the preamble to the confraternity's 1545 constitutions. López Muñoz, "Las ordenanzas de la hermandad de Nuestra Señora de las Angustias de Granada en el siglo XVI," *Chronica Nova* 17 (1989) 397.

59. Ibid., 413.

60. Archivo de la Cofradia de Nuestra Señora de las Angustias, Libro 2, f. 2.

61. José Gutiérrez Galdo, *La Virgen de Angustias: Patrona de Granada* (Granada: San Rita, 1983), 137.

62. López Muñoz, "Las ordenanzas," 383. López Muñoz later corrected himself, speculating on the basis of an eighteenth-century history of the brotherhood, and also not entirely accurately, that the early *cofrades* were "peasants and/or artisans:" Miguel Luis López-Guadalupe Muñoz and Juan Jesús López-Guadalupe Muñoz, *Nuestra Señora de las Angustias y su hermandad en la época moderna* (Granada: Editorial Comares, 1996), 19. There is, however, no documentary evidence of "peasant" membership in the brotherhood.

63. Diego Sánchez Saravia, *Compendio histórico del origen y culto en Granada de Nuestra Señora de las Angustias* (Granada: Santísima Trinidad, 1777), 5.

64. These constitutions, one of only two surviving sets of sixteenth-century Granadan confraternal bylaws, are published in their entirety in López Muñoz, "Las ordenanzas."

65. Sánchez Saravia, *Compendio histórico*, 7–8; Gutiérrez Galdó, *La Virgen de Angustias*, 111.

66. The 1556 additions to the constitutions are included in López Muñoz, "Las ordenanzas," 410–415.

67. Flynn, *Sacred Charity*. Flynn adds that many recruits to such confraternities in Spain were *judeoconversos*.

68. López Muñoz, "Las ordenanzas," 414–415.

69. Archivo de la Cofradía de Nuestra Señora de las Angustias, Libro 2, f. 12–12v. This history falsely identifies Cabrera as one of the confraternity's founders; he was not among the twenty members of the confraternity listed in the 1545 constitutions themselves. This deception is strong evidence that Cabrera himself may have been among the authors of this history.

70. APG, Libro 104, protócolos of Juan de Padilla, f. 741.

71. Ibid., Libro 208, protócolos de Bartólome Díaz, f. 436–440v.

72. Ibid., Libro 171, protócolos de Alonso de Alcalá, f. 108v.–111.

73. Ibid., Libro 210, protócolos de Luis Díaz, f. 290v–293.

74. Archivo de la Cofradía de Nuestra Señora de las Angustias, Libro 2, f. 12–12v.

75. AMG, legajo 1198, año 1567.

76. Gutiérrez Galdó, *La Virgen de Angustias,* 117.

77. Henríquez de Jorquera, Francisco, *Anales de Granada: Descripción del reino y ciudad de Granada. Crónica de la Reconquista. Sucesos de los años 1588 a 1646,* ed. Antonio Marín Ocete, 2 vols. (Granada, 1934; repr. Granada: Universidad de Granada, 1987), 1:229.

78. Archivo de la Cofradía de las Angustias, Libro 2, f. 1–16.

79. Hurtado de Mendoza, *Guerra de Granada,* 13–14.

80. García Pedraza, "El otro morisco," 231–232.

81. Ibid., 231–233.

82. Miri Rubin, *Corpus Christi: The Eucharist in Late Medieval Culture* (Cambridge: Cambridge University Press, 1991).

83. Orozco Pardo, *Christianópolis,* 85.

84. Garrido Atienza, *Antiguallas granadinas,* 7.

85. AHN, Inquisición, legajo 1953, no. 99, penitent #13.

86. Garrido Atienza, *Antiguallas granadinas,* 99–124.

87. Ibid., 9–10.

88. AMG, Libro de Ordenanzas, f. 12v.–13.

89. ACG, Libro 3 de Actas, f. 8v., actas of May 18, 1543.

90. Flynn, *Sacred Charity,* 122–123.

91. The first mention of such a brotherhood in Magdalena parish is in the testament of Cristóbal Frayle, dated April 30, 1537: APG, 1537 protócolos of Martín de Olivares, f. 255v. In San Justo, the first mention is in the testament of Catalina González, dated July 20, 1539: APG, 1539 protócolos de Martín de Olivares, f. 634. Impetus for the foundation of the confraternity in San Justo, however, had already been given in the 1537 testament of Catalina Hernández. See discussion below. In Santiago parish, the first mention is in the testament of Teresa Hernández, dated December 15, 1540: APG, 1540 protócolos de Martín de Olivares, f. 1027v.

92. ACG, legajo 84, p. 5. The constitutions mention 1538 as a "year to come" and indicate that they were written and approved during a period of *sede vacante.* Before 1538, the last time when the archiepiscopacy had been vacant was 1529, before the arrival of Archbishop Gaspar de Avalos.

93. Flynn, *Sacred Charity,* chapter 6.

94. APG, 1548 protócolos de Martín de Olivares, August 23, 1548 testament of Pedro Pizarro; ACG, legajo 84, p. 5.

95. APG, Libro de protócolos de Martín de Olivares, 1537, f. 262, April 21, 1537 testament of Catalina Hernández.

96. Ibid., Libro de protócolos de Martín de Olivares, 1537, f. 634, July 20, 1537 testament of Catalina González.

97. AMG, Libro de Ordenanzas, f. 246v.–247.

98. The first reference to this festival is a municipal ordinance issued in December 1514: AMG, Libro de Ordenanzas, f. 12v.

99. Ibid., Libro de Ordenanzas, f. 12v.–13.

100. ACG, Libro 3 de asuntos varios, f. 262. Charles argued in this *cédula* that payment for these memorial masses was included in the chapter's regular incomes, which were endowed by Isabella herself. The chapter thus had no reason to refuse to participate in her memorial masses.

101. AMG, legajo 1930, año 1542

6. DEFINING REFORM

1. Holy Roman Emperor Charles V (1519–1556) also ruled Aragon and Castile from 1516 to 1556 as King Charles I.

2. Prudencio de Sandoval, *Historia del Emperador Carlos V,* ed. Carlos Seco Serrano (Biblioteca de Autores Españoles, vols. 80–82, Madrid: Real Academia Española, 1955), 81:172.

3. Ibid., 81:173; Agustín Redondo, "El primer plan sistemático de asimilación de los moriscos granadinos: El del doctor Carvajal (1526)," in *Les morisques et leur temps* (Paris: Éditions du Centre National de la Recherche Scientifique, 1983), 113.

4. Beside Avalos, the other members of the visitation team included the royal chronicler, philosopher, and political theorist Fray Antonio Guevara as well as three officials from Granada's cathedral chapter: Dr. Utiel, Dr. Quintana, and Pedro López: Bermúdez de Pedraza, *Historia eclesiástica*, 213.

5. Along with Avalos and the royal secretary and former *regidor* on Granada's municipal council, Francisco de los Cobos, participants in the Royal Chapel Congregation included many of Spain's most powerful and influential clergymen: Archbishop of Seville and Inquisitor General Alonso de Manrique; Archbishop of Santiago and President of the Council of Castile Juan de Tavera; Archbishop-elect of Granada and former prior of Granada's Hieronymite monastery Fray Pedro Ramiro de Alva; Bishop of Osma and Royal Confessor Fray García de Loaysa; Bishop of Almería Diego de Villalán; Dr. Lorenzo Galíndez de Carvajal; Ldo. Luis de Polanco; the *comendador* of the military order of Calatrava Don García de Padilla; the Bishop of Mondoñedo Dr. Hernando de Guevara; and Ldo. Valdés of the Council of the Inquisition. Bermúdez de Pedraza, *Historia eclesiástica*, 213.

6. ACG, Libro 3, f. 75–77, mandates #5, 16, and 22.

7. Ibid., #19; Galán Sánchez, "Notas para una periodización de la historia de los moriscos granadinos."

8. ACG, Libro 3, f. 75–77, mandates #15 and 17.

9. Ibid., Libro 3, f. 75–77, mandates #8, 11, and 13. See also the more specific recommendations regarding clerical discipline in Charles V's instructions to Granada's new archbishop Pedro Ramiro de Alva in the wake of the 1526 Royal Chapel Conference: ACG, Libro 3, f. 77–79v.

10. Sandoval, *Historia del emperador Carlos V*, 81:172; Bermúdez de Pedraza, *Historia eclesiástica*, 212.

11. See the account by the elector's personal physician Iohannes Lange de Löwenberg, cited in Luque Moreno, *Granada en el siglo XVI*, 243.

12. Marmol Carvajal, *Rebelión y castigo*, 64; Garrad, "The Original Memorial of Don Francisco Núñez Muley," 207, footnote #2. The archival reference Garrad makes to ACG, Libro 3, f. 34–35 is incorrect.

13. ACG, Libro 3, f. 75–77. A prohibition of the *leylas* may have been implied, however, by a (perhaps intentionally?) vaguely phrased allusion to morisco wedding customs in a set of instructions given by the emperor at the end of his 1526 visit to Granada's new archbishop Fray Pedro Ramiro de Alva: See ACG, Libro 3, f. 77–79v., #2: "Asi mesmo tened muncho cuidado q de aqui adelante en los desposorios e velaciones e vodas que hicieren los dhos nuebamente convertidos no se hagan las ceremonias e ritos moriscos que hasta aqui hacian."

14. Sandoval, *Historia del emperador Carlos V*, 81:173: "Aposentóse en el Alhambra, y como mirarse con curiosidad los edificios antiguos, obras moriscas, y los ingenios de las aguas, y la fuerza del sitio, y la grandeza del pueblo, si bien de todas las ciudades de su reino mostró tener gran contento, de ésta en particular recibió mucho gusto." Of course, it should also be remembered that even as he resided in the Alhambra, he ordered plans drawn up for his own new Italian Renaissance-style palace within the old fortress's walls—an imposing edifice that today physically and symbolically dwarfs the old Nasrid royal residences next door: Earl Rosenthal, *The Palace of Charles V in Granada* (Princeton: Princeton University Press, 1985).

15. See Núñez Muley's recollection of the emperor's visit in Garrad, "The Original Memorial of Don Francisco Núñez Muley," 210–211.

16. The "epicenter" metaphor is particularly appropriate; a strong earthquake shook Granada and its royal guests on July 4, 1526: Bermúdez de Pedraza, *Historia eclesiástica*, f. 214v.

17. Sandoval, *Historia del emperador Carlos V*, 81:170–231.

18. Ibid., 81:185–187.

19. Garrad, "The Original Memorial of Don Francisco Núñez Muley," 207. In footnote #3, Garrad notes that Avalos in taking such a harsh stand on the *leylas* was supported not only

by the spirit of the 1526 royal mandates, which had after all been suspended, but also more specifically on the authority of a 1530 royal order addressed to him by the Empress Isabella (who evidently was not as much an admirer of morisco dance traditions as her husband). Núñez Muley does not identify the date of this incident, but he mentions the involvement of the city's *corregidor* Hernán de Arias Saavedra, who arrived in the city in or around 1535: López Nevot, *La organización institucional,* 27; Córtes Peña and Vincent, *Historia de Granada,* 161.

20. For biographical background on Avalos, see Miguel López, *Los arzobispos de Granada: retratos y semblanzas* (Granada: Santa Rita, 1993), 55–59; Bermúdez de Pedraza, *Historia eclesiástica,* f. 218v.

21. See Núñez Muley's scathing description of Avalos's policies and local reaction in Garrad, "The Original Memorial of Don Francisco Núñez Muley," 206–207.

22. Edward Cooper, *Castillos señoriales en la corona de Castilla* (Salamanca: Junta de Castilla y León, 1991), 143; Garrad, "The Causes of the Second Rebellion," 205.

23. Garrad, "The Original Memorial of Don Francisco Núñez Muley," 206–207; 210–211.

24. ACG, Libro 3 de asuntos varios, f. 78v, recommendation #13.

25. Ibid., Libro 3 de asuntos varios, f. 128–128v. The minutes of cathedral chapter meetings are sparse from 1528 to 1532, and they contain no mention of Avalos' synod: ACG, Libro 2 de actas capitulares. For a copy of Avalos's constitutions: Ibid., Libro 3 de asuntos varios, f. 84v.–112v.

26. Marín López, *El cabildo,* 55.

27. Jorge Díaz Ibáñez, "Fray Alonso de Burgos y el sínodo conquense de 1484," *Hispania Sacra* 47 (1995): 307–309.

28. Nalle, *God in La Mancha,* 10, 24–25.

29. On residence, see ACG, Libro 3 de asuntos varios, f. 87–87v.; on regular reading and study, especially during Lent, see f. 110v–101; on standards of dress, exemplary morality and the concubinage issue, see f. 95v. and 104v–105. On coverage of all of these issues by previous synods elsewhere, see e.g. Díaz Ibáñez, "Fray Alonso de Burgos," 312–313, 314, 316. At roughly the same time that Avalos was writing his Granada constitutions, Bishop Diego Ramírez de Villaescusa enacted a very similar 1531 set of synod decrees in his diocese of Cuenca. Interestingly, Ramírez de Villaescusa had been, like Avalos, a student in Talavera's innovative Colegio eclesiástico de San Cecilio in Granada in the years around 1500. Before moving to Cuenca, moreover, he had also previously been bishop of Málaga—like Granada a recently conquered part of the old Nasrid sultanate—where he had written that diocese's first postconquest synodal constitutions in 1515: Nalle, *God in La Mancha,* 22–30.

30. ACG, Libro 3 de asuntos varios, f. 96. On the use of similar policies elsewhere, see Díaz Ibáñez, "Fray Alonso de Burgos," 321; Nalle, *God in La Mancha,* 25.

31. ACG, Libro 3 de asuntos varios, f. 85v.

32. Ibid., 85v.–86.

33. Ibid., 86.

34. Mary Elizabeth Perry, "Behind the Veil: Moriscas and the Politics of Resistance and Survival," in *Spanish Women in the Golden Age: Images and Realities,* ed. Magdalena S. Sánchez and Alain Saint-Saëns (Westport: Greenwood Press, 1996), 37–53; Ronald Surtz, "Morisco Women, Written Texts, and the Valencia Inquisition," *Sixteenth Century Journal* 32 (2001): 421–433.

35. ACG, Libro 3 de asuntos varios, f. 86.

36. Ibid., f. 99v: "Pero porque muchos xpianos a nra sta fee catolica nuebamente conuertidos no pueden ni deven comulgar por no estar tan instructos y edificados en la fe como devrian y para resçibir tan alto sacramento se requiere no incurren en las dichas penas aunque no comulguen porq no dexan comulgar por rebelde."

37. Ibid., f. 95.

38. Ibid., f. 92–93v.

39. Documents and court rulings pertaining to this case are collected in ACG, Libro 3 de asuntos varios, f. 114–137v.

40. Nalle, *God in La Mancha*, 81.

41. ACG, Libro 3 de asuntos varios, f. 110v. The *beneficiados*' argument appears to be at least partly valid. In the baptismal registers of all eight urban parishes that I have examined, the *beneficiados*' names appear at least as often and in many cases more often than those of the *curas* well into the 1560s, even though the duty to administer the sacrament of baptism was supposed pertain exclusively to the *cura*. The 1548 archiepiscopal visitation report for the parish of Santa María in the Alhambra, moreover, listed all three of the principal parish clergymen as *beneficiados,* without mentioning which of the three if any was actually the *cura:* Archivo de la Parroquia de San Cecilio, Libro de Visitas de la Parroquia de Santa María del Alhambra, 1548 visitation. Evidently, some confusion and overlap existed regarding the nomenclature and duties of the two positions.

42. ACG, Libro 3 de asuntos varios, f. 131v.

43. Ibid., f. 110–110v.

44. Ibid., f. 123v.

45. Ibid., f. 111.

46. Ibid., f. 131v.–132.

47. Cortés Peña and Vincent, *Historia de Granada*, 191.

48. On Juan de Avila and the *Colegio de Santa Catalina,* see the final section of this chapter.

49. Bermúdez de Pedraza, *Historia eclesiástica*, f. 218v–220.

50. ACG, legajo 8, p. 19.

51. *Don Pedro Guerrero: epistolario y documentación,* ed. Juan López Martín (Rome: Instituto Español de Historia Eclesiástica, 1974), 25: Juan de Avila to Pedro Guerrero, April 2, 1547.

52. One way in which he may not have been typical of Granada's immigrant community was that he may have been Portuguese, as all of the traditional accounts of his life report: Francisco de Castro, *Historia de la vida y sanctas obras de Iuan de Dios y de la institución de su orden, y principio de su hospital* (Granada, 1585), in *San Juan de Dios: Primicias Históricas Suyas,* ed. M. Gómez Moreno (Madrid: S. Aguirre, 1950), 31; Antolínez de Burgos, *Historia eclesiástica,* 345.; Bermúdez de Pedraza, *Historia eclesiástica,* f. 231. However, Linda Martz, *Poverty and Welfare in Habsburg Spain: The Example of Toledo* (Cambridge: Cambridge University Press, 1983), 40, notes that he may have actually been from Covarrubias del Monte, a village near Toledo.

53. Castro, *Historia de la vida,* 11–128. Additional biographical background on Juan de Dios's life before coming to Granada can be found in Antolínez de Burgos, *Historia eclesiástica,* 345–346; Bermúdez de Pedraza, *Historia eclesiástica,* f. 231–231v.; and Martz, *Poverty and Welfare,* 40.

54. Castro, *Historia de la vida,* 40–41; Antolínez de Burgos, *Historia eclesiástica,* 345–346.

55. Bermúdez de Pedraza, *Historia eclesiástica,* f. 231–231v.

56. Antolínez de Burgos, *Historia eclesiástica,* 352, includes an account of the 1550 funeral of Juan de Dios, to which multitudes of people came in hope of obtaining a relic or two from the body. The first textual reference to Juan de Dios as a "saint" that I have seen is in the 1577 testament of María González, who left one ducat in alms to the "pobres de San Juan": APG, Libro 210, protócolos de Luis Díaz, f. 577–580. Usually, bequests to Juan's hospital were phrased "al hospital de Juan de Dios."

57. Martz, *Poverty and Welfare,* 43.

58. David Coleman, "Moral Formation and Social Control in the Catholic Reformation: The Case of San Juan de Avila," *Sixteenth Century Journal* 26 (1995): 17–30.

59. Bermúdez de Pedraza, *Historia eclesiástica,* f. 231v; Castro, *Historia de la vida,* 45.

60. Antolínez de Burgos, *Historia eclesiástica,* 346. See also Castro, *Historia de la vida,* 45–46.

61. Bermúdez de Pedraza, *Historia eclesiástica,* f. 231v.; Martz, *Poverty and Welfare,* 40–41.

62. Antolínez de Burgos, *Historia eclesiástica,* 347.

63. Ibid.; Bermúdez de Pedraza, *Historia eclesiástica*, f. 231v.

64. "Hay quién haga bien para sus mismos hermanos?" and "Quién haze bien para si mismo?": Antolínez de Burgos, 348; Bermúdez de Pedraza, *Historia eclesiástica*, f. 231v. In his 1585 biography of Juan de Dios, Francisco de Castro underlined the uniqueness of this method of begging alms, saying that the residents of the city "salían maravilladas a las puertas y ventanas, de oír la nueva manera de pedir," Castro, *Historia de la vida,* 58.

65. Antolínez de Burgos, *Historia eclesiástica,* 348: "Salía la gente a las puertas y ventanas, y maravillados de tan nueva manera de pedir, y más del rigor con que se tratava, de la gran caridad que usava con los pobres, le davan mucha limosna con grande amor y voluntad." Concerning his popularity among the moriscos, see Ronald Cueto, "Logic in Madness: St. John of God's Game of *Birlimbao,*" *Portuguese Studies* 5 (1989): 27–44.

66. Bermúdez de Pedraza, *Historia eclesiástica*, f. 231v.–232.

67. Castro, *Historia de la vida,* 69–70; Antolínez de Burgos, *Historia eclesiástica,* 349–350.

68. Martz, *Poverty and Welfare,* 43. One exception was the nobleman Rodrigo de Sigüenza. Later, in 1586, when the hospital found itself at odds with the archbishop over the issue of independence from archiepiscopal oversight, the vicar-general of the archdiocese called the brothers "imposters, who take money from the faithful for their own ends. This is not surprising since they are all the dross of society who do not work, so they take the habit to enrich themselves quickly, and afterwards they leave and marry." AGS, Patronato Eclesiástico, legajo 140.

69. The 1556 foundation document of this confraternity is transcribed in the 1568 archiepiscopal visitation of the hospital: ACG, legajo 85, p. 6. The thirty founding members included "el licenciado Juan Nuñez, "el bachiller Alonso Gómez," "Hernando Hurtado, tesorero de la casa de la moneda de Granada," and "Juan Juarez, escribano público." The visitation also includes other indications that there may have been a large *letrado* presence in the confraternity. The visitor's orders include the following (order #4): "yten mando que pues en esta casa ay copia de hermanos y en(tre) ellos hombres que pueden bien exercer y usar el oficio de mayordomo de obras sin que la casa pague salario por ello a otra persona."

70. Antolínez de Burgos, *Historia eclesiástica,* 353; Bermúdez de Pedraza, *Historia eclesiástica,* f. 232v.

71. Henríquez de Jorquera, *Anales de Granada,* 2: 258.

72. Of the twenty-three testaments that mention the hospital of Juan de Dios, only five include indications of the profession or social class of the testator. Among these five, two are laborers, two are bureaucrats, and one is a merchant.

73. In a letter to the duchess of Sesa, called the duke of Sesa his largest benefactor: Juan de Dios, *Cartas y escritos de N.P.S. Juan de Dios,* ed. P. Octavio Marcos (Madrid: Tipografía Artística, 1935), 15.

74. Cueto, "Logic in Madness," 42.

75. Archivo de la Diputación Provincial de Granada, legajo 532/H.

76. Bermúdez de Pedraza, *Historia eclesiástica*, f. 232.

77. Castro, *Historia de la vida,* 71–72; Antolínez de Burgos, *Historia eclesiástica,* f. 351.

78. *Cartas y escrituras del N.P.S Juan de Dios,* 50: letter to Gutierre Lasso.

79. Antolínez de Burgos, *Historia eclesiástica,* 350.

80. Martz, *Poverty and Welfare,* 41. As a result of the visitation, Guerrero ordered that the hospital be brought under stricter archiepiscopal supervision.

81. Cueto, "Logic in Madness," 37–44 attributes the local success of Juan de Dios in Granada above all to the way in which his appeal crossed all of the city's ethnic and religious boundaries.

82. Bilinkoff, *The Avila of Saint Teresa,* 58–60, discusses the foundation of a number of new poor-relief institutions in Avila.

83. On these issues see especially Martz, *Poverty and Welfare.*

84. AGS, Patronato Eclesiástico, leg. 39, cited in Martz, *Poverty and Welfare,* 36. Emphasis added.

85. The Hospital of Corpus Christi had been established by Antonio de Cáceres and Ed-

uardo Correa in 1517, and the Hospital de la Caridad had been founded by a group of nobles and upper clergy in imitation of that of Corpus Christi: Bermúdez de Pedraza, *Historia eclesiástica*, f. 209.

86. Martz, *Poverty and Welfare*, 52. A 1518-1519 crown-mandated visitation of Granada's Royal Hospital uncovered these abuses, but the reforms ordered by the visitors were ignored in subsequent years.

87. Ibid., 65. Also, on page 42, Martz explains that in the context of the debates of the era, Juan's views on this matter should be considered conservative—that is, in accordance with those of the Salamanca professor and Dominican theologian Domingo de Soto.

88. "Más dar acá, dar allá, todo es ganar; mientras más moros, más ganancias." *Cartas y escritos de N.P.S. Juan de Dios*, 20.

89. "[G]ozaban tanto del fruto desta caridad que unos convidaban a otros, y otros a otros, tanto, que era cosa mucho de ver la gente que al hospital iva: corregidor, veinticuatros, jurados, caballeros, dean canónigos, racioneros, colegiales, doctores teólogos, canonistas, y legistas, escribanos, procuradores, mercaderes, y cabdadanos, los qual an ido y van y sirven a los pobres, y les dan ellos mismos la comida, puesta una toalla al hombro, como maestresalas, incándose de rodillas al dar el plato, besando primero el plato que lo diesen al pobre, considerando jhu xristo en él.": MHSI, Litterae Quadrimestris, 6:742-743, 31 August 1560 report from Navarro to Laínez.

90. AMG, Libro de Ordenanzas, f. 242v. This order was in accordance with a 1387 Castilian law: Martz, *Poverty and Welfare*, 19-20.

91. AMG, Libro de Ordenanzas, f. 241-241v.

92. Castro, *Historia de la vida*, 71.

93. These expressions are repeated as the regulation means of begging alms in the 1587 constitutions of the Hospital of Juan de Dios, written by Archbishop Méndez de Salvatierra: ACG, Libro 3 de asuntos varios, f. 379-406, título 8, número 12.

94. Ibid., título 8, constitución 12.

95. A 1568 visitation of the hospital notes that the members of the *cofradía de las Cinco Plagas de Jesús* were required not only to assist in the hospital's primary activities of caring for the resident poor and sick, but also to care for orphans and widows, and to counsel married couples and prostitutes: ACG, legajo 85, p. 6. The 1587 constitutions of the hospital prohibited the brothers from serving as tutors or executors of testaments without explicit archiepiscopal permission, implying that they had up to that date engaged in such activities with at least some regularity: ACG, Libro 3 de asuntos varios, f. 379-406, título 8, número 8. Juan de Sigüenza, one of the brothers of the hospital, served as godfather for Mariana, the daughter of Andrés de Vergara and Francisca del Campo, at her baptism on April 6, 1567: Archivo de la Parroquia de San Ildefonso, Libro 1 de bautismos.

96. ACG, Libro 3 de Actas, f. 121, Actas of November 4, 1552.

97. Martz, *Poverty and Welfare*, 42.

98. The 1568 visitation contains a variety of documents that chronicle the agreements by which the Hieronymites gained the right of supervision over the hospital and the conflicts that arose between the Hieronymites and the hospital as a result: ACG, legajo 85, p. 6.

99. A copy of the 1571 bull granting the brothers of Juan de Dios the status of "congregation" is in ACG, legajo 85, p. 4; Martz, *Poverty and Welfare*, 42-43.

100. Martz, *Poverty and Welfare*, 43. The 1586 grant of independence from archiepiscopal control was itself an aberration in that era, when the Council of Trent and Counter-Reformation trends generally supported the authority of the prelate over the religious life of his diocese or archdiocese.

101. Antolínez de Burgos, *Historia eclesiástica*, 354; Bermúdez Pedraza, *Historia eclesiástica*, f. 232v.

102. Martz, *Poverty and Welfare*, 43.

103. Luis Sala Balust, "Introducción biográfica," in *Obras completas del Santo Maestro Juan de Avila*, ed. Luis Sala Balust and Francisco Martín Hernández, 2d ed., 6 vols. (Madrid: Católica, 1970-1971), 1:144. The most clear statement of Avila's Jewish ancestry is in MHSI, Epistolae mixtae, 2: 786.

104. Sala Balust, "Introducción biográfica," 68, 78, 90–91, 95.

105. Bermúdez de Pedraza, *Historia eclesiástica*, f. 224v.; Luis de Granada, *Vida del P. Mtro. Juan de Avila y las partes que a de tener un predicador del evangelio*, ca. 1580, in *Vidas del P. Maestro Juan de Avila*, ed. Luis Sala Balust (Barcelona: Juan Flors, 1964), 106.

106. Marcel Bataillon, "Jean de Avila Retrouvé," *Bulletin Hispanique* 57 (1955): 7, 40.

107. Juan de Avila, *Obras completas del Santo Maestro Juan de Avila*, ed. Luis Sala Balust and Francisco Martín Hernández, 2d ed., 6 vols. (Madrid: Católica, 1970–1971). Volume 6 contains complete transcriptions of the reform treatises Avila submitted to the Council of Trent.

108. Biographies of Juan de Avila include: Luis de Granada, *Vida del P. Mtro Juan de Avila*; Luis Muñoz, *Vida y virtudes del venerable varón el P. Mtro. Juan de Avila, predicador apostólico; con algunos elogios y virtudes y vidas de algunos de sus más principales discípulos,* 1655, in *Vidas del Padre Maestro Juan de Avila,* ed. Luis Sala Balust (Barcelona: Juan Flors, 1964); Sala Balust, *"Introducción biográfica"*; Rafael Arce, *San Juan de Avila y la reforma de la Iglesia en España* (Madrid: Ediciones Rialp, 1970).

109. Granada, *Vida del P. Mtro. Juan de Avila,* 104–113; Quote from Muñoz, *Vida y virtudes,* 190.

110. Sala Balust, "Introducción Biográfica," 38.

111. Camilo María Abad, "El proceso de la Inquisición contra el Beato Juan de Avila: Estudio crítico a la luz de documentos desconocidos," *Miscelánea Comillas,* 6 (1946): 136–138.

112. Avila, *Obras,* 6:33.

113. Ibid., 6:34–36.

114. Ibid., 6:155–158. See also Nalle, *God in La Mancha,* 122.

115. Avila, *Obras,* 6:454–480 for a copy of his *Doctrina cristiana.*

116. Ibid., 6:39.

117. Sala Balust, "Introducción biográfica," 64–107.

118. Arce, *San Juan de Avila,* 51–52; Avila, *Obras,* 1:700, 705.

119. Avila, *Obras,* 5:52, 750.

120. Coleman, "Moral Formation."

121. Avila, *Obras,* 5:52.

122. Ibid., 3:426–427; 6:39, 89, for three examples of his use of this metaphor. See also Coleman, "Moral Formation," 25–29.

123. Cited in Bermúdez de Pedraza, *Historia eclesiástica,* f. 223.

124. Ibid., f. 223v.–224.

125. Sala Balust, "Introducción biográfica," 91–92.

126. Bermúdez de Pedraza, *Historia eclesiástica,* f. 223–224; Sala Balust, "Introducción biográfica," 76–77.

127. Avila, *Obras,* 5:666–667; Camilo María Abad, "Escritos de Beato Juan de Avila en torno al Concilio de Trento," *Maestro Avila* 3 (1947): 274, 289.

128. Calero Palacios, *La enseñanza y educación,* 209–210; Sala Balust, "Introducción biográfica," 75.

129. Calero Palacios, *La enseñanza y educación,* 163–164.

130. Sala Balust, "Introducción biográfica," 72–76, 109; Luis de Granada, *Vida del P. Mtro Juan de Avila,* 106. Bilinkoff, *The Avila of Saint Teresa,* 84–86, explains the impact of Juan de Avila's sacerdotal school in the city of Avila, which, despite his name, Juan de Avila never visited.

131. Coleman, "Moral Formation," 29–31.

132. Sala Balust, "Introducción biográfica," 73.

133. Bilinkoff, *The Avila of Saint Teresa,* 84–86. Gaspar Daza's sacerdotal team in Avila was connected directly to the Granadan movement by the figure of Julián de Avila, who had been exposed to Juan de Avila and his followers during trips to Granada and Seville in the 1540s.

134. Ibid., 83–85.

135. *Don Pedro Guerrero: Epistolario y documentación,* ed. Juan López Martín (Rome: Instituto Español de Historia Eclesiástica, 1974), 25–26.

136. See chapter 1.

137. Álvaro Huerga, *Fray Luis de Granada. Una vida al servicio de la Iglesia* (Madrid: Católica, 1988).

138. Sala Balust, "Introducción biográfica," 65.

139. Muñoz, *Vida y virtudes*, 325.

140. Sala Balust, "Introducción biográfica," painstakingly traces Avila's path during his wanderings in the 1530s and 1540s and notes the numerous occasions when he and Fray Luis were in the same place. For correspondence between the two men, see Avila, *Obras*, vol. 5.

141. Elizabeth Rhodes, "Spain's Misfired Canon: The Case of Luis de Granada's Libro de la oración y meditación," *Journal of Hispanic Philology* 15 (1990): 43–66; Keith Whinnom, "The Problem of the Best-Seller in Spanish Golden-Age Literature," *Bulletin of Hispanic Studies* 57 (1980): 189–198.

142. Rhodes, "Spain's Misfired Canon," 50, n. 15.

143. Ibid., 47, 57; Bruno Jereczek, *Louis de Grenade disciple de Jean d'Avila* (Fontenay-le-Comté: Lussaud, 1971).

144. Luis de Granada, *Vida del P. Mtro. Juan de Avila*, 28; Sala Balust, "Introducción biográfica," 30.

145. Bermúdez de Pedraza, *Historia eclesiástica*, f. 226v.–227

7. NEGOTIATING REFORM

1. Constancio Gutiérrez, *Españoles en Trento* (Valladolid: Consejo Superior de Investigaciones Científicas, 1951), 955.

2. Cited in Ricardo G. Villoslada, "Pedro Guerrero representante de la reforma española," in *Il Concilio di Trento e la riforma tridentina: Atti del convegno storico internazionale: Trento—2–6 settembre 1963*, 2 vols. (Rome: Herder, 1965), 117.

3. Ibid., 118.

4. *Don Pedro Guerrero, Epistolario*, 50.

5. Antonio Marín Ocete, *El arzobispo Pedro de Guerrero y la política conciliar española en el siglo XVI*, 2 vols. (Granada: Consejo Superior de Investigaciones Científicas and University of Granada, 1970), 2:3.

6. For biographical information on Guerrero, see Bermúdez de Pedraza, *Historia eclesiástica*, 226v.–227v.; Marín Ocete, *El arzobispo Don Pedro Guerrero*.

7. Although it should be noted that in the Spain of Charles V and his son Philip II, such previously unheard of men were increasingly preferred for upper-level government and ecclesiastical posts.

8. *Don Pedro Guerrero: Epistolario*, 25–26.

9. Ibid., 87–95; 98–102; 104–105; and 111–112 for various letters from Avila to Guerrero.

10. Ibid., 25.

11. The only surviving copy of Guerrero's reform constitutions, dated January 1548, is located in the visitation book of the parish of Santa María del Alhambra: Archivo de la Parroquia de San Cecilio, Libro 1 de visitaciones de Santa María del Alhambra, 1548 visitation.

12. The only traces that I have seen of archiepiscopal visitors' activities in the parishes before Guerrero's 1546 arrival have been marginal notes in parish baptismal records, where the parish mayordomos often recorded incomes from baptisms. For example, see Archivo de la Parroquia de Santa Ana y San Gil, Libro I de Bautismos de Santa Ana, marginal note beside the baptism entry of June 14, 1545: "hasta aquí está visitado por el S. Visitador Cabezas." For comparison to the situation in Cuenca, see Nalle, *God in La Mancha*, 26.

13. Archivo de la Parroquia de San Cecilio, Libro 1 de visitaciones de Santa María del Alhambra, 1548 visit. Listed among the exhaustive inventory of goods pertaining to the parish are numerous books, including "this book in which visitations are recorded" and no other visitation records are listed. The 1548 visitation begins on the first page of the intact book, suggesting that this was the first time such records had been kept.

14. Ibid. This book includes detailed visitation records for the years 1550, 1552, 1553, 1554, 1556, 1559, 1561, 1564, 1566, 1568 and 1569.

15. Ibid., 1548 visitation, constitutions #1 and #2.

16. Ibid., constitution #10.

17. Ibid., constitution #13.

18. *Don Pedro Guerrero, Epistolario*, 26.

19. ACG, legajo 298, p. 11.

20. Ibid., Libro 3 de asuntos varios, f. 600. The question-list also asks both lay people and clergy to denounce publicly all forms of heresy and public sin among the laity, including Jewish and Muslim practices, witchcraft, concubinage, blasphemy, and use of Church property for secular activities

21. MHSI, Litterae Quadrimestris, 3: 502.

22. Ibid., 6:251. See also López Martín, "D. Pedro Guerrero como obispo del tiempo de la contrarreforma," *Archivo Teológico Granadino* 31 (1968): 208.

23. Guerrero, like Juan de Avila, frequently recommended mental prayer: MHSI, Litterae Quadrimestris, 5:122, Navarro to Laínez.

24. *Don Pedro Guerrero: Epistolario*, 26.

25. Coleman, "Moral Formation," 25–27.

26. Manuel Ruiz Jurado, "San Juan de Avila y la Compañia de Jesús," *Archivum Historicum Societatis Iesu* 40 (1971): 159.

27. Sala Balust, "Introducción biográfica," 162–163, 177–182.

28. The twenty-eight are listed in Ruiz Jurado, "San Juan de Avila y la Compañia de Jesús," 158 n. 8. Many of Avila's followers who became Jesuits may have done so because they were of *judeoconverso* descent, and membership in the Society of Jesus could provide them some measure of protection from persecution: Sala Balust, "Introducción biográfica," 154–158; William Bangert and Thomas McCoog, *Jerome Nadal, S.J: Tracking the First Generation of Jesuits* (Chicago: Loyola University Press, 1992), 107–108.

29. Sala Balust, "Introducción biográfica," 73, 109, 118–120, 173.

30. López Martín, "El arzobispo de Granada D. Pedro Guerrero y la Compañia de Jesús," 459–460.

31. Sala Balust, "Introducción biográfica," 75–76.

32. Bermúdez Pedraza, *Historia eclesiástica*, f. 227; López Martín, "El arzobispo de Granada D. Pedro Guerrero y la Compañia de Jesús," 456; Marín Ocete, *El arzobispo Pedro Guerrero*, 2:378.

33. Marín Ocete, *El arzobispo Pedro Guerrero*, 2:377.

34. Sala Balust, "Introducción biográfica," 73, notes that Navarro was a native of Lucena, and had lived in Granada, where he met Juan de Avila in the late 1530s.

35. MHSI, Litterae Quadrimestris, 3:499–500, Navarro to Loyola.

36. MHSI, Litterae Quadrimestris, 4:625, Ruiz to Laínez.

37. MHSI, Litterae Quadrimestris, 6:292, Navarro to Laínez; López Martín, "El arzobispo D. Pedro Guerrero y la Compañia de Jesús," 221.

38. Marín Ocete, *El arzobispo D. Pedro Guerrero*, 2:380.

39. Ibid., 2:398.

40. On the Loarte brothers, see Sala Balust, "Introducción biográfica," 73. On the morisco Jesuits, see López Martín, "El arzobispo de Granada D. Pedro Guerrero y la Compañia de Jesús," 460–463; Castillo Fernández, "La asimilación de los moriscos," 352.

41. Evennett, *Spirit of the Counter-Reformation*, 74.

42. MHSI, Litterae Quadrimestris, 6: 352, Navarro to Laínez.

43. Ibid., 249–252, Navarro to Laínez.

44. J. Rosaura Álvarez Rodríguez, "La Casa de Doctrina del Albaicín: Labor apostólico de la Compañía de Jesús con los moriscos," *Cuadernos de la Alhambra* 19–20 (1983–1984): 241.

45. Ibid., 242.

46. Ibid., 231–238; López Martín, "El arzobispo D. Pedro Guerrero y la Compañia de Jesús," 460–464.

47. Mármol Carvajal, *Rebelión y castigo*, 91.

48. MHSI, Litterae Quadrimestris, 6:292, 419, Navarro to Laínez; López Martín, "El arzobispo D. Pedro Guerrero y la Compañia de Jesús," 205.

49. MHSI, Litterae Quadrimestris, 6:743, August 31, 1560, Navarro to Laínez; Marín Ocete, *El arzobispo Pedro Guerrero*, 2: 425.

50. López Martín, "El arzobispo D. Pedro Guerrero y la Compañia de Jesús, 469.

51. Marín Ocete, *El arzobispo D. Pedro Guerrero* 2:382.

52. MHSI, Litterae Quadrimestris, 3:743.

53. Marín Ocete, *El arzobispo D. Pedro Guerrero*, 2:382.

54. Bermúdez de Pedraza, *Historia eclesiástica*, f. 227–227v. Though they shared the same last name, Padre Basilio was not related to Juan de Avila.

55. López Martín, "El arzobispo D. Pedro Guerrero y la Compañia de Jesús," 469; Bermúdez de Pedraza, *Historia eclesiástica*, f. 227v.

56. MHSI, Litterae Quadrimestris, 3: 744–745, Navarro to Loyola.

57. The municipal council passed a series of ordinances in 1538 and 1539 in which the mistreatment of prostitutes by Sánchez and his wife was explained and denounced. The ordinances went on to regulate the treatment of the women, ordering that Sánchez provide them with adequate food, clothing, work conditions, and pay for their services: AMG, Libro de ordenanzas, f. 243v.–245. On the Jesuit campaign, see MHSI, Litterae Quadrimestris, 3: 745, Navarro to Loyola.

58. On the social functions of prostitution reform efforts in Seville, see Mary Elizabeth Perry, *Gender and Disorder in Early Modern Seville* (Princeton: Princeton University Press, 1990), 140.

59. MHSI, Litterae Quadrimestris, 3: 745.

60. Bilinkoff, *The Avila of Saint Teresa*, 91.

61. Constance Jones Mathers, "Early Spanish Qualms about Loyola and the Society of Jesus," *The Historian* 53 (1991): 686.

62. MHSI, Litterae Quadrimestris, 3:499; Marín Ocete, *El arzobispo Pedro Guerrero*, 2:380–381.

63. This argument is made by Marín Ocete, *El arzobispo D. Pedro Guerrero*, 2:381. See also MHSI, Litterae Quadrimestris, 5:499; Epistolae Mixtae, 5:81.

64. Marín Ocete, *El arzobispo Pedro Guerrero*, 2:445.

65. Ibid., 2:381.

66. MHSI, Litterae Quadrimestris, 3:743. Though the evidence for the popularity of the Jesuits among Granada's laity is strong, it does not include numerous or substantial bequests or requests for funeral masses. In general, the Society of Jesus discouraged the saying of masses for individual donors: Bilinkoff, *The Avila of Saint Teresa*, 89. In this way, the Jesuits did not conform to lay expectations. As a result, mentions of the Jesuits are rare among testators; they appear only four times in the eighty-three testaments included in this study's database for the years after the Jesuits' arrival in Granada in 1554.

67. MHSI, Litterae Quadrimestris, 3:746, Navarro to Loyola; 4:622, Navarro to Laínez. Kamen, *The Phoenix and the Flame*, 380.

68. MHSI, Epistolae Mixtae, 5:168, Araoz to Loyola.

69. AMG, Libro V de actas capitulares, various actas from spring and summer 1556 speak of these crises.

70. Marín Ocete, *El arzobispo D. Pedro Guerrero*, 2:384.

71. Surviving firsthand accounts of the 1556 murder and controversy that followed are few. One such account is by an anonymous official who claimed to have entered into Archbishop Guerrero's service in 1556—the same year as this incident. His testimonial concerning the events of that fall was written down sometime after Guerrero's death in 1576, and probably around 1600, as the official admitted that he could not remember all of the minute details of the incident because it had happened nearly fifty years before. This text appears to have been part of a larger effort to gather information for the writing of a biography of the archbishop: Biblioteca Nacional, Madrid (BNM), ms. 6948, f. 453–453v. The friar's name is mentioned in Garrad, "The Causes of the Second Rebellion," 187.

72. BNM, ms. 6948, f. 453; Bermúdez de Pedraza, *Historia eclesiástica*, f. 228v.–229.

73. BNM, ms. 6948, f. 453. The archiepiscopal official reported that the two judges who

died were named Lebrija and Juarez, though he could not remember which of the two men had died first. See also Bermúdez de Pedraza, *Historia eclesiástica*, f. 228v.–229. Marín Ocete states that the death of the first judge and Padre Basilio occurred between October 17 and October 19: *El Arzobispo Pedro Guerrero*, 2: 387–388.

74. BNM, mss. 6948, f. 453; Bermúdez de Pedraza, *Historia eclesiástica*, f. 228.

75. Marín Ocete, *El arzobispo Pedro Guerrero*, 2:388.

76. Bermúdez de Pedraza, *Historia eclesiástica*, f. 228.

77. ACG, Libro 3 de actas capitulares, f. 295, actas of April 27, 1557.

78. Bermúdez de Pedraza, *Historia eclesiástica*, f. 228v.

79. Over the three years following the execution, the monastery was mentioned by one-fourth of testators. Only the houses of Santísima Trinidad and La Victoria—both of which were included among the *mandas acostumbradas* at that time—surpassed La Cabeza over the same period.

80. López Martín, "El arzobispo D. Pedro Guerrero y la Compañía de Jesús," 471.

81. Cortés Peña and Vincent, *Historia de Granada*, 51.

82. Neither the Jesuit's nor the woman's name is mentioned in the available sources. For general narrative accounts of the controversy that followed, see Antonio Astraín, *Historia de la Compañía de Jesús en la asistencia de España*, 7 vols. (Madrid: Razón y Fe, 1912–1925), 2:86–94; Marín Ocete, *El Arzobispo Pedro Guerrero*, 2:403; López Martín, "El Arzobispo D. Pedro Guerrero y la Compañía de Jesús," 471–477. On confessional solicitation in general, see Stephen Haliczer, *Sexuality in the Confessional: A Sacrament Profaned* (New York and Oxford: Oxford University Press, 1996).

83. Astraín, *Historia de la Compañía de Jesús*, 2:88.

84. Marín Ocete, *El arzobispo Pedro Guerrero*, 2:401–402.

85. Astraín, *Historia de la Compañía de Jesús*, 2:89; Marín Ocete, *El arzobispo Pedro Guerrero*, 2:403.

86. Astraín, *Historia de la Compañía de Jesús*, 2:89–90.

87. Ibid, 2:90.

88. Ibid., 2:90.

89. Ibid., 2:90–92.

90. Marín Ocete, *El arzobispo Pedro Guerrero*, 2:408–409.

91. ACG, Libro 4 de actas capitulares, f. 197, actas of February 22, 1563.

92. ACG Libro 4 de actas capitulares, f. 240–241, actas of February 18 and March 7, 1564.

93. MHSI, Litterae Quadrimestris, 6: 419, Navarro to Laínez.

94. Astraín, *Historia de la Compañía de Jesús*, 2:93–94.

95. *Don Pedro Guerrero: Epistolario*, July 14, 1558, letter from Guerrero to Pope Paul IV; López Martín, "El arzobispo D. Pedro Guerrero y la Compañía de Jesús," 483.

96. *Don Pedro Guerrero: Epistolario*, 38, July 2, 1559, letter from Guerrero to Paul IV. Haliczer, *Sexuality in the Confessional*, 42.

97. López Martín, "El Arzobispo D. Pedro Guerrero y la Compañía de Jesús," 485; Nalle, *God in La Mancha*, 65.

98. ACG, Libro 4 de actas capitulares, f. 129v, actas of August 16, 1561.

99. This is the total number of Spanish prelates who attended third Trent over its two-year span 1562–1563, although because of frequent travel back and forth to Rome and back to Spain, there were never more than twenty-four actually physically present in Trent at any given time: Jedin, *Crisis and Closure*, 29.

100. Jedin, *Crisis and Closure*, 31; *Don Pedro Guerrero: Epistolario*, 27, 21 April 1562 letter from Guerrero to the Marqués de Pescara.

101. H. Outram Evennett, *The Cardinal of Lorraine and the Council of Trent: A Study in the Counter-Reformation* (Cambridge: Cambridge University Press, 1930); Don Pedro González de Mendoza, "Lo sucedido en el concilio de Trento," in *Concilum Tridentinum: Diariorum, Actorum, Epistularum, Tractarum*, 3d ed., 13 vols. (Freiburg: Herder, 1963–1967), 2:661, 669–670.

102. See acts throughout *Concilum Tridentinum*, vols. 8 and 9.

103. Don Pedro González de Mendoza, "Lo sucedido en el Concilio de Trento," 707. See also Sforza Pallavicino, *Istoria del Concilio di Trento* (Rome, 1656–1657; repr. 6 volumes, Faenza, 1792–1798), 5:275.

104. ACG, Libro 3 de asuntos varios, f. 628.

105. Martín Pérez de Ayala, "Discurso de la vida del ilustrísimo y reverendísimo señor Don Martín de Ayala," in *Nueva biblioteca de autores españoles,* ed. M. Serrano y Sanz (Madrid, 1905) 2:232, 224–225, 232–234.

106. *Don Pedro Guerrero: Epistolario,* 86, 30 May 1564 letter from Guerrero to Philip II. Martín Pérez de Ayala's overall evaluation of the achievements of the council was far less flattering than that of Guerrero. Pérez de Ayala even accused Guerrero of having backed down on some of the most important reform proposals forwarded in the council's final sessions: Pérez de Ayala, "Discurso," 234.

107. González de Mendoza, "Lo sucedido en el concilio de Trento," 635.

108. Marín Ocete, *El arzobispo Don Pedro Guerrero,* 2:510–516.

109. González de Mendoza, "Lo sucedido en el concilio de Trento," 641–642; Jedin, *Crisis and Closure,* 15–16.

110. Jedin, *Crisis and Closure,* 17.

111. González de Mendoza, "Lo sucedido en el concilio de Trent," 639; Jedin, *Crisis and Closure,* 47–50.

112. González de Mendoza, "Lo sucedio en el concilio de Trento," 642.

113. This exchange is recorded in Pallavicino, *Istoria del Concilio di Trento,* 6:398–399, and González de Mendoza, "Lo sucedido en el concilio de Trento," 664.

114. González de Mendoza, "Lo sucedido en el concilio de Trento," 667.

115. Ibid., 669–670.

116. Jedin, *Crisis and Closure,* 113.

117. Guerrero's tract is transcribed in *Concilium Tridentinum,* 13:572–574. The January 18, 1562, protest is noted in *Concilium Tridentinum,* 8:291.

118. *Don Pedro Guerrero: Epistolario,* 78–79.

119. Villoslada, "Pedro Guerrero," 145–146; Marín Ocete, *El arzobispo Pedro Guerrero,* 2:530.

120. Jedin, *Crisis and Closure,* 107.

121. Marín Ocete, *El arzobispo Pedro Guerrero,* 2:574.

122. The three reform tracts, titled "De la reformación del estado eclesiástico" (1551), "Lo que se debe avisar a los obispos" (1551), and "Causas y remedios de las herejías" (1561) are published in Avila, *Obras,* 6:33–195.

123. These petitions are published in *Concilium Tridentinum,* 13:624–629; 629–630.

124. Ibid., 13:539–550.

125. The original Latin version of this document is published in *Concilium Tridentinum,* 12:134–144. An English translation is published in John C. Olin, *The Catholic Reformation: Savonarola to Ignatius Loyola. Reform in the Church 1495–1540,* (New York: Harper and Row, 1969), 182–197; Gleason, *Gasparo Contarini,* 67–68. The other members of the commission were the Theatine leader Gian Pietro Carafa, bishop of Verona Gian Matteo Giberti, bishop of Carpentras Jacopo Sadoleto, Abbot Gregorio Cortese of San Giorgio Maggiore in Venice, the English cardinal Reginald Pole, bishop of Gubbio Federigo Fregoso, papal nuncio and archbishop of Brindisi Jerome Aleander, and the Dominican master of the sacred palace Tommaso Badia.

126. González de Mendoza, "Lo sucedido en el concilio de Trento," 668.

127. Jedin, *Crisis and Closure,* 121–126.

128. Ibid., 120.

129. The original text of the seminary decree presented for debate at Trent is published in *Concilium Tridentinum,* 9:483. See also Camilo María Abad, "Escritos del Beato Juan de Avila en torno al Concilio de Trento," *Maestro Avila* 3 (1947): 273–295; Jedin, *Crisis and Closure,* 117–118.

130. Coleman, "Moral Formation," 25–27.

131. For text of the debates on the original seminary decree, see *Concilium Tridentinum*, 9:493–512. Also see the points on clerical education in the archbishop of Braga's aforementioned reform petitions: *Concilium Tridentinum*, 13:542.

132. Abad, "Escritos del Beato Juan de Avila," 289.

133. Ibid., 289; Avila, *Obras*, 6:47: "vale más elegir pocos y que no sea menester desechar ninguno, que no abrir la puerta a recebir a quien sea cargoso a los otros, y sea menester echarlo o ordenarlo siendo indigno." Also see Avila, *Obras*, 5:666–667, for another example of such a plea from Avila.

134. Jedin, *Crisis and Closure*, 117. Guerrero's 1547 constitutions for the Colegio eclesiástico required that each student admitted must be "tal que se espere dél que será solícito en el servicio del Señor y en los oficios que le fueren encargados." ACG, leg. 298, p. 11, f. 1. See also Martín Hernández, *Un seminario pretridentino*, 48.

135. Avila, *Obras*, 6:39.

136. *Decrees and Canons of the Council of Trent*, 187.

137. Ibid., 188.

138. Olin, *The Catholic Reformation*, 193.

139. Avila, *Obras*, 6:56–57; 75.

140. Ibid., 6:186–189.

141. "Petitiones comunes," #20: "Examinetur vita et doctrina eorum, qui praeficiuntur confessionibus a regularibus de mandato episcopi": *Concilium Tridentinum*, 13:625.

142. "Quoad monachi claustrales et reformati examinentur ab ordinariis, quando sunt promovendi ad ordines vel ad praedicandum vel ad audiendam confessiones." (IV, #22 of Martyris's reform tract): *Concilium Tridentinum*, 13:541. See also VIII, #10 of the same document (13:544).

143. *Canons and Decrees of the Council of Trent*, 185.

144. *Canons and Decrees of the Council of Trent*, 211.

145. See earlier discussion in chapter 5.

146. "Petitiones comunes,"#8, #17 and papal gloss in footnote #11: *Concilium Tridentinum*, 13:625.

147. *Canons and Decrees of the Council of Trent*, 252 (session 25, chapter #22 of the "Chapters on the Reform of the Regulars").

148. Ibid., 270.

149. Ibid., 277 (session 25, reform chapter #21).

8. REBELLION, RETRENCHMENT, AND THE ROAD TO SACROMONTE

1. ACG, Libro 3 de actas capitulares, f. 125, actas of January 17, 1553.

2. Ibid., Libro 4 de actas capitulares, f. 245, actas of May 2, 1564.

3. Domínguez Ortiz and Vincent, *Historia de los moriscos*, 28–29; Andrew Hess, "The Moriscos: An Ottoman Fifth Column," 1–5.

4. David Coleman, "Spain," in *The Reformation World*, ed. Andrew Pettegree (London: Routledge, 2000): 301–305.

5. Garrad, "The Causes of the Second Rebellion," 176–177; 476.

6. On Dr. Santiago's commission, see Garrad, "The Causes of the Second Rebellion," 53.

7. The incident is discussed in great detail in Mármol Carvajal, *Rebelión y castigo*, 82–84.

8. Antonio Marín Ocete, "El concilio provincial de Granada en 1565," *Archivo Teológico Granadino* 25 (1962): 23–95. A complete transcription of the text of the council's decrees is in Ignacio Pérez de Heredia y Valle, ed., *El concilio provincial de Granada en 1565. Edición crítica del malogrado concilio de Arzobispo Guerrero* (Rome: Publicaciones del Instituto Español de Historia Eclesiástica, 1990).

9. See ACG, Libro 3 de asuntos varios, f. 615–616: an anonymous eyewitness account of the council's proceedings that underscores the archbishop's firm and exclusive control over the agenda.

10. The municipal council's 1565 official protest letter is found in ACG, legajo 310, p. 3.

11. Ibid., Libro 5 de actas capitulares, actas of January 25, 1566. See also the 1565 complaint letter from the chapter to the archbishop in ACG, legajo 310, p. 3.

12. Marín Ocete, "El concilio provincial de Granada en 1565," 92.

13. ACG, legajo 321, p. 8.

14. Ibid., legajo 12, p. 34.

15. Data are drawn from rosters of *curas* and *beneficiados* contained in the baptismal records of eight local parishes spread throughout the city (San Ildefonso, San Cecilio, Santa Ana, San José, San Gil, San Juan de los Reyes, San Pedro y San Pablo and San Nicolás). The post-1550 figures are slightly higher than those of the clergy of the city of Cuenca, where local reformers' efforts to educate parish-level clergymen enjoyed some success in the same time period: Nalle, *God in La Mancha*, 93.

16. Cited in Juan López Martín, "D. Pedro Guerrero como obispo del tiempo de la contrareforma," *Archivo Teológico Granadino* 31 (1968): 193-231.

17. Juan López Martín, "El concilio provincial de Granada de 1565 y sus provisiones sobre los moriscos del reino de Granada," *Anthológica Annua* 36 (1989): 509-541.

18. The letter is transcribed in the documentary appendix of Marín Ocete, "El concilio provincial de Granada en 1565," 155-160.

19. Ibid., 158.

20. Domínguez Ortiz and Vincent, *Historia de los moriscos*, 33.

21. Garrad, "The Causes of the Second Rebellion," 317.

22. The incident is narrated in detail in Hurtado de Mendoza, *Guerra de Granada*, 65-66.

23. The most detailed account of this meeting and the debate is Mármol Carvajal, *Rebelión y castigo*, 164-165.

24. Hurtado de Mendoza, *Guerra de Granada*, 80.

25. Mármol Carvajal, *Rebelión y castigo*, 183.

26. Hurtado de Mendoza, *Guerra de Granada*, 79; Mármol Carvajal, *Rebelión y castigo*, 183-184.

27. Mármol Carvajal, *Rebelión y castigo*, 184.

28. Ibid.; Hurtado de Mendoza, *Guerra de Granada*, 79.

29. Hurtado de Mendoza, *Guerra de Granada*, 79-80.

30. Mármol Carvajal, *Rebelión y castigo*, 184.

31. Domínguez Ortiz and Vincent, *Historia de los moriscos*, 53-54.

32. Hutado de Mendoza, *Guerra de Granada*, 80.

33. Ibid., 79.

34. Domínguez Ortiz and Vincent, *Historia de los moriscos*, 55.

35. Bernard Vincent, *Andalucía en la edad moderna: economia y sociedad* (Granada: Diputación Provincial, 1985), 268-269. Vincent cites a 1580 royal survey according to which there were at that point a total of 3,851 moriscos living either in the city of Granada or the nearby countryside to the west.

36. Hurtado de Mendoza, *Guerra de Granada*, 80.

37. Córtes Peña and Vincent, *Historia de Granada*, 142.

38. Ibid., 143.

39. ACG, Libro 3 de asuntos varios, f. 546-551.

40. See López Nevot's incomplete list of new *regidores* and the dates on which they obtained their positions: *La organización institucional del municipio de Granada*, 112-113.

41. Ibid. These "new" elite lineages included: Ayala, Caicedo, Cuéllar, Monte, Ordóñez, and Varela.

42. Ibid., 187-190.

43. Manuel Barrios Aguilera, *Moriscos y repoblación en las postrimerias de la Granada islámica* (Granada: Diputación Provincial, 1993).

44. *The Avila of Saint Teresa*, 152. For similar trends in Cuenca and Catalonia, see also Nalle, *God in La Mancha*, 171; and Kamen, *The Phoenix and the Flame*, 437.

45. Archivo de la Parroquia de San Cecilio, Libro de visitas de Santa María de la Alhambra, 1568 visitation, constitution #3.

46. *El Concilio Provincial de Granada de 1565*, 229 (título 23, constitution #10).

47. Méndez's order also specifies that other confraternities had circumvented the ban on night processions by beginning during the day and lengthening their procession-route in order to insure that they did not finish until well after dark: ACG, legajo 84, p. 4.

48. Ibid., legajo 84, p. 4.

49. Ibid., Libro 5 de actas capitulares, actas of April 14, 1566. The invitation had first been issued by the confraternity in 1540 and frequently repeated since. See discussion of the confraternity and the local popularity of its procession in the first part of chapter 3 in this book.

50. The most vocal twentieth-century defender of the Sacromonte cause was the abbot of the Sacromonte Abbey from 1956 to 1971, Zótico Royo Campos. See his *Reliquias martiriales y escudo del Sacromonte,* ed. Miguel L. López Muñoz (Granada, 1960; facs. ed., Granada: Universidad de Granada, 1995).

51. The tower was finally destroyed in 1588 in order to make room for continuing construction on the walls of the new cathedral's south nave: Miguel Luis López Muñoz, "Estudio preliminar," in Zótico Royo Campos, *Reliquias martiriales y escudo del Sacromonte,* ed. Miguel L. López Muñoz (Granada, 1960; facs. ed., Granada: Universidad de Granada, 1995), xiii; Francisco Javier Martínez Medina, "Los libros plúmbeos del Sacromonte," in *Jesucristo y el Emperador Cristiano: Catálogo de la exposición celebrada en la catedral de Granada con motivo del año jubilar de la encarnación de Jesucristo y del V centenario del nacimiento del Emperador Carlos. Granada, 8 de julio al 8 de diciembre,* ed. Francisco Javier Martínez Medina (Córdoba: Publicaciones Obra Social y Cultural Cajasur, 2000), 619.

52. A. Katie Harris, "Forging Identity: The *Plomos* of the Sacromonte and the Creation of Civic Identity in Early Modern Granada," Ph.D. diss., Johns Hopkins University, 2000, 51.

53. On the 1588 Turpiana discoveries, see ACG, Libro 8 de actas capitulares, f. 113–113v.; Antolínez de Burgos, *Historia eclesiástica,* 489–493; Bermúdez de Pedraza, *Historia eclesiástica,* f. 261v.–262.

54. Martínez Medina, "Los libros plúmbeos," 621

55. López Muñoz, "Estudio preliminar," XVIII ; Julio Caro Baroja, *Las falsificaciones de la historia (en relación con la de España)* (Barcelona: Seix Barral, 1992), 119–120. The book is also mentioned in Antolínez de Burgos, *Historia eclesiástica,* 475, and Bermúdez de Pedraza, *Historia eclesiástica,* f. 266v.

56. For detailed narrative overviews of the Sacromonte discoveries, see Bermúdez de Pedraza, *Historia eclesiástica,* f. 266v.–273v.; Antolínez de Burgos, *Historia eclesiástica,* 475–515; Miguel José Hagerty, *Los libros plúmbeos del Sacromonte* (Madrid: Editora Nacional, 1980), 29–39; Martínez Medina, "Los libros plúmbeos," 623–630; Julio Caro Baroja, *Las falsificaciones de la historia (en relación con la de España)* (Barcelona: Seix Barral, 1992), 117–121; Harris, "Forging Identity," 56–62.

57. The nineteenth and final *plomo* was unearthed in May 1599: Martínez Medina, "Los libros plúmbeos," 629.

58. Antolínez de Burgos, *Historia eclesiástica,* 488; Martínez Medina, "Los libros plúmbeos," 627.

59. Marín López, "Estudio preliminar," xviii–xix. The term had also appeared on the plaque concerning the death of San Hiscio, another of the martyrs: Bermúdez de Pedraza, *Historia eclesiástica,* f. 267v.–268v.

60. Antolínez de Burgos, *Historia eclesiástica,* 479.

61. Ibid., f. 268v.; Harris, "Forging Identity," 60–61.

62. Harris, "Forging Identity," 61.

63. Archivo y Biblioteca de Zabálburu, Madrid, carpeta 161, p. 110.

64. For an overview of arguments made against the veracity of the *plomos,* alongside Royo Campos's energetic twentieth-century attempts to refute each objection, see Royo Campos, *Reliquias martiriales,* 73–93. Although initially skeptical, Mármol Carvajal over the next few years himself may have been transformed into a defender of the Sacromonte cause: López Muñoz, "Estudio preliminar, xxiii–xxiv, note #21.

65. Hagerty, *Los libros plúmbeos,* 48.

66. Darío Cabanelas Rodríguez, *El morisco granadino Alonso de Castillo,* 2d ed. (Granada: Patronato del Alhambra, 1991), 293; Hagerty, *Los libros plúmbeos.*

67. For a good overview of the question of authorship of the forgeries, and some intriguing possible alternative suspects, see Harris, "Forging Identity," 240–248.

68. Marín López, "Estudio preliminar," xvi–xvii, note #9; Hagerty, Los libros plúmbeos, 34–35; Caro Baroja, Las falsificaciones, 127.

69. AHN, Inquisición, legajo 1953, no. 5, penitent #26.

70. This book, titled in its Castilian translation Historia de la verdad del Santo Evangelio, is transcribed in Hagerty, Los libros plúmbeos, 119–130.

71. Martínez Medina, "Los libros plúmbeos," 641; Harris, "Forging Identity," 240.

72. The image is found in the Archivo y Biblioteca de Zabálburu, carpeta 161, p. 126.

73. Harris, "Forging Identity," chapters 3 and 5.

74. Ibid., 243.

75. ACG, Libro 9 de actas capitulares, f. 114v.

76. Harris, "Forging Identity."

77. The first mention that I have seen of this claim is in the minutes of the chapter's June 16, 1559, meeting: ACG, Libro 4 de actas capitulares, f. 53.

78. ACG, Libro 9 de actas capitulares, f. 199. The chapter again petitioned the archbishop to transfer the relics to the cathedral on May 16, 1600, and their request was again rejected: ACG, libro 9 de actas capitulares, f. 246.

79. ACG, Libro 9 de actas capitulares, f. 342v.

80. Bermúdez de Pedraza, Historia eclesiástica, f. 273.

81. Cited in Harris, "Forging Identity," 204 (her translation).

82. Ibid., 199.

83. Ibid., 205–216.

84. The municipal council apparently did send representatives to the archbishop in April 1595 in order to communicate to him their joy over the recent discoveries: Harris, "Forging Identity," 205.

85. Bilinkoff, The Avila of Saint Teresa, 174–179.

86. Nalle, God in La Mancha, 169–170.

87. Archivo y Biblioteca de Zabálburu, carpeta 161, p. 131; ACG, Libro 9 de actas capitulares, f. 345v.–346.

88. ACG, legajo 25, p. 13.

89. Martínez Medina, "Los libros plúmbeos," 622; Harris, "Forging Identity," 55–56.

90. Archivo y Biblioteca de Zabálburu, carpeta 161, p. 93

91. Harris, "Forging Identity," 60.

92. Archivo y Biblioteca de Zabálburu, carpeta 161, p. 110.

93. Harris, "Forging Identity."

94. Archivo y Biblioteca de Zabálburu, carpeta 161, p. 118.

95. Ibid. Discussion of Castro's inquiry with the confessors comes in the final sections of this lengthy report of all the miracles associated with the Sacromonte findings.

96. Hagerty, Los libros plúmbeos, 33

Bibliography

Below, in the archival and primary sources, I have added the abbreviations found in the notes for the most frequently used sources.

ARCHIVES

Archivo de la Catedral de Granada (ACG)
Archivo de la Cofradía de Nuestra Señora de las Angustias, Granada
Archivo de la Curia Arzobispal de Granada
Archivo de la Diputación Provincial de Granada
Archivo de la Parroquia de San Cecilio (Granada)
Archivo de la Parroquia de San Ildefonso (Granada)
Archivo de la Parroquia de San José (Granada)
Archivo de la Parroquia de San Pedro y San Pablo (Granada)
Archivo de la Parroquia de Santa Ana y San Gil (Granada)
Archivo de Protócolos de Granada (APG)
Archivo de la Real Chancillería de Granada (AchG)
Archivo General de Simancas (AGS)
    Cámara de Castilla
    Patronato Real
Archivo Histórico Nacional, Madrid (AHN)
    Inquisición
Archivo Municipal de Granada (AMG)
Archivo y Biblioteca de Zabálburu, Madrid
Biblioteca Nacional, Madrid (BNM)
    Manuscritos
    Raros

PRINTED PRIMARY SOURCES

Antolínez de Burgos, Justino. *Historia eclesiástica de Granada*. Edited by Manuel Sotomayor. Granada: Universidad de Granada, 1996.

Avila, Juan de. *Obras completas del Santo Maestro Juan de Avila*. Edited by Luis Sala Balust and Francisco Martín Hernández. 2nd ed. 6 vols. Madrid: Católica, 1970–1971.

Bermúdez de Pedraza, Francisco. *Historia eclesiástica de Granada*. Granada, 1568. Reprint, Granada: Editorial Don Quijote and Universidad de Granada, 1989.

Canons and Decrees of the Ecumenical Council of Trent. Translated by J. Waterworth. London: C. Dolman, 1848.

Concilum Tridentinum: Diariorum, Actorum, Epistularum, Tractarum. 3rd ed. 13 volumes. Freiburg: Herder, 1963–1967.

Castro, Francisco de. *Historia de la vida y sanctas obras de Iuan de Dios, y de la institución de su orden, y principio de su hospital.* Granada, 1585. In *San Juan de Dios: Primicias Históricas Suyas,* edited by M. Gómez Moreno, 11–128. Madrid: S. Aguirre, 1950.

Dios, Juan de. *Cartas y escritos de N.P.S. Juan de Dios.* Edited by P. Octavio Marcos. Madrid: Tipografía Artística, 1935.

Fernández de Madrid, Alonso. *Vida de Fray Fernando de Talavera, Primer Arzobispo de Granada.* Granada, 1530. Reprint, Granada: Universidad de Granada, 1992.

Fernández Navarrete, Martín, Miguel Salvá, and Pedro Sainz de Baranda, eds. *Colección de documentos inéditos para la historia de España.* 113 vols. Madrid: Viuda de Calero, 1842–1895. (CODOIN).

Gómez Moreno, Manuel, ed. *San Juan de Dios: Primicias históricas suyas.* Madrid: S. Aguirre, 1950.

González de Mendoza, Don Pedro. "Lo sucedido en el concilio de Trento." In *Concilum Tridentinum: Diariorum, Actorum, Epistularum, Tractarum,* 3d ed. 13 vols, 2:635–719. Freiburg: Herder, 1963–1967.

Granada, Luis de. *Vida del P. Mtro. Juan de Avila y las partes que a de tener un predicador del Evangelio.* In *Vidas del P. Maestro Juan de Avila,* edited by Luis Sala Balust, 3–135. Barcelona: Juan Flors, 1964.

———. *Fray Luis de Granada: Epistolario.* Edited by Alvaro Huerga. Córdoba: Monte de Piedad y Caja de Ahorros de Córdoba, 1989.

Guerrero, Pedro. *El concilio provincial de Granada en 1565. Edición crítica del malogrado concilio de Arzobispo Guerrero.* Edited by Ignacio Pérez de Heredia y Valle. Rome: Instituto Español de Historia Eclesiástica, 1990.

———. *Constituciones sinodales del arzobispado de Granada.* Granada, 1572, Reprint, Madrid: Sancha, 1805.

———. *Don Pedro Guerrero: Epistolario y documentación.* Edited by Juan López Martín. Rome: Instituto Español de Historia Eclesiástica, 1974.

Henríquez de Jorquera, Francisco. *Anales de Granada: Descripción del reino y ciudad de Granada. Crónica de la Reconquista. Sucesos de los años 1588 a 1646.* Edited by Antonio Marín Ocete. 2 vols. Granada: Universidad of Granada, 1934. Reprint, Granada: Universidad de Granada, 1987.

Hurtado de Mendoza, Diego. *Guerra de Granada.* Granada, 1610. Reprint, Granada: Impredisur, 1991.

Mármol Carvajal, Luis de. *Rebelión y castigo de los moriscos.* Málaga, 1600. Reprint, Málaga: Editorial Arguval, 1991.

Meneses García, Emilio, ed. *Correspondencia del Conde de Tendilla.* 2 vols. Madrid: Real Academia de la Historia, 1973.

Monumenta Historica Societatis Jesu. *Epistolae Mixtae.* 5 vols. Madrid: Editorial Ibérica, 1898–1901. (MHSI)

Monumenta Historica Societatis Jesu. *Litterae Quadrimestris.* 7 vols. Madrid: A Avrial, 1894–1932.

Muñoz, Luis. *Vida y virtudes del venerable varón el P Maestro Juan de Avila.* In *Vidas del P. Maestro Juan de Avila,* edited by Luis Sala Balust, 137–603. Barcelona: Juan Flors, 1964.

Münzer, Jerónimo (Hieronymus Münzer). *Viaje por España y Portugal 1494–1495: Reino de Granada.* Edited by Fermín Camacho Evangelista. Granada: Ediciones TAT, 1987.

Pallavicino, Pietro Sforza. *Istoria del Concilio di Trento.* Rome, 1656–1657. Reprint, 6 vols. Faenza, 1792–1798.

Pérez de Ayala, Martín. "Discurso de la vida del ilustrísimo y reverendísimo señor Don Martín de Ayala." In *Nueva Biblioteca de Autores Españoles,* Vol. 2. *Autobiografías y Memorias,* edited by M. Serrano y Sanz, 211–238. Madrid, 1905.

Sandoval, Prudencio de. *Historia del Emperador Carlos V.* Edited by Carlos Seco Serrano. Biblioteca de Autores Españoles, vols. 80–82. Madrid: Real Academia Española, 1955.

Torres, Alonso de. *Crónica de la Provincia Franciscana de Granada.* 1683. Reprint, Madrid: Cisneros, 1984.

SECONDARY SOURCES

Abad, Camilo María. "El proceso de la Inquisición contra el Beato Juan de Avila: Estudio crítico a la luz de documentos desconocidos." *Miscelánea Comillas* 6 (1946): 95–168.

——. "Escritos del Beato Juan de Avila en torno al Concilio de Trento." *Maestro Avila* 3 (1947): 269–295.

Aldea Vaquero, Quintín, Tomás Marín Martínez, and José Vives Gatell, eds. *Diccionario de historia eclesiástica de España.* 4 vols. Madrid: Consejo Superior de Investigaciones Científicas, 1972–1975.

Altman, Ida. *Emigrants and Society: Extremadura and America in the Sixteenth Century.* Berkeley: University of California Press, 1989.

——. "Spanish Society in Mexico City After the Conquest." *Hispanic American Historical Review* 71 (1991): 413–445.

——. *Transatlantic Ties in the Spanish Empire: Brihuega, Spain, and Puebla, Mexico.* Stanford: Stanford University Press, 2000.

Álvarez Rodríguez, J. Rosaura. "La Casa de Doctrina del Albaicín: Labor apostólico de la Compañía de Jesús con los moriscos." *Cuadernos de la Alhambra* 19–20 (1983–1984): 231–246.

Amelang, James. *Honored Citizens of Barcelona: Patrician Culture and Class Relations, 1490–1714.* Princeton: Princeton University Press, 1986.

Andrés Martín, Melquíades. *Los recogidos: Nueva visión de la mística española (1500–1700).* Madrid: Fundación Universitaria Española, 1976.

Arce, Rafael. *San Juan de Avila y la reforma de la Iglesia en España.* Madrid: Ediciones Rialp, 1970.

Astraín, Antonio. *Historia de la Compañía de Jesús en la asistencia de España.* 7 vols. Madrid: Razón y Fe, 1912–1925.

Baer, Yitzhak. *A History of the Jews in Christian Spain.* Translated by Louis Schoffman. 2 vols. Philadelphia: Jewish Publicaton Society of America, 1961–1966.

Baernstein, P. Renée. "In Widow's Habit: Women between Convent and Family in Sixteenth-Century Milan." *Sixteenth Century Journal* 25 (1994): 787–805.

Bangert, William, and Thomas McCoog. *Jerome Nadal, S.J.: Tracking the First Generation of Jesuits.* Chicago: Loyola University Press, 1992.

Barrios Aguilera, Manuel. *Moriscos y repoblación en las postrimerias de la Granada islámica.* Granada: Diputación Provincial de Granada, 1993.

Bataillon, Marcel. "Jean d'Avila, Retrouvé." *Bulletin Hispanique* 57 (1955): 5–44.

———. *Erasmo y España: estudios sobre la historia espiritual del siglo XVI.* Translated by A. Altorre. 2d ed. Mexico: Fondo de Cultura Económica, 1966.

Beinhart, Haim. "The Conversos and Their Fate." In *Spain and the Jews: The Sephardi Experience, 1492 and After,* edited by Elie Kedourie, 92–122. London: Thames and Hudson, 1992.

Bennassar, Bartolomé. *Valladolid au siècle d'or: une ville de Castille et sa campagne au XVIe siècle.* Paris: Mouton, 1967.

Bilinkoff, Jodi. *The Avila of Saint Teresa: Religious Reform in a Sixteenth-Century City.* Ithaca: Cornell University Press, 1989.

———. "A Spanish Prophetess and Her Patrons: The Case of María de Santo Domingo." *Sixteenth Century Journal* 23 (1992): 21–34.

———. "Confessors, Penitents, and the Construction of Identities in Early Modern Avila." In *Culture and Identity in Early Modern Europe (1500–1800): Essays in Honor of Natalie Zemon Davis,* edited by Barbara Diefendorf and Carla Hesse, 83–100. Ann Arbor: University of Michigan Press, 1993.

Black, Christopher. *Italian Confraternities in the Sixteenth Century.* Cambridge: Cambridge University Press, 1989.

Bosque Maurel, Joaquín. *Geografía urbana de Granada.* Zaragoza: Departamento de Geografía Aplicada del Instituto Juan Sebastián Elcano, 1962.

Boyd Bowman, Peter. "Patterns of Spanish Emigration to the Indies until 1600." *Hispanic American Historical Review* 56 (1976): 580–604.

Burns, Kathryn. *Colonial Habits: Convents and the Spiritual Economy of Cuzco, Peru.* Durham, N.C.: Duke University Press, 1999.

Burns, Robert Ignatius. *The Crusader Kingdom of Valencia: Reconstruction on a Thirteenth-Century Frontier.* Cambridge, Mass.: Harvard University Press, 1967.

Cabanelas Rodríguez, Darío. *El morisco granadino Alonso de Castillo.* 2d ed. Granada: Patronato del Alhambra, 1991.

———. "Los moriscos: vida religiosa y evangelización." In *La incorporación de Granada a la Corona de Castilla,* edited by Miguel Ángel Ladero Quesada, 497–512. Granada: Diputación Provincial de Granada, 1993.

Calero Palacios, María del Cármen. *La enseñanza y educación en Granada bajo los reyes austrias.* Granada: Diputación Provincial de Granada, 1978.

Cardaillac, Louis. "El enfrentamiento entre moriscos y cristianos." *Chrónica Nova* 20 (1992): 27–37.

Caro Baroja, Julio. *Los moriscos del reino de Granada: Ensayo de Historia Social.* 4th ed. Madrid: Ediciones Istmo, 1991.

———. *Las falsificaciones de la historia (en relación con la de España).* Barcelona: Seix Barral, 1992.

Castillo Fernández, Javier. "La asimilación de los moriscos granadinos: un modelo de análisis." In *Disidencias y exilios en la España moderna,* edited by Antonio Mestre Sanchís and Enrique Giménez López, 347–361. Alicante: Universidad de Alicante, 1997.

Castro, Américo. *España en su historia: cristianos, moros, y judíos.* 2nd ed. Barcelona: Editorial Crítica, 1983.

Chejne, Anwar. *Islam and the West: The Moriscos, A Cultural, and Social History.* Albany: State University of New York Press, 1983.

Christian, William. *Local Religion in Sixteenth-Century Spain*. Princeton: Princeton University Press, 1981.

Coleman, David. "Moral Formation and Social Control in the Catholic Reformation: The Case of San Juan de Avila." *Sixteenth Century Journal* 26 (1995): 17–30.

———. "Spain." in *The Reformation World*, edited by Andrew Pettegree, 296–305. London: Routledge, 2000.

Contreras, Jaime. "Aldermen and Judaizers: Cryptojudaism, Counter-Reformation, and Local Power." In *Culture and Control in Counter-Reformation Spain*, edited by Anne J. Cruz and Mary Elizabeth Perry, 93–123. Minneapolis: University of Minnesota Press, 1992.

Cooper, Edward. *Castillos señoriales en la corona de Castilla*. Salamanca: Junta de Castilla y León, 1991.

Cortés Peña, Antonio Luis. *Iglesia y cultura en la Andalucía moderna: Tendencias de la investigación, Estado de las cuestiones*. Granada: Proyecto Sur, 1996.

Cortés Peña, Antonio Luis, and Bernard Vincent. *La época moderna: Siglos XVI, XVII, y XVIII*. Vol. 3. *Historia de Granada*. Granada: Editorial Don Quijote, 1986.

Cueto, Ronald. "Logic in Madness: St. John of God's Game of *Birlimbao*." *Portuguese Studies* 5 (1989): 27–44.

Dandelet, Thomas. "Spanish Conquest and Colonization at the Center of the Old World: The Spanish Nation in Rome, 1555–1625." *Journal of Modern History* 69 (1997): 479–511.

Davis, Natalie Zemon. "From Popular Religion to Religious Cultures." In *Reformation Europe: A Guide to Research*, edited by Steven Ozment, 321–341. St. Louis: Center for Reformation Studies, 1982.

Delanty, Gerard. "The Frontier and Identities of Exclusion in European History." *History of European Ideas* 22 (1996): 93–103.

Díaz Ibáñez, Jorge. "Fray Alonso de Burgos y el sínodo conquense de 1484." *Hispania Sacra* 47 (1995): 299–346.

Domínguez Ortiz, Antonio. *La sociedad española en el siglo XVII*. 2 vols. Madrid: Concejo Superior de Investigaciones Científicas, 1970.

Domínguez Ortiz, Antonio, and Bernard Vincent. *Historia de los moriscos: vida y tragedía de una minoría*. 2d ed. Madrid: Alianza Universidad, 1993.

Donelly, John Patrick, S.J., and Michael W. Maher, S.J., eds., *Confraternities and Catholic Reform in Italy, France, and Spain*. Kirksville, Mo.: Truman State University Press, 1998.

Edwards, John. *Christian Córdoba: The City and Its Region in the Late Middle Ages*. Cambridge: Cambridge University Press, 1982.

Ehlers, Benjamin. "Christians and Muslims in Valencia: The Archbishop Juan de Ribera (1532–1611) and the Formation of a *Communitas Christiana*." Ph.D. diss., Johns Hopkins University, 1999.

Evennett, H. Outram. *The Cardinal of Lorraine and the Council of Trent: A Study in the Counter-Reformation*. Cambridge: Cambridge University Press, 1930.

———. *The Spirit of the Counter-Reformation*. Cambridge: Cambridge University Press, 1968.

Fernández Martínez, Fidel. *La España imperial: Fray Hernando de Talavera, confe-*

sor de los Reyes Católicos y primer Arzobispo de Granada. Madrid: Biblioteca Nueva, 1942.

Flynn, Maureen. *Sacred Charity: Confraternities and Social Welfare in Spain, 1400–1700.* Ithaca: Cornell University Press, 1989.

Forster, Marc. *The Counter-Reformation in the Villages: Religion and Reform in the Bishopric of Speyer, 1560–1720.* Ithaca: Cornell University Press, 1992.

Friedman, Ellen. *Spanish Captives in North Africa in the Early Modern Age.* Madison: University of Wisconsin Press, 1983.

Friedrichs, Christopher. *The Early Modern City 1450–1750.* London: Longman, 1995.

Galán Sánchez, Ángel. "Notas para una periodización de la historia de los moriscos granadinos de las capitulaciones de la conversión a las medidas de la Capilla Real." In *Actas del III Coloquio Histórico Medieval Andaluz,* 77–98. Jaen, 1984.

——. *Los mudéjares del reino de Granada.* Granada: Universidad de Granada, 1991.

——. "Los vencidos: exilio, integración y resistencia." In *Historia del reino de Granada I: De los orígenes a la época mudéjar,* edited by Rafael G. Peinado Santaella. Granada: Universidad de Granada, 2000.

Gallego y Burín, Antonio, and Alfonso Gámir Sandoval. *Los moriscos del reino de Granada según el sínodo de Guadix de 1554.* Granada: University of Granada Press, 1968.

Gallego Roca, Francisco Javier. "Mezquita del Hatabín e iglesia de San Gil (Del urbanismo musulmán al urbanismo cristiano: Granada)." *Chrónica Nova* 5 (1991): 111–129.

Gan Giménez, Pedro. "Los prebendados de la iglesia granadina: Una bio-bibliografía." *Revista del Centro de Estudios Históricos de Granada y su Reino.* 4 (1990): 139–171.

García Arenal, Mercedes. *Los moriscos.* Madrid: Editora Nacional, 1975.

——. "El problema morisco: Propuestas de discusión." *Al-Quantara* 13 (1992): 491–503.

García Ivars, Flora. *La represión en el tribunal inquisitorial de Granada, 1550–1819.* Madrid: Akal, 1991.

García Pedraza, Amalia. "El otro morisco: Algunas reflexiones sobre el estudio de la religiosidad morisca a través de fuentes notariales." *Sharq al-Andalus* 12 (1995): 223–234.

——. "La asimilación del morisco Don Gonzalo Fernández el Zegrí: edición y análysis de su testamento." *Al-Quantara* 16 (1995): 39–57.

Garrad, K. "The Original Memorial of Don Francisco Núñez Muley." *Atlante* 2 (1954):199–226.

——. "The Causes of the Second Rebellion of the Alpujarra (1568–1571)." Ph.D. diss., Cambridge University, 1955.

——. "La industria sedera granadina en el siglo XVI y su conexión con el levantamiento de las Alpujarras (1568–1571)." *Miscelánea de Estudios Árabes y Hebráicos* 5 (1956): 73–98.

——. "La inquisición y los moriscos granadinos (1526–1580)." *Miscelánea de Estudios Árabes y Hebráicos* 9 (1960): 55–72.

Garrido Aranda, Antonio. *Organización de la iglesia en el reino de Granada y su proyección en Indias.* Seville: Escuela de Estudios Hispano-Americanos, 1979.

———. *Moriscos e indios: Precedentes hispánicos de la evangelización en México.* Mexico City: Universidad Nacional Autónoma de México, 1980.

Garrido Atienza, Miguel. *Las capitulaciones para la entrega de Granada.* Granada: Paulino Ventura Travaset, 1910.

———. *Antiguallas granadinas: Las fiestas del Corpus.* Granada: Granada, 1889. Reprint, Granada: Universidad de Granada, 1990.

Gilman, Stephen. " 'Judea Pequenna:' Granada ante la Inquisición." *Nueva Revista de Filología Hispanica* 30 (1981): 586–593.

Gleason, Elizabeth. *Gasparo Contarini: Venice, Rome, and Reform.* Berkeley: University of California Press, 1993.

Glick, Thomas F. "Reading the *Repartimientos:* Modeling Settlement in the Wake of Conquest." In *Christians, Muslims, and Jews in Medieval and Early Modern Spain: Interaction and Cultural Change,* edited by Mark D. Meyerson and Edward D. English, 20–39. Notre Dame: University of Notre Dame Press, 1999.

Gómez-Moreno Calera, J. M. *La arquitectura religiosa granadina en la crisis del Renacimiento 1560/1650.* Granada: Universidad de Granada, 1989.

González Jiménez, Manuel. "Frontier and Settlement in the Kingdom of Castile (1085–1350)." In *Medieval Frontier Societies,* edited by Robert Bartlett and Angus MacKay, 49–74. Oxford: Clarendon Press, 1989.

Graña Cid, María del Mar. "Reflexiones sobre la implantación del franciscanismo feminino en el reino de Granada (1492–1570)." In *I Congreso Internacional de Monacato Feminino en España, Portugal, y América 1492–1992,* 2 vols., 2:523–538. León: Universidad de León, 1993.

Gutiérrez, C. *Españoles en Trento.* Valladolid: Consejo Superior de Investigaciones Científicas, 1951.

Gutiérrez Galdó, José. *La Virgen de Angustias: Patrona de Granada.* Granada: San Rita, 1983.

Hagerty, Miguel José. *Los libros plúmbeos del Sacromonte.* Madrid: Editora Nacional, 1980.

Haliczer, Stephen. *Sexuality in the Confessional: A Sacrament Profaned.* New York: Oxford University Press, 1995.

———. "The Expulsion of the Jews as a Social Process." In *The Jews of Spain and the Expulsion of 1492,* edited by Moshe Lazar and Stephen Haliczer, 237–251. Lancaster, Calif.: Labyrinthos, 1997.

Hamilton, Alastair. *Heresy and Mysticism in Sixteenth-Century Spain: The Alumbrados.* Toronto: University of Toronto Press, 1992.

Harline, Craig. "Official Religion-Popular Religion in Recent Historiography of the Catholic Reformation." *Archive for Reformation History* 81 (1990): 239–262.

Harline, Craig, and Eddy Put. *A Bishop's Tale: Mathias Hovius among His Flock in Seventeenth-Century Flanders.* New Haven: Yale University Press, 2000.

Harris, A. Katie. "Forging History: The *Plomos* of the Sacromonte of Granada in Francisco Bermúdez de Pedraza's *Historia Eclesiástica.*" *Sixteenth Century Journal* 30 (1999): 945–966.

———. "Forging Identity: The *Plomos* of the Sacromonte and the Creation of Civic Identity in Early Modern Granada." Ph.D. diss., The Johns Hopkins University, 2000.

Henáres Cuéllar, Ignacio, and Rafael López Guzmán. *Arquitectura mudéjar granadina.* Granada: Caja General de Ahorros y Monte de Piedad, 1989.

Henáres Cuéllar, Ignacio, and Rafael López Guzmán, eds. *Mudéjar iberoamericano. Una expresión cultural de dos mundos.* Granada: Universidad de Granada 1993.

Henningsen, Gustav. "The Archives and the Historiography of the Spanish Inquisition." In *The Inquisition in Early Modern Europe: Studies on Sources and Methods,* edited by Gustav Henningsen and John Tedeschi, 54–78. De Kalb: Northern Illinois University Press, 1986.

Hernández, Mauro. *A la sombra de la corona: Poder local y oligarquía urbana (Madrid, 1606–1806).* Madrid: Siglo veintiuno, 1995.

Hess, Andrew. "The Moriscos: An Ottoman Fifth Column in Sixteenth-Century Spain." *American Historical Review* 74 (1968): 1–25.

Hillgarth, J. N. *The Spanish Kingdoms, 1250–1516.* 2 vols. Oxford: Oxford University Press, 1978.

Hoffman, Philip T. *Church and Community in the Diocese of Lyon, 1500–1789.* New Haven: Yale University Press, 1984.

Homza, Lu Ann. "Erasmus as Hero, or Heretic? Spanish Humanism and the Valladolid Assembly of 1527." *Renaissance Quarterly* 50 (1997): 78–118.

——. *Religious Authority in the Spanish Renaissance.* Baltimore: The Johns Hopkins University Press, 2000.

Huerga, Álvaro. *Fray Luis de Granada. Una vida al servicio de la Iglesia.* Madrid: Católica, 1988.

Huerga, Álvaro, José Mendez Asensio, Antonio García del Moral, and Agustín Turrado, eds. *Tres estudios sobre Fray Luis y una crónica de su IV centenario en Granada.* Granada: Diputación Provincial de Granada, 1989.

Jedin, Hubert. *A History of the Council of Trent.* Translated by Ernest Graf. 2 vols. Edinburgh: Thomas Nelson and Sons, 1957–1961.

——. *Crisis and Closure of the Council of Trent: A Retrospective View from the Second Vatican Council.* Translated by N. D. Smith. London: Sheed and Ward, 1967.

Jereczek, Bruno. *Louis de Grenade disciple de Jean d'Avila.* Fontenay-le-Comté: Lussaud, 1971.

Kagan, Richard L, ed. *Spanish Cities of the Golden Age: The Views of Anton van den Wyngaerde.* Berkeley: University of California Press, 1989.

Kagan, Richard L., and Geoffrey Parker, eds. *Spain, Europe, and the Atlantic World: Essays in Honour of John H. Elliott.* Cambridge: Cambridge University Press, 1995.

Kamen, Henry. *The Phoenix and the Flame: Catalonia and the Counter Reformation.* New Haven: Yale University Press, 1993.

——. *The Spanish Inquisition: A Historical Revision.* New Haven: Yale University Press, 1997.

Kriegel, Maurice. "La prise d'une décision: l'expulsion des juifs d'Espagne." *Revue Historique* 260 (1978): 49–90.

Ladero Quesada, Miguel Ángel. "La repoblación del reino de Granada anterior al año 1500." *Hispania* 28 (1968): 489–562.

——. *Granada: Historia de un país islámico (1232–1571).* Madrid: Editorial Gredos, 1969.

——. *La Ciudad Medieval (1248–1492).* Vol. 2. *Historia de Sevilla.* Seville: Universidad de Sevilla, 1976.

——. *Granada después de la conquista: Repobladores y mudéjares.* Granada: Diputación Provincial de Granada, 1988.

——. *Los mudéjares de Castilla y otros estudios de historia medieval andaluza.* Granada: Universidad de Granada, 1989.

——. *La incorporación de Granada a la corona de Castilla.* Granada: Diputación Provincial de Granada, 1993.

——. *Castilla y la conquista del reino de Granada.* 2d ed. Granada: Diputación Provincial de Granada, 1993.

——. "Spain 1492: Social Values and Structures." In *Implicit Understandings: Observing, Reporting, and Reflecting on the Encounters Between Europeans and Other Peoples in the Early Modern Era,* edited by Stuart B. Schwartz, 96–133. Cambridge: Cambridge University Press, 1994.

Lavrin, Asunción. "Women in Colonial Mexico." In *The Oxford History of Mexico,* edited by Michael C. Meyer and William H. Beezley, 245–273. Oxford: Oxford University Press, 2000.

Lea, Henry Charles. *The Moriscos of Spain: Their Conversion and Expulsion.* New York: Burt Franklin, 1901.

Liss, Peggy K. *Isabel the Queen: Life and Times.* Oxford: Oxford University Press, 1992.

Lockhart, James. *Spanish Peru 1532–1560.* Madison: University of Wisconsin Press, 1968.

López, Miguel. "El colegio de los niños moriscos de Granada." *Miscelánea de Estudios Árabes y Hebráicos* 25 (1976): 32–68.

——. *Los arzobispos de Granada: retratos y semblanzas.* Granada: Santa Rita, 1993.

López de Coca Castañer, José Enrique. *El reino de Granada en la época de los Reyes Católicos: Repoblación, comercio, y frontera.* 2 vols. Granada: Universidad de Granada, 1989.

——. "Las capitulaciones y la Granada mudéjar." In *La incorporación de Granada a la corona de Castilla,* edited by Miguel Angel Ladero Quesada, 263–305. Granada: Diputación Provincial de Granada, 1993.

López-Guadalupe Muñoz, Miguel Luis, and Juan Jesús López-Guadalupe Muñoz. *Nuestra Señora de las Angustias y su hermandad en la época moderna.* Granada: Editorial Comares, 1996.

López López, Roberto J. *Comportamientos religiosos en Asturias durante el Antiguo Régimen.* Gijón: Silverio Cañada, 1989.

López Martín, Juan. "D. Pedro Guerrero como obispo del tiempo de la contrarreforma." *Archivo Teológico Granadino* 31 (1968): 193–231.

——. "El Arzobispo de Granada D. Pedro Guerrero y la Compañia de Jesús." *Anthología Annua* 24–25 (1977–1978): 453–498.

——. "El concilio provincial de Granada de 1565 y sus provisiones sobre los moriscos del reino de Granada." *Anthología Annua* 36 (1989): 509–541.

López Muñoz, Miguel Luis. "Las ordenanzas de la hermandad de Nuestra Señora de las Angustias de Granada en el siglo XVI." *Chrónica Nova* 17 (1989): 381–415.

——. *Las cofradías de la parroquia de Santa María Magdalena de Granada en los siglos XVII–XVIII.* Granada: Universidad de Granada, 1992.

——. "Estudio preliminar." In Zótico Royo Campos, *Reliquias martiriales y escudo del Sacromonte,* edited by Miguel L. López Muñoz, ix–civ. Granada: Universidad de Granada, 1995.

López Nevot, José Antonio. *La organización institucional del municipio de Granada durante el siglo XVI.* Granada: Universidad de Granada, 1994

Luna Díaz, Juan Andrés. "La parroquia de Santa María Magdalena de Granada, un barrio en expansión hacía la vega durante el siglo XVI." *Chrónica Nova* 11 (1980): 187–233.

Luque Moreno, Jesús. *Granada en el siglo XVI: Juan de Vilches y otros testimonios de la época.* Granada: Universidad de Granada, 1994.

MacKay, Angus. "The Ballad and the Frontier in Late Medieval Spain." *Bulletin of Hispanic Studies* 53 (1976): 15–33.

Marías, Fernando. "City Planning in Sixteenth-Century Spain." In *Spanish Cities of the Golden Age: The Views of Anton van den Wynegaerde,* ed. Richard L. Kagan, 84–105. Berkeley: University of California Press, 1989.

Marín López, Rafael. "El cabildo eclesiástico granadino y las obras de la catedral en el siglo XVI." *Chrónica Nova* 22 (1995): 211–241.

——. *El cabildo de la catedral de Granada en el siglo XVI.* Granada: Universidad de Granada, 1998.

Marín Ocete, Antonio. "El concilio provincial de Granada en 1565." *Archivo Teológico Granadino* 25 (1962): 23–95.

——. *El arzobispo Pedro Guerrero y la política conciliar española en el siglo XVI.* 2 vols. Granada: Consejo Superior de Investigaciones Científicas and Universidad de Granada, 1970.

Martín Hernández, Francisco. *Un seminario español pretridentino: El Real Colegio Eclesiástico de San Cecilio de Granada (1492–1842).* Valladolid: Universidad de Valladolid, 1960.

Martínez Justicia, María J. *La plaza pública como elemento urbanístico. Seis ejemplos en la ciudad de Granada.* Granada: Galería Virtual, 1996.

Martínez Medina, Francisco Javier. *Cultura religiosa en la Granada rencentista y barroca (estudio iconológico).* Granada: University of Granada Press, 1989.

——. "Estudio Preliminar." In Alonso Fernández de Madrid, *Vida de Fray Fernando de Talavera: Primer Arzobispo de Granada,* edited by Félix G. Olmedo, ix–lxxxviii. Granada: University of Granada Press, 1992.

——. "Los libros plúmbeos del Sacromonte." In *Jesucristo y el Emperador Cristiano: Catálogo de la exposición celebrada en la catedral de Granada con motivo del año jubilar de la encarnación de Jesucristo y del V centenario del nacimiento del Emperador Carlos. Granada, 8 de julio al 8 de diciembre,* edited by Francisco Javier Martínez Medina, 619–643. Córdoba: Publicaciones Obra Social y Cultural Cajasur, 2000.

Martínez Ruiz, Juan. "Ausencia de literatura aljamiada y conservación del hispano-árabe y de la entidad arabo-musulmana en la Granada morisca (siglo XVI)." *Chronica Nova* 21 (1993–1994): 405–425.

Martz, Linda. *Poverty and Welfare in Habsburg Spain: The Example of Toledo.* Cambridge: Cambridge University Press, 1983.

——. "Toledanos and the Kingdom of Granada, 1492–1560s." In *Spain, Europe and the Atlantic World: Essays in Honour of John H. Elliott,* edited by Richard L. Kagan and Geoffrey Parker, 103–124. Cambridge: Cambridge University Press, 1995.

——. "Implementation of Pure-Blood Statutes in Sixteenth-Century Toledo," in *In Iberia and Beyond: Hispanic Jews Between Cultures,* edited by Bernard Dov Cooperman, 245–271. Newark: University of Delaware Press, 1998.

Mathers, Constance Jones. "Early Spanish Qualms about Loyola and the Society of Jesus." *The Historian* 53 (1991): 679–690.

——. "The Life of Canons in Sixteenth-Century Castile." In *Renaissance Society and Culture: Essays in Honor of Eugene F. Rice, Jr.,* edited by John Monfasani and Ronald Musto, 161–176. New York: Italica Press, 1991.

Maurenbrecher, Wilhelm. *Geschichte der katholischen Reformation.* Nördlingen: C. H. Beck, 1880.

Meseguer Fernández, Juan. "Fernando de Talavera, Cisneros, y la Inquisición en Granada." In *La Inquisición española: Nueva visión, nuevos horizontes,* ed. Joaquín Pérez Villanueva, 371–400. Madrid: Siglo veintiuno, 1980.

Meyerson, Mark. *The Muslims of Valencia in the Age of Fernando and Isabel: Between Coexistence and Crusade.* Berkeley: University of California Press, 1991.

——. "Introduction," in *Christians, Muslims and Jews in Medieval and Early Modern Spain: Interaction and Cultural Change,"* edited by Mark D. Meyerson and Edward D. English, xi–xxi. Notre Dame: University of Notre Dame Press, 1999.

Moreno Olmedo, Maria Angustias. *Heráldica y genealogía granadina.* Granada: Universidad de Granada, 1976.

Nader, Helen. *The Mendoza Family in the Spanish Renaissance.* New Brunswick, N.J.: Rutgers University Press, 1979.

——. *Liberty in Absolutist Castile: The Habsburg Sale of Towns, 1516–1700.* Baltimore: Johns Hopkins University Press, 1990.

——. "The Spain That Encountered Mexico," in *The Oxford History of Mexico,* ed. Michael C. Meyer and William H. Beezley, 11–45. Oxford: Oxford University Press, 2000.

Nalle, Sara T. "Inquisitors, Priests, and the People during the Catholic Reformation in Spain." *Sixteenth Century Journal* 18 (1987): 557–583.

——. "Literacy and Culture in Early Modern Castile." *Past and Present* 125 (1989): 65–96.

——. *God in La Mancha: Religious Reform and the People of Cuenca, 1500–1650.* Baltimore: Johns Hopkins University Press, 1992.

——. "The Millennial Moment: Revolution and Radical Religion in Sixteenth-Century Spain." In *Toward the Millennium: Messianic Expectations from the Bible to Waco,* edited by Peter Schäfer and Mark Cohen, 153–173. Leiden: Brill, 1998.

——. *Mad for God: Bartolomé Sánchez, The Secret Messiah of Cardenete.* Charlottesville: University of Virginia Press, 2001.

Nirenberg, David. *Communities of Violence: Persecution of Minorities in the Middle Ages.* Princeton: Princeton University Press, 1996.

——. "Religious and Sexual Boundaries in the Medieval Crown of Aragon." In *Christians, Muslims, and Jews in Medieval and Early Modern Spain: Interaction and Cultural Exchange,* edited by Mark D. Meyerson and Edward D. English, 141–160. Notre Dame: University of Notre Dame Press, 1999.

Olin, John C. *The Catholic Reformation: Savonarola to Ignatius Loyola. Reform in the Church, 1495–1540.* New York: Harper and Row, 1969.

——. *Catholic Reform from Cardinal Ximénes to the Council of Trent 1495–1563.* New York: Fordham University Press, 1990.

O'Malley, John. *Trent and All That: Renaming Catholicism in the Early Modern Era.* Cambridge: Harvard University Press, 2000.

Orozco Pardo, José Luis. *Christianópolis: Urbanismo y contrarreforma en la Granada del 600.* Granada: Diputación Provincial de Granada, 1985.

Osorio Pérez, María José. "Notas y documentos sobre un caballero veinticuatro granadino: Gómez de Santillán," In *Las ciudades andaluzas (siglos XIII–XVI): Actas del VI Coloquio Internacional de la Historia Medieval de Andalucía,* edited by José Enrique López de Coca Castañer y ángel Galán Sánchez, 483–493. Málaga: Universidad de Málaga, 1991.

Parejo Delgado, María Josefa. *Baeza y Úbeda en la baja edad media.* Granada: Editorial Don Quijote, 1988.

Parker, Geoffrey. *Philip II.* Boston: Little, Brown, 1978.

Peinado Santaella, Rafael G. *La repoblación de la tierra de Granada: los montes orientales (1485–1515).* Granada: Universidad de Granada, 1989.

Peinado Santaella, Rafael G., and José Enrique López de Coca Castañer. *Historia de Granada.* Vol. 2. *La época medieval, siglos VIII-XV.* Granada: Editorial Don Quijote, 1987.

Perry, Mary Elizabeth. *Gender and Disorder in Early Modern Seville.* Princeton: Princeton University Press, 1990.

——. "Behind the Veil: Moriscas and the Politics of Resistance and Survival." In *Spanish Women in the Golden Age: Images and Realities,* edited by Magdalena S. Sánchez and Alain Saint-Saëns, 37–53. Westport Conn.: Greenwood Press, 1996.

Pike, Ruth. *Aristocrats and Traders: Sevillan Society in the Sixteenth Century.* Ithaca: Cornell University Press, 1972.

Poska, Alyson. *Regulating the People: The Catholic Reformation in Seventeenth-Century Spain.* London: E. J. Brill, 1998.

Powers, James. *A Society Organized for War: The Iberian Municipal Militias in the Central Middle Ages, 1000–1284.* Berkeley: University of California Press, 1988.

Pullan, Brian. *Rich and Poor in Renaissance Venice: The Social Institutions of a Catholic State to 1620.* Oxford: Oxford University Press, 1971.

Ravid, Benjamin C. I. "From Geographical Realia to Historiographical Symbol: The Odyssey of the Word *Ghetto.*" In *Essential Papers on Jewish Culture in Renaissance and Baroque Italy,* edited by David B. Ruderman, 373–385. New York: New York University Press, 1992.

Redondo, Agustín. "El primer plan sistemático de asimilación de los moriscos granadinos: El del doctor Carvajal (1526)." In *Les morisques et leur temps,* 113–123. Paris: éditions du Centre National de la Recherche Scientifique, 1983.

Rhodes, Elizabeth. "Spain's Misfired Canon: The Case of Luis de Granada's *Libro de la oración y meditación.*" *Journal of Hispanic Philology* 15 (1990): 43–66.

Rosenthal, Earl. *The Cathedral of Granada: A Study in the Spanish Renaissance.* Princeton: Princeton University Press, 1961.

——. *The Palace of Charles V in Granada.* Princeton: Princeton University Press, 1985.

Roth, Norman. "Coexistence and Confrontation: Jews and Christians in Medieval Spain." In *The Jews of Spain and the Expulsion of 1492,* edited by Moshe Lazar and Stephen Haliczer, 1–24. Lancaster, Calif.: Labyrinthos, 1997.

Royo Campos, Zótico. *Reliquias martiriales y escudo del Sacromonte.* Edited by Miguel L. López Muñoz. Granada: Universidad de Granada, 1995.

Rubin, Miri. *Corpus Christi: The Eucharist in Late Medieval Culture.* Cambridge: Cambridge University Press, 1991.

Ruiz, Teofilo. *Spanish Society, 1400–1600.* New York: Longman, 2001.

Ruiz del Rey, Tomás. *Vida del Padre Maestro Beato Juan de Avila, Apostol de Andalucía y Patrono del Clero Secular de España.* 2d ed. Madrid: Editorial Apostolado de la Prensa, 1954.

Ruiz Jurado, Manuel. "San Juan de Avila y la Compañía de Jesús." *Archivum Historicum Societatis Iesu* 40 (1971): 153–172.

Ruiz Martín, Felipe. "Movimientos demográficos y económicos en el reino de Granada durante la segunda mitad del siglo XVI." *Anuario de Historia Económica y Social* 1 (1968): 127–183.

Ruiz Rodríguez, Antonio Angel. *La Real Chancillería de Granada en el siglo XVI.* Granada: Diputación Provincial de Granada, 1987.

Sala Balust, Luis. "La espiritualidad española en la primera mitad del siglo XVI." *Cuadernos de Historia* 1 (1967): 169–187.

———. "Introducción biográfica." In *Obras completas de San Juan de Avila,* edited by Luis Sala Balust and Francisco Martín Hernández, 6 vols., 1:3–358. Madrid: Católica, 1970.

Sánchez Saravia, Diego. *Compendio histórico del origen y culto en Granada de Nuestra Señora de las Angustias.* Granada: Santísima Trinidad, 1777.

Schwaller, John Frederick. *The Church and Clergy in Sixteenth-Century Mexico.* Albuquerque: University of New Mexico Press, 1987.

Soria Mesa, Enrique. "La familia Pérez de Herrasti. Un acercamiento al estudio de la elite local granadina en los siglos XV al XVII." *Chrónica Nova* 19 (1991): 383–404.

———. "De la conquista a la asimilación. La integración de la aristocracia nazarí en la oligarquía granadina, siglos XV–XVI." *Areas* 74 (1992): 51–64.

———. "Crianza Real y clientelismo nobilario: Los Bobadilla, una familia de la oligarquía granadina." *Meridies* 1 (1994): 129–160.

———. "La asimilación de la élite morisca en la Granada cristiana. El ejemplo de la familia Hermes." In *Mélanges Louis Cardaillac,* edited by Abdeljelil Temimi. 2 vols., 2:649–658. Zaghouan: Fondation Temimi, 1995.

———. *Señores y oligarcas: Los señoríos del Reino de Granada en la edad moderna.* Granada: Universidad of Granada, 1997.

Spivakovsky, Erica. "Some Notes on the Relations between Don Diego Hurtado de Mendoza and Don Alonso de Granada Venegas." *Archivum* 14 (1964): 212–232.

Stow, Kenneth R. "The Consciousness of Closure: Roman Jewry and Its *Ghet.*" In *Essential Papers on Jewish Culture in Renaissance and Baroque Italy,* edited by David B. Ruderman, 386–400. New York: New York University Press, 1992.

Suberviola Martínez, Jesús. "La erección parroquial granatense de 1501 y el reformismo Cisneriano." *Cuadernos de Estudios Medievales* 14–15 (1985–1987): 115–144.

———. *Real Patronato de Granada. El arzobispo Talavera, la iglesia, y el estado moderno (1486–1516). Estudio y documentos.* Granada: Caja General de Ahorros de Granada, 1985.

Surtz, Ronald. "Morisco Women, Written Texts, and the Valencia Inquisition." *Sixteenth Century Journal* 32 (2001): 421–433.

Tueller, James B. "Good and Faithful Christians: Moriscos and Catholicism in Early Modern Spain." Ph.D. diss., Columbia University, 1997.

Van Deusen, Nancy E. *Between the Sacred and the Worldly: The Institutional and Cultural Practice of Recogimiento in Colonial Lima.* Stanford: Stanford University Press, 2002.

Vassberg, David. *The Village and the Outside World in Golden Age Castile: Mobility and Migration in Everyday Rural Life.* Cambridge: Cambridge University Press, 1996.

Vázquez Cano, Andrés A. "Los Pissas." *Revista del Centro de Estudios Históricos de Granada y su Reino* 4 (1914): 157–170.

Villoslada, Ricardo G. "Pedro Guerrero representante de la reforma española." In *Il Concilio di Trento e la riforma tridentina: Atti del convegno storico internazionale: Trento, 2–6 settembre 1963,* 2 vols., 1:115–155. Freiburg: Herder, 1965.

Vincent, Bernard. "L'Albaicín de Grenade au XVI siecle." *Mélanges de la Casa de Velázquez* 7 (1971): 187–222.

——. "Le Tribunal de Grenade." In *Les morisques et l'Inquisition,* edited by Louis Cardaillac, 199–220. Paris: Publisud, 1990.

——. *Minorías y Marginados en la España del siglo XVI.* Granada: Universidad de Granada, 1990.

——. "De la Granada mudéjar a la Granada europea." In *La incorporación de Granada a la corona de Castilla,* edited by Miguel Angel Ladero Quesada, 307–319. Granada: Diputación Provincial de Granada, 1993.

Whinnom, Keith. "The Problem of the Best-Seller in Spanish Golden-Age Literature." *Bulletin of Hispanic Studies* 57 (1980): 189–198.

Index

CPSIA information can be obtained
at www.ICGtesting.com
Printed in the USA
LVHW08s2120280718
585251LV00002B/68/P

9 780801 478833